Project Self-Esteem

A Parent Involvement Program for Improving Self-Esteem and Preventing Drug and Alcohol Abuse, K-6

Sandy McDaniel
Peggy Bielen

ɟ

Jalmar Press

PROJECT SELF-ESTEEM

Jalmar Press

P.O. Box 1185 Torrance CA 90505

Phone: (800)662-9662 (310)816-3085 Fax: (310)816-3092

e-mail: blwjalmar@worldnet.att.net
website: www.jalmarpress.com

Published by Jalmar Press

PROJECT SELF-ESTEEM

Author: Sandy McDaniel and Peggy Bielen
Photography: Marvin Steindler
Artwork: Mary Button, Darlene Landis and Orange County Department of Education, PAL Program

Manufactured in the United States of America
First edition printing: 10 9 8 7 6
Library of Congress Catalog Card Number: 89-84056
ISBN: 0-915190-59-1

Acknowledgements

Whereas, it is impossible to recognize every single person who has contributed to the creation of *Project Self-Esteem,* the following people assisted us significantly in the beginning years

Susan K. White   Marilyn Slaughter   Andrea Pfister
Susan Clendenen   Peggie Collins   Diane Wood
Sister Regina Gniot   Diane Linderman

Jean Aldrich, Dr. Pat Allen, Carolyn Alexander, Judy Allison, Susan Anderson, LuAnn Baker, Luis Barrenechea, Brenda Black, Vicki Bollenback, Linda Boris, Judy Brown, Sue Calabretta, Barbara Carr, Sheri Cagle, John Campbell MFC, Charlotte Cerrutti, Peggy Clark, Virginia Copp, Franky Cote, Judy Coyne, Dr. Mary Cruz, Nancy Donaldson RNC, MSN; Elana Donnavon, Monsignor Michael Driscoll, Dee Dunham, Shearlean Duke, Pat Eikerman, Frank Feller, Penne Ferrell, Kim Fisher, Marianne Fitzpatrick MFC, Karen Fratentaro, Stephanie Godby, Dr. Charles Godshall, Diane Gorney, Sue Hitchman, Linda Hart, Lisa Hinshaw, Candy House, Lynda Hughes, Carolyn Irvine, Peggy Johnson, Shari Jones, Karen Kendall, Gail Kerwin, Darlene Landis, Joan Lyons, Judy Mertz, Margo Misterly, Elke Muller, Diane Newberry, Dr. John Nicholl, Sister Linda Nicholson C.S.J., Jeanne Osborne, Ozzie Osborn, Alice Rail, Jeri Rimel, Kay and Philip Salisbury, Tina Sims, Dr. Bert Simpson, Charlotte Sinclair, Pinky Stanley, Robbie Stickler, Katherine Stuart, Sally Sullivan, Jo Lane Thomas, Lisa Triebwasser, Joan Thumb, Art Valentine, Jo Vandervort, Susan B. Valesquez, Jane Venard, Marion Walters, Bonnie Webster, Jan Wood.

Special "Smiley" Thanks To:

Janet Lovelady, Suzanne Mikesell, Bradley L. Winch for believing in us.

Jody Bergsma for designing the PSE logo

Sally Warrick for successful distribution of PSE in Orange County

Peg Rademaker and Kathleen Spurgeon...our mothers

And especially to Kathleen and Scott McDaniel...Bob, Janet and Brian Bielen for their uncompromising love and assistance — to Bob Bielen and Dick McDaniel for understanding.

Contents

Forewords

by Bill Beacham and Art Fisher

BILL BEACHAM *is Executive Director of the Center for Drug-Free Communities.*

It is truly a great honor and a joy to have been asked to write a foreword for the revised and expanded edition of *Project Self-Esteem*. During my twenty years of working with young people in schools (as a teacher/counselor), in hospitals (as a treatment specialist), in law enforcement (as a trainer for the DARE program), and in administration (as Executive Director of the Center for Drug-Free Communities), I have observed that the number one precursor of drug abuse is low self-esteem. While the issues of chemical abuse are complex and rarely attributed to a single cause, in most instances the use of drugs among young people correlates significantly with a lack of understanding of themselves, a lack of self-esteem, and a lack of supportive skills needed to resist drugs. *Project Self-Esteem* **directly addresses these three areas.**

The increasing availability and accessibility of chemicals to our children, along with the decrease in the age of onset of use, make it very clear to all working in the field that prevention strategies must begin as early as possible. Drugs have become the number one crisis facing our youth and challenging the basic fabric of our nation. When we look at the significant research on comprehensive prevention programs in our schools, the most effective programs contain the following components:

- Activities that strengthen the students' inner emotional/psychological resources and improve self-worth by assisting youngsters to become more knowledgeable about their own feelings along with the feelings of others.

- Techniques that provide young people with relevant and appropriate responses to resist social pressures from peers, family, and the media to use alcohol or other drugs.

- Instruction in a school atmosphere that stresses the importance of the total community by including the school staff, students, and parents in a unified effort. This approach recognizes that everyone has an important role to play in changing school and community norms regarding drug use and building positive self-esteem.

Project Self-Esteem **is a leader in all these areas!** Schools that begin with PSE and continue with the DARE program in the older grades, provide a powerful one-two punch in substance abuse prevention. PSE in its purest form is an education of the heart. This program will develop healthy, capable, and responsible young people and make a positive impact in the way young people feel about themselves and life.

—Bill Beacham

ART FISHER, Ed. D. *is Superintendent of the Cold Spring School District of Santa Barbara, California.*

My interest in student self-esteem is motivated by the fact that teachers today must deal with self-esteem problems before they can teach! Children bring problems from the home and the playground into the classroom. The teacher can choose to deal with these problems "proactively" or be faced with the loss of instructional minutes "reacting" to low self-esteem behavior. I am convinced that a routine classroom pattern of teaching self-esteem building skills is a necessary prerequisite for learning.

Ten years ago, as the principal of an elementary school chosen to be a Project Self-Esteem pilot school, I saw PSE grow from a two-person idea to a thriving program in over 210 county-wide classrooms. Lessons were in the "ditto format" and Peggy and Sandy literally trained all the volunteers. When the Orange County Office of Education adopted PSE as part of its drug prevention strategy, Peggy and Sandy continued to expand their efforts. It was our experience that the parents who presented the lessons gained parenting skills and enhanced their own self-esteem.

Many schools and districts today include self-esteem in their mission statements. But how can a superintendent or principal provide a cost effective and time effective vehicle to implement this goal? My experience shows that Project Self-Esteem offers that vehicle to the schools and teachers that care about self-esteem in grades kindergarten through sixth. The advantages of this program are:

- Effective grade-level, sequential lessons
- Explicit lesson plans designed for volunteers
- Low cost, high impact, ongoing program ideas for the classroom
- Thematic teaching strategies that overlap curriculum areas
- Humor-filled playacting for active learning
- Life-long skills for coping successfully with diversity
- A program which builds individual self-esteem and community responsibility
- A parent program to keep parents informed and involved in their child's training

Motivation researcher Abraham Maslow states that for people to reach their highest order need, self-actualization, they must have the confidence that comes with high self-esteem. This program was designed for parents and educators who care and want to make the self-esteem difference in their children. Congratulations on choosing PSE for your students!

—*Art Fisher*

Introduction

Kim has a stable home and a supportive family. But she doesn't do well in school, has difficulty making friends, and uses drugs. Why? This is a question educators and those who work with children in trouble ask themselves constantly.

There are no pat answers, but so often the real problem with children who are having trouble coping stems from their own lack of self-esteem. Kim is not alone. Experts agree that low self-esteem can be linked to substance abuse, learning problems, truancy, destructive behavior, and suicide. A recent report by the National Institute on Drug Abuse (1980), highlights this finding: "Low self-esteem. . .(was) found prior to the onset of drug use."[1] On the other hand, students with high self-esteem do better academically, are more likely to make positive independent choices, tend to respect the rights and feelings of others, and are confident in their own feelings of self-worth. This confidence enables young people to say no to drugs and alcohol.

The correlation between academic achievement and self-esteem is summed up by Erik Erikson:

> *Study after study has shown that children with superior intelligence but low self-esteem may do poorly in school while children of average intelligence but high self-esteem can be unusually successful.*[2]

Self-esteem then is the feeling a person has about him/herself. It is a general, overall perception of self-worth. Though one's sense of self-worth may fluctuate, high self-esteem is predominantly a feeling of well-being. Every human being needs to feel lovable and capable. The lovable side comes from being loved unconditionally by significant others. The capable side is enhanced by being able to do something well. High self-esteem, then, is a balance of feeling lovable and capable. As Dorothy Corkille Briggs states:

> *A person's judgment of self influences the kinds of friends he chooses, how he gets along with others, the kind of person he marries, and how productive he will be. It affects his creativity, integrity, stability, and even whether he will be a leader or a follower. His feeling of self-worth form the core of his personality and determine the use he makes of his aptitudes and abilities. His attitude toward himself has a direct bearing on how he lives all parts of his life. In fact, self-esteem is the mainspring that slates each of us for success or failure.*[3]

---

1. "Parental Support as an Approach to Primary Prevention of Chemical Abuse," St. Paul, Minnesota; the Companies, 1980.

2. "Our Children's Self-Esteem," *Florida Educator*, Summer 1983, pp. 5-7.

3. Briggs, Dorothy Corkille. *Your Child's Self-Esteem. (New York: Doubleday, 1970), p. 3.*

Our own involvement with the value of a self-esteem program in the schools began with a comprehensive study of every known book in the field. Study after study indicated a child who feels good about him/herself does better in school. We wanted to find a school program that would promote children's self-esteem in a meaningful way. After looking at several in existence, our response was, "That's fine, but it isn't what we would do." Ultimately, we asked ourselves, "What would we do?"

In order to answer this question three surveys were taken. Teachers, children, and parents were asked questions concerning the social and academic school problems consistent with each age group. For the most part, we discovered that a few central issues occurred at each grade level. From these trouble areas we began to create the PSE program. All of the program topics came from this survey.

At this point, we met with anyone interested in our program (as well as some people who had never heard of it — or us)! In the eight years since *Project Self-Esteem's* creation, the list of advisors and consultants is endless. We are especially grateful to Dorothy Corkille Briggs, Dr. Mary Dugan, Dr. Leo Buscaglia, Dr. Nathaniel Branden, Dr. Vicki Dendenger, L. S. Barksdale, Gene Bedley, Dr. Judith Annette Milburn, Susan K. White, and Marilyn Slaughter for the information and guidance which kept us soundly on track.

PSE is a program for grades K-6. It is designed to be taught in the classroom by a team of four parents. The program for grade 6 may be taught by two parents. The lesson topics include:

- *Realizing Your Uniqueness*
- *Attitude*
- *Compliments*
- *Rumors*
- *Stress Reduction*
- *Feelings*
- *Person and Action are Separate*
- *Friendship*
- *Tattling and Cheating*
- *Remembering to Be Kind to Each Other*
- *Goal Setting*

- *Listening*
- *Learning*
- *Stealing and Teasing*
- *Communication Skills*
- *Learning about Handicaps*
- *Social Skills*
- *Assertive Training*
- *Peers and Conformity*
- *Alcohol and Drug Abuse*
- *Preparation for Junior High*

There are five separate programs: a program for grades K, 1, 2/3, 4, 5, and 6. The Kindergarten and First Grade programs have 5 twenty-five minute lessons and can be taught every other week, beginning in January, February, or March. The Second/Third Grade program has 12 forty-minute lessons to be taught on an every other week basis, as well. It can be started in the fall. The Third Graders repeat the 2/3 lessons for extra emphasis. Fourth and Fifth Grades have 11 forty-minute lessons each, and the Sixth Grade program contains 9 forty-minute lessons. A chart on the next page shows a suggested schedule for presenting Project Self-Esteem. It is recommended that the 2/3 lessons be started in 2nd, 3rd and 4th grades the first year to make it easier for the volunteers. We have included a separate Teacher's Guide for individual teacher use. This Guide is provided in case schools have difficulty in recruiting parent volunteers.

The most effective means of reinforcement is school and home working together. So, for home reinforcement, we've added a supplementary Parent Program. This guide also gives parents a vehicle to incorporate their own personal experience and values into the overall philosophy.

Suggested Schedule

Grade Level	Number of Lessons	Number of Minutes	Limited Program – First Year	Regular Program – First Year	Regular Program – Second Year
K	5	25	K	K	K
1	5	25	1	1	1
2	12	40	2/3	2/3	2/3
3	12	40	2/3	2/3	2/3
4	11	40	2/3	2/3	4
5	11	40	0	5	5
6	9	40	0	6	6

* Possibility: Begin in only one classroom the first year.

The first PSE pilot program began in the Newport-Mesa Unified School District, Newport Beach, California in 1978. The pilot program was implemented in ten schools in southern California. Within a two year period, as an extension of the pilot program, *Project Self-Esteem* mushroomed to being introduced in over 200 schools in Orange County. Schools have discovered the innumerable benefits of the PSE program. In 1985, *Project Self-Esteem* was awarded the Disneyland Community Service Award for its outstanding contribution to youth.

This program is inexpensive, practical, easy to understand and easy to implement. Teachers have appreciated the efforts by the parent volunteers, and parent involvement has aided in community home-school relationships. This fun, warm program is working!

A part of our outreach has included presenting workshops and talks to groups of all types. We have compiled a list of the most frequently asked questions about PSE.

Do you feel our children have low self-esteem? Is that why you are bringing this program to our school?

Not at all. Though every single one of us would benefit from self-esteem training, our intent is: (1) To raise the self-esteem of each individual child. (2) To assist high self-esteem children in maintaining their sense of well-being. (3) To give all children tools for handling the ups and downs of daily life.

Doesn't an extra program take away from time for the basic subjects?

Statistics overwhelmingly prove children who feel good about themselves learn more easily and retain information longer. They do better in school. This program involves no more than 12 forty-minute periods throughout the year on what really needs to be a daily course. Balance is what we need. Producing masses of intellectual giants who have no fundamental resources for day-to-day living will result in an even more stressful world than we now have.

Shouldn't self-esteem be taught at home?

Absolutely! In this rapidly-expanding world, there doesn't seem to be any such thing as too much positive reinforcement. We have no intention of taking over the parent's job. As parents ourselves, we know we cannot have too much support!

What does this program cost?

An itemized list is included in Chapter I. Depending upon the number of teams and classrooms involved in the first year, implementation of the PSE program could cost under $200. This cost does not include the optional purchase of a training video. Maintenance costs, once the program has been introduced, is less than a hundred dollars. Some ways to raise money for the PSE program are through: PTA and PFO funds, local service groups and merchants, private donations, or fundraisers at school.

Can these materials be used in the home?

Yes. The Parent Program is a guideline for teaching the PSE principals in the home. The most effective means of teaching occurs when school and home combine to give support to children.

How do you know this program works?

Time is the best measure of success, especially in subjective areas such as self-esteem. Feedback from former students has been very positive. Principals note a distinct attitude change in schools using PSE. Individual teachers are tremendously supportive, saying the program gives them enough tools to work with all year long. A program which grows from ten schools to 160 schools in one year and has been in use for eleven years has its own success record. Self-esteem is not easily measured but we know if seeds are planted in a field, some will grow.

Does PSE work well with low-achieving, minority, and limited-English speaking students?

There has been wonderful, proven success in communities that have low-achieving, minority, and limited-English speaking students. Because PSE addresses the social needs of youth and gives them a specific way to do more than cope, this program is especially effective in these communities.

Can we begin the PSE program in January?

Yes. You may want to (1) Teach the lessons on an every week basis rather than every other week basis. It is more difficult to assimilate the material, but will work. (2) Begin teaching on an every week basis for four lessons, then skip to every other week. (3) Skip three lessons the first year.

Usually the 2/3 program is begun in grades 2, 3, and 4 the first year. Can you start all six programs the first year?

Of course! It does take more volunteers as well as a lot more coordination and work to begin all the programs the first year. However, this has been successfully accomplished at many schools.

Why do you repeat the same lesson in grades 2 and 3?

Do you know how many times children have watched "The Brady Bunch?" Repetition is a great teacher. Also, it assists new students coming into the school to keep current with the PSE philosophy.

Do we need parent volunteers to teach the PSE program?

No. We have included an individual Teacher's Guide for use by the teacher or in some areas, where parent resources are limited, local women's groups have taught the program as their service project. The program is designed to be taught by volunteer men and women or the classroom teacher.

It has taken twelve years of research, writing, and testing to create this program. Though the two of us have been the "die-hards" in terms of actually creating the program, innumerable people have assisted us. We are excited about the potential outreach of this work and thank you heartfully, for your energized caring. The world won't get better unless we make it better. *Project Self-Esteem* is one way to assist in creating that better world. We send you love on your adventure.

Sandy McDaniel & Peggy Bielen

Memo to All PSE Volunteers

If you find your stomach
       has giant butterflies
And your knees both wobble
       with fear you can't disguise

If you wake up each day
       going over your part
And get the golly-womps
       knowing it's time to start

If you wonder how you
       will ever make it through
You've proved you are normal—
       we were once just like you!

You'll survive the first class
       and all your hearts will soar
The fun will have begun
       it will no longer be a chore.

We just want to tell you
       be certain you don't forget
To enjoy every minute
       the trivia do not sweat.

No one expects perfection
       mistakes are always all right
If it makes you feel better
       we still get first-class fright.

The care that brought you here
       through children's life will flow
Bringing satisfaction
       wherever you may go.

We're sending you our thoughts
       and love for all your caring
Be sure to let us know
       how each of you is faring!

Chapter

I

Team Leader's Guide

Chapter I

Team Leader's Guide

Letter to Team Leader:

You have chosen to go the extra mile by taking on the leadership of Project Self-Esteem. This whole program was created by people dedicated to going beyond the expected measure and giving more. We want you to know how much we appreciate you! Without your dedication and drive, PSE is just an idea. We've designed this chapter to assist with the implementation of the program in a comprehensive and efficient manner.

Self-esteem is an intangible commodity and not easily measured. You might never fully know how much good your efforts will bring; however, we've found the feedback from former PSE students to be continuous and positive. Those of us who created PSE feel we cannot provide too much assistance to youngsters growing up in this complex world.

> Lack of awareness is the same as no choice. If we give new choices to the youngsters of today, they may create a better tomorrow.

Being involved in a parent support group has many rewards. You will gain a closer relationship with the faculty of the school as you and the principal work closely together to make the program successful. You will also know you made PSE possible for many children. This is a feeling no words can describe.

It is important to get this program started in a manner which works best for you. There is no right or wrong way to implement Project Self-Esteem into a school, but there are difficulties that you can avoid if you follow our suggestions. Three vital steps are needed for implementing Project Self-Esteem. Begin by establishing a rapport with the principal of your school and providing him/her materials to rely on in support of the program. (See Principal's Packet, pp. 22 to 26.)

It will also be important to build a cooperative effort with the teaching faculty. (See Introducing Program to School Staff, p. 27.) Remember, there would be no Project Self-Esteem without a school in which to teach. Your job is to enhance the quality of education for the individual child and to do so as a positive addition to the school program. This is accomplished by continually respecting your position as a guest in the school.

Finally, it is mandatory that you introduce the program to the parents. (See Introducing the Program to Parents, p. 29.) It is ABSOLUTELY VITAL that notices, including the right to excuse a child from the program, be sent home prior to teaching the first lesson. (See Parent Permission Slip, p. 24.) In addition, it's important to have a parent coffee prior to teaching the first lesson at which you may address any questions parents may have. Questions you are unable to answer may be sent to the authors. (See Questions Page, p. 42.)

Probably the first issue you will want to address is: How many classrooms and how many grades will be involved in the program? A school may begin using the 2/3 program in grades 2,3, and 4 the first year. During our first year we taught in seven classrooms, scientifically chosen — by where our children were! The idea is to begin with a number which is comfortable for you and grow into full use of the program. Some schools have begun with all six programs in the first year and have done so with relative ease. Having enough volunteers to teach, prepare materials, and help organize the program are the primary considerations.

Again, we send you oceans of appreciation for choosing to work with the Project Self-Esteem program. We invite you to send any feedback about the implementation and effects of the program.

Organizational Outline for Team Leader

1. Read entire program and become familiar with PSE concepts.
2. Meet with principal of school and submit Principal's Packet for review. (See pp. 22 to 26.)
3. Meet with principal of school for a second time.
4. Introduce PSE to school teaching staff. (See p. 27.)
5. Set up scheduling for lessons. (See pp. 31 to 32.)
6. Introduce PSE to parents. (See p. 29.)
7. Recruit team members. (See p. 30.)
8. Train team members. (See pp. 33 to 41.)
9. Begin teaching...and enjoy!

Expenses for Implementing and Maintaining the Program

One of the most surprising features about Project Self-Esteem is that it is so inexpensive to implement and operate in comparison to other programs of a similar nature. The basic expenses include:

1. Copies of the book, *Project Self-Esteem* (recommended: one for each team member, and a copy for both the principal and the superintendent)
2. Paper for worksheets and award certificates (Often the school will allow you to use their supplies for this need. Be sure to discuss this with the principal.)
3. Poster board for bulletin board strips (Again, check with the school principal.)
4. Yarn for making a Smiley for each child in the 2/3, 4th, and 5th grade programs.
5. Harmony Bear hand puppet
6. Coffee and rolls for initial parent meeting
7. Name tags and notebooks for team members (optional)

Funding is not as complicated as you may imagine. Check with the Parent Teacher Organization. This group can be very supportive if given enough time for appropriate budget planning. Another area to explore is local civic groups or large companies who often sponsor special programs in the interest of bettering community relationships. Don't overlook private donations as a source of funding. Finally, one of the most successful ways of raising money is to hold a fundraiser at school. The enthusiasm generated in creating a fundraiser spills over into the excitement for the program itself.

Materials to be Used in the Program

The materials used in the Project Self-Esteem program are inexpensive and easy to assemble. They may be put together by team members and other parent volunteers or may be purchased. All materials are to be prepared in advance of each lesson to avoid stress and possible lack of quality.

The following will be needed:

1. **Principal's Packet**
   The packet includes a letter to the principal, sample forms to be used, and a copy of the book. It is designed to give him/her an overview and basic understanding of the program.

2. **Teacher pages**
   These sheets include an Agreement Form, a Friendly Reminder Form, and a Teacher Evaluation Sheet. (You need to give an Evaluation Sheet to every teacher FOR EACH LESSON.)

3. **Student worksheets**
   The 2/3 program has student worksheets for Lessons 2, 6, 7, 9, and 12. The fourth grade program has student worksheets for Lessons 2 and 3, 5, and 11. The fifth grade program has student worksheets for Lessons 3, 4, 5, 9, and 11. There are no student worksheets for the sixth grade program. Award certificates and evaluation sheets may be reproduced for the K, 1, 2/3, 4, and 5th grade programs. (Reproducible masters can be found at the end of the appropriate chapter.)

4. **Notices for the coffee**

5. **Parent permission slip for each child**
Parent permission slips must be returned to the teacher before the program begins.

6. **Home reinforcement sheets**
The Parent Program (Chapter IX) is provided to give parents an opportunity to discuss their own values and teachings. The reproducible sheets for the Parent Program are to be prepared well in advance of each lesson. We have chosen not to have worksheets for each lesson on the Kindergarten–First Grade levels. The parent page for the Kindergarten and First Grade programs consists of a one-page explanatory letter. This same letter can also be sent home to parents of students in grades 2–6 who are new to the PSE program. Don't forget to date and sign the master before sending the letter home. The parent pages for the 2/3, 4th, 5th, and 6th grade programs cover each individual lesson.

Discuss with the principal and faculty the best means of sending these sheets home so they are received by the parents. Whether a family chooses to use the Parent Program is an individual decision. Be certain the parents, staff, and children understand this point.

7. **Bulletin board strips**
It is important that these strips be printed neatly and in large letters so they are readable. We do not recommend script, cursive, or calligraphy writing for these signs. The following are the bulletin board strips:

Kindergarten Program

Lesson 1:   You Can Always Be a Friend to You.
Lessons 2–5:   I Have Self-Esteem It's True. I Won't Hurt Me, and
                I'm Kind to You.

1st Grade Program

Lesson 1:   Friends Are Kind to Each Other.
Lesson 2:   I Can Always Be a Friend to Me.
Lessons 3–5:   I Have Self-Esteem It's True. I Won't Hurt Me, and
                I'm Kind to You.

2/3 Grade Program

Lesson 1:   Grade 2 — I Am Special.
              Grade 3 — There is Nobody Just Like Me!

Lesson 2:   Grade 2 — You're Special.
              Grade 3 — Attitude is the Difference.

Lesson 3:   Grade 2 — Compliments Bring Smiles.
              Grade 3 — Everybody Likes Compliments.

Lesson 4:   Grade 2 — Stress Can Be Valuable and
              Harmful.
              Grade 3 — Rumors Can Be Harmful.

Lesson 5:   Grades 2 & 3 — Everybody Has Feelings.

Lesson 6:   Grades 2 & 3 — I Can Like Someone and Not
              Like What He/She Does.

Lesson 7:   Grades 2 & 3 — #1. Say How You Feel.
              #2. Say What You Want.

Lesson 8:   Grade 2 — Listen to Other People's Tone of
              Voice.
              Grade 3 — Tone of Voice/Body Language/
              Words Are Ways to Communicate.

Lesson 9:   (Student created)

Lesson 10:   Grades 2 & 3 — Choose an Appropriate
              Time, Place, and Way to Express Your
              Upsets.

Lesson 11:   Grades 2 & 3 — Write Ten Ways to Be Good
              to Yourselves and Ten Ways to be Good to
              Each Other.

4th Grade Program

Lesson 1:   I Am Special. It Is Important to Listen to Others Because They Are Special, Too.

Lesson 2:   A Journey of a Thousand Miles Begins With a Single Step.

Lesson 3:   We All Like Compliments. Let's Give One to Mother, Father, Brother, Sister, Teacher, Friends, You!

Lesson 4:   Listening is Important; Stress Reduction, Too. Why?

Lesson 5:   Make School Easier: Learn to Memorize.

Lesson 6:   One Person's Feelings Can Be Different From Another Person's Feelings.

Lesson 7:   A Person With High Self-Esteem Feels Good About Self. (with happy face) A Person With Low Self-Esteem Doesn't Feel Good About Self. (with sad face) What Small Behaviors Can I Change to Help Me Feel Better About Myself?

Lesson 8:   Learn to Say No When You Want to Say No.

Lesson 9:   To Have A Friend, Be One!

Lesson 10:   (Use the two Poem Charts from Activity D and F.)

5th Grade Program

Lesson 1:   Set Reasonable Goals for Improving Your Self-Esteem.

Lesson 2:   (Use the states and capitals listed in Activity D.)

Lesson 3:   Juneau, Alaska and Austin, Texas

Lesson 4:   Think What You'd Hear If You Listened More Often.

Lesson 5:   "You" Messages are War Words.

Lesson 6:   Find an Appropriate Way to Handle Your Anger.

Lesson 7:   Don't Hang onto Anger.

Lesson 8:   Broken Record = Kind Statement Plus Policy Statement.

Lesson 9:   It's Important to Respect the Differences in Others.

Lesson 10:   (Use the two Poem Charts from Activity D and F.)

6th Grade Program

Lesson 1:   Stress — Deal With It.

Lesson 2:   Weigh the Risk and Gain In Making a Choice.

Lesson 3:   Saying No is OK.

Lesson 4:   If Someone Puts You Down, Fog Them.

Lesson 5:   Choose Your Friends Wisely.

Lesson 6:   Recipe for Having a Friend: Be One!

Lesson 7:   Say NO to Drugs.

Lesson 8 and 9:   (none)

8. Charts

Charts are an important visual aid for students. We are providing smaller versions of these charts. Please reproduce them on poster size boards for clear student visibility. If they are laminated, they may be used year after year. The following are the charts to be used in the PSE program:

2/3 Grade Program

Lesson 3, Activity D: Molly

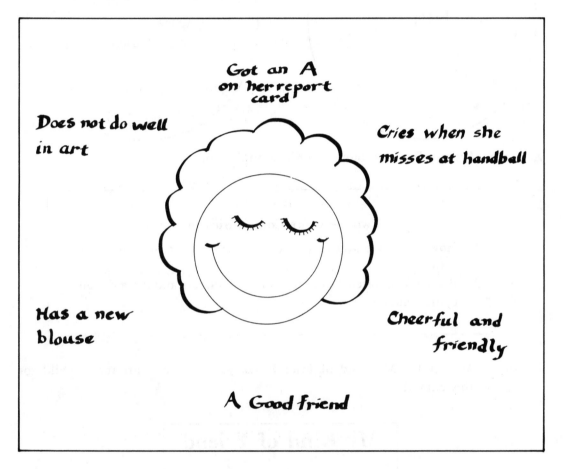

Lesson 5, Activity C: Feelings Sentences   (The word "feelings" goes in each blank.)

Everybody has _____.

_____ are based upon a past experience.

One person's _____ can be different from another person's _____.

_____ can change.

Lesson 7, Activity G: Wants and Feelings

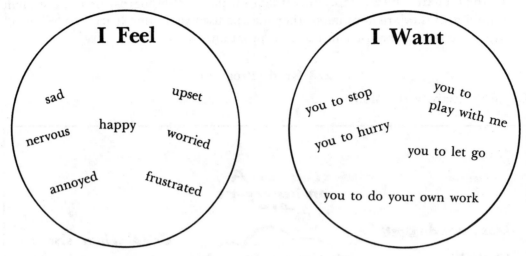

I Feel

sad   upset

nervous   happy   worried

annoyed   frustrated

I Want

you to stop   you to play with me

you to hurry

you to let go

you to do your own work

Lesson 8, Activity D: Two Steps For Communication

Two Steps for Communication

1. How you say something is an important part of communication.
2. If you do not listen carefully, you won't understand the message being sent.

Lesson 9, Activity C: My Kind of Friend (Draw an outline around a child for this chart.)

My Kind of Friend

Lesson 10, Activity E: Appropriate Sentences

> Choose an appropriate time.
> Choose an appropriate place.
> Choose an appropriate way.
> Have a friend you can talk to,
> So your upsets cannot stay.

Lesson 11, Activity C: Poems

> If you like to tattle
> Believe it or not it's true
> You're minding other's business
> You don't feel good about you!

> Cheaters never prosper
> It's true as it can be
> For when you cheat the one you hurt
> Is you...it isn't me!

4th Grade Program

Lesson 2, Activity D: Goal Setting

> **Goal Setting**
>
> 1. Set a reachable goal.
> 2. Write out steps for reaching that goal.
> 3. Keep going until you reach your goal.
> 4. Give yourself a reasonable time limit.
> 5. Evaluate — check your progress.
> 6. Compliment yourself.

Lesson 4, Activity B: Signs for the Pioneer Game

Group 1: Pioneers — "That's Us!"

Group 2: West — "Thata way!"

Group 3: Oxen — "Click, Clack"

Group 4: Wild Animals — "Grrr-Grrr"

Group 5: Afraid — "Help! Help!"

Group 6: Attitude — "You can if you think you can!"

Whole Class: Soldiers — "Do-do-do-doot-do-do, charge!"

Lesson 5, Activity D: U.S. Presidents

Washington, Adams, Jefferson, Madison, Monroe,
Adams, Jackson, Van Buren, Harrison, Tyler

Lesson 6, Activity C: Feelings Sentences   (The word "feelings" goes in each blank.)

Everybody has _____.

_____ are based upon a past experience.

One person's _____ can be different from another person's _____.

_____ can change.

Lesson 7, Activity D: High/Low Self-Esteem   (Draw an outline around a child for this chart's two figures. See phrases for strips in the lesson under Activity D.)

Lesson 8, Activity C: Types of Communicators

KING KONG — Aggressive: shouts, threatens, calls names, throws a fit, stormy, swears

DOORMAT — Passive: does nothing, withdraws, pouts, feels sorry for self, sulks, whines, begs, cries

ASSERTIVE — Says how he/she feels and states what he/she wants

---

Lesson 9, Activity C: My Kind of Friend   (Draw an outline around a child for this chart.)

Lesson 9, Activity D: Cinquain

Cinquains   (sin-cane)
First line...name or a noun
Second line...two adjectives describing line one
Third line...three verbs
Fourth line...one adjective
Fifth line...three words which describe

Lesson 10, Activity D: Poem

If you like to take things
That don't belong to you
You may end up behind bars
And it won't be at the zoo!

Lesson 10, Activity F: Poem

> If you do not talk straight
> Use teasing without end.
> You'll damage someone's feelings
> And might even lose a friend!

5th Grade Program

Lesson 1, Activity C: Success Questions

> 1. What happened?
> 2. What are three facts about the incident?
> 3. How did you feel about it?

Lesson 1, Activity E: Goal Setting Sentence Strips

> Set a reachable goal.

> Write out steps for reaching that goal.

> Keep going until you reach your goal.

> Give yourself a reasonable time limit.

Evaluate — check your progress.

Compliment yourself.

Lesson 2, Activity D: Eleven States and Their Capitals

Harrisburg, Pennsylvania   Nashville, Tennessee
Little Rock, Arkansas   Frankfort, Kentucky
Concord, New Hampshire   Springfield, Illinois
Topeka, Kansas   Hartford, Connecticut
Salt Lake City, Utah   Jefferson City, Missouri
Columbus, Ohio

Lesson 3, Activity D: Lovable, Capable Character

Lesson 4, Activity D: Signs for the Space Game

Group 1:   Space Voyager — "That's us!"

Group 2:   Shuttle — "Chooo!"

Group 3:   Space Station — "Mmmmmmmmmmm"

Group 4:   Afraid — "Red alert! Red alert!"

Group 5:   Attitude — "You can if you think you can!"

Whole class: Earth — "That's where we live!"

Lesson 8, Activity C: Types of Communicators

KING KONG — Aggressive: shouts, threatens, calls names, throws a fit, stormy, swears
DOORMAT — Passive: does nothing, withdraws, pouts, feels sorry for self, sulks, whines, begs, cries
ASSERTIVE — Says how he/she feels and states what he/she wants

---

Lesson 10, Activity D: Poem

> If you like to take things
> That don't belong to you
> You may end up behind bars
> And it won't be at the zoo!

Lesson 10, Activity F: Poem

> If you do not talk straight
> Use teasing without end.
> You'll damage someone's feelings
> And might even lose a friend!

6th Grade Program

Lesson 3, Activity C: Types of Communicators

> **KING KONG** — Aggressive: raise voice, shout, threaten, calls names, hit
> **DOORMAT** — Passive: sit, do nothing, hide from, yell "ouch" a lot, pout
> **ASSERTIVE** — Positive: confident in most everything, will claim or defend his/her rights

9. **Harmony Bear hand puppet**
   This puppet is available for purchase from the publisher and/or the authors. Harmony is a male brown bear. It is important that he be soft and furry. Eyes and nose need to be firmly attached. You may use doll clothes to give him even more personality.

10. **Name tags (These may be made or purchased)**
    It is important to have name tags and use them for each presentation. They let the school staff know you belong on campus and allow the children to learn your name. Be sure the printing on each tag is large and legible. Inexpensive tags may be purchased from a stationery store. Trophy shops will print plastic tags at a reasonable cost.

Directions for Making a Smiley

Use Roving or other braided yarn that combs out easily. You will need one 3-yard strand plus one 5-inch strand per child. If bought on spools, figure one spool (100 yards) per classroom.

STEP 1

Take three yards of yarn. Wrap loosely around your hand or an object (cardboard). Carefully take yarn off of your hand.

STEP 2

Tie the five inch strand in a knot around the center of the yarn, leaving loops on both sides of the knotted area.

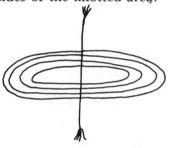

STEP 3

Cut the loops.

STEP 4

Unbraid each strand.

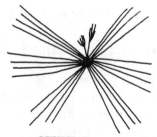

STEP 5

Brush the ends so they are fluffy. Brush away from the tie.

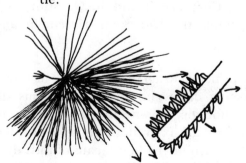

STEP 6

Cut off any long pieces or ends so the Smiley is round and fluffy.

11. **Smileys**

These fluffy reminders for giving compliments are used in the 2/3, 4th and 5th grade programs. It is wise to have a "Smiley Chairperson" who will buy the yarn, instruct volunteer mothers on the process of making them, and make sure the Smileys are available when needed. It is fun to have a "Smiley Party." Some local groups may choose to make Smileys as a service project. Smileys are to be bagged in groups of thirty-five. It is recommended that the Smileys in each bag be the same color.

HINT: Do not wear dark clothing while making these. You will turn into a human fuzz ball!

12. **Flannel Boards and Cut Outs**

The Kindergarten and First Grade programs use a flannel board and cut-outs for some of the lessons. Patterns for the cut-outs are included at the end of Chapters II and III.

Flannel boards are often in use by the teacher at the Kindergarten and First Grade level, but you might prefer to make your own. Use a heavy base for the flannel board. A children's blackboard, a piece of plywood, or even heavy poster board will do. The size varies, but the flannel board can be approximately 3' × 4'. You will want to cover the board with a pastel-colored flannel material. Be sure to stretch the material tight so it won't sag with usage.

Introduction of the Program to the School Principal

Before you contact the school principal be sure you have thoroughly read the PSE program as well as the pages you will be submitting for review. (See pp. 22 to 26.) It is important you have in mind an understanding of the program and your objectives for the year.

Set up your first meeting. Take along both the Principal's Packet and a copy of the book, *Project Self-Esteem*, for the principal to review. Ask him/her to read the Introduction, the Parent Program section (see Chapter IX), and the Question Page (see p. 42). It is imperative that your principal tells the district superintendent and the school board about the program.

Set up a time for a second meeting. Ask the principal to agree to review all materials prior to that meeting. During the second meeting, discuss how many classrooms will be involved during the first year. Usually a school begins with the 2/3 program in Grades 2, 3, and 4 but it is possible to begin with all six grades right away. Review possible scheduling with your principal and determine the best means of introducing the PSE concept to the teaching staff. (See pp. 27 to 28.) STRONGLY ENCOURAGE THE PRINCIPAL TO OFFER PSE ONLY TO THOSE TEACHERS WHO VOLUNTEER TO HAVE IT IN THEIR ROOMS.

Decide how the program will be introduced to the parents. A notice in the school newspaper, a flyer, and a coffee gives parents an opportunity to be informed about the PSE program and its concepts. (See pp. 29 to 30.) A permission slip is mandatory and is to be sent home with each child in the PSE program. (See p. 24.) As noted on the form, any parent who chooses to remove his/her child from the classroom is free to do so. Discuss with the principal what is his/her plan for any child not included in the program (library, etc.).

THE SELECTION OF TEAM MEMBERS IS THE MOST IMPORTANT DECISION TO BE MADE. It is vital to choose appropriate people so the integrity of the program is maintained. (See pp. 30 to 31.) Compile a list of suggested names from the principal, the classroom teachers (if appropriate), and your own sources. Including the principal in the final selection is imperative to the strength of the program. Also, it allows you a comfortable way of telling someone they were not selected, this year. We cannot overemphasize the need to be extremely careful in your selection. It is difficult to "fire" a volunteer, and the choice of team members really is the most important decision you will make.

The Parent Program is a vital link to the outreach potential of Project Self-Esteem. The details including the cost of sending this program home and how to make sure it gets home need to be discussed ahead of time.

Sample Principal's Letter

(for Principal's Packet)

Message to School Principal:

You have just been contacted about Project Self-Esteem. We appreciate the time you have taken to meet with the team leader and to acquaint yourself with this material. The intent of this packet is to inform you about the PSE goals and objectives. Project Self-Esteem is not just another program; here are some of its unique features:

- PROJECT SELF-ESTEEM has been thoroughly tested— approximately 800 schools and 200,000 people are already involved in the program.

- PROJECT SELF-ESTEEM is practical — it may be implemented entirely by trained parent volunteers thus requiring no extra time from the teaching staff.

- PROJECT SELF-ESTEEM is inexpensive — the program can be implemented for less than three hundred dollars.

- PROJECT SELF-ESTEEM will not interfere with present curriculum — there are never more than 12 forty-minute lessons throughout the entire year.

- PROJECT SELF-ESTEEM builds strong community and parent involvement relationships — it can be used as the basis of a Substance Abuse Program.

In a recent survey of school administrators across the country, student self-esteem was listed as the NUMBER ONE need. Studies have proven that students who feel secure about themselves do better academically. Therefore, self-esteem and strong choice-making skills need to be fostered as much as academic skills.

Project Self-Esteem is designed to build self-assurance and increase the choice-making potential of each individual student. PSE teaches coping skills. It is fun and it works!

You will note there is a Parent Permission Slip, an Agreement Form for Teachers and Teacher's Evaluation Sheet in your packet. All of these are necessary components of the PSE program. They have been developed to insure the rights of both the home and school. The Parent Permission Slip gives parents the option of having their child participate in the PSE program. The Teacher Agreement Form allows the individual teacher the right to decide whether he/she wants to participate in this program. The Evaluation Sheet ensures that the teacher, who is legally responsible for his/her class, is attentive and monitoring each lesson.

Please send any questions which you or the PSE volunteer staff are unable to answer to the authors directly. The address is: P.O. Box 16001, Newport Beach, CA 92659. (714) 756-2226. A Question Page is included on page 42. It is designed to provide information to any parents who might be concerned about the philosophy, application, or effects of the program. Please feel free to contact us if we may assist you in any way.

We trust you will see the immense potential for positive change that this program will bring to your school. Your support is essential and deeply appreciated by all the people connected with Project Self-Esteem. Thank you for your interest and your vision.

Warmly,

Sandy McDaniel and Peggy Bielen
Founders of Project Self-Esteem

Materials for Review:

Project Self-Esteem book   (Introduction and Parent Program marked)
Parent Permission Slip
Agreement Form for Teachers
Evaluation Sheet for Teachers

Sample Parent Permission Slip

Date

Dear Parent(s) or Guardian;

As a part of our school curriculum in grades K-6, we are offering a coping skills program called Project Self-Esteem. This program will be taught by volunteer parents from our school.

The K-1 program is based on personal safety and being kind to others.

For grades 2 and 3 the lesson topics include: Realizing Your Uniqueness, Gratitudes and Changes/Attitude, Compliments, Rumors, Stress Reduction Exercises, Feelings, Person and Action are Separate, Friendship, Tattling/Cheating, and Communication Skills.

For grades 4 and 5 the lesson topics include: Realizing Our Uniqueness, Goal Setting, Compliments, Listening, Stress Reduction Exercises, Learning to Memorize, Feelings, Friendship, Stealing/Teasing, Understanding Handicaps, and Communication Skills.

For grade 6 the lesson topics include: Social Skills I & II, Broken Record, Fogging, Assertive Apology, Making Choices, Drug Abuse, and Introduction to Junior High School.

The Project Self-Esteem curriculum materials were available for review at our parent coffee. They will also be available at Back-to-School Night and Open House. Parents who wish to review the curriculum on campus may make an appointment to do so. Questions about PSE may be address to: (name and phone number of PSE team leader).

Sincerely,

(Principal)

- -

_____ Yes I want my child to participate in the PSE program.
_____ No I do not want my child to participate in the PSE program.

Comments: _____

_____

_____ Yes I am interested in reviewing the PSE curriculum.

Parent/Guardian _____

Name of child _____   Teacher's Name _____

PLEASE RETURN THIS FORM BEFORE _____

Agreement Form for Teachers

Dear Classroom Teacher,

Welcome to Project Self-Esteem! The objectives and goals of PSE have been explained to you. We are looking forward to working with you and your class.

THE PSE TEAM ASSIGNED TO YOUR ROOM AGREES TO:

1. Arrive and leave on time. We respect that your schedule is being interrupted and are on a tight time schedule ourselves.

2. Let you know, in advance, if there is ever a schedule change.

3. Handle the classroom discipline in a manner consistent with your own.

4. Remember we are guests in your room and let you know how much we appreciate this time with your class.

THE FOLLOWING IS ASKED OF EACH CLASSROOM TEACHER:

1. Leave space for a twenty-five to forty-minute lesson consistent with the lesson schedule given to you at the first of the year.

2. Be in active attendance at every lesson and support the program with any of the follow-up activities. (It is distracting for the team and children if you correct papers.)

3. Allow chalkboard space and a bulletin board for each PSE lesson.

4. Have your class ready to go when the team arrives.

5. Stay in the room during the entire lesson. In most states this is a legal requirement.

— —

AGREEMENT BETWEEN THE CLASSROOM TEACHER AND PSE

Having PSE in your classroom occurs only on a volunteer basis. Please detach and return this part of the form if you want your classroom to be included in the program for the _____ school year.

Yes! I wish to participate in the Project Self-Esteem Program and agree to support the program as listed above. I understand the lessons will not be taught if I am not in the room.

_____   _____
                Teacher Signature   Grade

Please indicate below if you use any specific methods for obtaining class attention/control.

Turn off lights   Stop and Wait   Other_____

Teacher Evaluation Sheet

Lesson # _____   Date _____

Topic _____   Teacher _____

Please hand this form to a team member as we leave today.

1. What parts did the students seem to like the best?

2. What parts did you like the best?

3. Did control or discipline seem a problem at any time?

4. Do you have any ideas or suggestions for improving the lesson?

5. How will you and your students use these concepts before our next lesson?

THANK YOU! THANK YOU! THANK YOU! THANK YOU! THANK YOU!

Introducing Program to School Staff

Arrange to talk to all of the faculty members at a staff meeting to describe the program, answer questions, and give information about the class sign-up procedure and the Teacher Agreement Form (see p. 25), etc. Talk to the entire faculty, not just the ones who will be using PSE. Let the teachers know that questions will be asked by parents such as: Why doesn't my child have PSE? Informing the whole faculty enables each teacher to address those questions. Pass out Teacher Agreement Forms to appropriate faculty members.

Ask the principal to make it extremely clear to the faculty members that IT IS ILLEGAL FOR VOLUNTEERS TO BE IN A CLASSROOM WITHOUT THE TEACHER BEING PRESENT. The team will not teach unless the teacher is in the classroom.   (A substitute qualifies as a teacher.)

Set up an early morning or lunch time meeting for additional questions and sign-up. Collect Teacher Agreement Forms. (See pp. 31 to 32 for detailed scheduling information.) It is helpful to post the complete PSE schedule in the faculty room and be sure the school secretary, as well as the principal, has a copy. If the school has a school calendar, mark the PSE schedule on it. Give each classroom teacher using the program a schedule. It is advisable, for the first lesson only, to send out a Friendly Reminder Memo with the day and time of that room's PSE lesson. (See p. 28.)

Remember, each teacher is giving you a precious gift — time with her students. Continually express your appreciation. You will soon discover that each teacher has his/her own way of conducting a class. Please do not use your exposure to the individual teacher as an opportunity to critique those methods. The purpose of PSE is to allow for differences.

NO INFORMATION about an individual teacher or student is to be discussed outside of the classroom. This is a matter of professional ethics. It is the classroom teacher, not a PSE volunteer, who is responsible for all communication to the parents about their children. PSE provides a safe place for the child to share and feel comfortable.

It is important, at this time, to inform the PTA President about the program's implementation. The PTA President is the primary representative of the parents in your school. Discuss with the principal the best means of doing this.

Friendly Reminder for the Teacher

This is a friendly reminder that Project Self-Esteem will be in your room on
_____ at _____. Please assist us by providing the
following:

> 1. Printed name tags on each student's desk
> 2. Chalkboard space
> 3. Wall space or bulletin board space for PSE strip

After Lesson 1, we will appreciate your taking the time to discuss with the class the bulletin board strip that we leave.

It would be helpful to start on time. We promise to be prompt and to keep within the time schedule provided. As you well know, some lessons are more predictable than others. . .so please bear with us.

We will give you an Evaluation Form before each lesson. Such feedback is vital to the quality and integrity of this program.

It is imperative that you are present in the classroom and actively participating in the lesson. You are the most vital link in this chain of caring adults.

Many thanks from the PSE team.

Introducing Program to Parents

Parents who are well-informed about the contents of PSE are more likely to support the program. A parent coffee is a friendly way to be informative and give the parents an opportunity to ask questions. The team leader might have a concern about being able to answer every question asked by parents. By reading the Project Self-Esteem book, she will be well-equipped to respond. The principal needs to be in attendance to cover any district or state policies.

One purpose of the parent coffee is to secure volunteers for making Smileys, preparing the bulletin board strips and charts, and acting as chairperson for a fundraising event.

Information needs to be available for individual parents who want to review the Project Self-Esteem program. Discuss with the principal a policy for having a copy of the book available for parent review. Let the parents know they are WELCOME TO WATCH A PSE LESSON IN ACTION. To avoid having more adults watching than children participating, it is necessary for parents to contact the principal for permission to be in a classroom.

Following the coffee, a Parent Permission Slip will be sent home with each child. The purpose is to guarantee the rights of each parent to have a say in the curriculum for his/her child. By requiring a signed Permission Slip from each child, you will be certain that no parent is uninformed about the existence of the program.

The procedure for giving the coffee is as follows:

1. Send a notice to the parents.
2. Include all parents in the school, even those whose children will not have PSE.
3. If there is a school newspaper, announce the PSE coffee there as well.
4. Invite the members of the PTA board to the coffee.

The purpose of the coffee is to inform the parents of the objectives, structure, and value of this program. Please do not neglect to hold the coffee because it seems unnecessary. Informed parents are far more supportive than uninformed parents. Remember, you always have the option of saying, "I don't know" and getting back to someone.

During the meeting for the parents be sure to:
1. Have the principal introduce the PSE team leader(s) and volunteers.
2. Explain which classes will have PSE and why.
3. Describe the need for volunteers and pass around a sign up sheet.
4. Introduce Harmony and do a portion of Lesson 1 from the 2/3 program.
5. Give the lesson topics and general information about the program. (Use the book's Introduction and Team Training sections for assistance here.)

Home and school working together to give each child every possible resource to fully be who he or she is — this is a primary purpose of Project Self-Esteem.

Team Recruitment and Training

The Project Self-Esteem team of volunteers is selected by the principal and you. It is by far the most important decision to be made in support of this program. You need to choose warm, friendly people who are outgoing and not highly biased or judgmental. It is very awkward to "fire" a volunteer, so selection needs to be a careful process. It is best not to have people who tend to lecture or are critical and rigid in personality. It is also vital to have a group of people who can work comfortably with feedback from the teachers and from each other. The integrity of this program cannot be maintained unless the volunteers abide by the principles as stated in the text.

It is helpful to have a former classroom teacher on each team. It is also helpful to have a really hammy, playful person on each team to keep the whole atmosphere light, relaxed, and fun.

Be certain each new PSE volunteer is aware of his/her total obligation (rehearsal, teaching day, etc.) before a commitment is made. No one likes to agree to a commitment which suddenly grows.

In recruiting the volunteers, the initial input and FINAL SAY GOES TO THE PRINCIPAL who is responsible for everything that goes on in your school. Individually asking the classroom teachers for names and putting a notice in the school bulletin are ways to gather names. But THE ULTIMATE DECISION IS THE PRINCIPAL'S.

Try to balance the teams as much as possible. If one team substantially outshines the other(s), it can create some negative feelings among team members. Each volunteer is to be given a sheet which includes: the names and phone numbers of all the PSE volunteers in your school, the dates and time for each lesson to be taught, and the names/room numbers of the classroom teachers who are participating.

If your school district has purchased the PSE training video tape, schedule a three-and-a-half hour meeting (maybe a potluck lunch) for viewing this tape. Otherwise, use the Training Guide section (see pp. 33 to 41), and plan to give your own three-hour workshop. The primary objective for this workshop is to put PSE volunteers at ease, to give them some backup information about the PSE philosophy, and to create an atmosphere of professionalism in the school.

Early Planning and Scheduling

Scheduling is totally dependent upon the number of classrooms, the setup, team member needs, etc. The following are guidelines, only:
1. It is suggested you begin with the 2/3 grade program the first year. All the classes in the second, third and fourth grades may be included. During the second year you may go into the expanded schedule and include all six programs.
2. Check the school calendar to choose the day(s) of the week most suitable for scheduling PSE. Mondays and Fridays often get bumped by holidays but are OK to use if you allow for that. Be sure the schedules of any other special classes (music, remedial reading, etc.) are considered as well.
3. Before you draft the PSE schedule, have the following: a regular calendar; a school calendar with all special events, holidays, school assemblies, and conference schedules listed; information about lunch hours, reading, and math times, etc.
4. Make a tentative schedule. Keeping in mind all the special school activities, set up the sessions for the year on an every-other-week basis. The first lessons usually start at the end of October or the first of November. For grades 2-6, the program may be started in January. The Kindergarten and First Grade programs should start in January, February, or March. Remember to allow for vacations and holidays.
5. Make a sign up sheet for teachers.
6. After teachers have signed up for the days and time they prefer, prepare a final schedule and give a copy to the teachers, team members, school secretary, and principal.
7. Get a child count for each classroom so you will know the amount of materials needed.
8. Send a Friendly Reminder Memo (see p. 28) before the first lesson begins.

Scheduling the Expanded Program

The scheduling for an expanded program is dependent upon the number of classrooms involved, the number of PSE teams, the school situation, etc. The following are guidelines only and are to be used for those schools using all three programs:
1. Arrange to talk to teachers at a school staff meeting. You will need to let the faculty know of the extended program which you and the principal have worked out.
2. Announce a sign up time for the teachers.

3. Distribute the Teacher Agreement Forms. (See p. 25.) Some teachers may want to fill out the forms at the meeting and hand them in immediately. Set a due date for the others.

4. Make a list of teachers desiring the program.

5. Separate classrooms according to the grade level of the six programs. It is best to have a separate team for each of the six programs. The sixth grade program may be taught by two or three volunteers.

6. Decide how many teams you will need.

7. Arrange for parent recruitment. (See pp. 30 to 31.) Depending upon the number of classrooms and volunteers, it is possible to have PSE classes being taught on more than one day.

8. Arrange for the extra materials you will need for the expanded program.

9. Draft a scheduling format in the same manner as was done the first year. You may have two teams teaching at the same time in different classrooms or you may have one team teaching Lesson 1 on the second week, etc.

10. Check with the principal about an appropriate meeting room for the PSE team (for lunch especially). Faculty rooms are not to be used at any time without specific permission.

Sample of an Extended Scheduling Program

Format will vary according to number of teams and classrooms. This is an example only. It is for two teams, two different programs.

2/3 Team			4 Team		
Cote	9:05-9:45	Rm. 3			
White	10:10-10:50	Rm. 9	Rail	10:10-10:50	Rm. 16
Slaughter	11:00-11:50	Rm. 2	L. Hughes	11:05-11:45	Rm. 19
Ferrell	1:05-1:45	Rm. 8	Gorney	1:05-1:45	Rm. 23

Lesson 1	November 1
Lesson 2	November 15
Lesson 3	December 6
Lesson 4	January 4
Lesson 5	January 18
Lesson 6	February 1
Lesson 7	February 15
Lesson 8	March 1
Lesson 9	March 15
Lesson 10	April 15
Lesson 11	April 26
Lesson 12	May 10

Training Workshop — Introduction

The following is information used by the founders of PSE for a volunteer training workshop. It is scripted for your convenience. Please use it as a guide to assist your volunteers in being prepared, professional, and pleased! These training sessions may have as few as four people and as many as twenty in them, depending upon your individual circumstance. You might consider joining together with other schools in your area to provide one workshop for all the volunteers.

Warm up

We are going to do a section from the 4th grade program to assist us in knowing each other's names. To do this you will choose a positive adjective which begins with the same letter as your first name. You then say that positive adjective and your name together. So I, being Sandy, might choose to say "I am Special Sandy" or I could say "I am Sensitive Sandy." The positive word begins with the same letter as your first name and is said in front of your name. Take a minute to think about your choice. Now, we are going around the group and each of you will say "I am" along with your chosen names. (Go around whole room.)

I am going to pair you off so you can interview each other. You will be given time to find out at least two facts about each other which you will later tell the rest of the group. To find out more about each other, you will conduct a two-way interview, then introduce each other to the group using the information you have learned. Please use a complimentary adjective plus your first name in your introduction. (Allow three minutes for the interviews, then have each pair introduce each other. Remind everyone to use their adjective-name.)

> *HINT: The more members of a team feel comfortable with each other, the more vibrant they become as a teaching team. Having lunch together, doing these warm up exercises, and meeting as a unit gives them a connectedness which will make a difference in the work they will be doing.*

Background Information

According to Madeline Hunter at the University of California, Los Angeles, every human being needs to feel lovable and capable.[1] As a Project Self-Esteem team member you assist the children in feeling lovable by making it quite clear you are in the classroom because you care about them. In this way you may become a significant other in the lives of children — someone who supports and loves them.

---

1. "Teaching to Develop Strong Self-Concepts" Conference, Madeline Hunter. University of California, Los Angeles, November 12, 1978.

> You'll find that PSE addresses the issue of feeling lovable and capable in a very practical way and with information applicable to daily life.

Although a child who likes him/herself does better in school, there is more to be gained from this program than academic achievement. As Dorothy Corkille Briggs says in *Your Child's Self-Esteem:*

> *What is self-esteem? It is how a person feels about himself. It is his overall judgment of himself — how he likes his person. A person's judgment of self influences the kinds of friends he chooses, how he gets along with others, the kind of person he marries, and how productive he will be. It affects his creativity, integrity, stability, and even whether he will be a leader or follower. His feelings of self-worth form the core of his personality and determine the use he makes of his aptitudes and abilities. His attitude toward himself has a direct bearing on how he lives all parts of his life. In fact, self-esteem is the mainspring that slates each of us for success or failure as a human being.[2]*

An idea is a seed. Some seeds sprout more quickly than others. It is impossible to measure the degree of value your contribution can make to an individual child's life. In the long run, not only the child's life will be bettered, but you will find positive changes occuring in your own life as well.

Project Self-Esteem is a program designed for use by adults who care about children. It is a volunteer program. Project Self-Esteem is an idea but you make it work.

Basic Program Information

Project Self-Esteem has six programs: one for each grade level, K-6th. The Kindergarten and First Grade programs include 5 twenty-five minute lessons. There are 12 forty-minute lessons in the 2/3 program, 11 forty-minute lessons in the 4th and 5th programs, and 9 forty-minute lessons in the 6th grade program. The reason for repetition in the 2nd and 3rd grades is to accommodate the influx of new students and to support repetition as a successful teacher. This workshop will be based on the 2/3 program.

---

2. *Your Child's Self-Esteem*, Dorothy Corkille Briggs, New York: Doubleday, 1970, p. 3.

We are going to take a look at the twelve lessons in the 2/3 program to understand some of the philosophy behind each lesson.

> *HINT: For visual learners, it might be helpful to have a chart with the twelve lesson titles listed. This chart would also be useful for the parent coffee.*

Lessons and Their Philosophy

Lesson 1 — Realizing Your Uniqueness

In a world which is "do" oriented (do this, do that), realizing you don't have to do anything to be special can give you a new perspective on yourself and on life. Each of us wants to feel important. Realizing we are each a one of a kind happening reminds us of our specialness. Being special is an incredible gift given to us the day we were born and no person or event can take it away. Competing with others in being special is unnecessary because each and every person is unique in his or her own way. Being one of a kind is as special as you can get.

Lesson 2 — Gratitude and Changes/Attitudes

PSE teaches "attitude is the difference." Though we would like it to be so, rearranging the world to suit our needs generally doesn't work. But we are always, in every given situation, in charge of our attitude. If a child has a problem in school, the first thing to consider is his/her attitude. Attitude is clearly a choice each of us makes. Children need to see that, by changing attitude, they can take appropriate responsibility for what happens to them. In the PSE 2/3 program, we do lots of playacting to clearly demonstrate attitude is the difference. The program begins with the use of pantomime and develops into actual speaking parts.

Lesson 3 — Smileys and Compliments

People often focus on what they and others do wrong. Acknowledging positive qualities and actions is important for enhancing self-esteem. Ask an audience of any age to make a list of ten things they like and ten things they dislike about themselves and you'll find most people have difficulty with the positive list. PSE teaches children to look for the good in others and in themselves. Part of this lesson has to do with receiving compliments and learning what to do with a compliment.

Smileys are unbelievably popular among the children. A Smiley is a symbol for a compliment. It is warm, feels good, you smile inside and out when you receive one, and you can either keep a Smiley or give it away.

The use of "I messages" is encouraged in giving compliments. This means, you begin a compliment with the word "I." Normally, people say "You look nice." Use of the word "you" is a judgment. Judging sets up a people-pleasing syndrome. People-pleasing decreases self-esteem. So from "You look nice," we change the "you" to an "I" and say "I really like that color on you!" To say, "You're a good friend!" is an empty phrase. It is much more personal to hear, "I feel better having talked to you. I'm glad we are friends."

Let's practice giving and receiving compliments. Pair off where you are sitting and give each other at least one compliment. Remember to respond to the compliment in an appropriate way and please use "I messages" for your compliments.   (Go around the room.)

Lesson 4 — Rumors and Optional Stress Reduction

The topics for the PSE lessons evolved from a survey conducted among teachers, parents and students. One of the topics listed by teachers was rumors. To show how rumors get distorted, the PSE program uses the old telephone game where a single message is passed along and passed along until it becomes unrecognizable. The point of this part of the lesson is that each of us has a responsibility in the passing of rumors: Don't start one, don't believe everything you hear, and don't pass them along. Rumors don't just happen, people create rumors. It is your responsibility to stop them.

Research clearly indicates the importance of learning to relax. For health and general effectiveness, PSE offers several ways to assist children in dealing with stress. These exercises are optional.

Lesson 5 — Feelings

One of the most difficult things for people to do is to share their feelings. It is important to get in touch with feelings before they can be shared. This lesson is about getting in touch with and sharing feelings. I have something inside this box. You are going to look into the box, and without any comment, are going to write on a piece of paper your first feeling about what you see.   (Have items in the box some people will like and some people will not such as a green pepper, a piece of cooked liver, onion, a snail, etc.)   Be careful not to choose something which might cause extreme alarm.

Let's go around the group and have each of you tell what your first feeling was. What was in the box? (Wait for group response.) If there is one (onion) in the box, how is it possible to have so many different feelings about that one item? (Everybody doesn't feel the same about any one thing.)

PSE Teaches

1. Everybody has feelings.
2. Feelings are based upon a past experience.
3. One person's feelings can be different from another person's feelings.
4. Feelings can change.

Lesson 6 — Person and Actions Are Separate

I am not what I do. What I do is what I am learning. If we separate the person from his/her actions, he/she has room to grow.

Do: Skit with Harry (Lesson 6, Activity D, 2/3 program). When Harry gets a "you" message, he is put into a box. He has no place to go, no space to grow. There is a lot of difference between the message "You are a warp!" and "You have warpy behavior!" When a person's being is judged, he/she feels helpless and has no idea what to do. Having warpy behavior can be changed or Harry can keep going until he finds someone who likes warpy behavior. This illustrates again the value of changing "you" to "I" messages. Instead of saying "Your behavior is rotten!" change to "I'm having a problem with your behavior today." Instead of "Don't you dare talk to me that way!" say "I don't like the tone of voice. Say it again in a different tone." Use "I" instead of "you" messages.

Lesson 7 and 8 — Communication Skills, Part I and II

Once students have learned how to get in touch with their feelings, two lessons teach them how to communicate those feelings. Psychologists say one of the most common problems they deal with is the communication of feelings.

The PSE process is simple: State your feelings and your wants. If your pencil is taken say "I'm upset you took my pencil and I want it back!" There is no guarantee you will get what you want, but it is more effective to state your want than to assume the other person knows what it is you want. This process allows the individual to practice standing up for him/herself — something which is difficult for most people to do.

Lesson 9 and 10 — Friendship, Part I and II

Peer pressure is a primary influence in the lives of young people. It is important to teach them to choose their friends wisely.

To protect and not hurt someone else, we hold our negative feelings inside until they explode. For the purpose of assisting with the pain of upsets between friends, there is a section about communicating feelings and wants to a friend.

Although anger and upsets are explosive emotions, there is an appropriate time, way, and place in which to express them. We give the students real-life situations in which they need to decide if expressing their upset would be appropriate.

Lesson 11 - Tattling and Cheating

Both of these topics were chosen from the PSE founders' survey taken among classroom teachers. These two topics have been dealt with in a fun-filled manner. The scene is a TV station and characters such as "Tammy-Tell-It-Like-It-Is" and "Pamela Problem Solver" present a lot of latitude for team members to "ham it up."

Basically, reporting means that information given is for safety reasons or to avoid harm to someone. Almost anything else is tattling. If a child comes up saying, "Tommy is on the flag pole!" that child is probably concerned with safety. If, on the other hand, a child says "Tommy and Betty are talking" the appropriate question to ask is "Are you tattling or reporting?" This process eliminates a lot of people minding other people's business.

Lesson 12 — Review: Final Lesson

This lesson is an opportunity for review with space for some special recognition and togetherness.

Teaching a Lesson

A lesson is usually divided into four parts. If three volunteers are teaching, there are three parts. You will have one part. To become familiar with the process of dividing parts it is helpful to:

1. Read the entire script aloud as a group.
2. Decide where the parts begin and end for your group.
3. Choose parts.
4. Transfer your part to a note card and practice your part.
5. Rehearse lesson together as a team.

Objectives and suggested readings are listed at the beginning of each lesson. They are included to enhance the volunteer's understanding of the principles used in that lesson. Materials needed for each lesson are also listed at the first of each lesson.

The better you know the lesson, the more relaxed you will be. Also, classroom control is better when you use eye contact and are not glued to your notes. Take your note cards with you to the orthodontist or to the supermarket and learn them there.

The stress reduction exercises, Lesson 11 in the 2/3 and Lesson 10 in the 4th and 5th grade programs, are to be read verbatim from the book. They are the only exceptions to the request NOT to use note cards. Since the scariest lesson is the first one. some of us are going to run through that lesson and get a feeling for it.

> *HINT: If you are a brand-new school, you can have team members take turns reading the script aloud. Divide the possible parts, choose the one you feel most comfortable with, and then take turns walking through each part. If your school has been using the program and is breaking in new members, have the experienced team do Lesson 1 as a demonstration for the new recruits.*

Professionalism

It is important that PSE team members are professional in the classroom. We are guests in the school and in each individual classroom. To the extent we honor that privilege will we be welcome. Much of that sense of being welcome has to do with how professional we are. The following tips come from the authors' experience as classroom teachers and as volunteers of PSE.

1. Arrive and leave on time. Take all your charts, purses, etc. with you so you do not disrupt the class and be sure to thank each teacher as you leave the classroom.

2. It is unprofessional to gossip with other parents about specific classroom discussions or responses. Remember, it is the classroom teacher's responsibility to answer any parent questions. Be certain to refer all outside queries to the teacher or principal.

Classroom Control

On the teacher agreement we have requested that each classroom teacher write any specific requests for group control on his/her Agreement Form. Remember to follow the teacher's desires in that area. Use note cards instead of scripts and keep lots of eye contact with the children. It helps to include the child who is being somewhat disruptive by saying "Isn't that true, Scott?" or "What do you think about that, Scott?" If necessary, follow up with "You need to listen, Scott."

Please rehearse your part. If you know your material you will be able to respond to individual questions and input with less concern. You will also be able to see and include someone who is not paying attention.

When it is not your turn to teach, be sure to move about the classroom. Do not sit together as the tendency is to chatter, and that is distracting. Taking a chair and quietly sitting down next to a disruptive child has noticeable results.

Raising your voice to quiet the children simply adds to the noise level. Here are a few ways to get the students' attention:

1. Turn the lights on and off
2. Wait. Compliment those who are quiet by saying, "I see Brian is ready...and Janet...and Bob...etc." Do not ask, "Are you ready" because some child is bound to retort "No!"
3. A child always has the right to refuse, to pass, or to question. Some children need a little extra encouragement to risk being in front of a classroom.
4. Name tags are created so you will use names! For classroom control, it is helpful to call each child by name. More importantly, using the name assists the child in feeling special because he/she is recognized.

Be careful not to select only those children in the classroom that you know. Do not ignore or over-select your own child. Once in a while, ask for the hands of children who have not yet had a turn. Try to include everyone in the room as much as possible.

It is sometimes difficult to know what to do with an inappropriate or a wrong response. Remember, if a child risks giving you an answer and you put down that response, he/she may not choose to participate again. To a wrong answer respond "That isn't what I'm looking for, keep thinking!" or "No, but you are close." Sometimes you can say "I like your idea and that's not what I had in mind."

To a correct answer, please refrain from saying "Good." The opposite of good is bad. Labeling something as good or bad is a judgment. Judgments teach a person to perform for compliments and may lead to extreme cases of people-pleasing. Statements for acknowledging a correct answer might be "Thank you!" or "Now you're thinking!" or "I hadn't thought of that one, thank you!" You praise and nurture in a lasting way through your body language, tone of voice, and acceptance.

Discourage anyone from laughing at someone else's mistakes by saying "We learn from our mistakes. No one likes to be laughed at when a mistake is made. No one is to laugh at anyone else's mistakes. Do you understand, Peggy?"

Stop any "acting out" behavior the moment it occurs or it will gather momentum. Using direct eye contact say "That's not an appropriate comment for this lesson or the classroom." Since the person knows he/she is out of line, a glare and a strong "Enough!" will deliver the message. A volunteer, walking by the disruptive student also can curtail the negative behavior. Often, it is the disruptive child who most needs your attention and probably has low self-esteem. If necessary, ask the teacher to remove the disruptive child from the classroom.

The sooner a classroom realizes you will enforce your discipline standards, the less problems will occur. With five adults in the room there are seldom discipline problems.

Group Work

The group work is designed to provide a significant other for each child. In a world lacking in heroes, each adult who touches the life of a child does so in a significant way. A caring adult gives this vital message: (1) You are not alone in this important job of growing up. (2) I support you, will guide you with the information I have. (3) I think you are really valuable.

Using eye contact, knowing names, and listening with genuineness — all lead to a safe atmosphere for sharing. If a serious personality difference occurs between you and a child, switch that child to another group. Remember to keep the noise level of your group low so you won't distract other students. Do not encourage any sense of competition between groups. Each person is special and has something to contribute to the program.

HINT: During the Stress Reduction exercise, you find this class has difficulty with this stress reduction exercise and you have followed the directions in the manual you might consider discontinuing them for this class.

Final Comments to Volunteers from the Authors

You are about to embark on one of the most delightful, rewarding experiences of your life. The PSE program has been carefully constructed to meet the growing needs of individual children. It is important that the integrity of the program be maintained by following the lesson plans. The love and caring you take into each classroom is so important to the lives of those children. Project Self-Esteem is about enabling children to be all that they are.

When a survey was taken in three elementary schools, PSE was found to be the most popular subject — even more popular than lunch. Why? We give children tools of understanding and awareness with which to live their lives more abundantly. The program is fun! Adults, who admit they care, go to a classroom to be with those children.

An idea is no more than an idea unless it is put to work. PSE is a great idea, and YOU, the volunteers in each school, make it work and give it life with your caring. Everyone talks about wanting a better world. You, who have chosen to teach this program, are assisting in creating that more loving world. The founders of PSE appreciate your contributions more than words can transmit. May all of your love, time, and caring be returned to each of your lives many times.

HINT: Some of the information in the Introduction to this book may serve as useful data for this training. The more informed everyone is in the purpose and philosophy of Project Self-Esteem the more fully it is shared.

*Be good to yourself
and to each other!*

Questions?

In the event you are asked a question that you are unable to answer, please invite the person to direct that question to the authors:

Enhancing Education
P.O. Box 16001
Newport Beach, CA 92659

Let Us Hear From You

Please send us the following information and you will receive our **NEWSLETTER.**

Name of school _____

Address of school _____

Phone number of school _____

Contact person _____

Grade levels using PSE _____

Number of students in the PSE program _____

Number of volunteers in the PSE program _____

How you heard about PSE _____

Thank you for your cooperation.

Chapter

Kindergarten

——————————————— **Lesson 1** ———————————————

Being a Friend to You

Objectives

- The child will listen to a story which concludes, "You Can Always Be a Friend to You."
- The child will count to two, look into a box, and see a friend.

Suggested Reading

Dyer, Dr. Wayne. *Pulling Your Own Strings*, p. 5. "The freest people in the world are those who have senses of inner peace about themselves."

Background

In a world which teaches us to be outer-dependent, PSE's intent is to remind children to be their own friend. It is here that they begin building the concept of self-esteem, along with caring for others.

Materials

Harmony, Flannel board, George and Grandma figures for flannel board, Decorated box with large mirror in the bottom, Bulletin board strip: You Can Always Be a Friend to You.

Activity A — PSE Volunteers Introduce Themselves, the Program, and Harmony

We're the Project Self-Esteem team. Self-esteem is how you feel about yourself. We want you to feel happy that you are you. If you are already happy that you are you, we want you to always feel that way. Self-esteem is how you feel about yourself.

Let's get acquainted. I am (team members introduce themselves, giving their names only). Now we want you to meet our special friend, Harmony.

(Bring out Harmony.)   Harmony feels better when the children wave to him and say, "Hi, Harmony." Let's wave and say, "Hi Harmony" together.   (Wait for class response.)   Harmony wants me to tell you he talks but he's more comfortable talking to me. So, for now, he will talk to me and I will tell you what he says.   (Have Harmony talk to volunteer.)   Harmony says he is excited to be here so he can make some new friends. Harmony says friends are very important.

Because friends are so important, we are going to be talking a lot about friendship. Today, we are going to talk about a very special friend to you.   (Harmony talks to volunteer.)   Harmony says he has a story for you. Would you like to hear Harmony's story?   (class response)

Activity B — Children Listen to a Story about Friendship

> *HINT: Read this story with lots of animation and enthusiasm. The figures are to be cut out, colored, and backed with Velcro for use on the flannel board. The purpose of the flannel board is to assist children in focusing. Objects are to be stationary, moved only as directed.*

(Put figure of George on the flannel board and begin to read.)

This is George. George has always lived in the country. Always, that is until his dad got a job in the city. Then George's family moved to the city.

George had never seen so many people! There were cars on every street, zooming back and forth. Instead of one market in the whole town, the city had lots of markets. Instead of little stores with a few things in them, city stores were HUGE, GIANT STORES with rows and rows of shiny things to buy. It was wonderful, and kinda scary.

The hardest thing for George was going to school. He was in Kindergarten. You see, George looked different with his long, straggly hair and he sounded different. George was really embarrassed when the teacher called on him because the children would laugh at the way he talked. George had been in school for two whole months and he hadn't made even one new friend. He felt lonely and sad. George just sat around after school. He didn't do anything. He didn't play. He just sat around feeling unhappy.

(Add Grandmother figure to flannel board.)   Finally, George's grandmother, who was George's special friend, asked him to talk about his feelings. She knew that if George talked about his feelings to someone he trusted, it would help him feel better. Sometimes, just having someone listen to your troubles is enough. But George's grandmother had an idea.

"Sometimes, it takes a long time to people to open their hearts and let you in," she began, "and you just need to be patient. Meanwhile, I have a special box for you which might help."

> *HINT: Bring in the box to be used for the children. Place this special box in front of the flannel board.*

"What's in the box?" George asked with the first sign of interest that he had shown in anything.

His grandmother almost sang, "Peek in the box at the count of two. You'll see someone who's a friend to you." And then she sang it again, "Peek in the box at the count of two. You'll see someone who's a friend to you."

"In here?" George asked as he sat up in the chair. "If I look in here I'll see . . . what was it again?" Does anyone remember what George was going to see in the box?   (class response: Someone who's a friend to you.)

Well, George looked in the box. At first he frowned, then he laughed. "I get it! Yes, I get it! Thanks, Grandma! Thanks! Can I keep the box?"

From that day on, George had his box and he was patient. Before long, he made a new friend.

Activity C — Children Look into the Box

George's grandmother gave him the box. George is all grownup now, and he gave us his box to share with you. When we call on you, you are going to come up to the box. You will count, "One, two . . ." and then you will peek into the box. You will see someone who's a friend to you.

We're going to do this very quietly. And you need to be very careful not to tell anyone what you saw. It's your secret. Don't give away your secret. At the count of two, you will peek into the box and see someone who's a friend to you.

> HINT: One volunteer stays with the class; another gathers a small group of children to wait, away from the box. One volunteer holds or sits by the box. Children take turns looking into the box. Have each child count to two before he/she looks inside. Caution each child to keep the secret.

(When everyone is finished)   You counted to two, looked in the box to see someone who's a friend to you. What did you see?   (class response)   Yourself? How can that be? Can you be a friend to you?   (class response)   When you go home tonight, be sure to share your secret with your parents. What is your secret?   (I am a friend to me.)

> HINT: This is not the time to get into a lengthy discussion. Take about three responses and then continue.

Activity D — Lesson Ending

It will be fun to share your secret. The next time we come to see you, we are going to talk about some other ways you can be a friend to you. Before we go, we are going to give you this bulletin board strip to put in your classroom. It says, "You Can Always Be a Friend to You." Sometimes, children like to draw pictures to go with the strips we leave. Say this after me, "You Can Always Be a Friend to You."

Lesson 2

Taking Care of You

Objectives

- The child will participate in a game about safety.
- The child will listen to a Project Self-Esteem poem about self-esteem.

Suggested Reading

Barun, Ken. *How to Keep the Children You Love Off Drugs*, p. 8. "I advocate *pre*action instead of *re*action. Indoctrinate your children against drugs at the earliest possible age..."

Background

Research indicates that a person with high self-esteem does not willfully harm him/herself. Part of caring for oneself is to make appropriate choices concerning one's own safety. Reminders are a friendly way to reinforce self-care.

Materials:

Harmony, New bulletin board strip: I Have Self-Esteem It's True. I Won't Hurt Me, and I'm Kind to You.

Activity A — Children Introduce Themselves to Harmony

Hello. We are your Project Self-Esteem team. I am...   (Review names of PSE volunteers.)   This is Harmony.   (Harmony waves, then hides his head.)   What's the matter with you, Harmony?   (Harmony talks.)   Harmony is feeling shy because he doesn't know anyone in this classroom. Let's go around the room so you can introduce yourself to Harmony. This is the way you will do it: "Hi Harmony, I'm   (name)."

> *HINT: Have each child introduce him/herself to Harmony. Gently remind the child of the whole phrase if needed.*

Thanks class. That was fun. Do you feel better now?   (Harmony nods and talks.)   He feels much better and he wants to know more about you. He likes honey. In fact, he loves honey. Harmony wants to know what food you like best. Think of one food you really like. You may like more than one food. We are sharing just *one food you like* this morning/afternoon.

HINT: Go around the group and let each child share. Repeats are fine. If a child balks say, "Shall I come back to you later?" If the children give a list of foods, gently remind them to give only one answer. It is only one food that is being shared today.

(Harmony talks to volunteer.)   Oh, I did, too. Harmony says he liked the lesson where you looked into the box to see someone who can always be a what to you? (class response: Friend.)   What did you see in the box? (class response: Me!)   Harmony doesn't understand how you can be a friend to you.

Activity B — Children Practice Thumbs Up and Thumbs Down

One way you can be a friend to you has to do with safety. Let's play a game so we can think more about safety. We are going to say something. If you think the answer is yes, you will put your thumbs up, like this.   (Illustrate closed fist, thumb pointed to the ceiling.)   Everyone show me a thumbs up, yes answer. Put your hands in your lap, please. If you think the answer is no, put your thumbs down, like this.   (Illustrate closed fist, thumb pointed to the ground.)   Everyone show me a thumbs down, no answer. That's great. Now you need to listen carefully. Put your hands in your lap. Listen carefully.

This is a kindergarten class. If your answer is yes, show me a thumbs up. If your answer is no, show me a thumbs down. This is a kindergarten class.   (Wait for class response.)   Thank you! It is a kindergarten class, so everyone gave a thumbs up. Listen again! Your teacher's name is Mrs. Snodgrass. Thumbs up for yes, thumbs down for no.   (class response)   Thank you. I see everyone has thumbs down for no. What is your teacher's name?   (class response)

Activity C — Children Participate in a Safety Game

Now, let's talk about you.

HINT: Follow the same procedure of having each child hold thumbs up for yes and thumbs down for no for each question. Be sure to remind children that mistakes are the way we learn, and discourage any put downs.

Questions for the game:

Yes or no: Can you run inside the classroom whenever you want?   (no)

Comment: It isn't safe for you to run in the classroom. You might fall and hurt yourself. It might not be safe for other people if you run into them.

Yes or no: A stranger stops in a car and wants to talk to you. Would you walk up close to the car?   (no)

Comment: If someone stops a car to talk to you, it is best for you to run away from that car.

Yes or no: Sometimes, can you run while playing a game? (yes)

Comment: It is best to play by the rules. If it is appropriate to run in a game, do so.

Yes or no: Should you eat or swallow something if you don't know what it is? (no)

Comment: It is dangerous to eat something when you don't know what it is.

Yes or no: Should you ever play with matches? (no)

Comment: It is not safe to play with matches or with fire.

Yes or no: Should you cross the street without looking both ways? (no)

Comment: It is important to look both ways before crossing any street.

Yes or no: Should you do something dangerous because your friend dared you to do it? (no)

Comment: It is not wise to take dares — even from friends.

Yes or no: Should you ever take drugs without your parents' permission? (no)

Comment: It is not safe or "cool" to take drugs without permission from your parents.

Yes or no: Should you take care of yourself and not hurt yourself? (yes)

Comment: All your life you will be taking care of you. We want to help you remember not to do things that will hurt you.

Yes or no: Should you ever go in swimming alone?

Comment: Never, never go swimming by yourself.

Activity D — Introducing the PSE Poem and Lesson Ending

Here is our Project Self-Esteem poem:

> I have self-esteem it's true.
> I won't hurt me and I'm kind to you.

Today, we talked about not hurting you. For your bulletin board we are leaving a strip that says, "I Have Self-Esteem It's True. I Won't Hurt Me, and I'm Kind to You." Next time, we will talk about being kind to others.

_____ Lesson 3 _____

Being Kind to Others, Part I

Objectives

- The child will learn a poem about self-esteem.
- The child will watch a skit about respecting property.
- The child will watch a skit about remembering not to laugh at other's mistakes.

Suggested Reading

Paul, Dr. Jordan and Dr. Margaret Paul. *Do I Have To Give Up Me To Be Loved By You?*, p. 150. "Most everyone fears looking foolish. Everyone has refrained at least once from asking questions out of fear that someone would say, 'You mean you don't know that?' We've all held back emotions — whether laughter or tears — for fear of being thought a fool, losing face, being humiliated, losing respect and position."

Background

Our research indicates that children who have been taught understanding along with rules tend to be more empathetic and self-disciplined. Also, children who have been encouraged through their mistakes, tend to be less afraid to try new things.

Materials

Harmony, Props for skits, Same Lesson 2 bulletin board strip.

Activity A — Children Review Previous Lessons

This is the third time we have been with you. The first time, everyone looked into a box and saw something. What did you see?   (class response: Me. Someone who can always be a friend to me.)   So we learned that you can always be a friend to you.

The next time we were with you, we played a game. You used thumbs up for what?   (class response: Yes.)   That's right. And thumbs down meant what?   (class response: No.)   We talked about safety. Some of the things we learned were:

Where do you look when you cross the road?   (both ways)
If a stranger comes up to you in a car, what should you do?   (run away)
Should you eat something if you don't know what it is?   (no)
Will you take drugs without your parents permission?   (no)

Activity B — Students Learn the PSE Poem

Harmony is with us today. (Bring out Harmony and have him talk.) He says that he wrote a PSE Poem. He thinks it will sound great when children say it. But he has never heard his poem, and he wants to know if we will say it for him. That would be fun!

Harmony's poem goes like this:

I have self-esteem it's true.
I won't hurt me and I'm kind to you.

Let's learn that together. I'll say a line and then you will say a line. Watch me.

(point to self) I have self-esteem it's true.
(point to children) I have self-esteem it's true.
(point to self) I won't hurt me.
(point to children) I won't hurt me.
(point to self) And I'm kind to you.
(point to children) And I'm kind to you.

HINT: Repeat the whole process of saying the lines with the children.

Now for the PSE challenge. Let's see if we can say it together: I have self-esteem it's true. I won't hurt me, and I'm kind to you.

HINT: Say the poem slowly, encouraging everyone to stay together.
Repeat the process until the class can do it somewhat uniformly.
Have Harmony clap and be excited to have heard his poem.

Activity C — Volunteers Present Skit on Respecting Property

Today, we are going to talk about being kind to others. We are going to do a skit for you.

HINT: Team members act out skit for the children. We suggest
you wear baseball caps to differentiate boys from girls. One volun-
teer reads story while the others act it out.

51

Alfred got into Tom's backpack and took his money.   (Act out taking money from backpack.)   Alfred wanted to buy something to drink for lunch. Tom and Alfred were friends but Alfred did not think about that. Alfred just thought about how much he wanted to buy something to drink.

When Tom went to get his money out for lunch, it wasn't there. Tom was really upset.   (Act out Tom going to backpack, finding nothing, and tearing his backpack apart saying, "I know that money was here. Where is it anyway? I'm starving. Where is that money?")   Alfred could tell how upset Tom was feeling. He didn't know what to do.   (Alfred looks puzzled, then shrugs his shoulders.)   Stop the action! Let's think about what's happening here. We have a problem.

I know, let's call Harmony in and see if he can help us. Do this with me: (Raise both hands into the air each time you say help.)   Help, Harmony, Help!   (class response)

(Harmony is brought into the group.)   We need your help with this, Harmony. What can Alfred do?   (Harmony talks.)   Harmony says this is a tough one. He wants to know what you think Alfred could do.   (class response: Give the money back and apologize.)

> *HINT: Remember, young children will often start to tell endless stories. If someone starts a story say, "I really want to hear your story,   (Mark), and we need to solve this problem for Harmony." Repeat the question and get back on track. Be patient and kind: these children are just learning to take risks with sharing.*

Harmony says that stealing means taking something which belongs to someone else. He says stealing hurts people so he wants to remind you never to steal. He also said that sometimes friends make mistakes. If Alfred gives the money back and says he is sorry, Tom might be angry. But do you think Tom and Alfred could still be friends?   (class response)   I think so, too.

Let's replay that skit with a different ending.

> *HINT: Replay skit. Have Alfred tell Tom he took the money and apologize. Have Tom be angry at first, and then let Alfred and Tom still be friends.*

Activity D — Volunteers Present Skit about Laughing at Others

Let's do another skit.

> *HINT: Have all volunteers sit together to look like a classroom situation. This skit is to be pantomimed as the reader says his/her part. There is no skit rerun.*

Mrs. Easley is teaching her class. The children are listening. Mrs. Easley calls on Carolyn, asking her a question. (pantomime) Carolyn gives an answer. (pantomime) One of the children laughs at Carolyn's answer. (pantomime) Some of the other children laugh, too. (pantomime) Carolyn slinks down in her chair. She is really embarassed. . .and hurt. (pantomime) Stop the action! We have a problem. Let's call in Harmony. (class response: Help, Harmony, Help!)

(Harmony comes in and talks.) Harmony says that lots and lots of children will not raise their hands in class. They are afraid someone will laugh at them. He wants to ask you to remember not to laugh at someone when he/she makes a mistake. What are some kind things you could say to a person who makes a mistake? (class response: Nice try, that's OK, etc.)

Activity E — Lesson Ending

Kindness is important. Sometimes, we forget to be kind. When you are feeling badly — for whatever reason — and someone is kind to you, do you feel better or worse? (better) When you feel better, you do better. (yes) So kindness is important.

Today we talked about remembering not to steal. We also talked about remembering not to laugh when someone makes a mistake. You have the same bulletin board strip as before. Let's say the PSE poem together:

I have self-esteem it's true.
I won't hurt me and I'm kind to you.

Some classes might want to put up more pictures or drawings to go with this poem. We'll see you next time.

———————————————— **Lesson 4** ————————————————

Being Kind to Others, Part II

Objectives

- The child will watch and listen to a skit about not hurting him/herself.
- The child will watch and listen to a skit about not hurting others.
- The child will recall the PSE poem.

Suggested Reading

Reasoner, Robert W. *Building Self-Esteem*, p. 1. "Individuals with high self-esteem demonstrate a high degree of acceptance of self and others."

Background

It is not enough to tell children to follow our morals, values, and standards of safety. We must teach them HOW to do so. "What would you do if . . ." teaching is a valuable tool to assist children in making appropriate choices for their lives.

Materials

Harmony, Prop for skits, Same Lesson 2 bulletin board strip

Activity A — Review of Lesson 3

Last time we were here, we talked about telling the truth and remembering not to steal. What did Alfred take from Tom? (Wait for class response: His money.) What did Alfred do? (class response: Apologized and gave the money back.)

Remember when Carolyn answered a question in class and everyone laughed? How did she feel? (class response: Embarrassed, sad, angry, etc.) So, we remember it isn't kind to laugh at someone.

Activity B — Review the PSE Poem

Let's do the PSE poem together. Stay together and let's have some fun with this. (class response: I have self-esteem it's true. I won't hurt me and I'm kind to you.) That's wonderful. Thank you. We have been talking about how to take care of you and how to be kind to others. Today, we are going to do some more skits.

Activity C — Skit about Not Hurting Yourself

HINT: Follow the same procedure as used in Lesson 3. Read and act out the skit. Follow directions for discussion, and replay the skit with the different ending.

We are going to act out a skit. You will watch the skit and listen to my words.

Brenda and Sam were playing at Sam's house. They found a red object on the floor. It looked like a pill. Brenda said it was candy. (Brenda: "This is candy.") Sam said he wasn't sure. (Sam: "I'm not sure. It could be medicine.") Brenda and Sam argued. (Sam and Brenda: "It's candy. It's not safe. It's OK. Don't eat it. etc.") Brenda grabbed the object and put it into her mouth. Stop the action! Looks like it's time to call Harmony. Let's do it together. (Raise both arms upward each time you say, "Harmony.") Help! Harmony, Help!

(Bring Harmony in. Have Harmony talk to the volunteer.) Harmony says he wants to hear what you think about what happened. Did Brenda make a mistake? (class response: Yes. You never put something into your mouth when you don't know what it is.) What could Brenda have done instead of eating it? (class response: She could have given it to Sam's mother.)

> *HINT: If children suggest throwing the object away, remind them that it might be something someone needs. The best thing to do when you don't know what something is is to take it to an adult.*

Let's rerun that skit with a different ending.

> *HINT: Rerun skit without the reader. After the argument, have Brenda and Sam decide to take the object to Sam's mother.*

The skit with Brenda and Sam reminds you to be careful so you don't hurt yourself. Let's do another skit.

Activity D — Skit about Being Kind to Others

> *HINT: Have three volunteers, as children, play together on the floor. They will roll a ball back and forth to depict playing a game.*

Three friends were playing together. Two of the children began to whisper. (Act out two children whispering.) The left-out person got upset. (Have one volunteer act out looking embarrassed, then hurt, and finally angry.)

Stop the action! Time to call in Harmony. (class response: Help! Harmony, Help!) Harmony, something unkind is happening here. We need your help. (Harmony talks.) Harmony says it is not kind to whisper about someone else. Let's all say that together. (class response: It's not kind to whisper about someone else.) Let's replay the skit with a different ending.

HINT: Replay the skit. Have two children start to whisper, then remember that it's not kind to whisper, and stop. Have all the children continue playing.

Activity E — Review the Lesson

Let's do thumbs up for yes, thumbs down for no and answer these questions: If you find something and you don't know what it is, do you eat it? Thumbs up for yes, thumbs down for no.   (class response, No.)

Let's do another one. You and two friends were playing. Would it be kind for you and another friend to whisper?   (class response: No.)

This is the last one. Are you going to remember to do things that won't hurt you? (class response: Yes.) and are you going to remember to be kind to others?   (class response: Yes.)

Activity F — Lesson Ending

Let's end today by saying our PSE poem together: I have self-esteem it's true. I won't hurt me and I'm kind to you. We'll be back next time for our last lesson.

_____ **Lesson 5** _____

Review and Awards

Objectives

- The child will participate in a review of the four PSE lessons.
- The child will receive a PSE Award.
- The child will participate in a rhythm band activity.

Materials:

Harmony, PSE Award for each child, homemade or classroom rhythm band instruments

Activity A — Review Lesson 4

In our first lesson, you looked into a box. What did you see? (Wait for class response: Myself.) We learned that you can ALWAYS be a what to you? (class response: Friend.) Repeat after me: I can always be a friend to me. (class response)

In the safety lesson we did thumbs up for what? (class response: Yes.) And we did thumbs down for what? (class response: No.) Get your thumbs ready, and listen! If someone your age wanted you to take drugs, would you do it? Thumbs up for yes, thumbs down for no. (class response: No.)

> *HINT: If any child puts a thumb up, respond with: "Remember, Jon, a person with high self-esteem won't hurt him/herself. You need to say no to drugs."*

Listen to this one: Your friend was playing with matches. Lots of matches were being lit. Your friend wanted you to light matches, too. Would you do it? (class response: No.) Matches make fire. Fire is dangerous. Playing with matches is dangerous.

Activity B — Skit about Swimming Alone

We are going to act out a skit for you. It is your job to solve the problem in our skit.

> *HINT: Several volunteers act out the skit while another volunteer reads the script.*

James and Margie were playing. It was a hot day. Pretty soon, James said, "I am sticky-hot. Let's go for a swim in the pool." Margie replied, "I'm not a very good swimmer." James said, "Don't worry; I know how to swim." Something is wrong here. I think it's time to call Harmony for help.   (Help! Harmony, Help!)

Harmony wants to know what you think about this problem. What do you think is wrong with this skit?   (It is not safe to go swimming without an adult.)   Harmony is reminding you that unexpected things can happen and it just is not safe to go for a swim without an adult watching you.   (Harmony continues to talk.)   Harmony wants you to remember NEVER, NEVER, NEVER go swimming or even play near the pool or water by yourself. Accidents do happen, and you could drown. Never go swimming by yourself.

Activity C — Repeating Words to Remember Them

Watch me and listen carefully. I am going to say some words and then you are going to say them. Try to stay together. Listen to me.

(Say with enthusiasm and animation.)

> I will be kind to others.
> (children repeat)
> I won't whisper about someone else.
> (children repeat)
> I will be kind to others.
> (children repeat)

Let's do another one. Listen carefully and watch me.

> I won't hurt me.
> (children repeat)
> I won't take drugs.
> (children repeat)
> I won't hurt me.
> (children repeat)

Activity D — PSE Band and the PSE Poem (Optional)

HINT: Check with the teacher as to the advisability of this section. A class with no rhythm band experience could turn this exercise into a negative experience.

You have learned the PSE poem. Let's have some fun with it today. Your teacher has some things that make musical sounds. Let's create a PSE band to go along with the PSE poem.

> *HINT: This exercise will be somewhat wild. Giving specific directions and containing the wildness is essential. Get the children lined up, with the promise that the children who do so quickly and quietly will get to have a music maker. Have only six instruments in all. Repeat the words, switching instruments to a different student each time. Demonstrate, saying the poem in a singsong manner so it lends itself to musical accompaniment. Have a parade with the children saying the poem over and over. One volunteer leads the parade. When you are finished, collect the instruments and quiet down the children before you give them the awards. Sometimes, sitting and taking deep breaths, in through the nose and out through the mouth, will assist in calming everyone down.*

Activity E — Volunteers Present PSE Awards

It has been so much fun coming into your room to share PSE with you. Special thanks to your teacher for having us. We thank you for being YOU! We want to remember this special Project Self-Esteem time, so we have a PSE award for you. (Show award to students.)   This awards says you were in Project Self-Esteem in Kindergarten. Listen for your name and come on down to get your award.

> *HINT: Each volunteer calls a name and hands out an award. Be sure to look each child in the eye and thank him or her for the fun time. Include the classroom teacher.*

Activity F — Lesson Ending

We've had a lot of fun with you this year. We shared some thoughts and ideas. You will have Project Self-Esteem next year with a new team. Remember to take good care of you, and remember to be kind to others.

Grandmother

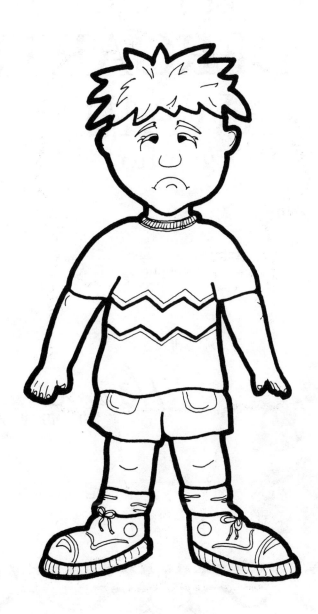

George

THE PROJECT SELF-ESTEEM

KINDERGARTEN AWARD

goes to

_____
student

_____
date

Harmony
PSE Official

_____
Team Leader

Chapter

Grade 1

―――――――――――――――― Lesson 1 ――――――――――――――――

Friendship

Objectives

- The child will introduce him/herself to Harmony.
- The child will participate in unscrambling a sentence.
- The child will sing a song about friends.

Suggested Reading

Anglund, Joan Walsh. *A Friend is Someone Who Likes You*, p.14. "Sometimes you don't know who are your friends. Sometimes they are there all the time, but you walk right past them and don't notice that they like you in a special way."

Background

As children begin school, an increasing amount of focus and importance is given to friendships. It is valuable to talk about the qualities desired in friends, and to continue to do so throughout the school years.

Materials

Harmony, Individual word strips   (backed with Velcro)   for chart: Friends are kind to each other, Bulletin Board strip: Friends Are Kind to Each Other.

> *HINT: If you have taught PSE in the upper grades, remember this age moves a lot slower. TAKE YOUR TIME in presenting these lessons.*

Activity A — Children Meet Harmony and Introduce Themselves

We want to introduce ourselves to you.   (Team members introduce themselves to the students.)   And now, we want you to meet our very special frend, Harmony.   (Bring out Harmony. Harmony waves to children, then hides his head in his paws.)   What's the matter, Harmony?

(Harmony talks to volunteer, then hides his head again.)   Harmony talks, but he's more comfortable talking to me, so I'll tell you what he says. Harmony said he feels really uncomfortable because he doesn't know some of you. I have an idea! Let's go around the room and have you tell Harmony your name. You will say, "Hi Harmony, I'm (Carol), or (Scott) or whatever your name is." Let's begin over here...

HINT: Keep the pace moving so the rest of the class doesn't lose interest. Gently assist children who have difficulty, since some children are able to risk sharing more easily than other.

(Harmony is upright, waving and talking.)   Harmony is really happy now because he has lots of new friends.

Activity B — Introduce Team and PSE

Raise your hand if you had Project Self-Esteem in Kindergarten.   (Wait for class response.)   Since there are a few people who don't know us, let me explain who we are and what we are doing. We are your PSE team. We will be coming into your room to share five lessons with you. Lessons on what? On self-esteem. Self-esteem is how you feel about yourself. If, most of the time, you like being you and feel good about the things you do, we say you have high self-esteem. People who have high self-esteem do better in school, have more friends, can take better care of themselves, and are happier. So, we will teach you things that will help you feel good or even better about being you.

Activity C — Students Assist Harmony in Unscrambling a Sentence

Harmony says he has a puzzle that he just can't figure out and wonders if you would like to work with him on solving it.   (class response)   He says he found this special sentence, but the words are all mixed up and he can't figure out what it says.

HINT: Each of the words in the sentence, "Friends are kind to each other." can be printed on poster board pieces or large index cards before the lesson. Be sure to back the pieces with Velcro. Use a large piece of poster board for a chart to display the words. Attach Velcro strips to the chart and put the individual words on the chart. Scramble them.

Whenever you solve a puzzle it's like a mystery. In every mystery there are clues. To find the first word we need to think, "Every sentence begins with what?"   (class response: A capital letter.)   Which word would be first?   (class response: Friends.)   We know that every sentence ends with a what?   (class response: A punctuation mark or a period.)   Then what is the last word in this sentence?   (class response: Other.)

HINT: Each class has its own learning pace. Work with the students until they unscramble the sentence. The sentence on the chart is to be in order when you are finished.

65

Friends are kind to each other. If everyone in this classroom were kind to each other, do you think it would be a friendlier place to be?   (class response: Yes.)   If everyone in this school were kinder to each other, do you think it would be a nicer place to be?   (class response: Yes.)   And if everyone in the whole world were kinder to each other, do you think it would be a nicer world in which to live?   (class response: Yes.)   I think so, too. We are going to talk lots about being kind to each other in our PSE lessons.

Activity D — Children Sing a Song about Being Special

HINT: This song is sung to the tune of "Frère Jacques." Sing the song all the way through, two times. Encourage the children to listen to the words each time. Then sing one line and have the children echo it. Finally, have the whole class sing the song. Repeat the song. Begin the song high enough for small, high voices.

The PSE Song about Being Special

I am special, I am special.
So are you, so are you.
Friends are special, friends are special.
It is true, it is true.

Activity E — Lesson Ending

Today we talked about being special and that friends are special. We remembered, friends are kind to each other.   (Show bulletin board strip.)   We are going to leave this bulletin board strip with you. Some classes like to draw pictures or write stories to go with the PSE saying. This one says, "Friends are kind to each other." Let's say that together.   (Repeat the sentence.)   We will be back again. Remember to be kind to each other.

Lesson 2

Being a Friend to You

Objectives

- The child will participate in a review of Lesson 1.
- The child will sing a self-esteem song.
- The child will listen to a story about being a friend to him/herself.

Suggested Reading

Keirsey, David and Marilyn Bates. *Please Understand Me,* p.1. "...and in understanding me you might come to prize my differences from you, and far from seeking to change me, preserve and even nurture those differences."

Background

We live in a very busy world. There is so much to do. Sometimes, we get so busy doing that we forget to take time for ourselves. It is like trying to write checks on an empty bank account to give-give-give-give all the time and do-do-do. Everyone needs some time, each day, to be with him/herself. In taking care of others it is important to remember to take care of you.

Materials

Harmony, Scrambled word chart from Lesson 1, Story for children, Flannel board and cut outs, New bulletin board strip: I Can Always Be a Friend to Me.

> *HINT: Cut out and color all the patterns at the end of this chapter. Put Velcro on the back of each pattern piece and on the flannel board. The purpose of using a flannel board is to assist children in focusing. Follow the directions that accompany the story for implementing each picture.*

Activity A — Review of Previous Lesson

Hello. We are your Project Self-Esteem team. Last time we were with you, we unscrambled this sentence. (Show chart with words scrambled.) Who remembers what the sentence said? (Wait for class response: Friends are kind to each other.) I will put the words in correct order (do so), and then we can read it together. (Read the sentence together.)

Last time, we learned a song. Listen and I will sing it for you. (do so) Let's sing it together, now. (Class sings song.)

That was fun. Is there anyone here today who has never seen us before?   (Introduce team members to any new children.)

Activity B — Harmony Has a Story for the Class

Let's bring in Harmony to be with us.   (Harmony waves to children. Encourage them to wave and say, "Hi, Harmony!" Introduce new child(ren) to Harmony. Harmony talks to volunteer.)   Harmony says he really likes your song. He thinks friends are very special and...what Harmony? (Harmony talks and points paw to class.)   Oh, yes, I agree. He says you are special, too.

Harmony says that he has a story to share and he wants to know if you would like to hear his story.   (class response)

> *HINT: Cut out and color all the patterns at the end of this chapter. Put Velcro on back of each pattern piece and on the flannel board. The purpose of using a flannel board is to assist children in focusing. Follow the directions that accompany the story for implementing each picture.*

Read the story to the class.   (Put Josie's unhappy face on flannel board.)

It was just the most awful day! Ever since Josie had gotten up, everything had gone wrong. Her brother, Cliff, spent the night with a friend, so there was nobody to play with. Later, when Josie went to Sara's house, she discovered that Sara wasn't home. Margie and Gail and Denise were all gone for the day, too. There was nobody, not even one person to play with, and there was a whole day with nothing to do. Josie was even bored with the television.   (Add television to flannel board.)   She didn't have a good book to read. It wasn't any fun to play video games by herself. What could she do? She didn't know...so she asked her mom.   (Add Mother to flannel board.)   Her mother said she was busy sewing and couldn't play with Josie, but suggested that Josie could learn to be a friend to herself. A friend to herself? Josie wondered what that meant. She started to laugh, thinking about how silly she would look, talking to herself.

For some time, Josie went from one thing to another. She just felt nervous, and couldn't find anything to do. Then she saw her new crayons.   (Add crayons to flannel board.)   She decided to draw a picture. Josie put a record on the machine and began to draw.   (Add a record to flannel board.)   It was fun to draw and very peaceful. Josie didn't feel nervous anymore.   (Change unhappy to happy face for Josie on flannel board.)

Josie did lots of things to keep herself happy. She built a house with blocks, looked at a magazine, and enjoyed listening to a record.   (Add record to flannel board.)   In the afternoon, Josie went for a walk. She saw the flowers and felt the warm sun on her shoulders. (Add flowers and sun to flannel board.) Josie even saw a butter-fly. (Add butterfly to flannel board.) When she walked with a friend she was busy talking. Walking by herself, she noticed everything. Josie felt peaceful inside because she had taken time to be with a very special friend...herself!

The next day, Josie was happy to see all of her friends again. They talked and played and talked and played. When Denise asked Josie who she had played with the day before, Josie said, "Oh, I made a new friend and we had lots of fun." Before Denise could ask who the new friend was, Josie changed the subject. But her mother smiled because Josie winked at her when she said it. Josie's mother knew that Josie's new friend was...Josie!

I really like your story, Harmony. (Harmony talks.) Harmony says it is impor-tant to learn to be a friend to you. He says you will be with you more than any other person. Harmony says it's important to be kind to others and it is important to be kind to Y-O-U...you! He hopes you will learn to take some time every day to be with your very special friend...M-E which spells what? (class response: Me.)

Let's see if you understand what Harmony said. Who will be with you more than any other person? (class response: Me.) So, when does Harmony want you to take time to be with you? (class response: Every day.) And who can always be a friend to you? (class response: Me.)

Activity C — PSE Song and Lesson Ending

> *HINT: Repeating the PSE song is optional, depending upon how much time is left. Discussion periods will vary in length from class to class.*

Let's sing our special song one more time before we leave. (Class sings song.) Today, we are going to leave a new bulletin board strip for you. It says, "I Can Always Be a Friend to Me." Sometimes, classes like to draw pictures or write stories to go with the bulletin board strip. Remember to be a friend to you, and we'll see you next time.

Lesson 3

Taking Care of You

Objectives

- The child will participate in a game about safety.
- The child will recite and talk about the PSE poem about self-esteem.

Suggested Reading

Briggs, Dorothy. *Your Child's Self-Esteem*, p. 280. "High self-esteem frees a youngster to play with a whole repertoire of possibilities, confident that he can choose those of greater merit. He can afford to stand up for his ideas and opinions."

Background

Research indicates that a person with high self-esteem does not willfully harm him/herself. Part of caring for oneself is to make appropriate choices concerning one's own safety. Games which involve making choices are a fun way to reinforce self-care.

Materials

Harmony, New bulletin board strip: I Have High Self-Esteem It's True. I Won't Hurt Me, and I'm Kind to You.

Activity A — Students Review Lesson 2

Last time we were with you we read Harmony's story about Josie. Remember, all of Josie's friends were gone for the day, so she played with a very special friend. Who was that friend?   (Wait for class response: Herself.)   We learned that you need to be a friend to you — to take take time to be with you. Who wants to share one thing you did since we were here last time that was just with you?

HINT: At this age, children have a one-track mind. If a child says he or she played the piano, and many other children want to talk about their musical instrument example, say "Lots of you played a musical instrument. Did anyone do something different?" If one child goes on and on with a story, remind the class that you want a short example like, "I went for a walk." The intent is to make good use of the limited time you have for the lesson, not to quell the children's enthusiasm for sharing.

Activity B — Students Practice Thumbs Up and Thumbs Down

One way you can be a friend to you is to take good care of you. Let's play a game so we can think more about safety and taking care of you. We are going to say something. If you agree with what is said, you will put your thumbs up like this.   (Illustrate closed fist, thumb pointed to the ceiling.)   Everyone show me a thumbs up, "yes" answer. Put your hands in your lap, please. If you do not agree with what is said, put your thumbs down, like this.   (Illustrate closed fist, thumb pointed to the ground.)   Everyone show me a thumbs down, "no" answer. That's great. Now you need to listen carefully. Put your hands in your lap. Listen carefully.

This is a First Grade class. If you agree, show me a thumbs up. If you do not agree, show me a thumbs down. Get Ready. This is a First Grade class.   (Wait for class response.)   Thank you! It is a First Grade class, so everyone gave a thumbs up. Listen again! Your school's name is Watercress Elementary School. Thumbs up for yes, thumbs down for no.   (class response)   Thank you. I see everyone has thumbs down for no. What is your school's name?   (class response)

Activity C — Children Participate in a Safety Game

Now, let's talk about you.

> HINT: Follow the same procedure of having each child hold thumbs up for yes and thumbs down for no for each question. Be sure to remind children that mistakes are the way we learn, and discourage any put downs. Please do not turn the "comment" section into a lecture series.

Listen to the examples and get your thumbs ready

Yes or no: Should you smoke a cigarette?   (no)

Comment: Cigarette smoke harms your body.

Yes or no: Should you drink water every day?   (yes)

Comment: Your body needs water to stay healthy.

Yes or no: Is it safe to play with a very sharp knife?   (no)

Comment: Sharp knives can be dangerous, even if you are careful.

Yes or no: Is it safe to run into the street before you look?   (no)

Comment: Always look both ways before you cross the street.

Yes or no: Should you sit down in a car with your safety belt fastened?   (yes)

Comment: Always fasten your safety belt when in the car.

Yes or no: Should you ever drink alcohol?   (no)

Comment: Alcohol is not good for your body.

Yes or no: Is it safe to play in a house where nobody lives anymore?   (no)

Comment: It is dangerous to play in an empty house.

Yes or no: Is it safe to play around the stove?   (no)

Comment: Burns hurt. It is best not to play near the stove.

Yes or no: Should you take drugs without your parents' permission?   (no)

Comment: It is not safe to take any medicine without the permission of a parent.

Yes or no: Should you go swimming by yourself?   (no)

Comment: It is not safe to swim alone.

Yes or no: Is it safe to play with matches?   (no)

Comment: Playing with matches or fire is dangerous.

Yes or no: Is it wise to take a dare from someone?   (no)

Comment: Taking dares is foolish. It could be dangerous.

That was fun. What we want you to remember is that a person with high self-esteem does not harm himself or herself. Learning to be safe is an important part of your life.

Activity D — Introducing the PSE Poem and Lesson Ending

Here is our PSE poem. If you heard it in Kindergarten, you might remember it. Our PSE poem goes like this: I have self-esteem it's true. I won't hurt me, and I'm kind to you.

Today, we talked about not hurting you. For your bulletin board, we are leaving a strip that says, "I Have Self-Esteem It's True. I Won't Hurt Me, and I'm Kind to You." Some of you might want to draw pictures or write a story about other ways to keep safe and not hurt yourself. Next time, we will talk about being kind to others.

—————————————————— **Lesson 4** ——————————————————

Being Kind to Others, Part I

Objectives

- The child will participate in a review about safety.
- The child will watch and listen to a skit about courtesy.
- The child will watch and listen to a skit about assisting.

Suggested Reading

Vitale, Barbara Meister. *Unicorns Are Real,* p. 35. ". . . we tend to forget that the child can learn only to the maximum of his own experience."

Background

Children need to see that courtesy and kindness are valued by the significant adults around them. This is one way children can learn to be more caring about people. Courtesy and kindness are best taught by example.

Materials

Harmony, Piece of tape for Harmony, Props for skits, Same Lesson 3 bulletin board strip

Activity A — Review of Lesson 3

In our first lesson, we remembered that friends are kind to each other. Say that with me: (Wait for class response.) In the second lesson, Josie learned that someone special could be her friend. Who could be Josie's friend? (class response: She could.) So we remembered to take time for you to be with you. You are your friend, too.

Last time, we talked about safety. Well, here's Harmony. Look! He has tape on his paw. How did you hurt yourself, Harmony? (Harmony talks.) Oh, dear, he says he was using a sharp knife and cut his paw. He says he was being really careful and it happened anyway. He wants me to remind you not to play with knives or sharp instruments because you might get hurt. We're sorry you got hurt, Harmony. Why don't you rest for a bit and take care of that paw.

Last time, we played a game using thumbs up for what? (yes) Thumbs down meant what? (no) Let's play thumbs up and down for these examples:

Yes or no: It will hurt you to smoke cigarettes. (yes)

Comment: Cigarettes are not good for your health.

Yes or no: You are special. (yes)

Comment: Not for what you do, but because you are the only Y-O-U, you are special!

Yes or no: You can always be a friend to you. (yes)

Comment: You will be with you for all of your life, so learn to be a friend to you.

Yes or no: It could hurt you to take drugs. (yes)

Comment: You need to have permission from one of your parents before you take any drugs.

Yes or no: We want to remember to be kind to others. (yes)

Comment: Being kind to others doesn't cost anything except remembering how much you like it when someone is kind to you.

Activity B — Volunteers Playact Skit about Courtesy

HINT: Volunteers act out the skit while it is being read, following the directions in the story. Optional: when the skit is rerun, ask for student volunteers.

Read the story slowly.

Maria and Sonia are coloring together. Maria reaches in front of Sonia and grabs a crayon. Sonia makes a mistake in her picture. She gets angry. (Sonia: "Oh, no! I've ruined it. You made me ruin it!") Maria gets angry, too. (Maria: "No, I didn't. I just reached to get a crayon.") Sonia and Maria begin to argue and fight. (Both: "Did so! Did not! It's ruined! No it isn't.")

Stop the action! I wonder what they can do about this problem. You know, Harmony has been very helpful in solving problems. But we need to call him. Let's do this together, "Help, Harmony, Help!" (Raise both hands over head as each "help" is said.)

(Harmony appears on the scene.) Did you hear the problem, Harmony? (Harmony nods.) Can you tell the boys and girls what Maria and Sonia could do? (Listen to Harmony.) Harmony says Maria could have asked Sonia for the crayon. If you were Maria, what words could you use to ask Sonia for the crayon? (class response: Would you please pass the pink crayon to me when you get a chance?)

HINT: Act out the same skit. This time, have Maria look for the crayon, wait for an appropriate time to ask for it, and then politely ask to use the crayon. Optional: have students act out the appropriate parts.

Activity C — Volunteers Playact Skit about Assisting Each Other

That was fun. Let's do another skit.

HINT: Pantomime skit as volunteer reads it.

Sam needs a ruler. Susie has a ruler on her desk. Sam takes the ruler. Susie notices the ruler is missing, sees that Sam has it, and tells the teacher. She says Sam stole the ruler. Sam says he was only borrowing it. Sam and Susie began yelling at each other. Stop the action!

Let's call Harmony. "Help! Harmony, Help!" (Harmony appears on the scene. Harmony talks to the volunteer.) Harmony says that Sam needs to ask whenever he borrows anything. What words could Sam use to ask Susie for the ruler? (I need to use a ruler, may I use yours?) Harmony says he doesn't like Sam and Susie yelling at each other. He thinks they could have talked about the problem until they worked it out. He thinks they could do so, without yelling and name calling.

Let's do another one: Carl is picking up the blocks and putting them where they belong. He is in a hurry to get them put away. Carl tries to pick up too many blocks and drops all of them. The faster Carl goes, the more mistakes he makes. Carl's friend is Martin. Martin is sitting nearby, watching Carl drop the blocks. Martin laughs at Carl, telling him to hurry. Stop the action!

There is a problem here. What can we do? Let's call Harmony. "Help, Harmony, Help!" (Harmony appears on the scene. Harmony talks to the PSE volunteer.)

Harmony says he didn't see what happened this time. Can someone tell Harmony what you saw in the skit? (class response) Harmony says that Carl could ask Martin to help him. Harmony also says that Martin could volunteer to help his friend. What else? (Harmony talks.) Oh, yes, I agree. Harmony says it wasn't kind of Martin to laugh at Carl. Let's look at a rerun of that skit.

HINT: This time Carl will ask Martin for help and the blocks will get put away quickly.

Thank you Harmony for helping us when we called on you.

Activity D — Lesson Ending

Kindness is important. Sometimes, we forget to be kind. When you are feeling badly and someone else is kind to you, do you usually feel better or worse? (class response: Better.) When you feel better, you do better. So kindness is important. Your bulletin board strip is the same one we left last time. Let's say it together: I Have High Self-Esteem It's True. I Won't Hurt Me, and I'm Kind to You. We'll see you next time.

_____ **Lesson 5** _____

Being Kind to Others, Part II

Objectives

- The child will listen to and watch a skit about being left out.
- The child will listen to and watch a skit about hitting.

Suggested Reading

Ungerleider, Dorothy Fink. *Reading, Writing and Rage,* p. 208. "In the research literature, one of the theories of juvenile delinquency is that anger, frustration, and aggressive behavior stem from feelings of powerlessness."

Materials

Harmony, Props for skit, Same Lesson 3 bulletin board strip

Activity A — Review Lesson 4

Last time we were here, we watched some skits. One had to do with asking to borrow crayons rather than taking them. That skit was about being polite and kind to your friends. We want you to remember to be kind to each other.

Another skit was about trying to put blocks away. We remembered to help someone who needs help. We also remembered that sometimes when you want help, you have to ask for it.

Activity B — Volunteers Playact Skit Dealing with Being Left Out

Today, we are going to playact something that might have happened to you. Watch closely so you can help Harmony solve the problem.

> *HINT: Several volunteers act out the skit, while one volunteer reads. Follow directions for dialogue.*

Joe and Bill are playing together. Mike comes up and wants to play.   (Mike: "Hi, can I play?")   Joe and Bill make lots of excuses. They even lie to Mike.   (Both: "This is a game for two. Well it's like this. . .ah. . .we have to go home soon so we're going to quit anyway.")   Mike feels left out. Stop the action!

Let's call Harmony for some help. (class response: Help, Harmony, Help!) We need your help with this problem, Harmony. (Harmony talks.) Harmony wants to know if something like this has ever happened to you. Show me thumbs up if this has ever happened to you. (class response) Harmony says it has happened to him, too, and he felt just awful. (Harmony hides head in paws.) Harmony hopes you will remember not to leave someone out, because it isn't kind.

There was another problem in this skit. Does anyone know what it was? (class response: Joe and Bill told a lie.) Harmony says it is hard to trust someone who doesn't tell the truth. It is important to tell the truth. Let's replay that skit.

> HINT: Repeat the skit. This time, Joe wants to leave Mike out but Bill remembers it isn't kind to leave someone out and says, "It's OK. There's room for one more. Let Mike play."

That was fun. Let's do some more playacting. (Put Harmony away.)

Activity C — Volunteers Playact about Hitting Each Other

Margaret and Sally want to get a ball for recess. There is only one kickball left. Both of them try to pick up the ball. They begin to argue. (Both: "It's my turn! No, it's mine. I got it first! You did not!") Margaret shoves Sally. Sally shoves Margaret. Sally raises her fist to hit Margaret. Stop the action!

Quick, let's call Harmony. (class response: Help, Harmony, Help!) Hi, Harmony. (Harmony talks.) Harmony says he wants to hear from you. What is the problem here? (class response: The two girls are fighting.) What is the problem with Sally and Margaret hitting each other? (class response: They might hurt each other.) Harmony says that people think hitting someone is tough and smart, but it isn't. To hurt someone or be hurt yourself over a kickball is just plain foolish. We need to use words to work out problems and be kind to each other. Let's replay that skit.

> HINT: Replay skit to the point where Margaret and Sally are starting to argue. Have Sally say, "Let's don't fight about this. We can work it out. We can either play together or take turns using the kickball."

Hitting each other is not kind. Let's remember to talk and work out our problems.

Activity D — Students Sing Self-Esteem Song

We're going to sing the PSE self-esteem song for the last time. Let's see if we can do something a little different this time. We are going to divide the class in half right here.   (Indicate with hand gesture, where the class will be divided.)   This song sounds like an echo. This group   (point to half of the class)   will start the song with the words, "I am special." This group   (point to other half of class)   will sing, "I am special" just like an echo. An echo is when you say something — sometimes in a canyon — and the same words bounce back. It might sound like this: Helloo! (Listen, then repeat the word as an echo.) We'll go slowly until you catch on. Watch me and remember, mistakes are the way you learn.

> *HINT: This may be a difficult concept for some classes. Have a volunteer be a leader for each group. Encourage the children to watch each leader closely. One group sings the first line, "I am special" and the second group echoes it. The first group then sings, "So are you" and the second group echoes it. Then, the first group sings, "Friends are special" and the second group echoes it. The first group ends with, "It is true" and the second group echoes it. Repeat the process, so the song is sung smoothly and easily.*

That was so much fun. I like the way you listened and I really like hearing you sing. Now we have something special for you.

Activity E — Volunteers Present PSE Awards

We have had so much fun coming into your room to share PSE with you. We thank your teacher for having us. We thank you for being you! We want you to remember this special Project Self-Esteem time, so we have a PSE award for you.   (Show award to students.)   This award says you were in Project Self-Esteem in First Grade. Listen for your name and come on down to get your award.

> *HINT: Each volunteer calls a name and hands out an award. Be sure to look each child in the eye and thank him or her for the fun time. Include classroom teacher.*

Activity F — Lesson Ending

Well, we've had a lot of fun. We shared some thoughts and ideas. You will have Project Self-Esteem next year with a new team. Let's say our PSE poem one last time. Stand up and we will say it together: I have self-esteem it's true. I won't hurt me, and I'm kind to you.

Remember to make choices which take good care of you, and remember to be kind to others.

Josie

Josie

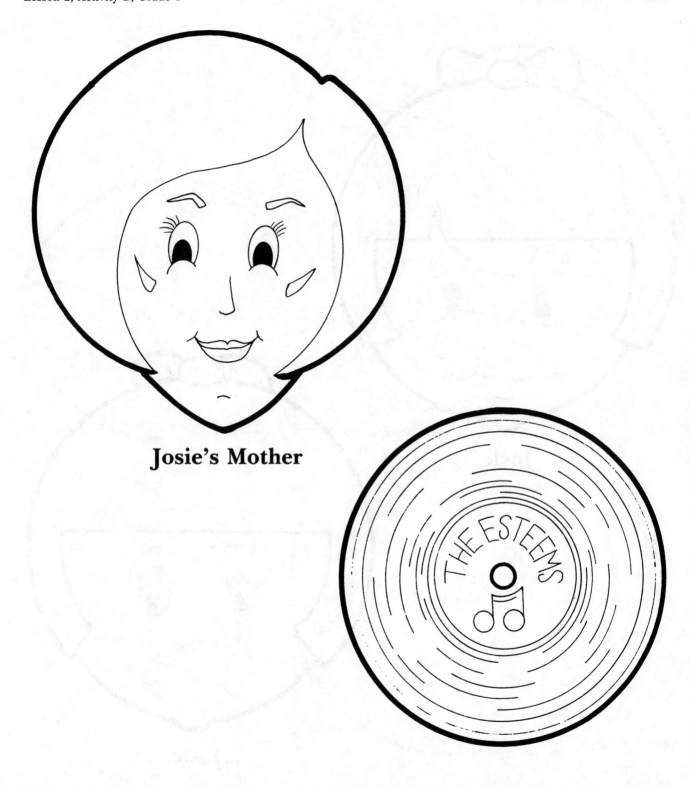

Josie's Mother

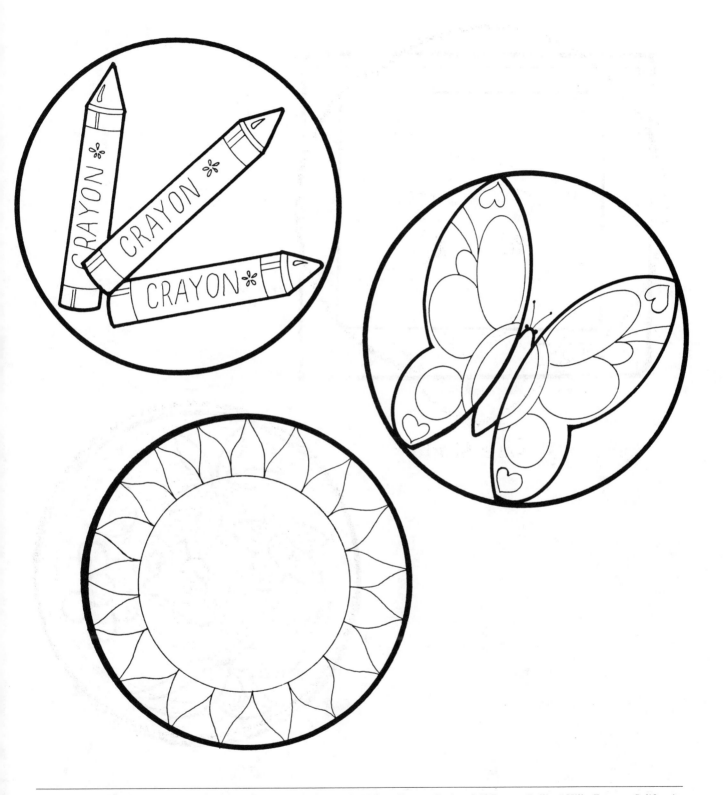

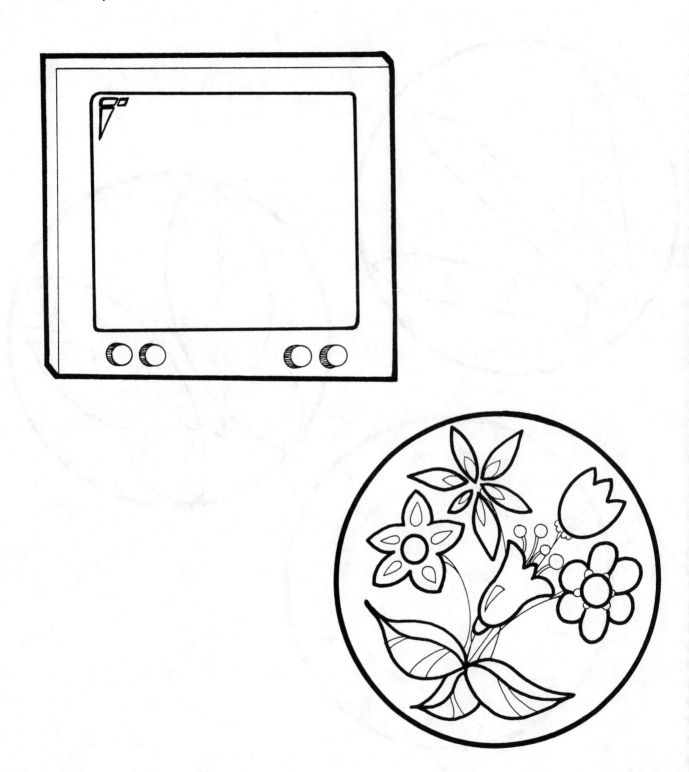

THE PROJECT SELF-ESTEEM

FIRST GRADE AWARD

goes to

_____
student

_____
date

Harmony
PSE Official

_____
Team Leader

Chapter

Grades
2 and 3

_____ Lesson 1 _____

Realizing Your Uniqueness

Objectives

- The child will state, "I am . . ."(with name) in a clear, audible manner.
- The child will contribute to a list of things that assist him/her in feeling good.
- The child will participate in "Harmony Says," a listening game.

Suggested Reading

Axline, Virginia M. Dibs *In Search of Self,* p. 67. "The child must first learn self-respect and a sense of dignity that grows out of his increasing self-understanding before he can learn to respect the personalities and rights and differences of others."

Bedley, Gene. *The ABC's of Discipline,* p. 19. "Every child is uniquely and wonderfully different."

Knight, Michael E.; Graham, Terry Lynne; Juliano, Rose A.; Miksza, Susan Robichaud; Tonnies, Pamela G. *Teaching Children to Love Themselves,* p. 3. "A child who is accepted, approved of, respected, and liked for himself or herself is better able to acquire an attitude of self-acceptance and respect."

Background

It is easy to become so critical of our shortcomings that we totally neglect to recognize our positive qualities. Knowing, really knowing inside, that you are one of a kind — an unrepeatable happening in the world — is not an ego trip. One person is not better than another because each of us are one of a kind. Think how differently each one of us would feel if we began the day with this thought, "I am special. No one can take being special away from me. I don't have to prove it. I am special!"

Materials

Harmony with pin or necklace attached, New bulletin board strip: Grade 2 — I Am Special. Grade 3 — There's No One Just Like Me! Optional: Commercial posters with sayings

Activity A — The PSE Volunteers Introduce Themselves, the Program, and Talk about Experience

(Names of PSE volunteers) and I are part of a volunteer group called Project Self-Esteem. Self-esteem means how you feel about yourself. We all have days when we don't like ourselves, but people with high self-esteem like themselves and feel good about what they do MOST of the time. All of us are going to be in your room from now until   (name the last month of the program). Why? Because we care about you and your job of growing up. Sometimes we adults forget to tell you we realize growing up can be hard. We sometimes forget that parts of growing up were difficult for us, too. We adults have one small advantage. It's called EXPERIENCE.   (Write the word "experience" on the board.)

1. We've been through all the years from being born to whatever age we are right now.
2. Things have changed a lot since we were in (second or third) grade. (Use examples consistent with your age.) Some of us didn't have TV because it hadn't been invented yet.
3. Some things have changed a lot, some have changed very little, and some are the same as they have been for many years.

Knowing about these things is called EXPERIENCE. PSE will share the experience of many grown-ups with you. Each lesson will be different. Sometimes you will have lots of talking to do. Other times you will have to do some listening. We will work hard to make each lesson fun.

> *HINT: When the PSE volunteers introduce themselves, they may wish to add a comment or two of a personal nature. (My children go to this school, etc.)*

Activity B — The Students Introduce Themselves

We are going to go around the room having each of you say, "I am..." and your name. We want to learn your names, so chins up! Speak clearly! Please don't talk faster than we can listen and be sure to say the whole sentence. I'll begin. "I am...." (Say your name and include PSE team members, too.)

(When everyone has participated) We began by having each of you say "I am and your name" for a reason. Even if you have the exact same name as another person — even if you are an identical twin — there is no one, no one in this whole wide world, EXACTLY like you. You are you, the rarest kind of rare. You are very special!

Activity C — Introduce Harmony

I want you to say hello to a special friend of mine. This puppet...(Make Harmony look upset.) What's the matter? Oh, I'm very sorry — he's quite sensitive. This bear... (looking at Harmony) is that better? (Harmony nods.) This bear's name is Harmony. He's going to become a special friend of yours. You see, Harmony has taken all the Project Self-Esteem lessons. He used to be shy (Harmony hides head), afraid to try new things (looks frightened), and always tried to be just like every other per... (Harmony looks at you)...er...bear. But now he has high self-esteem. His life is in harmony and he will help bring more harmony into your lives. What does it mean when your life is in harmony? (Write "harmony" on board and wait for class response.) By the way, Harmony talks, but he only talks to the person holding him. So for now, he will talk to me and I'll share what he says with you.

(Talking to Harmony) That's a beautiful necklace (or pin) you are wearing. (listening to Harmony) Your grandmother gave it to you? She said it is an antique, but you don't know what an antique is? Let's ask the children — what's an antique? (Wait for class response.) It's something that there isn't very many of — a person might collect an antique because it is rare. You know Harmony, there's something in this room that is more rare than any antique could ever be. (Harmony rubs ear with one paw.) Yes, more rare...anyone know what it is? (class response) You're right, it's a human being...or a human bear! (Harmony claps paws.)

No matter how hard you try, no matter how far you look, you will never find another human being just like you. Even if you have an identical twin — someone who looks exactly like you — one of you may like chocolate ice cream and the other might like strawberry ripple. One of a kind! You don't need to hide your face. It's supposed to be that way. Feeling good about being you is one of the best feelings in the world! It begins by knowing you are special, not by what you do, but by being — just being — you! This doesn't make you better than someone else. That other person is one of a kind, too. So, by being you, you are special.

Activity D — List Items That Assist You in Feeling Special

Think about some of the things you do that assist you in feeling special. We are going to make a list on the chalkboard of things you do that you feel good about. Tell me some special things you do. (Put class ideas on board.).

These items are important because they ASSIST you in feeling special, but are you special because of them? (no) If you can't (take one example from the chalkboard), does that mean you're not special? (no) If you can't (take another example from the board), does that mean you're not special? (no) You are special because there is no one just like you. No one can take being special away from you. You were special the day you were born and you will always be...why? (You are one of a kind.)

Activity E — Introduce Listening Tool and Harmony Says

We human beings have parts of us that help us in being special. We are going to call them tools. Tools are things you use to make your life better and easier. Your dad and uncle or your mom use tools to make a certain job easier. An important tool we need to practice using is our LISTENING tool. You spend a lot of time listening. Give me some examples. When I say "go" everyone tell me of times in your life when you need to listen. Go. (home, school, parents, people, radio, television, records, etc.) Stop! You see, so much of what we do depends upon listening.

How many of you have ever played Simon Says? (show of hands) Today, we are going to play Harmony Says. The rules are the same; if I begin with "Harmony says" you must do what I say. If I do not say "Harmony says" you must not do it. Harmony and I have been practicing for weeks so you need to listen. Before we begin our game, raise your hand if you have ever made a mistake. (show of hands) Leave your hand up if you wanted someone to laugh at you when you made a mistake. If you liked being laughed at, leave your hand up. Look around. Mistakes are OK. We do not need to laugh, make fun of, or point at anyone else who makes a mistake. During this game, no one will sit down if he/she makes a mistake.

(Begin slowly) Everyone stand up! (most children get up) Oops! I didn't say "Harmony says." Be careful! Harmony says, "Everyone stand up!" (Give the directions, changing back and forth from commands with Harmony says and commands without.) Left hand up. Right hand up. Both hands up. Both hands down. Put one hand on top of your head. Put the other hand on top of your head. Put both hands down. Jump on both feet. Bend over. Stand up straight. Sneeze. Turn around. Bend your knees. Shout, "I am special!" Shout it again. Sit down. What tool did we use to play this? (listening)

> *HINT: PSE volunteers will monitor the class, reminding individual children not to tease when mistakes are made.*

Activity F — Introduce Bulletin Board and Reasoning Tool

Another tool we humans have is our thinking and reasoning skill. We are going to practice using this thinking and reasoning tool throughout the year. We will leave a special bulletin board which will assist us in doing this. Every lesson will have a different bulletin board. Who wants to read this for us? (Show appropriate bulletin board strip: Grade 2 — I Am Special. Grade 3 — There's No One Just Like Me!)

We want you to share your ideas with us. You might draw a picture or write your ideas about what this strip means or you might even write a story about being special. Wouldn't it be fun to collect pictures from magazines and put them all around this strip? Whatever you decide to do, we want you to put what you do around this sentence on the bulletin board. Then you can share your thoughts with us and that way we will all be learning together!

What was one of the tools we talked about today? (listening) What was the other tool we talked about today? (thinking and reasoning skill)

We have had fun being here with you today. This lesson is the shortest one we have. Next time we will be here for forty minutes and that will be in two weeks. Between now and the next time we come, be good to yourself and to each other and smile! YOU ARE SPECIAL!

_____ Lesson 2 _____

Gratitudes and Changes/Attitudes

Objectives

- The child will state at least one idea about being special.
- The child will write and share at least one gratitude.
- The child will write and share at least one change.
- The child will state that a change in attitude can change a given situation or result in acceptance of that situation.
- The child will write at least one way he/she can alter his/her attitude.

Suggested Reading

Bedley, Gene. *ABCD's of Discipline,* pp. 24-25. "If you treat an individual as he is, he will stay as he is; if you treat him as if he were what he ought to be and could be, he will become what he ought to be and could be."

Coopersmith, Stanley. *The Antecedents of Self-Esteem,* pp. 22-23. "Attitude substantially affects the motivation of every individual." Lincoln, Abraham. "Folks are about as happy as they make up their minds to be."

Background

In any given situation, each person has a choice of attitude and attitude IS THE DIFFERENCE. It is infinitely easier to play victim than to take responsibility for oneself. Learning to look for, acknowledge, and amend one's attitude is the primary way of learning to be independent in a fulfilling way.

One means of solving a problem, be it with a person or a situation, is to first examine attitude. A child with a learning difficulty needs to be approached FIRST in terms of his/her attitude.

Materials

Harmony, Gratitudes and Changes worksheet, Chalkboard space, Shoe box, New bulletin board strip: Grade 2 — You're Special. Grade 3 — Attitude Is the Difference. Optional: guitar, costumes, glasses for "The Esteems"

Activity A — Children Introduce Themselves Using "I Am"

Today we are going to talk about gratitudes and attitudes, and the difference your attitude makes in life. We are going to begin this lesson the same way we began the last one. We are not going to begin every lesson this way; today will be the last time. Each of you will say, "I am..." and your name. Beginning with me...(Wait for class response.) The point of doing this is to remind each of you: there's no one just exactly like you. So you are what? (class response) That's right. Special!

Activity B — Review Bulletin Board Materials Provided by the Students

Let's look at your bulletin board and see what you added to our strip. What does the strip say? (class response) Does anyone want to share what you added? (class response)

> *HINT: Keep this section brief. If there are too many children who wish to share, break off the discussion with, "We have time for one more person to share."*

> *You may choose to have PSE folders in which the children can put their contributions as well as any worksheets they do. If you collect the worksheets, please do not judge them in any way. Happy faces are considered judgmental. "I enjoyed reading this" or "Thank you for sharing" are appropriate word choices.*

Activity C — Discuss Gratitudes and Changes

Today, we are going to talk about the things for which we are grateful in our lives — things which help us feel happy or special. Who wants to share one thing for which you are grateful?

> *HINT: If child names a bird, for example, say, "OK, a pet. What's a different kind of thing for which you are grateful?" If students continue to stay on the same subject, suggest a different category.*

(After two examples) We are giving you a piece of paper. (Distribute worksheets.) Put your finger on the word "Gratitudes." (Check each child.) Put a circle around the things for which you are grateful. Then, on the line, write two or three things about which you feel glad or happy. Do it now. (Allow a few minutes.) Who wants to share what you wrote? (class response)

> *HINT: While children write, one PSE volunteer puts the word "gratitudes" on the board. During the class discussion, this volunteer will write what each child says on the chalkboard. If one child gives the same example as someone else, put a check by that item, thus acknowledging the contribution. Do the same for "changes."*

On the lower half of your paper, it says the word "Changes." Now we are going to think about things for which we are not so grateful — things you would change or things you don't like to do. Put your finger on the lower half of your page, on the word "Changes." Put a circle around the things which you would change. Then, on the line, write one or two things you want to be different in your life. Do it now. (Allow a few minutes.)

Thank you for sharing all your thoughts with us. Please put your name and today's date on your paper. A PSE volunteer will collect it later. Turn it face down for now.

Activity D — Skit About Nancy: Illustrating Attitude Changes

It's a fact. There are some things in our lives we just cannot change. We are going to put on a skit for you. Last time we were with you, you used your listening skills to play Harmony Says. You need to pay attention and really listen now because there will be an important question at the end.

HINT: PSE volunteers act out each segment: washing face, combing hair, etc. Note: ending #1 and ending #2 are clearly marked. The first time through, read ending #1. The second time through read ending #2. READ VERBATIM! It is advisable to practice this segment so it is not read too quickly or slowly, giving the PSE volunteer time to complete each action.

Nancy's Story

Once there was an eight year old girl named Nancy. She was all ready for school. She had washed her face, combed her hair, eaten her breakfast, brushed her teeth, made her bed, and she still had twenty minutes until it was time to go to school. So Nancy decided she would work on a picture she wanted to color. She went to her room, got out everything she needed, and began to color. Just then Nancy's sister called to remind her that her clock was slow and it was almost time to leave for school. Nancy was annoyed and upset! She really wanted to color. She began to put away her crayons, but there was a frown on her face. About that time her friend Betsy called her on the phone. Betsy wanted Nancy to come over after school and bake cookies.

ENDING #1: Nancy was so out of sorts she said, "I can't!" and went on sulking.

ENDING #2: Nancy stopped sulking, thought about it, knew it would be fun, and said "Wait, I'll ask my mom."

Her mom said, "Sure!" After school Nancy and Betsy had fun baking cookies and eating them.

In the second ending did Nancy get to color?   (no)   Who can tell me what changed? (class response)

> HINT: If the children do not say the word "attitude" in six tries ask them, "Have any of you heard of the word 'attitude'?"

What does attitude mean?   (how you feel about something)   Nancy's attitude changed. She still didn't get to color, but she changed her attitude.

Activity E — Skit Illustrates Attitude Is the Difference

We need two girls and two boys to put on a skit.   (Choose volunteers. Have them come to the front of the room.)

> HINT: Read the following story all the way through before having the volunteers act it out. When you read the story to the class the first time, include ending #1. The second time through, read ending #2. READ VERBATIM. Have the students act it out using first one ending, then the other.

Once there was a nine year old girl named...(Use first volunteer's name.)   She had saved her money to buy a new soccer ball. She and her friend (use second volunteer's name), were kicking the ball back and forth...back and forth...when (second volunteer's name) kicked it out into the street. A truck ran over the ball. The ball popped. (Second volunteer) said she was sorry, but (first volunteer) was so sad. Her ball was ruined. She picked up the flattened ball and started walking home. She was so unhappy she couldn't even speak to (second volunteer). On the way home, two other friends (boy volunteers) came up asking (second volunteer) and (first volunteer) to get ice cream. The friends said they would treat.

ENDING #1: (First volunteer) shook her head no, and went on home. (Second volunteer) and the other two friends went for ice cream without her.

Now we will do an instant replay, but the ending will change. Listen, so you can tell the difference.

ENDING #2: (First volunteer) explained what had happened to her ball. She told her friends how badly she felt, but (first volunteer) said she would like to get ice cream anyway. All four of them went for ice cream and they had a terrific time.

What changed this time? (class response) Right, her attitude. (First volunteer) still felt badly about her popped ball, but she knew there wasn't any point in sulking about it. She couldn't change the fact that the ball was ruined but she could change her attitude, and she felt better about the situation once she shared her feelings with someone. The whole point of this lesson today is to show you that there are things in your life you cannot change, but you are always in control of your attitude. You can sulk all day because you can't do something or you can say, "I can't change it, but I can make the most of it!"

Activity F — Children Write Specific Ways to Alter an Attitude

Let's go back to the section of your paper on the things you would change. Turn your papers over. Some of you said you would change homework. How do you think you might begin to change your attitude about homework? (Make a game out of it. Do it right away and get it over with. Do it with a friend. Tell yourself when you're through with it you can do something fun.) Take one thing you would change from your list. Write it on the back of your paper. List some ways you could change your attitude about the one thing you chose. Raise your hand for assistance. Do it now.

> *HINT: While children are writing, erase the chalkboard. After two minutes ask for volunteers to share ideas. Write the different methods children suggest on the board.*

Now you have one way you know you can change your attitude. In the next two weeks we want you to work on the one change you wrote down.

Activity G — Harmony Teaches "You Are Special and You Know It" Song

I wonder why Harmony is in this shoe box? (Knock on the box.) Harmony won't come out. (Put ear next to box.) He says he didn't wear something special so he doesn't feel special. What can I tell Harmony? (Wait for class response, then slowly bring Harmony out of the box.)

HINT: Many of the social problems which occur can be addressed via Harmony. In this case, the children will tell Harmony (and each other): You aren't special because of what you wear but because you are you. Some teams have put doll clothes on Harmony and have had a lot of fun improvising in this manner. In this instance, a non-brand name shirt will get the point across.

Harmony is going to do a song with us today. First he wants to know why you think you are special. (class response) How many of you know a song which goes, "If you're happy and you know it, clap your hands?" We are going to change it a little. Listen and tell me the difference. You are special and you know it, clap your hands. (repeat) You are special and you know it, and your life really shows it. You are special and you know it, clap your hands. What was different? (Wait for class response and then repeat new words.) Class sings: Clap your hands/Stomp your feet/pat your head/ wiggle your nose/shout I'm special/shout hooray/make a face/quietly sit down. (Remember to use the word "special" in place of word "happy.")

HINT: (Optional) PSE volunteers dress up in hats, glasses, necktie, etc. One member may carry a guitar. The volunteer who is the announcer could say, "Ladies and gentlemen, live from . . .(name of school) school, we bring you 'The Esteems'!" The children will join us in singing this song with you. This hint is really successful in classes which are ho-hum about singing.

Activity H — Lesson Ending and Review

We have a new sentence for your bulletin board. Who wants to read it? (Grade 2 — You're Special. Grade 3 — Attitude Is the Difference.) Remember to add to it with your pictures and we will be back again in two weeks with a special lesson which will be fun, and we will have a present for each of you. Remember to be grateful for all that is in your life — especially being able to change your attitude. Next time we will talk about one way you can choose to change your attitude.

Be good to yourself and to each other and remember: If you feel yourself pouting about doing something, take a look! Maybe you can change your attitude.

Lesson 3

Smileys and Compliments

Objectives

- The child will state the idea that a Smiley is a symbol for a compliment.
- The child will differentiate between a materialistic and non-materialistic gift.
- The child will accept compliments with an appropriate response.
- The child will construct compliments in teacher-given situations.

Suggested Reading

Buscaglia, Dr. Leo. *Love*, p. 87. "...for part of the responsibility lies with each of us to reach out."

Ginott, Haim. *Between Parent and Child*, p. 45. "The single most important rule is that praise deal only with the child's efforts and accomplishments, not with his character and personality."

Palmer, Pat. *The Mouse, The Monster, and Me*. p. 61. "A compliment is a gift."

Background

Everyone likes compliments. However, the tendency is to focus more on what we and what others do incorrectly, and so correspondingly little attention is given to what is done correctly. This lesson teaches there is good in everyone. People thrive on encouragement. Sincere compliments assist people with feeling good about themselves.

We encourage the use of "I" messages in giving compliments. This means, you begin a compliment with the word "I." Normally, people say, "You look nice." Use of the word "you" is judgmental. Judging sets up people-pleasing. People-pleasing decreases self-esteem. So, from "You look nice," we change the "you" to "I" and say, "I really like that color on you!" To say, "You're a good friend!" is an empty phrase. It is much more personal to hear, "I feel better having talked to you. I'm glad we are friends."

Materials

Harmony, The Molly chart (see Activity D), One giant Smiley, A small Smiley for each child, Wrapped box for small Smileys, 3x5 cards with situations for group work (see Activity F), New bulletin board strip: Grade 2 — Compliments Bring Smiles. Grade 3 — Everybody Likes Compliments.

Activity A —
Introduction and Review Bulletin Board Strip from Lesson 2

Today we are going to talk about giving and receiving compliments. (Acknowledge and go over class contributions to PSE bulletin board. Be brief. Collect contributions for folders, if appropriate.)

We would like to share the one way you worked on changing an attitude. (Ask for volunteers and thank them for sharing.)

Activity B — Discussion of Materialistic and Non-Materialistic Gifts

Some presents are items to play with, wear, or use. Give me some examples of these types of presents. (Wait for class response.) Sometimes gifts don't come in boxes with wrapping paper. There are, in fact, gifts you cannot wrap. Often these are the best gifts of all. Use your thinking and reasoning tool and give me examples of the types of gifts which cannot be wrapped. (class response)

> HINT: When the children's responses are: a train, car, etc., the PSE volunteer might say, "If you had enough paper you could wrap that. We're looking for something you couldn't ever wrap such as hugs or friendship."

Activity C — Define a Compliment and Discuss Possible Responses to Receiving a Compliment

This is a Smiley. (Show class a small Smiley.) It represents or stands for a compliment. What's a compliment? (class response) That's right, a compliment is when you say something nice about someone else that you believe is true. Just like a Smiley, it is warm and it feels good. You may keep it or give it away; but every single human being wants one and when you receive a compliment, you want to smile inside and out. Compliments are so important. Today we will talk about how to give compliments and what to do with a compliment when you get one.

The biggest problem in getting a compliment is, what do you say? Even if you like what the person is saying, you might feel embarrassed. Let's think together and come up with what might you say when someone gives you a compliment? (Thank you, or thank you and return the compliment.)

Activity D — Finding Good in Everyone: the Molly Chart

It's very easy for each of us to think of things we don't like about people. Sometimes we are so busy seeing what we don't like that we forget to think about what we DO like in someone. Every single person has something about him or her which is valuable. It's important that we learn to look for the good in people.

> HINT: It is helpful to use a large poster board for the Molly chart so that the words will be big enough to be seen by all the students.

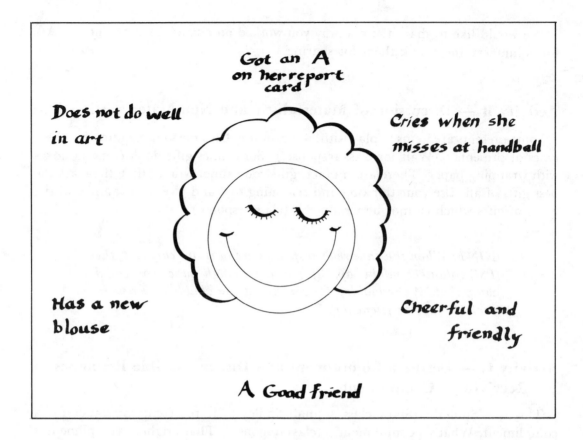

(Show the Molly chart.)   This is Molly. These (pointing to the words written around her), are not all there is to Molly, but these are some of the things we know about her. (A PSE volunteer reads them, pointing to each.)   We would like you to choose one thing about Molly to compliment. Please start your sentence with the word "I." (Choose volunteers to give compliments.)

> HINT: The children will choose Molly's positive aspects to
> compliment. Have them give several examples. Some child may
> choose one of Molly's negative aspects to compliment, which is
> fine as long as it is kind and true. Example: Molly, I like the way
> you keep trying to handball even though you don't do well.

Activity E — Practice Giving Compliment as a Class

Let's use this giant Smiley to practice giving compliments. (Take out a giant Smiley.)   A compliment needs to be kind and true. We'll begin with two of the PSE volunteers. I know that (first PSE volunteer) likes to teach PSE with...(second PSE volunteer.)   They are going to give each other a compliment. (Be sure each volunteer responds to the compliment with "Thank you.")

Now, we are going to read an example and ask for class volunteers to give compliments. Remember to begin each compliment with the word "I."

HINT: Read the situation first, then ask for volunteers. Remind children to respond to compliments in an appropriate way. Have the children pass the giant Smiley back and forth as they give compliments.

Grade 2

Your friend wore a new shirt to school. (I like your shirt.)

Your teacher taught a fun lesson. (I really like your lesson.)

Grade 3

Your younger brother or sister did something he/she had never done before. (I'm glad you did that.)

Your mom fixed a new dinner you really did like. (Thanks Mom, I really like this dinner. I hope you fix it again.)

HINT: The only instructions which needs to be given when a "you" message is used is "I like what you said and I want you to do it again," and "Begin your sentence with 'I.' "

Activity F — Group Work: Children Practice Giving Compliments

We promised we'd have a present for each of you, so I need a volunteer to open this giant box and see what's inside. (One student opens a box full of Smileys.)

HINT: It is easier if PSE volunteers do not take Smileys from the large box. Instead, have baggies with about thirty Smileys in each.

We are going to practice using a Smiley and giving compliments. We will give each of you your own Smiley before we leave. First, I'm going to count off the class by fours...1, 2, 3, 4; 1, 2, 3, 4; etc. The ones go with...(name of PSE volunteer). The twos go with...(name). The threes go with...(name) and the fours go with...(name).

*HINT: It is helpful to put situations listed below on 3x5 cards.
You will need a set for each adult group leader. The group leader
reads each situation then asks for two student volunteers to act
it out. Be sure to give each child a turn. If there are more children
than situations, have the additional children give each other a
compliment. Remind students to begin with "I." The object in
this exercise is to practice using "I" messages — not simply to say,
"Thank you."*

Grade 2 Situations

1. Your mother has fixed your favorite dinner. (I really liked dinner tonight, Mom.)
2. Your friend got a haircut. You like it. (I really like your new haircut.)
3. Your father or uncle took you for a ride. (I had a fun time.)
4. Your friend is fun to be with. (I like to be with you.)
5. Your friend draws well. (I like the way you draw.)
6. You like your friend. (I like being your friend.)
7. Your friend is wearing a new shirt. (I like your new shirt.)
8. Your friend lets you ride his/her new bike. (I'm glad you let me ride your new bike.)

Grade 3 Situations

1. Your sister or brother let you wear her/his new shirt. (I like wearing this shirt.)
2. Your friend stood up for you when someone was teasing. (I'm glad you are my friend.)
3. Your friend has a brand new bicycle. (I like your bike.)
4. Your friend has a wonderful sense of humor. (I like your sense of humor or I like being with you.)
5. Your friend asks you to play but you can't. (I like playing with you, but I can't.)
6. Your friend kicks a home run in a kickball game. (I like the way you kicked the ball.)
7. You go somewhere with your friend and have a wonderful time. (I had a fun time.)
8. Your friend threw the ball hard, but the runner was safe. (I'm sorry you missed, but nice try.)
9. Your teacher helps you with your spelling. (I'm glad you helped me.)

(While still in small groups) Now I am going to give each of you a Smiley to keep for your very own. With it I want to give each of you a compliment. (Be sure to begin each compliment with "I.")

That was fun. Let's see how quietly you can return to your desks.

*HINT: In most classes the students will be excited about receiv-
ing their Smileys. Give them a minute or two to enjoy them and
then ask them to put the Smileys in their desks and out of sight.*

Activity G — Harmony Shares a Story with the Class

I bet Harmony is dying to get into this lesson. Why don't we get him out and see what he has to say. Hi, Harmony. (Look at each other.) What? Where's your Smiley?

(Give him the giant Smiley.) A special bear needs a special Smiley. (Harmony talks.) What? Thanks, you really like Smileys. Well, you're welcome, Harmony. (Harmony whispers in volunteer's ear.) You have a present for the children, too? It's a story you wrote? Let's ask the children if they would like to hear it. (class response) Harmony wants me to read it for him.

The Rarest Gift

The decree came straight from the king. "Hear ye! Hear ye! In celebration of the king's birthday, a contest will take place throughout the land. The citizen who makes or builds something which is the symbol for the rarest treasure in the world will get a prize. Forty thousand bluegots (which is a lot of loot in any language) goes to the winner. Bring all entries to the palace on November 15th."

Well, the carpenters began to build, the whittlers whittled, and all the ladies worked day and night sewing, crocheting, and knitting. Each person began to make something with his or her chosen talents.

Poor Allison didn't know what to do. She was only ten years old, and she knew there were artists who could paint better than she, craftsmen who could make better clay pots, and singers who could sing better. Ordinarily, Allison wouldn't care about the money that would go to the winner, but her father had had a bad year with the farm and Allison had heard her parents talking about their money troubles.

She thought and thought, but each time she thought of something she could do, she also thought of someone who could do it better. What could she make or show that would be the only one of its kind, the best it could be, the rarest kind of rare? She was walking by the lake, thinking and wondering, when suddenly she began jumping up and down with joy. "I know!" she squealed and dashed home.

Allison got a giant box. She covered it with red paper. Carefully, she cut hundreds of snowflakes of all sizes and glued them onto the box.

The king's birthday arrived. The red box with white snowflakes was delivered to the royal palace. People were assembled everywhere. Excitement filled the air. One-by-one, each contestant brought his or her contribution. When it came time for the king to open her present, Allison's throat was dry and her heart pounded in her chest. The king opened the card which was attached to the box and read, "There is no duplicate for this gift. It is one of a kind — the rarest kind of rare. It is the greatest treasure in the world. It may be shared, but no one can own it."

101

As King Alfredo pulled the red and white ribbon, all four sides of the box dropped to the ground. A surprised gasp popped out of the king's mouth — and then a laugh. "I declare this gift the winner!" he shouted. Standing ever-so-shyly-but-proudly in the middle of the box was Allison — the rarest kind of rare, a unique and priceless treasure, a one-of-kind human being!

1. What was inside the box?   (Allison)
2. What did Allison stand for or represent?   (The rarest treasure in the world.)
3. Who, besides Allison, is the only symbol of the rarest treasure in the world?   (We are.)

Activity H — Lesson Ending

Here is your new bulletin board strip for next time: Grade 2 — Compliments Bring Smiles. Grade 3 — Everybody Likes Compliments. (Have a student read them to the class.)   Remember to add your stories and pictures to the bulletin board. We will be back soon with some more PSE lessons.

Meanwhile, you'll want to try to look for the good in each person, practice your compliments and of course, be good to yourself and to each other.

_____ Lesson 4 _____

Rumors and Stress Reduction

Objectives

- The child will define a rumor.
- The child will participate in a rumor-passing game.
- The child will verbalize how statements of fact can change through the passing of rumors.
- The child will state why it is important to learn about stress reduction.
- The child will participate in a stress reduction exercise.

Suggested Reading

James, Muriel and Jongeward, Dorothy. *Born to Win,* p. 48. "Listening is one of the finest strokes one person can give another."

Miller, Mary Susan. *Childstress!,* p. 21-22. "Since most adults view a child's world from their own frame of reference, it is difficult for them to imagine any life but their own as stressful. However, adult recognition or nonrecognition of the stress under which children live changes nothing. The stress is there."

Selye, Dr. Hans. *Foreword of Childstress!,* p. vii. "Without being aware of it, for example, parents sometimes expose their children to tremendous stresses whose results may be carried into adulthood. Children are often pressured to conform to their parents' aspirations and ambitions. If these are different from the children's desires, or beyond their capacities, deep feelings of guilt, unworthiness and suppressed anger may develop in the children."

Background

The tendency is to say "rumors happen," but each of us has a responsibility in dealing with rumors:

1. Not to believe everything we hear
2. Not to pass a rumor
3. Not to "mirror" passing rumors to children, especially those designed as gossip.

People think they relax by watching TV or reading a book. Though these activities can be relaxing, they are not enough. Research tells us that we are a stress-oriented nation. Several types of techniques have been developed to reduce stress in our lives. In this program we will be concentrating on muscle tensing techniques. Scientific research indicates that being able to handle stress affects health, attitudes and performance in all walks of life.

Materials

New bulletin board strip: Grade 2 — Stress Can Be Valuable and Harmful. Grade 3 — Rumors Can Be Harmful.

Activity A —
Define Rumors and Review Bulletin Board Strip from Lesson 3

Today we will be talking about two different things: rumors and how to reduce stress in our lives. (Acknowledge and go over class contributions to the PSE bulletin board.) In November (or most recent month), we had a lesson about Gratitudes and Changes. We talked about things we would change and realized there are some things in our lives we cannot change. But we are always in control of our what? (Wait for class response.) Right. We decided attitude is the difference.

The Project Self-Esteem teams have been talking about something we would change. It has to do with rumors. What's a rumor? (class response) A rumor is something someone tells you, usually about someone else, which may or may not be true. Why do you think people tell rumors? (get someone in trouble, revenge) Why would you want to get someone in trouble? (make self look better) Why would you want to look better? (don't feel good about self) FACT: You are not as likely to be mean to others when you feel good about yourself. What do you think that sentence means? (When you feel good about yourself, putting people down and being mean isn't something you would do.)

Activity B — The Rumor Game

To show you how rumors happen, we are going to play a game you have probably played a lot. It is called the telephone game. This is the same game and we call it the Rumor Game. We are going to divide you into groups (Divide class into two to three groups.) I will tell the person in front a sentence. He or she will tell the person behind him/her. That person will tell the next person and so on until you get to the end of the row. If you do not hear, you must say what you think you heard. The sentence may only be said one time. The rest of you need to be quiet.

> *HINT: When you divide the class into groups, have each group stand to play the game. The students stand only for this part of the lesson.*

Sentences for the Rumor Game

Grade 2

1. Elephants wear large tennis shoes.
2. Starting rumors will hurt someone.

Grade 3

1. Fish swim in schools; they learn while they travel.
2. People who start rumors do not feel good about themselves.

(After the Rumor Game is finished, ask students to quietly return to their seats and then discuss the results.) The point of this game is: Be careful about the information you pass along, especially when you hear it from someone else. You cannot stop others from passing rumors, but you can refuse to pass one. Just as important, you can be the one who doesn't believe everything you hear about someone else.

Activity C — Defining Stress and Discussing the Value of Decreasing Stress

You and I live in a busy world. We move fast. Sometimes, it seems as if there are more things to be done than there is time to do them. Everyone tell me what you do with your time. TELL ME ALL AT ONCE. (Wait for class response.) Stop! I'm getting tired just listening! It is a busy world. We need to learn to relax.

Let's think about a car. People don't drive it ALL THE TIME at ninety miles per hour. First of all, it wouldn't be safe. They would get tickets and it wouldn't be good for their engines. Your body is nothing like an engine, really, but we can use an engine as our example. If you race your engine, which is your heart, at full speed ALL THE TIME and never give it a chance to slow down, you will have trouble staying healthy. What else do we need to do to stay healthy? (Eat proper foods. Drink lots of liquids. Get plenty of sleep.) There is more to keeping healthy than that, and it has to do with learning to reduce the stress in your life. What is stress? (upsets and demands) Not all stress is harmful. Stress is harmful when you feel so upset you can not think straight.

Lots of people in the world do stress reduction exercises. Many of the best athletes do stress reduction exercises. You might have noticed when someone is about to do something like pitch a ball or hit a golf ball, they do some sort of stress reduction exercise just before the activity.

> *HINT: Disruptive individuals need to be reminded, if they cannot use this tool to help their lives, they need to allow other children in the class to make their own choice.*

Activity D — Learning to Breathe Properly

We will begin by learning to breath in a new way. As you may know, you have two lungs. When you breathe, your lungs fill up with air and then empty. You do this properly by breathing as deeply as you can. Most of us have not been taught how to breathe so our body will get enough air. I want you to put your feet flat on the floor and sit up so your spine and your back are straight. Place both of your hands just above your stomach. We do this so we are able to feel the air filling the lungs.

Watch me the first time. Using only my nose I take a long, slow breath, bring in as much air as I can, and hold it for just a second. Now slowly I begin to let it out, but this time through my mouth. If your fingers move apart and stomach moves out when you breathe in through your nose, you are doing this exercise properly. Let's do it together. (Repeat four times.)

When you are upset, nervous, or just sometime when you need to calm down, try this simple breathing exercise. It works!

Activity E — Stress Reduction Exercise (read verbatim)

We are going to do what is called a tensing exercise. That means that you will make a muscle really tight, hold it tightly, and then relax it. Listen so you know what to do. Everyone hold up your left hand. (If possible, turn in same direction the children are sitting and hold up your left hand.) Drop your arms to your sides. Squeeze your left hand into a fist. Hold it as tightly as you can while I say TIGHT! TIGHT! TIGHT! TIGHT! TIGHT! Now open your hand and let it hang to your side. Let's do your other hand. Squeeze your right hand into a fist. Hold it as tightly as you can while I say TIGHT! TIGHT! TIGHT! TIGHT! TIGHT! Now, open your hand and let it hang by your side. Bring your fists up by your shoulders like you're showing how strong you are and make your upper and lower arm muscles TIGHT! TIGHT! TIGHT! TIGHT! TIGHT! Now drop your arms and let them hang by your sides.

We're going to tighten the muscles in your head. Frown, squeeze your eyes really tight, press your lips together, push your chin down to your chest, and hold all those muscles TIGHT! TIGHT! TIGHT! TIGHT! TIGHT! Now, let your head hang loose, relax your mouth, and just be still for a few seconds.

Slowly bring your shoulders up and try to touch your ears. Pull them up hard, hold them there, and drop them. Pull in your chest muscles and stomach muscles. Hold them TIGHT! TIGHT! TIGHT! TIGHT! TIGHT! Now, let those muscles relax and just sit quietly for a few seconds.

Pull the muscles tight in your upper and lower leg. TIGHT! TIGHT! TIGHT! TIGHT! TIGHT! Tighten the muscles in your feet. TIGHT! TIGHT! TIGHT! TIGHT! TIGHT! Now just relax.

Just feel how relaxed your arms feel. And your chest. And your stomach. And the lower part of your body. And your legs. And your feet. Bringing air in through your nose, take a long slow breath. Hold your breath for a second and then slowly let the air out through your mouth.

We will be doing an exercise like this at the beginning of each lesson from now on. You might want to practice this exercise at home.

Activity F — New Bulletin Board Strip and Ending

We have a new strip for your bulletin board. (Grade 2 — Stress Can Be Valuable and Harmful. Grade 3 — Rumors Can Be Harmful.) We will be looking forward to seeing the stories and pictures that you add to this bulletin board. We will be back in two weeks with the Feelings Lesson. Between now and then we ask you to remember to be good to yourself and to each other.

_____ **Lesson 5** _____

Feelings

Objectives

- The child will read aloud four sentences about feelings.
- The child will listen to a story which talks about feelings being based upon past experiences.
- The child will participate in an activity with surprise boxes and write his/her feelings.
- The child will be able to state that one person's feelings can be different from another person's feelings.
- The child will hear about a situation where feelings can change.

Suggested Reading

Ginott, Haim. *Between Parent and Child*, p. 30. "The best help we can give a child is to show him we understand his general feelings."

Palmer, Pat. *Liking Myself*, p. 20. "Feelings let us know what is happening, what we want, what is important to us."

Rubin, Theodore Isaac. *Reconciliation; Inner Peace in An Age of Anxiety*, p. 59. "It is almost never possible to repress one emotion without repressing others. It is impossible to experience prolonged relative peace of mind when a great deal of repression is taking place."

Wahlroos, Sven. *Family Communication*, p. 153. "Accept all the feelings expressed by another person and try to understand them; do not accept all actions, but try to understand them."

Background

Feelings are a barometer for each of us with important insight into our perception of the world. Therefore, it is important to understand that people do have different feelings and then to accept their feelings as valid for them. To say to a child, "You're a big boy, you shouldn't be too shy to be in the school play" is invalidating that child and not allowing him to be who he truly is. It is better to say, "I understand how scary getting up in front of others can be."

Many experts believe that all feelings are related. If one denies, represses, or buries one feeling, all the other feelings will be affected. It is like a string of lights. Turn off anger and you will also turn off love — and other emotions. It is important for us to discover a safe way to express each of our feelings.

Materials

Feelings chart (see Activity C), Five strips with the word "feelings" written on them. Masking tape for the back of these, Small piece of paper for each child, A box for feelings activity, Chalkboard space, Bulletin board strip: Grade 2 and 3 — Everybody Has Feelings.

Activity A —
Introduction and Review Bulletin Board Strip from Lesson 4

We are really happy to be here with you today because we know you are special and we care about you. (Review bulletin board. Acknowledge several students' work and thank all students who contributed. Collect contributions for folders if appropriate.)

Today we are going to talk about feelings. Everyone has feelings. Sometimes you are not aware of how you feel about things. We are going to take a look at how you feel about specific things.

Activity B — Stress Reduction Exercise (read verbatim)

Last time we were with you, we did our first stress reduction exercise in which we made our muscles tight then let them relax. We took different parts of our body, made the muscles tight, and then relaxed. Did anyone try to do it on your own? (Have a brief class discussion.)

Today, we are going to use our imaginations and do another tensing exercise during which you will make your muscles tight. Pretend you are a wooden soldier. While sitting at your desk, make your body really straight. Put your feet flat on the floor. Sit up straight...straighter. Pull in your stomach muscles. Put your chin close to your chest. Put your shoulders towards your chair. Tense all the muscles in your body. TIGHT! TIGHT! TIGHT! TIGHT! TIGHT! Now relax.

Pretend you are a rag doll. Your neck is filed with cotton. Let your head roll from side to side and then stop and drop it to your chest. Let your arms swing just a little from side to side and then stop. Let your feet roll out to the side. Feel your knees relax. You are soft and relaxed throughout your whole body. By tensing muscles and then relaxing them you can teach your body how to relax.

Take a deep, slow breath, holding it for a moment, and then slowly let it out. Sit quietly and just relax.

Activity C — Introduction to Feelings Sentences

On this chart I have four sentences. Each one has a blank space into which one word will fit. The same word will fit into each of the four sentences. (Read the sentence saying "blank" where appropriate.)

HINT: It is helpful to use a large poster board for the Feelings chart so that the words are big enough to be seen by all the students.

Feelings Chart

1. Everyone has _____.
2. _____ are based upon past experience.
3. One person's _____ can be different from another person's _____.
4. _____ can change.

What one word would fit into each of these sentences?   (feelings)

HINT: When the appropriate word is discovered, have a child read the first sentence, come to the chart, and place the word in the blank. Complete all four sentences this way.

Activity D — Story to Illustrate Feelings Are Based upon Past Experience

Let's look at the third sentence, "Feelings are based upon a past experience." Here we have a boy named Jack (Draw a circle-face on the chalkboard. Put a frown on the face.) When Jack was three years old, his mother took him to a park. A big black dog ran up and jumped on him, knocking him flat. He wasn't hurt, but he cried. How did Jack feel about dogs?   (afraid)

On the other hand, let's take a look at Dick. (Draw a circle-face with a smile for Dick.) When Dick was three years old, his parents gave him a puppy and Dick and the puppy grew up together. Dick played with his dog, loved it, and took it everywhere. How did Dick feel about dogs? (liked them) Jack and Dick feel differently about dogs because of what happened to them when they were very young.

Now what if Jack's parents decided to give him a puppy when he was ten years old. He played with the puppy, took it for walks, and the puppy followed Jack everywhere. How would Jack feel about dogs now? (might like them) So Jack's feelings about dogs changed. Will he like all dogs now? (maybe yes, maybe no) The important thing to remember is that feelings can change.

Think of something you once were afraid of but you aren't any more. Who wants to share? (Wait for class response.)

HINT: (Optional) Have children write one idea before sharing, to prevent coattailing. Perhaps a PSE volunteer would like to share how scarey the first day of school was for her when she was young. Keep the sharing brief.

Activity E —
Show Box Containing Object; Students Write First Feelings

We said everybody has feelings. People have many different kinds of feelings. Let's make a list of all the different feelings we can think of.   (class response)

> *HINT: (Optional)   Draw faces which correspond to feelings rather than using words.*

You are being given a piece of paper.   (Team member distributes paper.)   When it is your turn, you will look into a box and write one word which describes how you felt when you saw what was in the box. You are not going to touch what is in the box. You will just look, and then write what you feel. You must not peek before it is your turn, or make a sound when it is your turn — because it will put ideas into the heads of your neighbors. We want your feelings only, so you must not make a sound. Put your head down, close your eyes, and do not open them until someone taps you on the shoulder.

> *HINT: Two adults move around the room. One holds the box and one taps the child on his/her shoulder whispering the child's name. Remind each child to look, be quiet, and write. The object inside the box must have the possibility of either a positive or negative feeling. Suggestions: a mirror, green pepper, celery, onion rings.*

Everyone open your eyes. What was in the box?   (class response)   We will go around the room. We want you to share your first feeling. If your first feeling is the same as someone else's you may say it again.

> *HINT: List feelings on chalkboard. If a student repeats an answer, put a check next to that feeling. If a student hesitates, say "We'll come back to you" and move on.*

We have   (count and tell the number)   feelings about one item.   (Ann)   you felt (disgusted)   while   (Jeff)   you felt   (delighted). But how could we get   (say the number)   different feelings about one item?   (Not everyone feels the same way about any one thing. Or, one person's feelings can be different from another person's feelings.)   Let's do it again! (Repeat the entire process a second time, using a different item in the box.)

Once again we have proven everyone does not feel the same about any one thing. That means, to put people down or make fun of them because they do not feel the same way you do isn't appropriate.

Activity F — Feelings Game

I'm going to read a sentence. You are to follow directions. Please listen carefully — make your choice from your own feelings.

HINT: After each statement, have the children sit down again.

Feelings Statements

1. If you were walking at night and a big gorilla came up to you, stand up if you would feel afraid.
2. If you are afraid of snakes, stand up.
3. If you were asked to go to Disneyland and you would feel happy about that, stand up.
4. If your mother served broccoli for dinner and you would feel happy about that, stand up.
5. If someone teased you in front of your friends and you would feel upset about that, stand up.
6. If you got a knot in your shoelace that you couldn't get undone and your friends were calling for you to hurry...and if you would feel upset about this, stand up.

Feelings are important. They tell us who we are. We will talk more about feelings in our next lesson.

Activity G — Lesson Ending

Let's take a look at the bulletin board strip for next time: Grade 2 and 3 — Everybody Has Feelings.

We will be looking forward to seeing the stories and pictures which you add to our new bulletin board. We will be back in two weeks. Meanwhile, be good to yourself and to each other.

_____ Lesson 6 _____

Person and Actions Are Separate

Objectives

- The child will participate in several activities that illustrate the separation of actions from the person.
- The child will state orally that he/she likes a person but not his or her actions.
- The child will complete a written worksheet entitled, "My Feelings."
- The child will share orally some feelings he or she wrote on a worksheet called, "My Feelings" with one partner.

Suggested Reading

Berksdale, L. S. *Building Sound Self-Esteem*, p. 7. "I am not my actions."

Briggs, Dorothy C. *Celebrate Your Self*, p. 204. "See your person as separate from your behavior, thoughts and feelings; otherwise your self-worth is lowered with each misstep." Dreikurs, Rudolf. *Children: The Challenge*, p. 115. "We must make a particular effort to separate the deed from the doer. When we realize that it is not the CHILD that is bad, but only what he does, the child senses it and responds to this distinction."

Background

To call someone a "jerk" is to put that person into a box. It is one thing to have "jerky" behavior and quite another thing to be a "jerk." We can, if we choose, change "jerky" behavior, but to change "BEING A JERK" is nearly impossible.

By focusing on changing behavior, we give others room to grow.

Materials

Harmony, My Feelings worksheet, Feelings chart with blank space from Lesson 5, Yardstick, Scarf, Cards with names of characters for skits. New bulletin board strip: Grades 2 and 3 — I Can Like Someone and Not Like What He/She Does.

Activity A —
Introduction and Review Bulletin Board Strip from Lesson 5

Today we are going to talk about how we can like someone and not like what they do. (Review bulletin board. Acknowledge several student's work and thank all students who contributed. Collect contributions for folders if appropriate.)

Did you try to do a stress reduction exercise on your own? Does anyone want to share his or her experience? (Wait for class response. Be brief.)

Activity B — Stress Reduction Exercise (read verbatim)

Today, we are going to use our imagination and do another tensing exercise during which you will make your muscles tight. Pretend you are a wooden soldier. While sitting at your desk, make your body really straight. Put your feet flat on the floor. Sit up straight. . .straighter. Pull in your stomach muscles. Put your chin close to your chest. Put your shoulders back towards your chair. Tense all the muscles in your body. TIGHT! TIGHT! TIGHT! TIGHT! TIGHT! Now relax.

Pretend you are a rag doll. Your neck is filled with cotton. Let your head roll from side to side and then stop and drop it to your chest. Let your arms swing just a little from side to side and then stop. Let your feet roll out to the side. Feel your knees relax. You are soft and relaxed throughout your whole body. By tensing muscles and then relaxing them you can teach your body how to relax. Just sit still. Enjoy feeling relaxed (allow thirty seconds.)

Activity C — Harmony Comes Out of Hibernation and Acts Up

We have news for you today! Harmony is out of hibernation! (Bring him out.) Everyone say hi to Harmony. (class response) Wait a minute! What's the matter, Harmony? (Bear's head is buried; he holds a yardstick.) Hey, what's going on? You're unhappy? I can see that, but I need you to use your words to tell me what's going on. (Harmony still holds head.) He won't talk. . .but I bet he just feels unhappy because he's been gone. Let's review. Maybe he will cheer up.

(Take Feelings chart from Lesson 5, with blank spaces, and hold in one hand.) The first sentence with the correct word is what? (Everyone has feelings.) We proved in the last lesson that you all had feelings about what was in the boxes. We. . .(Harmony begins banging the yardstick on a desk.) What? Harmony, stop that! (Take stick away. Harmony hides head again.) What are you doing? (no response) Harmony, you need to talk. (no response) Well then, you need to be quiet so I can work with the children.

Where was I. . .let's go on. What is sentence number two? (Feelings are based upon a past experience.) Remember we decided. . .(Harmony grabs onto volunteer's scarf and won't let go.) Harmony! Harmony, let go! I don't know what has gotten into you today (pulling him off of scarf — glaring at him), but I'm beginning to feel frustrated. (Harmony hides face.) Are you going to use your words to tell me what is going on? (silence) Then you need to be quiet.

Our third sentence is, one person's feelings can be different from another person's feelings. What is the last sentence? (Feelings can change.) That's right and. . . (Harmony knocks chart out of volunteer's hand — volunteer looks really annoyed.)

That's it! You have a choice: either talk to me or be put out of the lesson. I have a job to do — to teach this lesson. (getting more upset) But I cannot do it when you keep interrupting. Do you want to talk about what's bothering you? (no response) Then I have no choice but to give you to. . .(name another PSE volunteer as you give Harmony to her). Then walk back to front of classroom. This PSE team member brings Harmony back up to the front of the classroom and says. . .) Wait a minute. Let's take a look at what's happening here.

Does (first PSE volunteer) still like Harmony? (yes) What's the matter then? (She doesn't like what he is doing or his actions.) The other problem is that Harmony won't use his words. You really need to talk Harmony. (Harmony talks in second PSE volunteer's ear.) He says he didn't like being in hibernation. He says he was lonely and he missed the children.

Activity D —
Skit with Harry: Illustrating Person and Actions Are Separate

(First PSE volunteer takes Harmony back.) I can understand why you were upset. I couldn't help you because I didn't know what was wrong. What? Oh, you don't understand how you can still like someone and not like what he or she does? Well, that's a new idea to think about. Maybe if we do some playacting, we can make it more clear. We are going to show how you can like a person even though you don't like his or her actions.

HINT: This skit is done by PSE volunteers.

Skit with Harry

A: I don't like Harry! I really don't like him, I really, really don't!

B: Tell me (name), what is it you don't like about Harry?

A: (Pouting) Well. . .he pinches and bites and teases and steps on my shoes and he calls me names.

B: If Harry didn't pinch, bite, tease, step on your shoes, and call you names, is it possible you might like Harry?

A: (Thinking) Yeah. . .then he'd be OK.

B: Then it's what Harry DOES that you don't like.

A: Yeah, I don't like what he does. . .but he can be nice, sometimes.

Activity E — Playacting: Liking Someone without Liking Actions

That may be a new idea. Why don't we do some playacting to help us think about liking someone even though we don't like his or her actions? These are things that happened in our school.

> HINT: Have cards with names of characters. Read each skit, then choose volunteers. Pin or hang card on appropriate child.

Grade 2

One day, after school, two close friends were playing hopscotch. The first girl threw her marker and took her turn. Just as the second person was going to throw her marker, another friend came along. "May I play, too?" the new friend asked.

"No, the game has already started," was the answer.

1. How did the new girl feel?
2. Is it possible the new girl still likes the other two?
3. What doesn't she like?   (actions)
4. Has this ever happened to you?
5. Do you remember how you felt?
6. Have you ever done this to others? How did they feel?

Chuck brought invitations to his birthday party. He passed them out at recess. He gave one to Anne, one to Joey, but he didn't give one to Ned.

1. Has anything like this ever happened to you?
2. How did Ned feel?
3. Is it possible that Ned and Chuck are still friends?
4. Could Ned still like Chuck? What doesn't he like?   (actions)

Grade 3

One day, two children who were really good friends, were playing together. They were playing catch. First one child threw the ball to the other and he/she threw it back. After a few minutes a third child came along and asked only one person to play. He/she showed the one child a new walkie-talkie. The two children who had been looking at the walkie-talkie walked off together, leaving the other person behind.

1. How many of you have ever been left like this?
2. How does the one who gets left behind feel?
3. Is it possible the two children who were playing in the first place will still be friends?
4. What is it that the child who is left behind doesn't like?   (actions)
5. What could they have done differently?

Sally and Martha were good friends. They had known each other for a long time. One day they decided to play handball. Martha served. Sally caught the serve and wouldn't accept it. She handed the ball back to Martha. Martha served again. Sally caught it again and wouldn't accept it. Martha served it a third time. Sally caught the ball. Martha stopped and glared at Sally "Well, what do you want?" she asked. Martha served the ball again. Sally hit the ball then deliberately stepped in front of Martha so she couldn't get the ball. Now Martha was really annoyed. She threw down the ball and left the game.

1. Is it possible that Martha and Sally are still friends?
2. Does Martha still like Sally?
3. Why did Martha leave?   (didn't like Sally's actions)

Sam's friend John was chosen to be captain of the class baseball team. John had chosen all but one player for the team. Only Bill and Sam were left. John could only choose one person. He chose Bill.

1. Has anything like this ever happened to you?
2. How did Sam feel?
3. Did Sam still like John?
4. Even though Sam's feelings are hurt, is there a chance he and John will still be friends?

> *HINT: Encourage children to get into their parts. There is no talking from the actors/actresses in these skits. Read slowly enough to have the children act out their parts like throwing the ball back and forth, etc.*

Activity F — Write a Specific Feeling and Share with a Partner

Do you understand now, Harmony, how you can like someone but not like his or her actions? (Harmony nods his head.) The second problem we had was getting you to talk. Sharing is such an important part of understanding feelings. Some people find it easy to share with others and some find it very difficult to share with anyone. There's an old saying: Practice makes...what? (Harmony whispers in volunteer's ear.) That's right, perfect. At least we know most things get easier when we practice.

Today, we are going to practice sharing. The PSE teachers are passing out a worksheet. You are going to do some writing. Then we will pair you off, and you can share those feelings with the person who is your partner. (Read the worksheet with the class.) The worksheet will help you when it comes time to share. Take a few minutes to fill out the worksheet. Raise your hand if you need help.

> HINT: *Allow time for the majority of the class to complete the worksheet. Those who finish early may begin to color the faces on the worksheet. Assist individual children.*

Now it's time to share. If you have not finished the worksheet you may do so later. (Pair off class.) Each of you will take turns sharing your example for each feeling. (Allow time for sharing.)

When we share our feelings with someone else, we find others may have the same feelings. More importantly, when we put a feeling into words and share it, often the feeling somehow changes. Or perhaps our attitude about it changes, which makes a difference. So it is important for each of us to share our feelings with friends.

Activity G — Lesson Ending and Review

Every PSE lesson has a reason. What do you think we wanted you to learn from today's lesson? (It helps to share feelings. You might not like someone's actions but you can still like the person.)

Here is your new bulletin board strip for next time: I Can Like Someone and Not Like What He/She Does. Remember to share your ideas, stories, and pictures on our new bulletin board. See you next time. Meanwhile, be good to yourself and to each other.

Lesson 7

Communication Skills, Part I

Objectives

- The child will orally name some of the characteristics of communication: giving each other messages with words, sounds, and body movement.
- The child will identify the two participants of any communication: the person who talks and the person who listens.
- The child will write the steps of communication in given situation: Say how you feel, and say what you want.

Suggested Reading

Briggs, Dorothy C. *Celebrate Your Self,* p. 166. "Openness does not mean dumping on others. It does mean letting the other know how you experience your world, what's in your heart. This means taking responsibility for your own feelings."

Ginott, Haim. *Between Parent and Child,* p. 71. "Feelings come through in word, and in tone, in gesture and in posture. All we need is an ear to listen, an eye to behold, a heart to feel."

Nierenberg, Gerard I. and Calero, Henry H. *How to Read a Person Like a Book,* p. 12.

"People can communicate different types of information at different levels of understanding. The communication process consists of more than the spoken or written language. When you are trying to communicate with a person, sometimes you get through and sometimes you do not . . . because many times the reception of your communication is based upon the degree of the listener's empathy for your nonverbal communication."

Background

The primary interpersonal relationship problem facing humans today is communication. Many people are unable to express their feelings. For this reason, an important part of Project Self-Esteem is to offer many opportunities for children to get in touch with their feelings and their wants. The program also teaches children how to express both feelings and wants.

The issue in this lesson is not to change the "victimizer" but to diminish the feeling of "being the victim" by standing up for oneself and thus raising self-esteem.

Materials

Harmony, Word cards for charades (see Activity D), Communication Is Important worksheet, Wants and Feelings charts (see Activity G), New bulletin board strip: Grades 2 and 3 — #1. Say How you Feel. #2. Say What You Want.

Activity A —
Introduction and Review Bulletin Board Strip from Lesson 6

Today we are going to talk about communication. Last time we talked about a person and his or her actions being separate. We found you could still like a person even if you didn't like what he/she was doing. If I got upset with this class for being noisy, would it be because I don't like the class? (no) What wouldn't I like? (the actions of the class)

(Review bulletin board from Lesson 6, acknowledge several students' work, and read one or two stories. Thank those students who contributed and save work for folders if appropriate.)

Activity B — Stress Reduction Exercise (read verbatim)

Today, we are going to use our imaginations and do another tensing exercise during which you will make your muscles tight. Pretend you are a wooden soldier. While sitting at your desk, make your body really straight. Put your feet flat on the floor. Sit up straight...straight. Pull in your stomach muscles. Put your chin close to your chest. Put your shoulders back towards your chair. Tense all the muscles in your body. TIGHT! TIGHT! TIGHT! TIGHT! TIGHT! Now relax.

Pretend you are a rag doll. Your neck is filled with cotton. Let your head roll from side to side and then stop and drop it to your chest. Let your arms swing just a little from side to side and then stop. Let your feet roll out to the side. Feel your knees relax. You are soft and relaxed throughout your whole body. By tensing muscles and then relaxing them you can teach your body how to relax. Just sit still. Enjoy feeling relaxed (about thirty seconds.)

Activity C — Body Language and Communication

Today, we are going to talk about communication. Communication takes two people — but first, tell me what the word communication means to you. (Wait for class response.)

> *HINT: Write the word "communication" on the chalkboard. Under it, write "talks" and "listens."*

Communication is giving each other messages with words, sound, or body movements. Let's get Harmony out and see if you can show him some of the ways to communicate. Moving only your head let me see how you show: yes/no/happy/sad/surprised/upset. Using only one hand, show me: OK/no/hope so. Moving your head and hands, show me: be quiet/come here/stay back/speak louder.

Activity D — Charades Game: Actions Speak Louder Than Words

You see, we think we communicate only in words, but our actions talk just as loudly, actually louder than words. Let's play an old game called "Charades" to show how much you can communicate without words.

HINT: Go over words to be used and define each word so its meaning is clear. Call up two or three students at a time to take a word card out of a box. The card indicates what is to be acted. Have students act out each.

Words for Grade 2

upset	shy	sad
annoyed	bored	happy

Words for Grade 3

afraid	silly	confident
happy	worried	proud

Activity E —
Explain Why We Use Different Types of Words for Different Ages

Learning to communicate is a BIG JOB! It is wise to know we talk to different people in different ways. We are going to teach you two steps for communicating. This method is a wonderful idea to use with your classmates. You need to decide if it is the way you want to talk to adults.

HINT: It is important that children understand that there is an appropriate time, place, and way to express feelings and wants. We wish to discourage any and all disrespectful communication between children and adults.

Activity F — Introduce Feelings and Wants Formula

People don't always know what you are thinking. Let them know! Wishing doesn't work; asking works better. What do you want? That's a big question, but just answer it with whatever pops into your mind. (Call on several children to get varied responses.) Saying you want something doesn't mean you will get it. Wants change. You might want a million dollars today; but if you got really sick tomorrow, you might want to be healthy.

HINT: Let students know it is OK to want — to ASK for what they want. But that doesn't mean they will GET what they want.

When you communicate, it is important to say what you feel (write "I feel" on the chalkboard), and to say what you want. (Write "I want" on the chalkboard.) Why is it important to let people know how you feel? Why do you think it is important to tell others what you want? (so they will know what you are thinking/might guess wrong/so you have a better chance of understanding each other)

Activity G — Feeling and Wants Game

Here is a chart with a circle of feelings. All the feelings you might have are not on it. A few feelings are written inside the circle. Who wants to read these feelings? (class response) Remember, the first step in communicating is: Say How You Feel. The second step is: Say What You Want.

HINT: It is helpful to use two large poster boards for these charts
so that words are big enough to be seen by all the students.

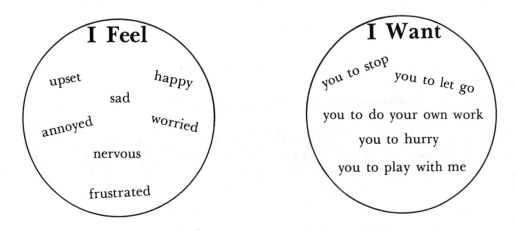

Let's play a game. I'll read a situation. You look at the I Feel chart and choose the feeling you might have in this situation. Tell me your feeling. Choose a want from this chart (pointing at the I Want chart) and tell me what you would want to happen in this situation. The only rule is: no name-calling! We call name-calling "war words." War words start fights, they do not communicate.

HINT: The student may chose any word from the I Feel chart
and any phrase from the I Want chart that go together to make
a complete thought. Assist any child who has difficulty reading.

1. Someone calls you a name you don't like.
    I feel   (sad)
    I want   (you to stop)

"I feel sad and I want you to stop" — does that mean the person will stop? (maybe, maybe not) It does get you to explain your feelings and to say what you want. Let's do some more.

2. Someone is looking at your paper during a test.
    I feel   (upset)
    I want   (you to do your own work)

3. You're waiting for a friend to go to school. You are worried about being late.
    I feel   (worried)
    I want   (you to hurry)

Now, let's practice a few more situations using your own words.   (Put charts away.)

4. A friend borrows your bike without asking.
    I feel   (upset)
    I want   (you to ask me first)

5. You share a problem with a friend. Your friend listens.
    I feel   (better)
    I want   (to thank you)

That was fun. Who can tell me what the two steps of communicating are? (class response) Remember: saying what you want doesn't mean you'll get it, but expressing your feelings and wants helps the people around you know you better. It assists you in communicating clearly.

HINT: If this exercise seems stilted, remember a formula gives children something to follow. Later the children will modify it to suit themselves.

Activity H — Communication Worksheet

Between now and next time, we want you to fill out this worksheet. We will use the worksheet for our next lesson, so be sure to finish it. Let's take a look at it.

HINT: Explain the worksheet. Ask the students and the teacher to do the last six examples on the page together at another time before the next lesson. Children may begin worksheet during class if time permits.

Activity I — Lesson Ending

Let's take a look at the bulletin board strip for the next time: Grades 2 and 3 — #1. Say How You Feel. #2. Say What You Want. Remember to practice your new way of communicating and be good to yourself and to each other.

_____ **Lesson 8** _____

Communication Skills, Part II

Objectives

- The child will orally name the two steps of communication.
- The child will participate in skills demonstrating how the two communication steps may be employed in real-life situations.
- The child will practice giving the same word message in several ways utilizing different voice tones.

Suggested Reading

Smith, Manuel. *When I Say No, I Feel Guilty*, p. 74. "...in expressing our feelings, even when we don't get what we want, we enhance self-respect."

Palmer, Pat. *The Mouse, The Monster & Me*, p. 41. "It's OK to ask for what you want but don't always expect to get it."

Wahlroos, Sven. *Family Communication*, p. 7. "Remember that actions speak louder than words; nonverbal communication is more powerful than verbal communication."

Background

The careless use of words causes many problems in interpresonal relationships. A knowledge of communication skills gives children an alternative in the way they speak to others. Students need to be aware that more is communicated through body language and tone of voice than through words. This knowledge helps children not only to become aware of what others are communicating, but also to understand what message they are sending to others.

Materials

Harmony, Word cards for Using-Tone-Of-Voice game: happy/sad/bored/upset/etc. (see Activity E), Bulletin board strip: Grade 2 — Listen to Other People's Tone of Voice. Grade 3 — Tone of Voice/Body Language/Words Are Ways to Communicate.

Activity A — Stress Reduction Exercise (read verbatim)

Today we are going to use our imagination and do a tensing exercise during which you will make your muscles tight. Pretend you are a wooden soldier. While sitting at your desk, make your body really straight. Put your feet flat on the floor. Sit up straight...straighter. Pull in your stomach muscles. Put your chin close to your chest. Put your shoulders back towards your chair. Tense all the muscles in your body TIGHT! TIGHT! TIGHT! TIGHT! TIGHT! Now relax.

Pretend you are a rag doll. Your neck is filled with cotton. Let your head roll from side to side and then stop and drop your head to your chest. Let your arms swing just a little from side to side and then stop. Let your feet roll out to the side. Feel your knees relax. You are soft and relaxed throughout your whole body. By tensing muscles and then relaxing them you can teach your body how to relax. Just sit quietly and enjoy feeling relaxed. (Allow thirty seconds.)

> *HINT: We have reversed the order of the stress reduction exercise and the review because this lesson is a continuation of Lesson 7. You may do the same or keep the review first.*

Activity B — Introduction and Review Bulletin Board from Lesson 7

Today we are going to continue talking about communication. First, let's look at our bulletin board from last time. Would someone like to read the first step for communication? Who would like to read the second step? The first step is: say how you what? (feel) Now, all together, what is the second step? (Say what you want.) Did anyone have a chance to use this method of communicating? (Call on one or two students, acknowledge work of those who added to the bulletin board, and save work for folders if appropriate.)

Activity C — Continuation from Lesson 7

> *HINT: Students need to have the worksheet from Lesson 7 on their desks.*

In our last lesson we began talking about communication. We discovered there are many ways we send messages. We do use words, but we discovered we also use our face and hands and body to help us communicate. Who remembers what we call it when we use our body to communicate? (body language) So I, for example, can say "Come here, please!" If I want you to hurry, I'd use body language to show you my feelings. (Use gestures to indicate speed wanted with hand, anxious look on face, etc.)

Sometimes when we're upset we don't say what we feel. We get into name-calling instead of talking about what's happening and we do not tell others what we want done. So PSE wrote the two steps for better communication: SAY HOW YOU FEEL. SAY WHAT YOU WANT. You've done a worksheet using these two steps and we are going to use that worksheet to practice communicating.

Harmony has had trouble using his words, so let's bring him out. Say hi. . .(Harmony waves.)

> *HINT: Talk to Harmony, but do not use eye contact. Instead, look all over the place. Have Harmony move to try to catch your eye.*

What are you doing, Harmony? (Harmony talks.) If I don't look at you when I talk you aren't sure if I'm talking to you or not? (Harmony nods.) You're right, Harmony. It is important to look at someone when you talk. It's called "eye contact." Boys and girls, let's be sure to use eye contact when you act out the situations on your worksheet. Instead of reading the situations we are going to ask for volunteers to act out each situation.

HINT: Encourage children to use eye contact when giving examples. Invite those students who seldom participate to do so. However, do NOT insist if a child is reluctant to volunteer.

---

1. Someone takes your ball at recess.

We need two volunteers to do this skit. A and B are playing when B takes A's ball. Who would like to be in this skit? (Choose two volunteers and assist them in setting up skit. Have them playact the skit.) Stop the action! (Call out names of children in the classroom.) (John) how does (A) feel? (frustrated) (Karen) what does (A) want done? (give ball back) Now (turning to A), put it together in a sentence. (I feel frustrated. I want you to give my ball back now, please!)

HINT: Don't let the lesson drag while one child tries to create two sentences. Instead, two different children can give one part of the total solution and the child, who is acting the starring role can put the parts together to create a single sentence. Encourage this student to use a tone of voice appropriate for the feeling.

It is important, with this example, to let the class know that the person might or might not give the ball back. The value of this lesson is in learning to release or let go of frustrations by putting feelings and wants into words.

---

2. Someone sticks up for you.

Two students are teasing a third one when a fourth student comes and sticks up for his/her friend. We will need three volunteers who will act out this scene for us. Mrs. (PSE volunteer) will be the person being teased. (Choose volunteers, assist them in setting up this situation, and ask them to playact the skit.)

Class, how do you think the person being teased would feel? (Wait for class response.) Now, what might the friend of the person being teased say to the other two? (Call on a child in the class.) What needs to be done? (Call on another child.) So (name of child defending friend), what might you say? (Example: It doesn't feel good to be teased. I want you to stop.)

---

3. Someone tattles on you.

We will need three volunteers. One to be a teacher, one to be the person who is tattled on, and a third to be the person who tattles. (Choose the three volunteers and assist them in setting up this situation. Have them playact the skit.) Class, what might the person being tattled on say to the tattler about how he/she feels? (Wait for class response.) What might she say about what she/he wants done? (Addressing the person in the skit), could you put this together? (I am annoyed that you tattled on me, and I don't want you to do it again.) Does this mean the person will not tattle again? (maybe so, maybe not) The point is that it is important to release feelings in an appropriate way instead of keeping them inside. It is helpful to say what you want done.

Sometimes we forget to tell people how much we value them and what they do for us. Let's try the two steps for communicating on this one.

---

4. You forgot your lunch, your friend shares.

This time we will need two volunteers. (Choose two volunteers and assist them in setting up situation. Have them playact the skit.) Class, how would you feel if someone shared his/her lunch with you? (Wait for class response.) What would you want done? (Addressing the sharing student in the skit), what would you tell your friend who shared his/her lunch? (I really feel happy that you shared with me and I hope I can share with you if you forget your lunch.)

Here is a new situation that is not on your worksheet.

---

5. Your brother or sister eats your piece of cake.

Let's take a look at this example. There is one piece of cake left; it is yours. Walking home from school, you think about how good it will taste. You can hardly wait to eat it. When you get home you find your brother or sister has just finished eating your piece of cake. (Choose two volunteers and assist them in setting up the situation. Have them playact the skit.) How do you feel (name)? What do you want done (name)? Put it all together for us (name). (I feel really upset. I don't want you to take what belongs to me!) Be really careful you don't slip into words like, "I feel really upset because you ate my cake, You are selfish!" Do you hear the war words in there? If you call people names, will they listen to your message? (probably not) What will happen? (argument)

You are to say how you feel about what happened, and say what you want done, but you may not call names.

Activity D — PSE Team Skit: Tone of Voice is Important

So far, we've talked about changing name-calling to talking about feelings and wants. There is something else we need to look at and that is HOW you say something. We will discover two important facts today:

1. How you say something is an important part of communication.
2. If you do not listen carefully you won't understand the message being sent.

We are going to do a skit for you. We want you to listen carefully.

> *HINT: PSE team will act out this skit. Do one sequence after another. Wait for student response after each section.*

Mother: How was your test?
Student: I don't know! (upset)

What's the message she's sending — how does she feel?

Mother: How was your test?
Student: I don't know. (bored — sigh, yawn)

127

What's she feeling?

Mother: How was your test?
Student: I don't know. (worried — frown, almost whispering)

What's the feeling? Each time the student said the very same words. Did she give the same message? How could you tell? (her tone of voice)

Activity E — Using-Tone-Of-Voice Game

We're going to play a game, but first we will run through one example to show you how it's done. (Use PSE volunteers.) The person standing is going to ask, "Are you upset?" The person sitting is going to answer "No." We are going to show the sitter a sign telling what message is going to be sent. Watch. Stander, close your eyes. (Show sitter a sign reading "worried.") Stander open your eyes. Now stander ask your question and sitter, give your answer... but remember to send your message. Stander, what do you think the sitter is feeling? (worried)

> HINT: For the next activity, pair off class into twos. One student
> stands by desk, the other sits.

We are going to have the whole class do the exact same thing. Standers will ask "Are you upset?" and sitters will answer "No." We will show the sitters a sign saying which message is to be sent. Ready now? Standers, close your eyes. (Show sign saying "happy" to sitters.) Standers, open your eyes and ask your question. (Wait for sitters response.) Sitters, answer the question and remember to send your message. Standers, what was the message? (Wait for class response.)

Let's do it again. Standers you are going to ask, "How was school today?" Don't ask it until we are ready to begin, but keep it in your mind. Sitters the only word you are going to say is, "Fine." We will show you a card telling you what message to send. Standers, close your eyes. (Show card saying "sad.") Standers, open your eyes and ask your question. Sitters, send your message. Standers, what message was being sent? (sad)

> HINT: Repeat the same procedure using the words "bored,"
> "upset," "afraid" etc. Switch standers and sitters. Standers ask
> "How was the party?" Sitters respond "It was OK." Messages to
> be sent: hurt, excited, silly.

128

We have discovered two important facts today:

1. How you say something is an important part of sending messages.
2. If you are not listening carefully, you will not hear the message being sent.

How you say something and how carefully you listen are important tools of communication. Another point to think about. . .how could you be SURE the other person understood your message when they asked you "How was the party?" (Instead of saying "OK," tell them exactly what you meant. "It was fun! We played tag, musical chairs, and had cake and ice cream.")

Activity F — Lesson Ending

We have a new bulletin board strip for you today. Would someone like to read it for us? (Have student read the strip.) Remember to add your stories and pictures around this strip. We will see you in two weeks. Meanwhile, be good to yourself and to each other.

_____ Lesson 9 _____

Friendship, Part I

Objectives

- The child will compile a list of things he/she likes in a friend.
- The child will compile a list of things he/she does not like in a friend.
- The child will construct a bulletin board strip about friendship.

Suggested Reading

Powell, John. *Why Am I Afraid to Love?*, p. 68 "All of us have the need for supportive friendship. We need to be able to express ourselves without fear or rejection by others."

Richards, Arlene Kramer and Willis, Irene. *Boy Friends, Girl Friends, Just Friends*, p. 15. "Telling something to a friend who hears it as someone close to you, but not identical with you, gives you a chance to check up on how your thinking matches up with that of others. In a sense, a friend is a bridge between you and the rest of the world."

Background

A significant influence in a child's decision-making process is his/her peers. Peer pressure steadily increases as children get older. Studies show that selecting friends who support one's individual values and morals make a significant difference in the choices that are made. Therefore, we begin our series on friendship by looking at the desirable and nondesirable qualities in a friend.

Materials

Harmony, Friends worksheet, Paper for student-made bulletin board strips, My Kind of Friend chart (see Activity C), Crayons, Pen or pencil

Activity A — Review of Lesson 8

Today we are going to discuss friendship. Last time we talked about communication. Who remembers what the word communication means? (Wait for class response.) We learned that we communicate with our tone of voice and our body language. We also learned how to communicate our feelings and our wants. Suppose someone took a pencil of yours and you wanted it back. How could you say this. (I feel upset that you took my pencil and I want you to give it back.)

Let's take a look at your bulletin board from last time. (Acknowledge students' work, read one of the stories, and ask students to share a time when they used the "I feel and I want" way of communication. Place students' work in folders if appropriate.)

Activity B — Stress Reduction Exercise (read verbatim)

HINT: It is important you keep the pace flowing when the children are tightening their muscles — continuous, like a wave — or they will not be able to hold their muscles tight long enough.

To begin today's exercise I want you to sit up straight, feet flat on the floor, but this time let your hands hang loosely at your sides. Beginning with your feet, we are going to tighten every muscle. Pull your feet in tight and hold them. Tighten the muscles in the lower part of your legs, and then the top part of your legs. Pull your stomach muscles in really tight. Tighten the muscles in your chest and your shoulders. Make a fist with your hands. Tighten your arms. Pull in your chin and make a face as you tighten those muscles. Pull every muscle in your body really tight TIGHT! TIGHT! TIGHT! Now let go and relax. Just sit still and enjoy feeling relaxed. (Allow thirty seconds.)

Activity C — Defining What Students Like and Don't Like in a Friend

Today, we are going to talk about what you like and don't like in a friend. Friends are important. What makes a friend important to you? (Wait for class response.)

Because friends are important, you need to think about what you like and don't like in a friend. Let's start with "It bothers me when a friend..." (Write "It bothers me when a friend..." on the chalkboard.) What words could I write under this sentence? (brags, teases, puts people down, etc.)

We are giving you a worksheet. Put your name and date on the top of your paper. Now we are going to fold the paper in half. (Demonstrate how to fold, monitor class.) Be sure the top of the page you are looking at says, "It bothers me when a friend..." Raise your hand if you have a question. You are going to choose the words from our class list that are true for you. Write the words inside the drawing of the person like this. (Show a worksheet with an example.) Choose as many words as you want. Please do it now. (Wait for two minutes.)

Turn your paper over. What does the top of your paper say? (I like it when a friend...) This time you are going to choose your own words to write INSIDE the drawing of the person. So you will think about the sentence "I like it when a friend..." and a word will pop into your mind. Write that word INSIDE your person. Think of as many words as you can. Raise your hand if you need assistance (Allow three minutes.)

As you can see, I have a giant chart that has a figure just like the person on your worksheet. The top of my chart says, "My Kind of Friend." If you want to share one of the things you wrote inside your "I like it when a friend" person, raise your hand.

> HINT: It is helpful to use a large posterboard for the My Kind of Friend chart and make the words you write on the chart big enough to be seen by everyone. Make a class composite of the qualities the students like in a friend. Leave the charts as the class bulletin board for this lesson.

We are going to leave this chart with you because it is your choice of a wonderful friend. It will be your bulletin board for this lesson.

For Third Graders Only

We're not finished with your worksheet. Open your worksheet so you can see both of the people. Turn your paper over. What do you think this means: "A way to have friends is to be one."? (Wait for class response.) So, if you want to have friends you need to be one. Make three spaces or lines in the middle of your worksheet. (Draw three lines on the chalkboard.) I want you to think of three ways you can be a friend. You might look at your worksheet to get some ideas. One way I can think of to be a friend is to listen. So I'll write the word "listen" on one of these three lines. (Write "listen" on one of the three lines on the chalkboard.) Now write your ways to be a friend. (Allow two minutes.) Who wants to share one way for you to be a friend? (class response) Put your paper inside your desk, please.

> HINT: If you have been collecting the students' work for folders it is appropriate to collect these worksheets now. The rest of the lesson is for grades 2 and 3.

Activity D —
Students Make Own Bulletin Board Strips or Bumper Stickers

Harmony is with me today. (Harmony waves to class then talks to PSE volunteer.) He says he liked the first part of this lesson. It will help him remember to listen, to talk to his friends, and to have fun. (Harmony talks to PSE volunteer.) Oh, that's true. I hadn't thought of that. Harmony says he would like to remember all the ideas for being a friend. He thinks he will forget so he suggests we make bulletin board strips about friendship and put them around the room. That's a great idea. Thank you, Harmony!

> *HINT: Calling the strips bulletin board strips or bumper stickers is an optional decision. In some areas of the country, bumper stickers will be more fun. The strips of paper used for the sentences are to be about twenty-four inches long.*

If we look at the My Kind of Friend chart, we can get some ideas about friendship. We could say (write on the chalkboard), "A Friend is Honest." Maybe we could say, "Friends Talk to Each Other." What else could we say?

> *HINT: Using the chart as a reference, write a list of slogans or sayings about friendship.*

We are going to pass out a long strip of paper to each one of you. You need to get out your crayons. (Allow time for all students to get out crayons.) When you get your slip, write your name on one side then put your crayon down and look at me so I will know you are ready. (Wait for class to finish.) Turn your strip over. Please look at me. You are going to choose one of these sayings (pointing to the chalkboard list) and you will write that saying on your strip. Please print or write it large enough to be easily read. Do it now. (Allow two minutes.)

We are going to collect your bulletin board strips and give them to your teacher. He/she will decide where to put them so everyone will remember some important ideas of being a friend. (Harmony talks.) Harmony says he wants to thank you for making so many reminders about friendship. Thank you, Harmony.

Activity E — Lesson Ending

Today, we talked about what we like and don't like in a friend. We also thought about ways we can be a good friend. Finally, we made bulletin board strips to remember ideas about being a friend. We will be back in two weeks. Between now and then, be good to yourself and to each other.

_____ Lesson 10 _____

Friendship, Part II

Objectives

- The child will listen to the story about Sam's balloon.
- The child will provide different alternatives to situations as the story is presented again.
- The child will decide whether a given action is appropriate.

Suggested Reading

Kuczen, Barbara. *Childhood Stress*, p. 128. "Children have to learn how to be a good friend. They sense it has something to do with being kind and loyal and having fun together."

Richards, Arlene Kramer and Willis, Irene. *Boy Friends, Girl Friends, Just Friends*, p. 135. "Conflicts with friends endanger the friendship only when they lower the self-esteem of one or both of the friends...And you can't keep up a friend's self-esteem by avoiding all criticism, because every conflict involves some criticism of each other and conflicts are necessary in friendship."

Zimbardo, Philip G. *A Parent's Guide to the Shy Child*. p. 58. "Friendship skills also involve being a friend who makes others feel special about themselves."

Background

In the survey we took of parents, teachers, and students, one of the areas which caused problems for most children was learning to cope with the upsets in friendships. It is important that children understand that such upsets happen in the best of friendships and that it is normal for friends to disagree at times. We think it is also important that children be given tools to help them cope with this challenging part of life.

Materials

Harmony and several pre-tested balloons, Pin to pop the balloon, Appropriate chart (See Activity F), Bulletin board strip: Grades 2 and 3 — Choose an Appropriate Time, Place, and Way to Express your Upsets.

Activity A — Introduction and Review Lesson 9

Today, we are going to talk about friendship. Last time we talked about things we liked and didn't like in a friend. (Review bulletin board and Friendship strips. Acknowledge students' work, reading one or two stories. Thank those who contributed and save work for folders if appropriate.)

134

Activity B — Stress Reduction Exercise (read verbatim)

> *HINT: Keep the pace moving on this exercise. Have the students tighten their muscles in a rhythm like a wave — from head to toe.*

Sit up straight, feet flat on the floor, but this time let your hands hang loosely at your sides. Beginning with your feet, we are going to tighten every muscle. Pull your feet in tight and hold them. Tighten the muscles in the lower part of your legs, and then the top part of your legs. Pull your stomach muscles in really tight. Tighten the muscles in your chest and your shoulders. Make a fist with your hands. Tighten your arms. Pull in your chin and make a face as you tighten those muscles. Pull every muscle in your body really tight. TIGHT! TIGHT! TIGHT! Now let go and relax. Sit quietly and enjoy the feeling of being relaxed. (Allow thirty seconds.)

Activity C — Sam's Balloon

Today, our lesson has to do with friends' upsets. We're going to begin with Harmony. Let's help him feel comfortable by saying hi. . .(Harmony buries his head.) Oh, no, not again! What's the matter, Harmony? (Harmony talks to PSE volunteer.) Your stomach hurts? I'm sorry to hear that. Maybe it was something you ate. (Harmony talks.) You barely ate at all today. . .I wonder what it could be? Have you been getting along with your friend Yogi lately? (Harmony nods no, talks, and hides his face again.) Oh, I see. You and Yogi had a fight and you aren't talking to each other. That's a tough one. Friends don't always get along. Sometimes, when friends don't talk to each other about what's bothering them it can turn into a huge fight over something very small. (Harmony scratches his head.) You don't understand? Let's tell a story to show you what I mean.

> *HINT: This sequence is most effective when animated and done with someone acting "hammy!" Optional: one person blows up the balloon and one person tells the story. Put a pin through Harmony's paw to pop the balloon at the appropriate moment.*

Sam's Balloon

Living in a town like this one is a boy named Sam. Sam's best friend is named Chris. Sam and Chris ride their bikes to school every morning. This morning Chris arrives ten minutes late to find Sam pacing around nervously. Sam says nothing to Chris about being late and dashes out the front door. (Blow into balloon.)

"Where is your bike?" Sam asks.

"Flat tire." Chris replies with a sigh.

A flat tire means they will have to walk to school. Sam hates to walk to school. (Blow into the balloon.) On the way to school, Chris keeps stopping to tie his shoelaces. Sam gets more and more nervous about being late but he doesn't say anything to Chris. (Blow into the balloon.) About halfway to school, Chris sees Doug walking along and runs over to talk to him. Sam is now walking by himself. Sam hates to walk by himself. (Blow into the balloon.)

Sam and Chris get back together and have to run to get into their classroom. And they are late. Their teacher scolds them in front of the whole class. Sam is embarrassed. (Blow the balloon.) Later, Chris turns around and makes a face at Sam. Sam laughs. The teacher scolds Sam again and Sam begins to argue with the teacher. (Blow into the balloon.)

At lunch, Chris had agreed to meet Sam at a certain place. Sam is there, Chris is not. (Blow into the balloon.) Then Sam asks Chris to give him back his mitt. Sam's team is in the playoffs today. Chris says he forgot to bring Sam's mitt. Sam yells, "What?" (POP the balloon.)

What happened? (Sam blew up.) Sam and Chris did have a lot of little upsets during the day, didn't they? Maybe, if Sam had told Chris about his feelings as they happened, he wouldn't have exploded. If he had talked about his feelings and his wants MAYBE he would have been less upset.

Activity D — Reviewing I Feel and I Want Communication Skills

If you remember, in an earlier lesson, we talked about saying what you feel and what you want. (Write "I feel..." and "I want..." on the chalkboard.) Let's take a look at the times Sam was upset with Chris and see what Sam might have said.

> HINT: Assist the students in forming the "I feel" and "I want" statements by asking questions and calling on several students to put the statements together.

1. When Chris arrived late Sam might have said...(I feel upset about being late. I want you to hurry.)
2. Chris told Sam his bike had a flat tire, and Sam might have said...(I feel upset about walking. I don't want to be late.)
3. Chris keeps stopping to tie his shoelaces so Sam could say...(I feel nervous about being late. I want you to hurry.)
4. Sam is walking alone because Chris went to see Doug. Sam might say...(I feel upset because you left me and I want us to hurry so we won't be late.) Sam could go with Chris to see Doug or Sam could go on without Chris.

5. Sam probably wouldn't say anything to Chris when they were late to class. He probably wouldn't say anything to Chris about getting in trouble for laughing, either.
6. Chris did not meet Sam at lunch. Sam might have said...(I feel really upset when you don't do what you say you are going to do. I want you to keep your word.)
7. Chris forgot to bring Sam's mitt. Sam might have said...(I feel really upset about the mitt. I want you to get a mitt for me to use in the game.)

With that many upsets in one day, it looks like Sam and Chris need to talk. Sometimes little upsets can be smoothed out by talking. Chris might not know Sam gets really upset when he is going to be late. Sam's talking to Chris might get Chris to be on time more often. If not, Sam and Chris might need to stop meeting to go to school together.

There were two places in the story of Sam where we decided Sam probably would not talk. One was when both boys were late to school in the morning. Does anyone remember what the second one was? (Wait for class response.) That's right it was when Chris made a face. Sam laughed and got into trouble with the teacher.

Activity E — Introducing Appropriate Chart

Remember, both boys were late for class. Sam could take time to tell Chris how upset he is about being late. But the teacher, who was already annoyed, would get even more irritated. We've said Sam needs to talk to his friend so the little upsets do not explode. What could Sam do? (class response) Raise your hand if you agree that it would be best for Sam to talk to Chris later. (class response) Sometimes, you need to WAIT to talk to your friend.

HINT: It is helpful to use a large posterboard for the Appropriate chart and make the words you write on the chart big enough to be seen by everyone.

Appropriate Chart

Choose an appropriate time.
Choose an appropriate place.
Choose an appropriate way.
Have a friend you can talk to,
So your upsets cannot stay.

Let's look at this chart. Who would like to read the first line for us? (Choose an appropriate time.) The second line? (Choose an appropriate place.) The third line? (Choose an appropriate way.) And the last two lines. (Have a friend you can talk to, so your upsets cannot stay.)

What does the word appropriate mean? (safe, acceptable, right, proper) Sam and Chris are late for class. If Sam begins to scold Chris which of these is he breaking? (time, place, and maybe way) Sam needs to talk to Chris later. Also, Sam had a choice to leave Chris and get to school on time. Sam needs to be responsible for himself and not blame Chris.

Later, Chris made a face. Sam laughed and got into trouble with the teacher. Sam began to discuss this with the teacher. Stop! look at the chart. Which of these is being broken? (time, place, and way) It is not appropriate to discuss this with a teacher in front of the whole class. Sam could ask to speak to the teacher after class.

The friend you can talk to might be your mom or dad. It might be someone your own age or an older friend. Question: If you are the person someone can talk to and you tell other people what your friend said, will he or she share with you again? (no) Is it possible that telling other people might hurt your friendship? (yes) People will only trust people who show they can be trusted.

Activity F — Playacting Using Appropriate Chart

Let's do a different kind of playacting and see if we can decide which of these (pointing to the Appropriate chart) is being used or broken.

HINT: Read each scene to class before asking for volunteers.

Taking Sides

Janice and Dan are friends. Janice is upset because Susan tattled on her. Janice is really upset. She tells Dan what happened. Which of these (pointing to chart) is being used? (Have a friend you can talk to.)

Arguing with a Friend

As they come in from recess, Pat and Rosa begin to argue. They get annoyed and keep on arguing. The teacher begins to teach. Pat and Rosa are still arguing. Which of these is being used or broken? (time, place and way) Pat and Rosa need to talk to each other, so what might they do? (Talk to each other later.)

Crying on the Playground

You get so upset you cry on the playground. Is that appropriate? If not, why? (Kids might make fun of you.) What could you do? (Go somewhere safe to cry.) Which of these (pointing to the chart) is being used or broken in this situation? (place)

Friend Calls You a Name

You and your friend disagree on a game to play at recess. You are accused of being selfish and of always wanting your own way. You feel this is not true. You become upset. You decide to jog around the playground to work out some of your upset. Is this appropriate behavior? Why or why not? (class response) If you decided to jog around the CLASSROOM which of these (pointing to the chart) would you be using or breaking? (time, place)

> HINT: If you like, choose an example relevant to your school. You can bring in Alcohol and Drug Use. Remember PSE stands for a strong NO USE statement "it is illegal for you to use alcohol or drugs."

There are no answers to handling upsets that will always work. Your life may be easier if you remember:

Choose an appropriate time.
Choose an appropriate place.
Choose an appropriate way.
Have a friend you can talk to,
So your upsets cannot stay

Activity G — Lesson Ending

We have a new bulletin board strip for you today. Would someone like to read it for us? (Have a student read the strip, "Choose an Appropriate Time, Place, and Way to Express Your Upsets.") Remember to add your stories and pictures around this strip. We will see you in two weeks. Meanwhile be good to yourself and to each other.

_____ Lesson 11 _____

Tattling and Cheating

Objectives

- The child will differentiate between tattling and reporting in given situations.
- The child will assist in compiling a list of possible reasons for tattling.
- The child will take part in a class discussion involving the topic of cheating.
- The child will demonstrate suggestions of what to do in a situation where someone is cheating.
- The child will compile a list of ten ways to be good to self and to others to be completed by the next lesson.

Suggested Reading

Briggs, Dorothy Corkille. *Your Child's Self-Esteem*, p. 207. "Consistent teasing, tattling, and sarcasm are indirect outlets for pent-up animosity.

Wahlroos, Sven. *Family Communication*, p. 164. "Do not preach or lecture; ask questions instead." p. 168. "It is through questions and posing problems that we teach children to think for themselves. At the same time we show our interest in what THEY have to say, thus helping them develop a positive self-concept. And we show confidence in their ability to work out problems on their own, a confidence they will eventually adopt and which will help them throughout life."

Background

The classroom teachers requested we include a lesson on tattling and cheating. Both of these serious topics have been dealt with in a light-hearted manner to prevent lecturing.

_____

Materials

Scripts, Cereal box, Hats, Microphones, Glasses and other props, Two Poem charts (see Activity C), New bulletin board strip: Write Ten Ways to Be Good to Yourselves and Ten Ways to Be Good to Each Other.

Activity A —
Introduction and Review Bulletin Board Strip from Lesson 10

Today we are going to talk about tattling and cheating. (Write "tattling" and "cheating" on the chalkboard.) (Review bulletin board strip. Acknowledge several students' work, reading one or two stories. Thank the students who contributed and save work for folders if appropriate.)

Activity B — Stress Reduction Exercise (read verbatim)

Sit up straight with your feet flat on the floor, but this time let your hands hang loosely at your sides. We are going to tighten every muscle, beginning with your feet. Pull your feet in tight and hold them. Tighten the muscles in the lower part of your legs, and then the top part of your legs. Pull your stomach muscles in really tight. Tighten the muscles in your chest and shoulders. Make a fist with your hands. Tighten your arms. Pull in your chin and make a face as you tighten those muscles. Pull every muscle in your body tight. TIGHT! TIGHT! TIGHT! Now let go and relax. Sit quietly and enjoy feeling relaxed.

This kind of relaxation really works before a test — or when you are feeling upset in any way. Try it. These exercises can keep your from exploding, like Sam's balloon.

Activity C — PSE-TV Station Discusses Tattling and Cheating

> *HINT: For the rest of this lesson, feel free to take on parts and really have fun with it. Hats, glasses, etc. add to the fun. Though the subjects are serious, a little sugarcoating makes them both palatable and memorable. It sometimes assists the children if you wear name tags.*

TV Announcer: Good (morning/afternoon.) I am Tammy-Tell-It-Like-It-Is. Today's program is coming to you from the PSE-TV studio. Our TV topics for today are tattling and cheating. First we will talk about tattling. We will need to understand another word: reporting. (Write "reporting" on chalkboard.) We will know the difference between tattling and reporting when we are finished with today's program.

In order to understand the difference between tattling and reporting we are going to take you to our roving reporter, Olive-On-The-Spot, who is on location. Switching now to PSE-TV, live to, (name) school.

Olive: Good (morning/afternoon) Ladies and Gentleman. This is your news reporter, Olive-On-The Spot, here to bring you the latest school news. We are broadcasting live from (name) school in... (teacher's name and grade) classroom, attempting to figure out the difference between tattling and reporting. First, we want to know the answer to some questions. Raise your hand when it is appropriate. Raise your hand if you have ever known ANYONE who tattled. Raise your hand if you have ever know ANYONE who cheated.

Do not raise your hand, but think the answer: Have you ever tattled! Have you ever cheated? We are going to talk about why we do these things.

Now, back to Tammy for some local news.

Tammy: (School name) was selected, in a statewide contest, as the winner of the "Cleanest School After Lunch" award. It's just wonderful to think all those (school name) children care enough to use the trash cans — and not school grounds — for trash.

Tammy: (Child's name) will represent (school) in the (city) annual chocolate egg eating contest. The contestant who succeeds in eating the most chocolate eggs without throwing up will have his or her name put onto a trophy which will be kept at the school.

We interrupt this report for a word from our sponsor. Here's Connie Commercial.

Connie: Boys and girls, here is the cereal you have been waiting for: Sugar! Not 10, 30, 60 or even 80% sugar...but 100% sugar! No vitamins, no minerals, nothing that's good for you to spoil it. If you hurry and get a box today, you will find a coupon on the back for one free trip to the dentist of your choice. Let's take a look at a typical family scene with two children eating Sugar for breakfast.

HINT: The PSE volunteers will act out this skit, too.

Person A: Boy am I hungry! I could eat this whole box of Sugar!

Person B: Gimme! Give it to me. I want that one!

Person A: Sit down, I got it first!

Person B: I want it now. Give it to me!

Person A: No, I'm not giving you any!

Person B: Mom! Mom! (Name) won't give me the cereal! Mom!

Tammy: That was a clear case of tattling. We're going to return to our commercial again with a similar scene. This time we'll show you a case of reporting. See if you can tell the difference between the two.

Person A: Boy, am I hungry! I could eat this whole box of Sugar!

Person B: Gimme! Give it to me. I want that one!

Person A: Sit down, I got it first!

Person B: I want it now! Give it to me!

Person A: No! Look out. Be careful with that milk. Watch out! (crash) Oh, no, the bottle broke! There's glass all over the floor. Stay in your chair. Mom! Mom! We need help.

Tammy: Clearly a case of reporting, Let's go to our Roving Reporter, Olive-On-The-Spot, and our kids in the classroom to tell us the difference between the two scenes. One was tattling, one was reporting, but what made the difference?

HINT: Write the word "safety" on the board. As the students respond, write their responses under the word.

Olive: Right! Olive here, in the classroom. Kids, what do you think is the difference between tattling and reporting? (Wait for class response.) You are absolutely correct, someone tattles when he or she has a stake in it. They will get something out of it. Reporting usually has to do with safety. Back to you, Tammy...

Tammy: So we have found out that reporting occurs when there is some danger or harm involved or someone is helpless. Tattling is minding someone else's business. The difference between reporting and tattling has to do with the reason behind your telling. Let's go back to Olive, our Roving Reporter, and the kids in the classroom to play the example game...

Olive: I am going to read an example of a true-life situation. If you think it is an example of tattling, stay in your seat. Stand up only if you think it is an example of reporting.

1. A lady drops her wallet in the market. You tell your mother.   (reporting)

2. Your brother takes a cookie and runs into his room. You tell your mother.   (tattling)

3. Your little sister is pouring all the hair shampoo on the bathroom floor. It is very slippery. You tell your mother. (reporting)

4. You see someone take someone else's lunch money. You tell your teacher. (reporting)

5. An upper grader takes the ball at recess. You need help. You tell the teacher. (reporting)

6. You see someone fall off his bike. He looks hurt. You tell the teacher.   (reporting)

> *HINT: If some students disagree with the answers given, remind them that the difference between tattling and reporting is found in the intention of the speaker.*

Olive: Now, kids in the classroom, the question is: Why do people tattle? Let's make a list of reasons people tattle. (Write answers on chalkboard: to put someone down/if I follow the rules, everyone else has to /revenge /jealousy /recognition /feel helpless /elevate self)

Tammy: Thank you kids in the classroom. That was very helpful. This week we have two winners for our poem-of-the-week contest. The one on tattling goes to Sarah Snodgrass for this:

> **Poem #1**
> If you like to tattle
> Believe it or not it's true
> You're minding other's business and
> You don't feel good about you!

Sarah will be sent a week's supply of Sugar, the new breakfast cereal.

> *HINT: PSE volunteer may read or choose a child from the class to read. The part of Sally-Sneak-A-Look needs to be melodramatic so that it is funny.*

Today, our special interview has to do with cheating. We have a special guest here in our studio, Sally Sneak-a-Look. Sally has spent six years fooling everyone by cheating on her reading, spelling, and math work. Sally, how does it feel to have gotten away with so much for so many years?

Sally: Not so hot.

Tammy: Not so hot? You didn't have to work hard all those years.

Sally: Yeah...I didn't learn anything either.

Tammy: Well, what's the difference? You got in all the high books and fast groups and your parents were happy.

Sally: But now I'm behind...in fact I'm lost. I didn't learn what I needed to know. Now the hard work is even harder. I'm in trouble.

Tammy: Ladies and Gentlemen, PSE-TV's research has shown that children who cheated in school wish they hadn't. They tell us small cases of cheating lead to big cases of cheating. PSE-TV is going to take you to our Olive-On-the-Spot to ask: Why do you think people cheat?

Olive: Here we are back in the classroom. Why do you think people cheat? (afraid of failure/win a game/parent pressure/avoid work/please teacher/don't know answer to or don't think they do) Kids in the classroom, how do you feel when you choose not to cheat? (class discussion)

Tammy: Now that you know why people cheat, Sally, do you have any last words for the children in the classroom?

Sally: I know this sounds silly, but you only cheat yourself when you cheat. If you get behind in school you can talk to your teacher, get a capable friend to help or talk to your parents. (weeping) I wish I could go back and do it all over. (sob) Besides, now I have a reputation and eveyone thinks I cheat even when I don't. (sob)

Tammy: Sally can't do it over but you can learn from her mistake. Now we switch to our other Roving Reporter, Pamela-Problem-Solver, for a report.

Pamela: Here is a typical classroom scene. Maggie and Agatha are doing their classwork. Maggie is copying from Agatha's paper. We are going to play a little game. First I need some volunteers to play the part of Maggie and Agatha. (Put two chairs next to each other. Put one child in each — one is working, one is cheating.) Ask the one who is working to give one response to the cheater. (We are assuming the worker does not want the other person to cheat.) Thank you for that response. (talking to the worker) Now you take your own seat. Does anyone else want to take this seat and give a different way of dealing with cheating? (Call on children as long as their answers are different. Remind students that punching or hitting are inappropriate ways of dealing with someone.)

HINT: Keep this part moving quickly. The advantages of this exercise are, adults don't lecture and children come up with numerous solutions to the problem.

Tammy: The kids in the classroom have done it again! A week's supply of Sugar goes to Harvey Haymaker for this poem about cheating:

Poem #2

Cheaters never prosper
It's true as it can be
For when you cheat the one you hurt
Is you. . .it isn't me!

TV Announcer: Thank you reporters and kids in (teacher's name and grade level) grade class. We have learned that the difference between tattling and reporting is the REASON you do it. We have also learned why people cheat. We are leaving these poems for your bulletin board. We want you, as a class, or individually, to make a list of ten ways to be good to yourselves and ten ways to be good to each other. We will begin our lesson by going over your list, so please remember to do it: ten ways to be good to yourself and to each other. We will be back in two weeks for the last time this year. Between now and then, be good to yourself and to each other.

_____ **Lesson 12** _____

Review: Final Lesson

Materials

Harmony, Butcher paper if needed, Special certificate awards for each student and for classroom teacher, Optional: Evaluation worksheets

Activity A — Discuss Ten Ways to be Good to Yourselves and to Others

Last time when we were with you, we asked you to write ten ways you could be good to yourselves and ten ways to be good to each other. We want you to share your thoughts and we will write them on the chalkboard (or butcher paper). (Wait for class response.)

Activity B — Hand Out "I Am Special" Award Certificates

(Harmony has small towel pinned to paw.) Hi, Harmony...what's the towel for? (Harmony talks.) You don't like to say goodby...the towel is to wipe away your tears? Well, you will see these children next year, so you don't have to be sad. (Harmony claps paws.) That cheered him up! He says he has something for each of you. It's an award for being special. (Read the award.) The PSE teachers will line up and call out the names on the awards. Please come and get yours when you hear your name. (Pass out awards.) You may color these later if you wish. They are a gift from Harmony and PSE to remind you that each of you are special.

> *HINT: The rest of this lesson is optional. You are welcome to use some of our ideas or create your own ending lesson. Plan for approximately twenty minutes. The following are suggestions only.*

1. Have a party. Parents may provide treats or you can have a foodless party. (Check with classroom teacher.)

2. Go over evaluation sheet and discuss the lessons for the year.

3. Play a game called "Guess the Lesson" using ideas from each lesson as a review.

4. Sing "You Are Special and You Know It" song.

5. Play "Rumor Game" again.

Activity C — Lesson Closing

We've had fun and hope you have, too. We hope you realize now that how you feel about yourself and how good you are to yourself, makes the difference in what kind of life you have. Be good to yourself. . .and since we're all in this big ol' world together, be good to each other.

Though we'll be seeing you next year, it is always difficult to say goodby. In doing so, we have a little rhyme to share.

HINT: Each PSE Volunteer can take a section or the entire team can read the following poem aloud:

We've had a lot a fun
Since October when we came,
To teach you about yourself
How to win the living game.

We've told all our stories
Even resorted to rhyme.
But best of all, students,
We've had a good time.

Now it's time to leave you
We'll try not to shed a tear,
But thanks to all of you
For such a wonderful year.

And just in case you're asked
Who else cares about you,
Be sure to tell them straight
Project Self-Esteem — we do!

YOU. . .ARE. . .SPECIAL!!!

Name _____

Date _____

Gratitudes

Put a circle around anything you are grateful for:

Family	Home	Brother	Sister
Pet Friends	Good health	School	
Food	Harmony	Compliments	

Other _____

Changes

Put a circle around anything you would change:

Being picked on   People being mean to each other

Being left out   Hunger in the world   Teasing

Stealing   Tattling   People cheating

Fighting   Put-downs   People not caring

Other _____

ATTITUDE IS THE DIFFERENCE!

Name _____

Date _____

My Feelings

1. One time I felt happy when a friend _____

_____

_____

2. One time I felt silly when _____

_____

_____

3. One time I felt upset at school when _____

_____

_____

4. One time I felt important when _____

_____

_____

5. One time I felt special when _____

_____

_____

6. Draw your own happy, silly, upset, important and special faces on the back of this paper.

Name _____

Date _____

Communication Is Important

Say: I FEEL   (it's important to get feelings out)
         I WANT   (people don't guess well, tell them what you want)
Know: It's OK to ask for what you want, but don't expect to always get it.

1. Someone takes your basketball at recess.

   I feel _____

   I want _____

2. Someone sticks up for you.

   I feel _____

   I want _____

3. Someone tattles on you.

   I feel _____

   I want _____

4. You forgot your lunch. Your friend shares.

   I feel _____

   I want _____

STOP! DO THE BOTTOM OF THIS PAGE LATER WITH YOUR TEACHER.

1. Someone cuts in front of you in line.
2. Somone borrows something from you and doesn't return it.
3. A friend helps you with your homework.
4. Someone pulls your hair.
5. Friends won't let you play in their game.
6. You have on a new outfit. Your friend doesn't notice.

Name _____

Date _____

I Like It When a Friend . . .

It Bothers Me When a Friend . . .

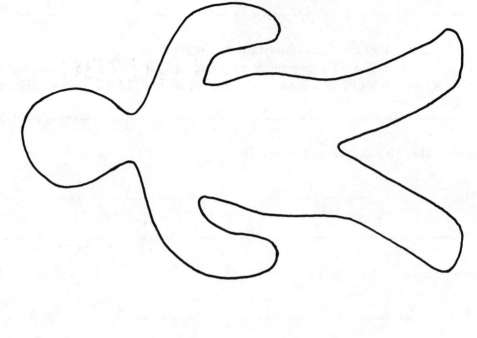

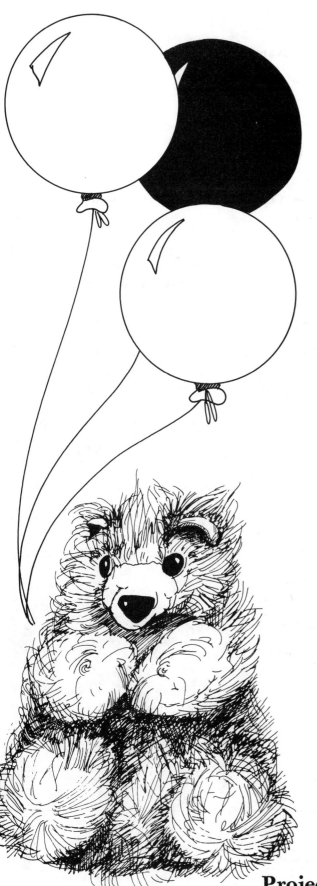

The
Harmony Award
is presented to

_____

FOR BEING

S
P
E
C
I
A
L

Project Self-Esteem

153

Name _____

Date _____

Program Evaluation

Pretend you are going to be a Project Self-Esteem teacher next year. Read each activity listed below. Draw a circle around YES if you would use a lesson. Draw a circle around NO if you would not use it. Draw a circle around ? if you don't remember the activity.

1. Bulletin Boards and Saying . . . . YES   NO   ?

2. List the things you are grateful for and the things in your life you would change   YES   NO   ?

3. Playacting (acting out a situation) . . . . YES   NO   ?

4. Song: "You Are Special and You Know It" . . . . YES   NO   ?

5. Story: "The Rarest Gift" . . . . YES   NO   ?

6. Looking in a box and writing your first feeling . . . . YES   NO   ?

7. Smileys and Compliments . . . . YES   NO   ?

8. Stress Reduction Exercises . . . . YES   NO   ?

9. Game: "Harmony Says" (like Simon says) . . . . YES   NO   ?

10. Game: "The Rumor Game" (like telephone game) . . . . YES   NO   ?

11. TV Program on tattling and reporting . . . . YES   NO   ?

12. Communication Lesson: Say what you feel & want . . . . YES   NO   ?

13. Story with Sam's balloon: Talking to a Friend . . . . YES   NO   ?

14. The Choice is Yours game about cheating . . . . YES   NO   ?

The Project Self-Esteem Lesson I Liked Best Was _____

_____

What I'd Like to Tell the PSE Team is _____

_____

Chapter

Grade 4

_____ **Lesson 1** _____

Realizing Your Uniqueness

Objectives

- The child will introduce him/herself using a positive adjective.
- The child will interview and introduce one classmate to the group.
- The child will contribute to a list of qualities admired in others and in self.
- The child will learn to give self compliments.
- The child will discuss the difference between compliments and bragging.
- The child will participate orally in a review and will contribute thoughts for the bulletin board in writing.

Suggested Reading

Briggs, Dorothy Corkille. *Celebrate Your Self,* pp 4-8. "How you feel about yourself directly affects how you live life, how you relate to others."

Buscaglia, Leo. *Love,* p. 133. "To love others, you must first love yourself."

Clames, Harris and Bean, Reynold, *Self-*

Esteem — The Key To Your Child's Well Being, pp. 44-51. "High self-esteem occurs when children experience the positive feelings of satisfaction that result from having a sense of Uniqueness. That is, a child acknowledges and respects the personal characteristics that make him special and different, and receives approval and respect from others from those characteristics."

Background

Self-esteem is feeling good about yourself. When you learn to quietly value your own positive behavior, you feel better about yourself. Balancing excessive criticism is one way to raise self-esteem.

Note: If you have not taught the 2/3 grade program, it is very important that you read those lessons. You will be called upon to review some of the concepts taught in the younger grades.

Materials

Harmony, List of adjectives, One piece of paper per student, New bulletin board strips: I Am Special. It's Important to Listen to Others Because They Are Special, Too.

Activity A —
PSE Volunteers Introduce Themselves, the Program, and Harmony

Welcome to another year of Project Self-Esteem! Raise your hand if you've had PSE before. What is self-esteem? (how you feel about yourself) If you feel good about yourself, how will it affect your life? (more friends, do better in school, be happier, etc.)

We are your PSE team. From now until May (or the last month of PSE), we will be coming into your room every other week. I am Mrs. Fallman. Each of the PSE volunteers will say their name and tell you one special fact about themselves.

*HINT: Take your time and be sure your introduction is clear.
Add a personal comment or two if you choose. (My children go
to this school, etc.)*

If we are going to be seeing you eleven times this year to talk about self-esteem, we want you to be sure what that is. What is Project Self-Esteem about? (learning things that assist you in feeling good about yourself) A person who feels good about him/herself learns more and is happier. We choose to come here and teach because we care about you and your job of growing up.

*HINT: You might want to show a board with photos of the PSE
volunteers when they were in school. Children will enjoy matching
the photos with each volunteer.*

(Bring out Harmony.) Welcome back, Harmony! It's great to see you again! Did you have a fun summer? (Harmony nods and talks.) You did, but you missed the children? We did too. It has been a long time since we were together. By the way, for those of you who are new, Harmony is a graduate of PSE. He's the bear who assists us with our lessons. (Harmony whispers.) You want to play the Name Game? OK, let's do!

Activity B — Positive Adjective and Name Game

We want you to introduce yourselves and to do this we'll play the Name Game. There's a rule in this game which says you need to listen so you will know how to play. We want you to choose a complimentary word which starts with the same letter as your first name, then put that word with your name when you introduce yourself. Let's use Harmony. His name starts with an "H", so think of a word starting with "H" that is complimentary. (happy) Now Harmony can say "I am Happy Harmony." (Write "Happy Harmony" on the chalkboard.) What if your name were Wanda? What is something positive you could say about yourself? (wise, witty, wonderful)

If Wanda introduced herself as Wise Wanda, or Harmony introduced himself as Happy Harmony, they would be giving themselves compliments. (Write the word "compliment" on the chalkboard.) What's a compliment? (discuss) You see Harmony (look at Harmony), sometimes it is difficult to say something nice about yourself in front of others. It seems like bragging.

What do you think the difference is between giving yourself a pat on the back and bragging? What is bragging? (showing off, using a look-at-me tone of voice, exaggerating your qualities, etc.) Why do people brag? (to look good because they don't feel good about themselves) How is a self-compliment or pat on the back different? (It's more like encouragement. It is a direct, honest comment about who you are or something you did.)

When you value who you are and what you do, you raise self-esteem. Since giving yourself compliments will help your self-esteem we are going to practice doing just that.

Paper is being passed out. Please write one or more complimentary words on the paper using the same letter which starts your first name. If you need assistance, raise your hand. (A PSE volunteer will assist where necessary. Allow two minutes.)

> *HINT: You will need to think through possible adjectives for each letter in the alphabet ahead of time so you are able to provide children with assistance. Example: V (Vanessa) = Very Nice.*

Beginning with the PSE volunteers, we will go around the room so each of us can introduce ourselves using a complimentary word name. "I am...(Special Sandy).

> *HINT: If you hear giggling or resistance say something like, "Some of you might feel embarrassed about doing this. Maybe it's hard to give yourself a compliment in front of others. We ask you do not add to that embarrassment by giggling or snickering."*

Thank you for sharing your names and for sharing one part of you. PSE teaches that each one of you is special. Are you special because of what you do? (no) Why are you special? (one of a kind/no one is just like you) Please turn your paper over. We will be using it again in this lesson. Pencils down, please.

Activity C — Students Practice Listening Skills

> *HINT: In this activity the class will be divided into small discussion groups. If classroom space is limited, move desks into clusters in appropriate numbers. If possible, ask the classroom teacher to divide the class into four compatible groups ahead of time. It will be helpful if the students are sitting in their clusters when you arrive. Otherwise, the groups may be selected by counting off by fours.*

We have shared and listened as a class, now we are going to share and listen using partners. First, we will divide you into four groups. A PSE team member will be with each group and each of you will be given a partner within your group. For now, all you need to do is listen.

> *HINT: The four PSE volunteers need to scatter around the room. As a team member's name is called, she raises her hand and leaves it up until she has her entire group. The purpose in establishing groups is to provide each child with a significant other with whom to share. It is important to establish your group rapport now, so take sufficient time to build a positive relationship with each child. PLEASE DO NOT ELIMINATE SMALL GROUP WORK.*

Pretend you are going to live on a space station orbiting the earth. There are three questions you need to answer before you can leave home.   (Write the categories "Food," "Sport or Hobby," and "Belonging" on the chalkboard.)

Each of you will ask your partner these three questions:

1. What's your favorite food?
2. What's your favorite sport or hobby?
3. What one thing that you own do you want to take along?

Listen carefully to the answers. Remember what you learn, because you will be given the opportunity to share that information with your group.

The team member in each group will start the group discussion by saying, "If you had asked me the three questions, I would say my favorite food is tacos, I like to play tennis, and I want to take my favorite book."

Her partner would take this information and introduce her to the group saying, "This is Mrs. Loftis. She loves to eat tacos, enjoys playing tennis, and wants to take her favorite book into the space station." As you can see, it is important to listen to what your partner tells you.

> *HINT: Allow two or three minutes for partners to interview. Then ask each student to introduce their partner to the group. When all the students have had a turn, have them return to their regular seats. It is wise to dismiss each group one at a time to keep the noise level down.*

Now we have found out information about each other. In addition, we have practiced our listening skills. We've found out, by listening carefully, that each of us is special in our own way.

Activity D —
Students List Qualities Admired in Themselves and Others

In PSE we want to focus on the things we like about ourselves and others. We want to become aware of these special qualities. By seeing the positive side of yourself, you will feel better about who you are. Also, your self-esteem will get higher and higher. Let's find out what qualities you like in yourself and in others. (Write this sentence on the chalkboard: I like him/her because he/she is a _____ person.) Tell me some adjectives that define a likable person. An adjective is a word that describes something. (Write the words given by the class on the chalkboard and discuss.)

> HINT: The purpose of this activity is to concentrate on what people
> ARE rather than what they do. For example, if a student wants
> to say that he likes a friend because the friend is a super soccer
> player, try to elicit the qualities a super soccer player possesses:
> courage, determination, enthusiasm, etc.

Activity E — Looking At Our Differences and Similarities

Let's bring Harmony back. Hi Harmony, are you enjoying the lesson? (Harmony talks.) You liked hearing about the difference between bragging and self compliments? You often forget to compliment yourself? (Harmony nods.) We all do, Harmony. Is there anything else you would like to talk about in today's lesson? (Harmony scratches his head, looks around, and talks.) Oh, that's an important thought. Harmony says he has been thinking about how people are alike in many ways and different in others. He wants to know more about that idea. (look at Harmony.) I think it would be fun for the whole class to think about ways they are different and ways they are alike.

(To the class) You are to use the back side of the paper on your desk. On the top part of the paper write the word "Alike." In the middle part of the paper write the word "Different." Under the word "Alike" write all the ways as you can think of that you are like boys and girls your own age. (Allow three minutes.) Now, under the word "Different" write all the ways you can think of that you are different from boys and girls your own age. You will not be asked to share this information with anyone in the class. (Allow two minutes.)

Which list was the longer? (alike) Which was the easier to write? (alike) We all tend to try to be alike. Mostly, we do this because of peer pressure. What's a peer?

(someone your own age) Peer pressure means doing things to fit into a group, belong to a group, or feel a part of the group. In what ways do we attempt to be alike so we can belong? (clothes, food, hobbies, slang words, how we act, etc.)

Let's imagine what the world would be like if all of us were exactly the same. In what ways would we be the same? (food, clothes, buildings, subjects taken in school, sports, television would have few channels, etc.) Would you like to live in a world that is all the same? (class response) It would be boring wouldn't it? So differences are important. Being alike in some ways and being different in some ways — that's the way life is! Thank you for the question, Harmony. (Harmony talks.) He said thanks to all of us for the answer!

Activity F — Stress Reduction Exercise (read verbatim)

If you had PSE in grades two and three, you know we included a stress reduction exercise in each lesson. What is stress? (anything that causes tension or anxiety) What do you think the word "reduction" means? (to make smaller or lessen) So, stress reduction exercises are designed to assist you to lessen the feelings of stress you might have.

All you need to do is listen and follow my words. Sit up tall, but comfortably — feet flat on the floor. Make a fist with each hand as tightly as you can. Now tighten all the muscles in your lower arms, upper arms, and shoulders. Keep those muscles tight as you tighten your chest, stomach, and now all the muscles in your legs. Pull every muscle as hard and tight as you can. Make your face and forehead muscles tight. Tighten the muscles in your eyes, mouth, and jaw. TIGHT! TIGHT! TIGHT! Now, all at once, relax. Breathe.

In your mind, tell your muscles to relax. Tell your forehead and eyes to relax. Tell your chin and neck to relax. Say relax to your shoulders, your arms and hands, your chest, your stomach, and the lower part of your body. Tell your legs to relax and say relax to your feet. Just sit still and notice how good it feels to be relaxed.

Activity G — Lesson Ending

Today, we have talked about how each one of us is a unique, special person. In the Name Game you gave yourself a compliment. You listened to a classmate and introduced him/her. You worked together to list qualities you like in yourself and others. Each of these ideas will assist you in feeling good about yourself. Your self-esteem will get higher and higher.

(Hold up bulletin board sentences and give a brief synopsis of each of these topics.) Here are two sentences to remind you about all we've learned today: I am Special. It's Important to Listen to Others Because They Are Special, Too.

Each time we come into your room, we will leave some sentences for you to think and write about. Between now and the time we return in two weeks, please write your thoughts or make up a story concerning one or all of these sentences.

We'll be back again in two weeks. Between now and then, be good to yourself and to each other.

HINT: Folders are optional at this grade level.

Lesson 2
Goal Setting

Objectives

- The child will introduce him/herself to the class.
- The child will contribute to a class discussion about the bulletin board.
- The child will learn to set individual goals.
- The child will learn to take one step at a time in reaching a goal.
- The child will set a goal and discuss how to reach that goal.
- The child will use a worksheet to set and achieve that goal.

Suggested Reading

Fensterheim, Herbert, Ph.D. and Baer, Jean. *Don't Say Yes When You Want to Say No*, p. 56. "Goals reinforce self-esteem. Achievement of goals strengthens your desire to achieve other goals. As a result, you attain a feeling of movement through life and a higher sense of self-worth."

Miller, Gorden Porter and Oskam, Bob. *Teaching Your Child to Make Decisions*, p. 96. "Each goal success will tend to whet the appetite for doing something a little more ambitious the next time. Along the way, success contributes to the child's sense of accomplishment and builds self-esteem."

Peele, Norman Vincent. *You Can If You Think You Can*, p. 110. "Law of Successful Achievement. And what is that law? First of all, it is to have a goal, not a vague fuzzy goal, but a sharply focused objective."

Background

Every human being needs to feel lovable and capable. Goal setting enables the individual to focus on the idea of achieving the feeling of being capable. A common deterrent to progress of any kind is the feeling of being overwhelmed by problems. Sometimes, even the everyday aspects of life can seem overwhelming. When students are taught to set goals, they learn to live life in one-step-at-a-time increments.

A common behavioral trait is to give up prior to reaching a goal. Teaching youngsters to see something through to completion by persistence and reevaluation gives them an important life resource.

Materials

Goal setting worksheet for each student, Harmony, Goal Setting chart (see Activity D), New bulletin board strip: A Journey of a Thousand Miles Begins With a Single Step.

Activity A — Stress Reduction Exercise (read verbatim)

We are going to repeat the stress reduction exercise we did in our last lesson. Sit up tall, but comfortably — feet flat on the floor. Make a fist with each hand as tightly as you can. Now tighten all the muscles in your lower arms, upper arms, and shoulders.

Keep those muscles tight as you tighten your chest, stomach, and now all the muscles in your legs. Pull every muscle as hard and tight as you can. Pull your face and forehead muscles tight. Tighten the muscles in your eyes, mouth, and jaw. TIGHT! TIGHT! TIGHT! Now, all at once, relax. Breathe.

In your mind, tell your muscles to relax. Tell your forehead and eyes to relax. Tell your chin and neck to relax. Say relax to your shoulders, your arms and hands, your chest, your stomach, and the lower part of your body. Tell your legs to relax and say relax to your feet. Just sit still and notice how it feels to be relaxed.

Activity B — PSE Teacher and Students Introduce Themselves

What is self-esteem? (how you feel about yourself) How does it affect your life to have high self-esteem? (more friends, do better in school, happier, etc.)

As you may remember, in the last lesson you chose a complimentary word beginning with the same letter as your first name and said it with your name. Someone named Sandy became "Special Sandy." Let's go around the room again and say each of our special names. Begin with the words "I am" and add your name.

Activity C — Review Bulletin Board Materials

We are going to review the two statements from last time: I Am Special. It's Important to Listen to Others Because They Are Special, Too. Let's see what you did with the sentences we left for you last time. (Give lots of positive reinforcement).

Activity D — Introduce Goal Setting

Last time, we talked about the qualities you like in yourself and others. (Bring out Harmony.) Hi, Harmony! You're just in time! We are going to talk about setting a goal. (Harmony scratches his ear.) A goal is something you want to reach or attain. Let's use something from your life as an example. What goal do you want to talk about, Harmony? (Harmony talks.) Oh, you want to improve your paw...er... handwriting. OK, you need to begin somewhere. Work on one change at a time and keep going until you reach your goal. (Harmony scratches head.) What? You don't understand? Here's a chart which will give us a place to start. (Invite different children to read each line of chart.)

Goal Setting

1. Set a reachable goal.
2. Write out steps for reaching that goal.
3. Keep going until you reach your goal.
4. Give yourself a reasonable time limit.
5. Evaluate — check your progress.
6. Compliment yourself.

The first one simply asks you to be reasonable and pick possible goals. For example, it wouldn't make sense to set this as a goal: Become friends with everyone in the school. It isn't possible. So, we begin by setting a goal which may be reached.

Harmony, you want to improve your paw...ah...handwriting? (Harmony nods.) That is a reasonable goal. What is one thing Harmony could do to improve his handwriting?

> *HINT: If several people give examples, choose one to write on the board such as: Hold your pencil correctly. Then draw a ladder big enough to encompass several of the suggestions given by the students. Continue this process until you have three to five examples.*

```
     |                                        |
4.   |                                        |
     |_____|
     |                                        |
3.   |                                        |
     |_____|
     |                                        |
2.   |                                        |
     |_____|
     |                                        |
1.   |   Hold your pencil correctly           |
     |                                        |
```

What we are doing is writing out steps for reaching this goal. (Point to the chart.) If Harmony tries to do these all at once it will boggle his mind. He wouldn't try to climb three steps on a ladder at one time. But he could start with the bottom one (hold pencil correctly), and WORK ONLY ON THAT ONE until he makes the change. Then he could work on the second one (sitting up straight), until it was automatic. Next, he could work on (writing slower). By taking one step at a time Harmony would reach his goal.

So, we've chosen a reasonable goal for Harmony and written out steps for reaching that goal. Let's look at number three: Keep going until you reach your goal. (Get Harmony out and talk to him.) It seems obvious you won't reach your goal if you stop at (sitting up straight). You will have made some improvement, but not as much as if you've taken all the steps. (Harmony nods.) Give yourself a reasonable time limit. You don't want to improve your handwriting in ten years. You want to do it in, for instance, one month. (Harmony claps.)

Finally, check your progress. In this case, each week. Ask yourself, "How am I doing?" (Harmony scratches his head.) "Is my goal still reasonable?" Evaluate your progress. Then compliment yourself, "I can see my handwriting has improved!" (Harmony hugs himself.)

(Speak to the class.) How do you think you would feel about yourselves if you reached that goal? (Wait for class response.) Would your self-esteem be higher or lower? (class response)

(Look at Harmony.) So, as you can see, Harmony, goal setting is important. We're going to practice goal setting with all of us using the same goal: MAKE A NEW FRIEND. To set as a goal "making friends with everyone in the school" would not be reasonable; but making one new friend sounds reasonable. (Point to the chart.) The next thing to do is to write out the steps for reaching this goal.

HINT: Draw another empty ladder on the chalkboard (to match students' worksheet).

Activity E — Children Experience Goal Setting Procedure

A piece of paper is being handed to you. Write your name on it. After the phrase "My goal is" write "make a new friend." Beginning at the bottom of the ladder, put your finger on step number one. What is the step you might take in order to make a new friend? (Discuss several examples, but choose only one to write onto the step.) We are going to give you a few minutes to write your next two steps for making a new friend. Write one idea on each step of your ladder. If you need assistance, raise your hand.

HINT: Allow two or three minutes.

Activity F — Group Work: Setting and Reaching Goals

The PSE team has spread out around the room. When I finish talking, not before, you will go to the same group you had in the last lesson. Take your goal-setting paper with you. (Call each team member's name one at a time, and wait until that entire group is settled.)

HINT: Much of the success of group work has to do with setting an atmosphere of cooperation. Early control of behavior is imperative to establish this. As the students come to the group, the adult leader will greet each child by name and ask him/her to sit down quietly. A difficult child may be given the alternative of sitting down, returning to his/her seat, or sitting next to the classroom teacher.

166

Group Work

1. Discuss the steps each child listed.
2. Discuss Goal Setting chart (keep going, reasonable time, evaluate).
3. Ask "What do you do if the person you choose doesn't want to be your friend?" (Pick someone else and start again.)
4. Ask "If you follow the Goals chart, is there a guarantee you will reach your goal?" (No, but the person with high self-esteem sets goals.)
5. (As time permits) Take a sports-oriented theme if you'd like. For example: Improve soccer skills. Use a blank ladder worksheet (PSE teacher only), discuss as a group, and set steps for reaching this goal. (Examples: practice kicking with left foot, practice with right foot, run each day to keep in shape, etc.)
6. Tell the group that the next lesson will continue use of this worksheet and each individual will set an individual goal. Let them know they will be working on their individual goal for several lessons, but it is important they think about and have chosen a personal goal for the next lesson. Discuss some of the topics they could think about: sports, school, home, personal, etc.

Activity G — Lesson Ending

Today, we've talked about setting goals. A goal is something we'd like to reach or attain. Each one of us will choose a personal goal to work on this year. We will work on goals again next time. Here is the bulletin board strip for next time: A Journey of a Thousand Miles Begins With a Single Step.

We will be back again in two weeks. Meanwhile, there are two things we always ask you to do between now and next time. Who can tell me one of them? (Be good to yourself.) And the other? (Be good to each other.) Great! Be good to yourself and to each other.

_____ Lesson 3 _____

Goal Setting and Compliments

Objectives

- The child will orally define a compliment.
- The child will practice giving him/herself a compliment.
- The child will hear a PSE teacher give him/her a compliment.
- The child will hear a story in which people see the good in each other.
- The child will discuss what a difference it would make if people saw the good in each other.

Suggested Reading

Briggs, Dorothy Corkille. *Your Child's Self-Esteem*, p. 3. "High self-esteem is not noisey conceit. It is a quiet sense of self-respect, a feeling of self-worth."

Clemes, Harris and Bean, Reynold. *Self-*

Esteem, the Key to Your Child's Well Being, p. 261. "Remember you can assist children to reach their goals."

Zimbardo, Philip G. and Radl, Shirley, *The Shy Child*, p. 233. "People who aren't shy know how to accept compliments gracefully."

Background

When you feel good about yourself, you do not waste time or energy trying to impress other people. You are already convinced of your worth. Often, the tendency is to focus more on imperfections. To avoid this, it is important to create a balance and gain a true sense of worth by complimenting yourself. By accepting your own value, you begin to feel lovable and capable.

Materials

Harmony, Magic Glasses story (Activity F), A Smiley for each child, A giant Smiley, Strips with the words: Mother/Father/sister/brother/teacher/friends/me on each one. Blank strips and felt pen, Paper for each student, Goal Setting worksheets, Single piece of paper for Harmony's compliment, New bulletin board strips: We All Like Compliments. Let's Give One to Mother, Father, Brother, Sister, Teacher, Friends, You!

Activity A — Stress Reduction Exercise (read verbatim)

Today, we are going to do a stress reduction exercise. All you need to do is listen and follow my words. Sit up tall, but comfortably — feet flat on the floor. Make a fist with each hand as tightly as you can. Now tighten all the muscles in your lower arms, upper arms, and shoulders. Keep those muscles tight as you tighten your chest, stomach, and now all the muscles in your legs. Pull every muscle as hard and tight as you can. Pull your face and forehead muscles tight. Tighten the muscles in your eyes, mouth, and jaw. TIGHT! TIGHT! TIGHT! Now, all at once, relax. Breathe.

In your mind, tell your muscles to relax. Tell your forehead and eyes to relax. Tell your chin and neck to relax. Say relax to your shoulders, your arms and hands, your chest, your stomach, and the lower part of your body. Tell your legs to relax and say relax to your feet. Just sit still and notice how it feels to be relaxed.

Activity B — Review of Goal Setting

(Review the Goal Setting chart.)   There are lots of different kinds of goals. Let's list as many topics as we can.   (List on chalkboard: sports, school, home, personal, etc.)

In our last lesson, we completed a worksheet on making a friend. Today, we are going to work on an individual goal. A new worksheet is being passed out to you. You need to decide on a goal you want to work with in your own life. If you have not chosen such a goal, please decide on one right now.   (A volunteer passes out the worksheets.)

When you get your worksheets, write your own goal in the appropriate place. Be sure your goal is reasonable. Raise your hand if you need assistance. Let's look at the chart to discover what to do next.   (Write out steps for reaching goal.)   Write four possible steps you might take in order to reach your goal. Your group leader will check your papers when you go to your group.   (PSE volunteers assist individual children as needed.)

Activity C — Practice Giving and Receiving Compliments

People who set goals and reach them feel good about themselves. Another part of high self-esteem is giving and receiving compliments. What is a compliment?   (when you say something positive about someone that you believe to be true)

Before we practice giving compliments, we want to review what to say when we get one.   (Elicit from class: Thank you/ Return the compliment if sincere.)

We want you to begin each compliment with the word "I." Instead of saying something like "You look nice," say "I like your blouse." Begin each compliment with the word "I."

> *HINT: The low self-esteem person finds it difficult to accept compliments. Compliments may become superficial, non-specific, and impersonal with "You" messages. When the sender starts with the word "I" he/she tells the receiver: This is a specific message from me and it belongs to you. The receiver might refute a general statement, but cannot so easily challenge a personal opinion. For instance, a child, remembering an unkind deed done the day before, might refute the "You" message "You are kind," but is more likely to accept "I noticed you helped your brother."*

Who would like to choose a friend, come up front, and give a compliment? (use four sets of children, reminding each to start the compliment with "I.")

> *HINT: Encourage children to vary their topics: sports, school, personality, etc. You may choose to use a giant Smiley in the exercise above. The advantage is that it entices reluctant volunteers and is fun — the disadvantage being, sometimes more attention is given to the Smiley than the words. If you choose to use a giant Smiley, its representation of a compliment needs to be discussed.*

Activity D — Students Practice Compliments

We know that compliments assist with self-esteem. Which person in your life has the greatest opportunity to compliment you? (Any answer other answer than "me" is to be treated with, "Even more than that.") We talk to ourselves. When we do it's called self-talk. This self-talk is usually done inside our heads, as a thought, but is NOT always complimentary. For example, many of us are quick to say "dummy" to ourselves when we make a mistake. Our self-talk is too often used as a put-down. It would be better to say: "I made a mistake. I wish I hadn't and I'll do it differently next time."

When you do a job well such as get a high grade on a test or do something kind for a friend, do you compliment yourself? It's OK to give yourself a compliment. You know the difference between a pat on the back and bragging.

Write at least five compliments you could give yourself on the paper being passed to you. Begin each compliment with the words "I am." Be careful to write what you ARE rather than what you DO. There's a difference between "I am thoughtful" and "I am a good soccer player." What do you need to do as a team member to be a good soccer player? (work as a team) So what quality do you need in order to be a good soccer player? (be cooperative)

Activity E — Harmony and PSE Volunteers Give Out Smileys

(Bring out Harmony.) Hi, Harmony! What? You're excited about today's lesson? (Harmony nods.) Well, if there ever was a bear who likes a present, it's you and if that present just happens to be a Smiley...(Harmony starts jumping around.)

Look at your list with the five compliments you could give yourself. Circle the one you would most like to hear. Oh, Harmony has his paper and wants me to give him a compliment. (Read from paper and be sure to begin with "I.") Harmony, I like your cheerful personality, (Listen to Harmony.) He says "Thank you!"

Take your compliment papers with you when you go to your groups.   (Move into groups in an organized manner.)

Group Work

1. Spend a little time just talking
2. Ask each student to give you his/her compliment sheet, observe which one is circled, transcribe to an "I" message, and give back with an "I" compliment. With each "I" message, give the child a Smiley.
3. Allow some play time with the Smileys.
4. Check each student's goal sheet and make an agreement to meet during the next lesson.
5. Ask students to return desks and chairs to regular placement

---

HINT: If all Smileys are the same color in each classroom, there is less disruption.

Activity F — Read and Discuss The Magic Glasses Story

I want you to put your Smiley into your desk. Harmony has a story to share. Any Smiley I see after I count to five is mine: 1, 2, 3, 4,...5.

Here's a special story about some magic glasses.   (read story)

The Magic Glasses

When Uncle Fred died he left a very strange command in his will, "To my niece and nephew, Kathleen and Scott, I leave my dark glasses with the gold rims."

"Big deal," said eight year old Scott, "who wants to wear dark glasses anyway!"

Kathleen, who was ten and so tended to think things out, responded, "But it seems strange, doesn't it, that Uncle Fred would put something ordinary in his will. I'm going to put them on and see what happens."

Kathleen and Scott were sitting on the porch of their home in Avalon. Up the street walked Grubby Girtie. GG, as she was called by some, only liked one shirt and pair of levis. Because she wore them all the time, they naturally got quite grubby — hence the name. Kathleen and Girtie were NOT the best of friends. In fact, they seldom spoke to each other. As Girtie approached the house, Kathleen peered through Uncle Fred's glasses.

"You got your hair cut, Girtie," Kathleen said happily. "I think it looks super!"

It was questionable as to whose mouth dropped open wider, Scott's or Girtie's.

Girtie muttered, "Uh...ah...thanks," and self-consciously brushed her hair out of her eyes.

Kathleen smiled and continued, "I can see why you wear that shirt all the time. It's the greatest! Why, I bet, if I had such a wonderful shirt, I'd want to wear it day and night. Yep, I would."

Scott almost got whiplash as he looked quickly at Girtie then back to Kathleen. His eyes were three times their normal size. Girtie, by now, had totally lost her composure. She began brushing off her sleeve with one hand, pulling the shirt down, and attempting to smooth out the wrinkles with the other.

"It's, it's nothing," she stammered, "just an old thing my father gave me. Gotta go now." Girtie smiled (something no one had ever seen her do before), and walked on up the street.

This time it was Scott who stammered. "Wha...What got into you?"

Kathleen had the dark glasses in her hands inspecting them, over and under, "I don't know. It was like...well, I couldn't help myself."

"Here," Scott commanded, "let me see those things."

Kathleen and Scott nearly jumped out of their shoes. It was Manny and Marcus, the town bullies. Manny and Marcus enjoyed driving Scott bonkers at the beach. They would splash Scott, tease him, and flop in front of his Boogie-Board just as a big wave came.

"Hi! Guys!" Scott almost sang, "I'm going to the beach in about an hour. Wanna go with me?" Scott's smile touched each ear. Manny and Marcus looked like turkeys — their eyes bulging, and heads snapped forward on their necks

"In fact," Scott continued, "you can take my Boogie-Board and I'll join you later."

The two boys took the board but were too dumbfounded to speak. They only muttered. "Sure...O.K..." to Scott's, "Have fun. See you later!"

Kathleen had been sitting quietly as she watched the strange phenomenon of Scott being nice to two boys he didn't like. "It's the glasses," she said slowly. "It's gotta be the glasses."

172

In attempting to hand the dark glasses to Kathleen, Scott dropped them. She grumbled, "Look what you've done! They broke!" Crouching down to inspect she muttered, "I guess they're not broken after all." But she saw the arm had opened up and a folded piece of paper dropped out.

"Read it out loud!" Scott shouted.

"Shh...I've got to unfold it, first." Carefully, Kathleen unfolded the long, skinny piece of paper and read aloud, "I am glasses as special as can be, for you see good in others when you look through me."

Well, it didn't take long for the word to get out. Soon, the whole town knew about the remarkable glasses. Kathleen and Scott loaned them to anyone who asked. All the families began to get along better — even brothers and sisters fought less. The demand became so great that there was a waiting list and that's when Kathleen got her idea. "Let's tell everyone it isn't the glasses that hold the magic, it's the ATTITUDE of the person wearing them. Let's tell them to take any pair of glasses and make an agreement to see good when they're worn. Attitude is the magic and the difference."

And that's what they did. They told everyone. Their plan worked and Avalon became known as the world's most friendly city.

What difference do you think it would make if people saw the good in each other? (discuss with class) How many of you know bullies like the ones in this story? Why do you think they act this way? (don't feel good about themselves) People who get negative attention don't think they can get positive attention or compliments. Everyone needs attention. Some people actually believe the only kind they can get is negative attention. Bullies, trouble-makers, and people who are not kind to others are telling you they need positive attention.

Activity G — Review Sentences for Bulletin Board

To review today's lesson, let's read these sentences. (Hold up "We All Like Compliments.") Who wants to read this sentence? (Wait for class response.) Which people in your life could you compliment?

> *HINT: (Put strips on board as students name them: mother,*
> *father, sister, brother, teacher, friend, self, etc. Blank strip and*
> *pen are for any other name.)*

For our next lesson, write two or three compliments for each of these people (Point to strips on the board.) Remember to begin each compliment with the word "I." Work on the goal you set for yourself in your group. And remember to be good to yourself and to each other!

_____Lesson 4_____

Listening and Stress Reduction

Objectives

- The child will compile a class list on the importance of listening.
- The child will practice good listening habits in the Pioneer Game.
- The child will experience a stress reduction exercise.

Suggested Reading

Buscaglia, Leo. *Living, Loving and Learning*, p. 58. "I think listening is tremendously important, and yet we abhor and are frightened of silence."

Fromm, Erich. *The Art of Loving*, p. 114. "Most people listen to others, or even give advice, without really listening."

Background

The PSE philosophy includes the belief that children learn facts and concepts more willingly and more lastingly when school is fun. Many necessary skills may be effectively taught through the use of a game.

When a child has a problem or a concern that is important to him/her, **take it seriously.** Do — STOP what you are doing. LOOK at the child's eyes, and LISTEN with your mind and heart. Don't — give advice unless asked, try to "fix it," or share how very difficult it was for you, way back then.

Materials

Signs for Pioneer Game, Props for game: cowboy hats/scarves/etc. New bulletin board strips: Listening Is Important; Stress Reduction, Too. Why?

Activity A — Review Bulletin Board Strips from Lesson 3

The sentence we left with you last time was, "We all like compliments." Who wants to share a compliment you thought of for your father, mother, brother, sister, teacher, friends, and you? (Ask for compliments for each person on the list.) Remember to begin with the word "I."

> HINT: If you have not met with the class for several weeks, as originally planned in the timing of the lessons, you may wish to form small groups and check on the progress of each student's goal. You could include this as a New Year's Resolution, reminding the class it is time to get going on reaching goals. Some students may wish to set new goals, etc.

174

Activity B — Practicing Listening Skills: Pioneer Game

In today's lesson, we will be talking about two separate topics which are important in our lives. If we can master these two aspects of living, our lives will be happier. The first of these is LISTENING.

Why is it important to listen well? (List student responses on the chalkboard: learn, follow directions, enjoyment of movies and music, assists you in friendships, etc.) Because listening is SO important in our lives, PSE is going to give you a chance to practice this skill today with a game.

> HINT: Divide the class into six groups. Have each group stand and say their part to be sure everyone understands. Each group will have a sign indicating its part. The words for each group are listed below. It is helpful to have a sign for each group.

Words for the Pioneer Game

Group 1:	Pioneers —	"That's us!" (Pointing to self with thumb.)
Group 2:	West —	"Thata way!" (Pointing to their left with their right hand.)
Group 3:	Oxen —	"Click, Clack" (Done with tongue.)
Group 4:	Wild Animals —	"Grrr-Grrr" (Hands like claws.)
Group 5:	Afraid —	"Help! Help!"
Group 6:	Attitude —	"You can if you think you can!"
Whole class:	Soldiers —	"Do-do-do-doot-do-do, charge!" (Musically, into side of closed fist.)

Whenever you hear me say the name of your group, you will stand and say your part. You need to LISTEN so your group stays together. Remember, the whole class does the part of the soldiers. Let's do a practice exercise and sentence to get our act together. When I say your group name, stand, say and do your part: pioneers, west, oxen, wild animals, afraid, attitudes, and soldiers. (Pause between each group.) Now we'll do it in a sentence. LISTEN carefully. We are going to do a story where the PIONEERS head WEST with their OXEN. Naturally, they have trouble with the WILD ANIMALS and many of them are AFRAID. In the end, the SOLDIERS rescue them and they find their ATTITUDE made the difference.

Now we are going to do a story using these parts. Pay attention! If you follow your neighbor and he or she gets lost, what will happen? (Wait for class response.) The success of this game depends upon listening.

Pioneer Game

Pioneers came out **west** in wagons pulled by **oxen**. Many of them were **afraid**; their **attitude** made the difference. The **pioneers** knew there would be many hardships. They felt they might starve, get lost, be beaten down by the weather, or that the **wild animals** would get them. The **pioneers** were **afraid** of the **wild animals**. Sometimes, the **wild animals** killed the **pioneers'** **oxen**. The **soldiers** tried to protect the **pioneers** who headed **west** with their **oxen**.

One group of **pioneers** who were headed **west** with their **oxen** killed a buffalo for food. The indians didn't like it when the **pioneers**, who were headed **west** with their **oxen**, killed their buffalo. It was the **pioneers' attitude** and actions the indians didn't like. The **wild animals** frightened the **pioneers**. But the **pioneers** kept heading **west**.

Just when it looked as if the **pioneers** or their **oxen** wouldn't make it west, the **soldiers** came! The **soldiers'** job was to protect **pioneers** heading **west** with their **oxen** and to help them not to be so **afraid**. Their **attitude** also made the difference. The **soldiers** taught the **pioneers** how to defend themselves from **wild animals**. The **pioneers** were happy! The **soldiers** were happy! **Oxen**...well, **oxen** are just **oxen**. The **pioneers** thanked the **soldiers**, gathered their **oxen**, and continued heading **west**.

Everyone take your seats, now.

HINT: The team may choose to wear cowboy attire. It's fun to repeat the game. If time permits, change parts, and remind students to listen carefully for their new parts.

Activity C — Stress Reduction Exercise (read verbatim)

We are going to do a tensing exercise. As you know, that means you will make a muscle really tight, hold it tight, and then relax it. Listen so you know what to do.

Drop your arms to your side. Look down in your lap so you can concentrate on what you are doing. Squeeze both of your hands into a fist. Hold them as tightly as you can while I say TIGHT! TIGHT! TIGHT! TIGHT! Now open, your hands and let them hang loosely to your sides.

Make a fist with both hands again. Bring your fists up by your shoulders like you're showing how strong you are and make your upper and lower arm muscle TIGHT! TIGHT! TIGHT! TIGHT! Drop your arms and let them hang to your side.

We're going to tighten the muscles in your head. Frown, squeeze your eyes really tight, press your lips together, push your chin down to your chest, and hold all those muscles TIGHT! TIGHT! TIGHT! TIGHT! Let your head hang loose, open your mouth, and just relax for a few seconds. (pause)

Slowly bring your shoulders up and try to touch your ears. Pull them up hard, hold them there, and then drop them. Pull in your chest, muscles and stomach muscles. Hold them TIGHT! TIGHT! TIGHT! TIGHT! Now let those muscles relax, and just sit there quietly for a few seconds.

Pull the muscles tight in your upper and lower legs. TIGHT! TIGHT! TIGHT! TIGHT! Then tighten the muscles in your feet. TIGHT! TIGHT! TIGHT! TIGHT! Now relax.

Just feel how relaxed your arms feel. And your head. And your chest. And your stomach. And the lower part of your body. And your legs. And your feet. Bringing air in through your nose, take a long, slow breath. Hold your breath for a second, and then let the air out. Please look at me.

Activity D — Lesson Ending

Today's lesson has been on two topics. Who remembers what they were? (listening and stress reduction) Why is it important to relax? (class discussion)

We will leave this bulletin board with you to help you remember these two important parts of life. Please add to it with your writings. Why not try an imaginative story where the use of one of these — listening or stress reduction — saves the day for the hero or heroine? We will be back in two weeks. Be good to yourself and to each other.

_____ Lesson 5 _____

Learning to Memorize

Objectives

- The child will use memory techniques to recall a list.
- The child will participate in memorizing the first fifteen Presidents of the U.S.

Suggested Reading

Buscaglia, Leo. *Love,* p. 130. "Love listens."

Crow, Lester and Alice, *How to Study,* p. 111. "It is important that you realize you cannot improve your memory in general by memorizing passages of prose or of poetry. Memory is not a general ability; memories are specific."

Lorayne, Harry and Lucas, Jerry. *The Memory Book,* entire book.

Background

School children are told, over and over, to learn. Some children are never given any assistance on ways to accomplish this task. This lesson includes three techniques for memorization. We have chosen learning the first fifteen Presidents of the United States because it is a common task many children will be asked to do during their schooling. The techniques we have used are so simple they may open a whole new world of discovery for the children; and, even more importantly, will make memorizing this material over again unnecessary. To learn this way is to know it forever! Listening carefully requires practice. We have chosen to practice this skill in a fun-filled manner.

Materials

One small piece of paper for each student, U.S. Presidents worksheet, U.S. Presidents chart (see Activity D), Bulletin board strip: Make School Easier: Learn to Memorize.

> *HINT: The length of time needed to complete this lesson is dependent upon the nature of the class. It is important to take enough time with the memorizing process to be certain the procedure is understood. Activity D may be taught in this lesson and E done as teacher follow-up work or the entire listening segment (D and E activities) can be taught in the beginning of Lesson 11.*

Activity A — Stress Reduction Exercise (read verbatim)

Sometimes, when you get to rushing around in your lives, it is helpful to just sit and listen. The object is to take yourself out of motion and simply listen. Sit up tall, but comfortably — feet flat on the floor. Bringing air in through your nose, take a long, slow breath. Hold your breath for a second then slowly let the air out through your mouth. Now, making no sound whatsoever, simply sit and listen. Relax and just listen to whatever there is to hear. (Pause thirty seconds.) As you sit there, take a breath in through your nose and then let it out through your mouth. Do this several times. One of the ways to relax is to just sit and listen.

Activity B — Memorizing by Picturing

A large part of learning is listening. There is another part of learning about which we are going to talk today — memorizing. In school, you are asked to memorize a lot of facts. There are many ways to memorize. We are going to talk about two ways: to learn something and to remember it forever.

Let's say your mother asks you to get certain items at the store, after school. She gives you a list, but you want to remember the items in case you lose the list. She asks you to get: apples, raisins, eggs, cereal, milk, and soap. (Write the words on the chalkboard.)

Write the first letter of each word: a, r, e, c, m, s. You are going to unscramble the letters and make a word, if possible. The letter c needs an e if it goes at the end of the word.

Let's start with the letter "c." You have the letters a, r, e, m, s left. Put r after c and that makes — cr. Add e and a and m and you have cream. Add an s to the front and you may scream if you forget something. You now have the word scream.

Each letter stands for something; S is for what? (soap) C is for ? (cereal) R is for ? (raisins) E is for ? (eggs) A is for ? (apples) M is for ? (milk) Remember the word "scream" and you have your list.

Let's say you don't have time to figure out a word from the first letter of each word. There is another way to remember this list. Make a silly picture using all the items on the list. I worked this out earlier and came up with this. (Draw a picture on the chalkboard which illustrates the words below.)

A milk carton sitting in a cereal bowl with an apple for a head, eggs for eyes, and raisins for the nose and mouth. The whole group is balanced on a bar of soap.

Now use your mind like a camera and take a picture of the whole thing. When you get to the market, see your picture in your mind and pick up the parts: apple, eggs, raisins, milk, cereal, soap. Any time you need to memorize a list, both of these ways will help you learn the words and remember them for a long time.

Activity C — More about Memorizing with Pictures

Sometimes, you can use pictures to remember two things that need to go together. For instance, you may be given the assignment to learn all the states and their capitals. That's a big job! Let's look at one way to make it a fun job.

Here are a list of five capitals and their states: Sacramento, California; Salem, Oregon; Topeka, Kansas; Little Rock, Arkansas; Harrisburg, Pennsylvania.

To learn the capital of California, you might picture a man sitting in a boat, rowing — his foot propped up on the side. He has a fat toe. All around him in the water are floating sacks. Put the pieces together: sack-row-man-toe. To link the silly picture you have just made with its state, you might have a California flag flying from the stern (back) of the boat. See the picture in your mind. Put the pieces together. Sack-row-man-toe is the capital of California.

Let's do another one. How about Harrisburg, Pennsylvania. Harris and "hairy" sound similar. Burg reminds me of an iceberg. So I see a hairy iceberg which I shorten to hairy-berg. Now to link this capital to its state, I see pens sticking out all over the hairy iceberg. Penn. is a short form for Pennsylvania. See that silly picture. Put the pieces together: Hairy-berg, Penn.

> HINT: If the student are confused with Penn., you might use a
> pencil with veins running through it — writing "ya" on the hairy
> berg: hairy-berg, pencil-vein-ya.

I want you to do one, now. A small piece of paper is being passed to you. Write this capital and its state: Little Rock, Arkansas. Play with the words to form a silly picture. Draw the picture you create. Turn your paper over and put your pencil down when you have it finished. (Wait for about four minutes.) Who will share your idea for learning this state and its capital?

> HINT: Take three to five ideas. Draw them on the chalkboard
> if you can. Otherwise, say the words and have the children form
> a picture. One example might be a small rock on top of an ark
> which is sitting in a pile of saws. Little Rock, Ark-in-saws.

That was fun. We are going to give you two states and their capitals to play with so we can discuss some silly pictures for learning the   We will do so in the next lesson.

Activity D — Learning to Memorize

(Question from PSE team member: What do you do if the first letters from each word don't unscramble into a word or you can't form pictures like we did with the states?) Thank you for that question. Let's say you need to learn the Presidents of the United States, in order. If I look them up, I find the first ten to be: Washington, Adams, Jefferson, Madison, Monroe, Adams, Jackson, Van Buren, Harrison, Tyler. (Have the presidents names printed on a chart large enough so the whole class can see.)

Let's take the first five Presidents and write the first letter of each name vertically. (Write these letters vertically on the chalkboard: W-A-J-M-M.)

We can't scramble the letters because our assignment is to learn them in order. This time take the first letter and have it stand for a word which creates a silly picture. (Write after appropriate letter.) **Whales Always Juggle Mice and Monkeys.** Take a picture with your mental camera.

Tell me each word and I'll write the first letter. (Whales) **W,** (Always) **A,** (Juggle) **J,** (Mice) **M,** (Monkeys) **M.** (Write vertically.) Now we need to learn each President's name that goes with the appropriate letter. W-Washington, A-Adams. Think: W-Washington, A-Adam, J-Jefferson. M-Madison. Think: W-Washington, A-Adams, J-Jefferson, M-Madison. M-Monroe. Think: W-Washington, A-Adams, J-Jefferson, etc. If you get the M's mixed up, remember they are in alphabetical order.

(Erase the chalkboard.) Tell me the silly sentence. Write the first letter. Tell me the Presidents' names that begin with W-A-J-M-M. Repeat over and over until you know all five names.

The next five Presidents are: Adams, Jackson, VanBuren, Harrison, Tyler.

Steps to Follow

1. First letters written vertically.
2. Make a sentence: **Ants Jump Very High Trees.**
3. Take a picture.
4. Erase chalkboard.
5. Say sentence.
6. Write first letter.
7. Learn names.

There are two Adams — one is John, one is John Quincy. Number one has one name (John). Number two has two names (John Quincy).

Are you ready for the PSE CHALLENGE? We are going to give you the next five Presidents: Polk, Taylor, Fillmore, Pierce, Buchanan. We want to practice this way of learning by memorizing the first fifteen Presidents of the U.S. in two weeks. We'll give you a worksheet so you can learn them.   (Hand out worksheet.)

You need to figure out a sentence for the last five Presidents and learn them. We talked about whales and ants. Be sure to keep in the category of animals. The point of this exercise is not to learn the presidents but to teach you how to memorize.

HINT: Go over the entire worksheet so instructions are clear.

We talked about:

1. Learning a list by making a word out of each first letter.   (Write scream on the chalkboard.)

2. Seeing items in a silly picture so you can remember them   (Draw a crazy picture of an apple, raisin, eggs, milk, cereal, and soap on the chalkboard.)

3. Seeing items in a silly picture so you can remember two things that belong together (Write "Sack-row-man-toe, California" on the board.)

4. Making a silly sentence out of first letter of each word or name. Tell me the first sentence. (Whales Always Juggle Mice and Monkeys.) (Write W-A-J-M-M on the board.) And the second sentence? (Ants Jump Very High Trees.) (Write A-J-V-H-T on the board.)

These three ways of learning take time but you will only have to learn them once. For better grades and remembering — MEMORIZE.

Activity E — Lesson Ending

Your new bulletin board strip is: Make School Easier: Learn to Memorize. Between now and next time, we want you to practice your new memory skills. You are going to figure out how to memorize two states and their capitals and five more presidents of the U.S.

Today was fun! We'll see you in two weeks for a lesson on feelings. Between now and then, be good to yourself and to each other!

_____ Lesson 6 _____

Feelings

Objectives

- The child will review the topic of feelings by orally reading the four sentences about feelings.
- The child will recall and discuss feelings which have changed.
- The child will play a game which illustrates different people have different feelings.
- The child will reevaluate his/her goal from a prior lesson.
- The child will share his/her feelings with one other person.

Suggested Reading

Powell, John. *Why Am I Afraid to Tell You Who I Am?*, p. 57. "Actually, the things that most clearly differentiate and individuate me from others, that make the communication of my person a unique knowledge, are my feel- ings or emotions."

Background

Most children were afraid the first time they rode a bicycle. Remembering that fear and recognizing it no longer exists can assist children in realizing that feelings change. When children are aware that feelings change they become more accepting of their current feelings.

Another fear a child might have is that he/she is the only one in a group who feels something in a certain way. Understanding that different people may have different feel- ings is the beginning of teaching respect for the rights of others. In a world with so many dif- ferent cultures, it is illogical to think we will all feel the same way. *Project Self-Esteem* sup- ports valuing differences.

Materials

Set of cards containing feeling words for each student: happy/lonely/upset/sad/afraid, Feelings chart (see Activity C), Five strips with the word "feelings" written on them, Extra Goal Setting worksheets, Masking tape for the chart, New bulletin board strip: One Person's Feelings Can Be Different From Another Person's Feelings.

Activity A — Review Bulletin Board from Lesson 5

Let's look at your bulletin board and see what you added. Will someone read the strip? (Wait for class response.) Can anyone name the first fifteen Presidents of the United States?

> *HINT: Choose two or three students and discuss key sentences for learning the last five presidents. Suggest to the teacher that the class might want to learn all the presidents this way.*

Did anyone figure out a way to learn the two states and capitols we left with you last time? (class response) What idea do you have for Salem, Oregon? (class response) And what about Topeka, Kansas? (class response)

> *HINT: Using the chalkboard where appropriate, create a picture for each of the two states. Take more than one idea. Compliment the students' ingenuity.*

We hope you will use these new memorizing tools in your schoolwork every day. You will be surprised at how much quicker studying for exams will be using these ways to memorize.

Activity B — Stress Reduction Exercise (read verbatim)

Sometimes, when you get to rushing around in your lives, it is helpful to just sit and listen. Sit up tall, but comfortably — feet flat on the floor. Bringing air in through your nose, take a long, slow breath. Hold your breath for a second then slowly let the air out through your mouth. Now, making no sound whatsoever, simply sit and listen. Relax and just listen to whatever there is to hear. (Pause thirty seconds.) As you sit there, take a breath in through your nose then let it out through your mouth. Do it several times. One of the ways to relax is to just sit and listen.

Activity C — Review and Discuss Feelings Sentences

The subject of today's lesson is also the answer that fits into the four sentences on this chart. The same word will fit into all four sentences.

> *HINT: Read the sentences or have the students read them saying "blank" where appropriate. When the right word is discovered, put the correct word into the blank one sentence at a time and have a child read each completed sentence.*

Everybody has _____. _____ are based upon a past experience. One person's _____ can be different from another person's _____. _____ can change.

What's the one word which fits into each sentence? (Wait for class response.)

Today, we are going to take a minute or two to think about the times your feelings have changed. Try to remember something you felt one way about but, for some reason, changed your feelings. It can be food, animals, an activity, or anything about which you changed your feelings.

> *HINT: Ask someone to share. If students are hesitant, the PSE volunteers might share.*

Activity D — How Would You Feel? Game

> *HINT: Give each student cards containing feeling words. Cards can be premade or children can make them.*

Let's go through the six cards each of you have been given: lonely, upset, happy, proud, sad, afraid. We are going to play a game called "How Would You Feel?" Listen while I read a possible happening in your life. Decide which card comes the closest to describing how you would feel and hold it up. Ready? Let's try one.

> *HINT: The point of this exercise is to illustrate that not everyone feels the same way about any given situation. Be sure to note differences and to clearly state that each difference is OK.*

How Would You Feel?

1. If you did something well. (happy, proud)
2. If you were at home alone after dark. (lonely, sad, happy, afraid)
3. If your friend asked you to hold his/her snake. (happy, proud, afraid)
4. If you were invited to have a Chinese dinner with your friend and his/her family. (happy, sad)
5. If you were left out of a game or conversation. (all cards possible)
6. Your dad has been elected President and you are going to Washington. (all cards possible)
7. You need to go onto the stage and receive an award in front of the whole school. (all cards possible)

We played this game to remind you that each of us is unique. Our own feelings change from time to time and we sometimes have feelings that are different from other peoples' and that's OK. Is it OK for me to have a feeling which is different from yours? (yes) Is it OK for you to have different feeling than any of us? (yes) And last, but not least, feelings change — yes or no? (yes)

Activity E — Check Goals: Progress to Date, Reevaluation

We are going to get into our small groups for a brief time to check your progress on your goals. As I call your group leader's name, please move quickly and quietly into your group.

> *HINT: Have each child state his/her goal. Discuss progress to date with the group, giving suggestions as to methods of reaching that goal. If any student has successfully achieved a goal, compliment him/her and discuss how it feels to have accomplished that goal. Children who have accomplished their goal may choose to do another one. It is defeating to reward excellence with another task, so be sure there is no pressure in this choice. Return students to their own seats as soon as all groups are finished.*

Activity F — Divide Class into Pairs and Share Feelings

It is important that we learn to share our feelings. So, we are going to break into pairs and play a sharing game. (Divide class into pairs.) Each of you has a stack of cards which you held up in the "How Would You Feel?" game. Each of you hold up your stack of cards right now. A PSE volunteer will take one person's cards. You will only need one set of cards per group for this exercise. (Wait for volunteers to collect cards.)

Hold the cards face down or lay them in a row face down. One person will draw a card, and share a time when he/she had that feeling. Please take turns drawing and sharing until all the cards are used. (Collect the cards when finished. Be sure to keep cards in sets.)

Activity G — Lesson Ending

What was today's lesson about? (feelings) Tell me four facts you know about feelings. (class response based on Feelings chart) Thank you. I like the way this class is listening today. We have said that everyone has feelings and today we named six different feelings. There are many more feelings than six. For next time, we want you to write some other feelings on a piece of paper. When we come for our next lesson, we'd like to see this bulletin board sentence, "One Person's Feelings Can Be Different From Another Person's Feelings," surrounded by the feeling words you choose to write. We will be back in two weeks. In the meantime, be good to your self and to each other.

_____ Lesson 7 _____

High and Low Self-Esteem/Review

Objectives

- The child will share feelings with classmates.
- The child will experience a relaxation exercise.
- The child will participate in a review game with classmates.
- The child will note the difference in the behavior of a high and low self-esteem person.
- The child will discover methods of changing behavior.

Suggested Reading

Barksdale, L. S. *Building Sound Self-Esteem,* pp. 1-4. "Self-esteem is how warm and loving we feel toward ourselves, based upon our personal sense of worth and degree of self-acceptance."

Knight, Michael E.; Graham, Terry Lynne; Julano, Rose A.; Miksza, Susen Robichaud; Tonnies, Pamela G. *Teaching Children to Love Themselves,* p. 4. "Children who see themselves as unliked, unaccepted, and unable to perform, frequently become maladjusted and are frustrated in society...A fundamentally positive self-concept gives the child a basic strength for dealing with situations in life."

Background

A child who knows that people who put others down do not feel good about themselves is less likely to allow others to dominate his/her life.

It is easy to allow others to determine how we feel. A comment like, "He made me unhappy" has no truth in it. No one makes anyone FEEL anything. We make continuous choices including whether to be happy, angry, sad, etc. The high self-esteemer takes responsibility for his/her own well-being. Understanding that a person with low self-esteem behaves in a certain way allows us to stop playing victim to that person.

Materials

Props appropriate for pantomime, High and Low Self-Esteem charts (see Activity D), Strips to tape onto the High/Low Self-Esteem charts (see Activity D), Masking tape, Harmony, New bulletin board strips: A Person With High Self-Esteem Feels Good About Self. (with happy face) A Person With Low Self-Esteem Doesn't Feel Good About Self. (with sad face) What Small Behaviors Can I Change to Help Me Feel Better About Myself? Optional: Name that Lesson banner

Activity A — Review the Bulletin Board from Lesson 6

Who wants to read the bulletin board sentence from the last lesson? (One person's feelings can be different from another person's feelings.) Raise your hand if you want to read one of the feelings that was put on the bulletin board. I am going to point to a feeling. Please say the feeling with the appropriate emotion. In other words, say "sad" sadly.

HINT: Keep the pace moving on this so it is not boring. Call a name, point to a feeling, and let that person say the word with the appropriate emotion.

Activity B — Stress Reduction Exercise (read verbatim)

Sometimes, when you get rushing around in your lives, it is helpful to just sit and listen. The object is to take yourself out of motion and simply listen. Sit up tall but comfortably — feet flat on the floor. Bringing air in through your nose, take a long, slow breath. Hold your breath for a second, then slowly let the air out through your mouth. Now, making no sound whatsoever, simply sit and listen. Relax and just listen to whatever there is to hear. (Pause thirty seconds.) As you sit there, take a breath in through your nose and then let it out through your mouth. One of the ways to relax is to just sit and listen.

Activity C — Name That Lesson Game

HINT: This lesson needs to be "hammy" or it drags. We suggest using your most enthusiastic team member as the announcer. Props and costumes add flavor and an air of fun. Invite the children to enjoy themselves.

Hello boys and girls. We're going to play a game today! To find out the name of the game, we direct your attention to the sign over there. (Point to the banner.) Who can tell me the name of this game? (class response) That's right and you are going to play Name that Lesson! The PSE team will be acting out or pantomiming some of the ideas from our lessons and you, yes (pointing) you, will be guessing the...name...of...the...lesson!

We are going to divide you into your four groups. To keep our show moving, each team needs to have a student group leader. Please select one now, and have your group leader raise his or her hand.

Hands down. Everyone listen carefully because here come the rules of this game! We, the PSE volunteers, will be acting out or pantomiming some of the ideas we've talked about in PSE this year. For example, if I were to do this (patting and hugging self), what message, from a PSE lesson, might you get? (I am special or I need to be good to myself.) Who remembers one thought or idea about being special? (I am special because I'm one of a kind.)

Listen carefully! Your group will watch the pantomime and discuss what you think is being acted out. Tell your team leader your idea and give the name of the lesson. When the whole team agrees, everyone except the team leader will sit down. The team leader will raise his/her hand. The team seated first will be called upon first.

One of the PSE volunteers will write the correct name of the lesson on the chalkboard. I will then ask many of you to share any ideas or thoughts you remember from that lesson. Put on your thinking caps! Work as a team! Are you ready? Let's begin! PSE volunteers will act out the following ideas using props and format of their choice.

1. Smiley — a compliment
2. Stress reduction exercise (idea: agitated, stop, sit down, relax, etc.)
3. Being alike is OK, so are differences
4. Goal setting
5. The Magic Glasses
6. Listening skills — Pioneer Game
7. Memorizing something and remembering it
8. Feelings change

HINT: Announcer will lead class discussion after each correct lesson title is given. A PSE volunteer will write the correct lesson title on the chalkboard. The heart of this activity is the discussion. Be sure to elicit as much information from each lesson as possible.

Announcer: Wonderful! Wonderful! Wonderful! You have been most wonderful in our Name that Lesson Game! For your efforts, we have some great prizes. (These may be changed to suit the individual classroom.)

Team 1: Gets an all-expense paid trip for each member to. . .
(name of their school)
Team 2: Each member gets 12 cans of. . .spinach!
Team 3: Gets a Veg-o-matic
Team 4: Gets one thousand. . .yes one thousand. . .fish sticks!

That's all for today for our Name that Lesson Game. Thanks for joining me. (Have class return to their seats.)

Activity D — Discussion of High and Low Self-Esteem Behavior

That game was fun. We've learned a lot about self-esteem. What kind of person has high self-esteem? A person with high self-esteem does what? (feels good about him/herself) A person with high self-esteem behaves differently than someone with low self-esteem. Think about it. When you're feeling happy and good about yourself, do you behave differently than in times when you are low and down on yourself? Of course you do! We're going to look at some differences between high and low self-esteem behaviors.

HINT: The charts for this exercise should be at least five feet tall, but may be whatever size works best for you. The following phrases can be used:

High Self-Esteem Strips:

Able to share self; makes positive comments about self; gives genuine compliments easily; doesn't feel he/she has to be good in everything; can laugh at self; listens; etc. (Be certain to use behaviors applicable to your school.)

Low Self-Esteem Strips:

Excludes others; frequently tattles; brags about accomplishments; continually puts self down; bullies others; starts rumors; frequently teases others; continually puts others down; etc., (Ask classroom teachers for list of qualities which are problems in her class.)

We have drawn two people. One is labeled high self-esteem and one low self-esteem. (Point to charts.)   On each of these strips, we have written different types of behavior. When I show you each strip, I want you to vote by using your thumbs. If you think the behavior described belongs to a high self-esteem person, put thumbs up for yes, thumbs down for no. We're looking for high self-esteem behavior.

HINT: This part can drag unless done with some enthusiasm. As each strip is introduced and voted upon, put a strip onto the appropriate figure. Have folded-over tape on the strips. Give lots of positive strokes such as "Whoa! Can't fool you! Let's try another one!"

Activity E — Discuss the Value of Attaining High Self-Esteem

Let's look at the person with low self-esteem. I need a volunteer to read some of the ways he/she behaves. (Choose a student to read the strips.)   How do you think this chart person feels about him/herself? (Use the chart for specific examples.) You now know that a person who teases others, brags, and puts down people doesn't feel good about himself or herself. Therefore, you have a new choice to make. Are you going to give someone who doesn't feel good about self the power to influence how you feel about yourself? Are you going to give that person the power to hurt or change you? Remember, the person who behaves this way doesn't feel good about himself or herself.

Now let's look at the high self-esteem chart person. How do you think he or she feels about self? (feels good about self) It's important to realize that no one is always here. (Point to High Self-Esteem chart.)   At one time or another, all of us have these feelings. (Point to Low Self-Esteem chart.)   But most of the time, the high self-esteemer is here.   (Point to the High Self-Esteem chart.)

The question is: If you have low self-esteem, how do you get high self-esteem? It isn't done overnight. In fact, it's done in the same way you eat an elephant — one bite at a time! Look at the chart (Low Self-Esteem chart) and if you see some of your own behavior your might say to yourself, "I do that sometimes!" Recognizing a place you could change is the beginning of changing. Next, just like your ladder in goal setting, you can begin to plan ways to change that behavior. In the beginning you may, for instance, hear yourself brag and say "Ooops! I did it again!" Change takes time. The beginning is to want to change. Then you take small steps and allow yourself to make mistakes. Change isn't easy, but it is possible and we do learn from our mistakes.

Activity F — Lesson Ending

Today, we've had fun reviewing some of the ideas we've been talking about in PSE this year. We've written three sentences to remind you of these ideas:

A Person With High Self-Esteem Feels GOOD About Self.
(with happy face)
A Person With Low Self-Esteem Doesn't Feel Good About Self.
(with sad face)
What Small Behaviors Can I Change to Help Myself Feel Better About Myself?

Think about these ideas for the next two weeks. We'll be back with another PSE lesson. Meanwhile, there are two things we always ask you to do. Who can tell me one of them? (Be good to yourself.) Who can tell me the other? (Be good to each other.)

_____ Lesson 8_____

Communicating Assertively

Objectives

- The child will practice a stress reduction exercise.
- The child will learn there are three types of communicators.
- The child will experience the three different types of communicators through playacting.
- The child will learn and practice the Broken Record method of communicating.

Suggested Reading

Palmer, Pat. *Liking Myself,* p. 9. "Being a good friend to yourself means that you can STOP doing something you don't like."
Smith, Manuel J. *When I Say No, I Feel Guilty,* p. 74. "One of the most important aspects of being verbally assertive is to be persistent and to keep saying what you want over and over again without getting angry, irritable or loud."

Background

Extensive research indicates many individuals find themselves in undesirable situations because they do not know how to say no. Learning how to say no when you want to say no is the primary focus of this lesson. The Broken Record method of communication is a valuable tool for each of us to know and use.

Materials

King Kong, Doormat, Assertive chart   (see Activity C), One piece of writing paper for each student, New bulletin board strip: Learn to Say No When You Want to Say No.

Activity A — Review Lesson 7

Last time, we discovered that a person with high self-esteem feels what about him or herself? (good) How does a person who brags a lot, teases a lot, and often puts people down feel about him/herself? (not good) So, when someone puts you down, you have a choice. Who knows what it is? (whether or not to let someone who does not feel good about him/herself ruin your day.)

Activity B — Stress Reduction Exercise (read verbatim)

Whenever you are upset and want to calm down, a simple way to do so is a breathing exercise. It is easy and it works. Please look into your lap and keep your head down. Slowly draw air in through your nose and let it out, very slowly, through your mouth. Do it with me. Breathe in through your nose, and breathe out through your mouth. Breathe in through your nose, and slowly breathe out through your mouth. Nose . . . in, mouth . . . out. Nose . . . in, mouth . . . out. (Repeat the words a few more times.) Now stop. When you are ready, please look at me.

Activity C —
Introduce King Kong, Doormat and Assertive Communicators

Types of Communicators

KING KONG — Aggressive: shouts, threatens, calls names, throws a fit, stormy, swears

DOORMAT — Passive: does nothing, withdraws, pouts, feels sorry for self, sulks, whines, begs, cries

ASSERTIVE — Says how he/she feels and states what he/she wants

On this chart we have listed three types of communicators. First is the KING KONG type. This communicator uses body language which is powerful and strong. You get an idea of what this person is like by the name, but here are some words which describe a KING KONG COMMUNICATOR: aggressive; shouts; threatens; calls names; throws a fit; storms around; swears loudly.   (Point to the chart.)

Then there's the DOORMAT COMMUNICATOR. This person is passive; does nothing; withdraws; pouts; feels sorry for self; whines; begs; cries a lot.

Finally, we have the ASSERTIVE PERSON. This kind of communicator says how he or she feels and states what he or she wants.

Thumbs up for yes, thumbs down for no. Do you think the King Kong Communicator has high self-esteem? (no) How about the Doormat? (no) Assertive? (yes)

These three types of communicators behave in certain ways. Let's do a skit and see how each of them would behave. (One PSE volunteer will be the brother or sister with a loud stereo.) You are trying to study but your brother or sister is playing the stereo so loudly you cannot think. Who wants to show the class how a King Kong Communicator would act?   (remind students; no swearing, even though it is on the list.) How about a volunteer to be the Doormat Communicator? Anyone want to be the Assertive Communicator?

Let's do another example. You are watching a movie in the theater. The person behind you continually kicks your chair and this bothers you.

> HINT: Have children come up to pantomime: King Kong threatens; Doormat does nothing and just gives a slight glance; the Assertive Communicator says, "That's annoying, please stop."

We need to be careful not to disguise King Kong and Doormat when using Assertive: "I feel upset because you took my pencil and I want you to give it back." You do not shout or threaten as King Kong does. You do not whine or sulk as the Doormat does. The Assertive Communicator is very matter-of-fact, has a strong-but-easy tone of voice, and doesn't use aggressive body language.

> *HINT: Demonstrate an assertive sentence using the King Kong tone first then the Doormat tone.*

Activity D — Introduce Broken Record Technique

Even if you choose to use assertive communication, you may get a King Kong or Doormat back. Watch this example:

> **A:** I feel upset because you took my pencil. I want you to give it back.
>
> **KK:** So what, nerd!

It is easy, in this situation, to jump right into name-calling. How would you handle this situation? Let's talk about it. Stick to your point and say your sentence again. (Repeat the dialogue for A.)

This technique is called the Broken Record. When a record has a scratch in it, it plays the same section over and over — the technique is the same, over and over. Let's do an example.

> *HINT: Sandy and Peggy meet each other. Sandy wants to borrow Peggy's van. Peggy does not want to loan it and makes one excuse after another: out of gas, dirty, might need it, don't know how to drive a van, etc. For each excuse, Sandy has a solution.*

Stop the action! Peggy is running out of excuses. Raise your hand if you ever said yes when you wanted to say no to a friend. (Wait for class response.) The Broken Record method works well for this and it has two parts. First, you have your policy statement or rule. If a store has a sign saying "No Eating in the Store," the rule is meant for everyone, not just you. A policy statement is a statement for everyone, not just the person you are talking to at the time. Before the policy statement or rule, you make a kind statement which shows you have some understanding, but your policy sticks. Let's replay the van scene. This time Peggy will have a policy statement.

HINT: If the class has a problem with the phrase "policy statement," change the word to "rule." The children love this scene if the borrower really hams it up and literally does anthing she can to get her friend to change her mind. The following are suggestions, only.

Suggested Dialogue

Sandy: Hi, Peggy, I'm glad to see you. You know my daughter is about to have her birthday. She invited a whole bunch of her friends to have a picnic on the beach. Fun, huh? Fun, except she invited more children than will fit into my car. So I thought, being that we're such good friends, you might loan me your van for the afternoon.

Peggy: I understand your problem, Sandy and I never loan my van.

Sandy: Of course you don't...not to others...but we're FRIENDS and have been for a long time.

Peggy: Being your friend is a neat part of my life, and I never loan my van. I'm sorry.

Sandy: What do I do? When the kids arrive do I line them all up and say "You go, you don't, you go, you don't...? Look, I need a favor. Remember the time I loaned you my best, not my junky one, but my best coffeepot for your party?

Peggy: I appreciated using your coffeepot, and my policy is I never loan my van.

Sandy: (Crying, getting angry, pouting, begging — all fair game.)

Stop the action! Peggy held in there with her policy statement. What were some of the kind statements she used? (class response) Let's do another one.

(Use a PSE volunteer and a student volunteer who is coached by another PSE team member.) Mrs. St.Clair, you are going to talk to Bobby about a book he borrowed and promised to return last week. Mrs. St.Clair's policy statement is, "You promised to return the book by Friday." (PSE volunteer and student act out the skit.)

Stop the action! The important thing to remember is to make a kind statement which may be different each time and a policy statement which is always the same. (Go around the room and ask different children if you may borrow whatever you see on their desk or person. Remind them to use kind and policy statement — making excuses is not allowed.)

Activity E — Broken Record Practice

I am going to divide you into pairs and let you practice this technique. (Divide class.) You decide who will do the Broken Record in the first example...ready? Your friend wants to borrow some money from you but you do not want to loan him or her any money. Remember to make a kind statement then a policy statement. Broken Record people think of your policy statement...and hold the line. Begin! (Allow three minutes.)

What were some of your policy statements? OK, switch parts and let's do this example. Your friend teases you about your clothes. Broken Record people get your policy statement ready. Remember a kind statement first and no war words...begin. (Allow three minutes.)

That one was different. The Broken Record is a great tool to use if someone is teasing you. I know one boy who drove a teaser bonkers by saying over and over, "I'm sorry, I didn't hear you." Whatever your statement or policy statement is, stick to it. It isn't any fun to tease a person who doesn't get upset.

Switch again and let's try this one: One of you wants to steal something from a store, the other does not want to do it. Broken Record communicators, think of your policy statement...begin! (Allow three minutes.) The only statement made is your policy statement. The other person always has his or her right to choose. What were some of your policy statements?

Here's another example: Your friends have some cigarettes and are going to smoke them. You know smoking is harmful and you don't want to join them. One friend tries to argue with you. (Ask students to switch partners and allow three minutes.) What were some of your policy statements?

Activity F — Lesson Ending

Today, we've talked about three different types of communicators. We know that body language, tone of voice, and choice of words are all important things to consider when we want to communicate. We learned the Broken Record technique as a means of saying no when we want to say no and we learned how to be assertive when someone else is doing a King Kong job on us.

Your bulletin board strip for next time is: Learn to Say No When You Want to Say No. See you in two weeks. Be good to yourself and to each other!

_____ Lesson 9 _____

Friendship

Objectives

- The child will learn to breathe to relieve stress.
- The child will list qualities desired in a friend.
- The child will express feelings about friendship by writing a cinquain.
- The child will participate in listening and responding to a story.

Suggested Reading

Anglund, Joan Walsh. *A Friend is Someone Who Likes You*, p. 14. "Sometimes you don't know who are your friends. Sometimes they are there all the time, but you walk right past them and don't notice that they like you in a special way."

Newman, Mildred and Berkowitz, Bernard. *How to Be Your Own Best Friend*, p. 39. "You can't do anything if you believe you can't."

Background

It is easy to believe that positive friendships "just happen." However, friendship, like any relationship, requires a conscientious effort on the part of the people involved.

An important aspect of friendship is listening. A person who thinks he or she is being heard feels valued. We find that listening is an art which requires some knowledge and lots of practice. So we have included teaching listening skills as a means of enhancing children's self-esteem.

Materials

Harmony, My Kind of Friend chart (see Activity C), Cinquain chart (see Activity D), Piece of paper for each child, New Bulletin board strip: Grade 4—To Have a Friend, Be One!

Activity A — Review Lesson 8

Last time we discovered there are three types of communicators. Who can tell me one of them? (King Kong) Another one? (Doormat) And the last one? (Assertive) We introduced an assertive training technique to be used when someone wants to borrow something or wants you to do something you do not want to do. What is that technique called? (Broken Record)

> *HINT: Choose three or four students. Practice the Broken Record technique by asking to borrow something or to do something.*

Activity B — Stress Reduction Exercise (read verbatim)

We've learned that whenever you are upset and want to calm down, a simple way to do so is a breathing exercise. Pay attention to your breathing, not to what's going on in the room. Look down into your lap. Draw air in through your nose and let it out, very slowly, through your mouth. Do it with me. Breathe in through your nose, and breathe out through your mouth. Nose . . . in, mouth . . . out. Nose . . . in, mouth . . . out. Nose . . . in, mouth . . . out. (Repeat the words a few more times.) Now stop. When you are ready, please look at me.

Activity C — Listing Qualities You Want in a Friend

Let's see how Harmony is today. Hi, Harmony! (Harmony waves and talks.) He says he loves PSE because he is making so many new friends. (Harmony talks again.) I'm with you, Harmony. He says that friendship is really important to him. Friendship is important to me, too. Raise your hand if it is important to you to have friends. (class response) Well, since friendship is important to all of us, we have decided to talk about it in today's lesson. In fact, we'll be talking about friendship for the next two lessons.

As you get closer to the teen years, your friends will be more and more important to you. Because of that you need to keep defining what it is you like and want in a friend. Thanks for your contribution, Harmony. We'll talk to you at the end of the lesson.

HINT: The chart for this exercise should be at least five feet tall, but may be whatever size works best for you. This poster will be left with each classroom after your lesson so you need to have one for each room.

We are going to do an exercise which is similar to one you have done before. (Point to the My Kind of Friend chart.) "My Kind of Friend" is the title of this chart. Think of qualities which are important to you in a friend. We are going to compose the ideal friend for (Mrs. White's) students. What qualities do you want in a friend?

> HINT: Write the words each student gives you inside of the drawing of the person. Be sure to keep the class on track with qualities and don't let them wander. For example, "a good friend" needs to be specifically defined as "someone who tells the truth."

We are going to leave this chart with you so you will be reminded of the qualities many people want in a friend.

Activity D — Writing a Cinquain about Friendship

We are going to write a cinquain (sin-cane) about friendship. "A what?" you ask. A cinquain. Let's look at this chart.

Cinquains (sin-cane)

First line . . . . . name or a noun
Second line . . . two adjectives describing line one
Third line . . . three verbs
Fourth line . . . one adjective
Fifth line . . . . three words which describe

A cinquain is like a poem, but it does not rhyme. You use words, follow these steps (pointing to chart), and it is a fun way to say something.

The best way to learn how to do this is to do one! Let's start with line one. Because we are writing about friendship, let's begin with the word FRIEND.

> HINT: Write "friend" on the board. Do the same with the other words in the poem.

For the second line we need two adjectives to describe the first word — friend. Who knows one word which describes a friend? (honest, fun, dependable, friendly, etc.) Now we have friend and for line two we have two words which tell about that friend. We now need three verbs, or action words, that tell what the friend does. Think of some words and raise your hand when you want to share. (talks, listens, plays) Starting from the top we have: friend, honest, fun, talks, listens, plays. For line four we'll use another adjective to describe the friend — all we need is one word. Who has an adjective? (helpful) Now we have; friend, honest, fun, talks, listens, helpful. To finish it off, we need three words which describe and bring this whole cinquain to an end. To show you what I mean by bringing it to an end, I could use the words "always supports you" for the ending. What three words can you think of that end this poem? (fun for you) To go through for the last time:

Friend

honest, fun

talks, listens, plays

helpful

fun for you.

You are going to write your own cinquain on friendship or a friend. A piece of paper is being given to you. Please put your name and teacher's name on the top right portion of the paper. If you have a question during this exercise, please raise your hand.

I want you to put "friend" or "friendship" as the first word. Look at me when you are finished so I know when to continue.

HINT: Wait for a few minutes between each step.

For the second line, you need two words that describe or two adjectives which talk about the first word. Think of your two adjectives and write them. Look at me when you are finished. OK, for the third line you need three action words or verbs. Write three action words then look at me. The fourth line takes one word — a word that describes. Write one word on the fourth line and then look at me. Finally, you need three words which describe. They need to be words which end the cinquain. Write your three words then look at me.

Who wants to read your cinquain? (Choose three or four students.) We are going to collect your cinquains and give them back to you in our next lesson.

Activity E — Introduction to Listening and Responding

An important part of communicating is listening. We probably aren't aware of how much listening we do. Just for fun, all at once, give me examples of times and places when you need to listen. (home, school, friends, TV, radio, records, someone calling for assistance, sirens, etc.) STOP!

What you may not realize is that over half of communicating is listening, but most of us are better talkers than listeners. Listening is more than hearing. It is trying to understand what we hear. Listening is an important way of showing people we are interested in them and care about them.

201

Most of us have not been taught to listen. Did you know we talk at a rate of 125 to 150 words per minute? (Write 125-150 per minute on the chalkboard.) We can listen to 400 to 700 words per minute. (Write 400 to 700 words per minute on the chalkboard.) How does that make listening difficult? (Wait for class response.) Listening isn't always easy. We tend to daydream, think other thoughts, or race ahead of the speaker instead.

Today, we are going to talk about listening for feelings. Some of you will remember when we talked about how your tone of voice carried a message. We did exercises in which part of the class was asked for example, "How was school?" The other half of the class answered, "Fine" every time but gave different messages by changing the voice tone. Listening includes hearing the tone of voice, seeing the body language, getting in tune with the person who is talking, and looking for the feelings behind the words.

Some simple rules for listening are:

1. Use eye contact by looking directly into the eyes of the person who is talking.
2. Respond to what the person is saying so he or she knows you are listening

Responding to someone isn't as easy as it sounds. Let's do a skit to show you how deflating it can be to talk without a response.

HINT: Two PSE volunteers stand face to face. One begins to tell the scarey story that follows. The other uses eye contact, but says nothing until the team member who is telling the story gives up.

First Version of the Scary Story

I was driving home from the meeting last night — you remember how dark it was last night — when I noticed that the same headlights had been behind me for some time. I began to watch them and sure enough, every time I turned, the headlights stayed with me. My heart began to pound. I turned off the radio. It was a very dark road. I drove faster. Then I looked down and realized my gas gauge read empty. I yelled, "No!"

I was nearer my home street now, but I didn't know if it would be wise to have whoever was behind me follow me home. I felt panicky, but decided to race for home. I tore around the corner and down the street. (Storyteller says to the other team member, "Are you listening?" Team member snaps back, "Oh, sure." Storyteller says sadly, "Never mind. I'll tell you later!")

Now, we are going to replay the situation and the listener is going to respond. Look for the difference. (Responses will be in parenthesis.)

Second Version of the Scary Story

I was driving home from a meeting last night — you remember how dark it was last night? (really dark) I noticed that the same headlights had been behind me for some time. (No kidding!) I began to watch them and sure enough, every time I turned, the headlights stayed with me. (Someone was following you?) My heart began to pound. (Mine's pounding now.) I turned off the radio. I was on a very dark road. (Oh-oh!) I drove faster. Then I looked and noticed my gas gauge read empty. (no!) That's what I yelled, "No!"

I was nearer my home street now, but I didn't know if it would be wise to have whoever was behind me follow me home. (Oh, I'm glad you thought of that, but what did you do?) I felt panicky, but decided to race for home. (OK!) I tore around the corner (Yes!), down the street (Yes!), opened the garage, tore inside, slammed on the brakes, and closed the garage door. (Whew!) On wobbly legs, I went inside and looked out the window to see if the car was there . . . (Was it? . . . Was it there?) Yes, it was there! (No!) But it was my next door neighbor coming home from her meeting. (Your next door neighbor . . . Oh, wow! I bet you almost cried from relief!)

> HINT: The above script was written to give you an idea of how to present this idea. It may not be effective if read verbatim. The point is to respond so the person telling the story knows you are listening. Use appropriate body language along with the words of response.

What difference do you feel there was between the story with no response and the one with responses? (class discussion) We're going to pair you off and give you a chance to practice responding.

Activity F — Tell a Scary Story and Respond

(Divide class into pairs.) Decide which one of you will tell a story and which one of you will respond. You can make up the story or tell something frightening that really happened to you. Think of something to use for your story. Questions to answer are: Where is this taking place? Are you alone? Are you inside or outside? Is it light or dark? What is happening that is frightening?

Storytellers, think of your story. Listeners get ready to respond. We will give three minutes for the story and one minute warning before time is up. Ready...begin!

> HINT: *Assist students who have difficulty thinking of a story. Encourage them to choose three scarey elements for their story. One choice could be the dark. Then ask "what is going on," "what goes wrong" etc. Give the class three minutes with a one-minute warning. Then, switch roles (responder tell story, storytellers respond), and repeat for three minutes.*

Telling a scary story makes giving responses easy. What we want you to remember is the importance of responding while you are listening. Responding tells the person you are with them and are listening to their feelings.

Activity G — Lesson Ending

Today, we wrote cinquains about friends and friendship and then we practiced listening and responding. We will return your cinquains in the next lesson which will be in two weeks. Your bulletin board strip for next time is: To Have a Friend, Be One!

Between now and then we want you to do two things. Who can remember what one of them is? (Be good to yourself.) And what is the other one? (Be good to each other.) Be good to yourself and to each other.

_____ **Lesson 10** _____

Stealing and Teasing

Objectives

Stealing:
- The child will demonstrate his knowledge of the difference between borrowing and stealing.
- The child will state the reasons why people steal.
- The child will understand that stealing hurts both himself and the person from whom he steals.
- The child will understand that stealing decreases self-esteem, even if the person stealing is not caught.

Teasing:
- The child will state why people tease.
- The child will conclude that it is often best to ignore the person doing the teasing.
- The child will state that people will tease about things that are different (size, shape, abilities).
- The child will conclude the person who teases most of the time has low self-esteem.

Suggested Reading

Briggs, Dorothy Corkille. *Celebrate Your Self*, p. 94. "Every low and shaky self-esteemer lives with the basic belief: 'I am what I do.' Separate your person from your behavior, thoughts, feelings."

Dreikurs Rudolf M.D. *Children: The Challenge*, p.278. "The act of lying or stealing are symptoms of deeper underlying rebellion."

Background

These lessons were developed at the request of seven classroom teachers who had PSE during our first year. The teachers felt that these subjects are part of the everyday life of a student, and one more approach might help students understand and cope with them. We have used the format of a TV program. You may use any format you wish. However, it has been our experience that it is beneficial to avoid anything that even slightly resembles "preaching" as most students will switch their listening skills to "off."

The information in this lesson gives the individual child another resource in dealing with the temptations and challenges of growing up. Lack of awareness is the same as no choice. Teaching children not to be "victim" to the behavior of others is important. By adding to the individual awareness, we give children a new choice.

Materials

Scripts, Props for skits: box of soap powder marked "CLEAN" and a large box marked "washer," Two identical shirts (one dirty), Hats, Glasses, Mikes for TV show, Signs or name tags with character names, New bulletin board: (Use the two Poem Charts from Activity D and F.)

Activity A — Review Lesson 9

Last time, you wrote a cinquain about friends and friendship. We have chosen three cinquains to share with you. (Read three cinquains from students.) It was fun to read what you wrote and we are giving these to your teacher so he/she can enjoy them, too. Maybe you will do some more cinquains as a class.

Activity B — Stress Reduction Exercise (read verbatim)

Whenever you are upset and want to calm down, a simple way to do so is a breathing exercise. Please look into your lap and keep your head down. Draw air in through your nose and let it out through your mouth. Do it very slowly. Let's practice together. Breathe in through your nose, and breath out through your mouth. Breathe in through your nose and breathe out through your mouth. Breathe in slowly through your nose, and out through your mouth. Nose . . . in, mouth . . . out. (Repeat several times.) Now stop. When you are ready, please look at me.

Activity C — Introduction of Lesson on Stealing and Teasing (read verbatim)

> *HINT: PSE volunteers will act out this skit. Visible name tags or signs assist in defining different characters.*

Tammy: In other years, we talked about tattling and cheating. Today, PSE-TV will take you to our studios to cover the important subjects of stealing and teasing. First a commercial, then to our PSE studios. Come in, Connie Commercial.

Connie: Boys and girls, we have a new miracle wash powder for you today. It is our new, outstanding, cleaning product. We took CLEAN (show box) to the National Laundry Contest and won first prize. Now for our demonstration. Here we have a very dirty shirt . . . grease spots, chocolate, even bubble gum stains. We place it in the washer (box with word "washer") with some of our spectacular wash powder CLEAN. We will return during our next commercial break and check on the cleaning power of CLEAN!

Activity D — Compare Stealing to Borrowing

Tammy: Good morning (afternoon) boys and girls, this is your very own Tammy-Tell-It-Like-It-Is here to bring you school news. We are broadcasting live from (school) in (teacher's name and grade of class) grade classroom. Today, we will discuss the difference between stealing and borrowing. Let's go to Olive-on-the-Spot and the kids in the classroom to ask, "What is the difference between stealing and borrowing?"

Olive: Olive-on-the-Spot here. Tell us kids, what's the difference between borrowing and stealing? (Stealing is taking something without permission. Borrowing is done with the intention of giving it back.) Thank you kids. But why do people steal? (want something, can't pay for it, to show off or act big, for the challenge, excitement.) Thank you kids. Now back to Tammy.

Tammy: Thank you Olive! Our researchers have put together a list of examples from real life. Would you and your kids in the classroom be willing to decide whether each example is borrowing or stealing?

Olive: How about it kids in the classroom. Would you like to make it into a game?

HINT: Some classes respond better if you simply tell them, "We are going to play a game!"

Olive: OK, if you think the example I read is stealing stand up. If you think the example is borrowing, stay seated. (Write "stealing — stand, borrowing — sit" on the chalkboard. Some classes have used thumbs up and down.) Remember . . . we all know that people make mistakes, so no one needs to laugh if someone makes a mistake. Ready, here's the first one:

1. Joe took a cookie from Tom's lunch tray. Is he borrowing or stealing? (stealing)

HINT: Under some circumstances, this could be either. Have one student who thinks it is borrowing explain why. (intention)

2. Carlos asked if he could use Todd's bike; he forgot to bring it back on time. (borrowing)

207

3. Sam takes his brother's T-shirt out of the drawer. (stealing)

4. You ask your mom if you can take her scissors. (borrowing)

5. John picked up the pencil up from Wong's desk. (stealing)

6. You take a library book without signing it out. (stealing)

7. You put candy in your pocket at the market. You do not pay for it. (stealing)

8. You ask your neighbor to use his skateboard for an hour. (borrowing)

Tammy: Thank you, Olive and kids in the classroom! This week we have two winners in the poem-of-the-week contest, and the first one goes to Nellie Nurd for this little ditty:

> If you like to take things
> That don't belong to you,
> You may end up behind bars
> And it won't be at the zoo!

Nellie will be sent a month's supply of CLEAN, the miracle cleaner. Let's check back with Connie Commercial and see how the miracle soap has worked. Connie?

Connie: Here we are, back at the washer demonstration. May I remind you that this laundry soap won first prize as the best stain remover of all laundry soaps. So, the exciting moment is here, where we demonstrate the removal of grease, chocolate, and bubble gum stains. TA-DAH!

HINT: PSE Volunteer playing Connie holds up second shirt which is dirtier than the first. Without looking at the shirt, she continues to talk about the greatness of CLEAN — until kids let her know something is wrong.

Oh, My! Back to the studio. . .(Looks at shirt in disbelief.)

Tammy: Thank you, Connie, ah, let's go on. . .Today, boys and girls, we have a special studio guest, Doctor Knows-A-Lot. Dr. Knows-A-Lot is here to give you the latest research data on what stealing does to the person who steals. . .Welcome, Doctor.

Doctor: Thank you, Tammy. Fact: There is an enormous amount of stealing going on in the world. Research shows many people have not been told what is going on when they choose to steal. My concern is with the fact that people are choosing to hurt other people. You need to realize: If you steal something, you are hurting someone because that's what happens.

Tammy: How does that apply to us, Doctor?

Doctor: For instance, let's say your dad owns (name of a local store) store. I remind you that not just one person, but many people are stealing from this store. In fact, your dad had to hire undercover people to walk around the store trying to catch people stealing. In order to put merchandise into the store, your dad had to buy it. If people steal an item, he spent money he won't get back. If many people steal, it might mean you and your family would not be able to buy something you need. Also, prices on other items will increase. Your father may need to raise the prices to help cover the loss on the things that are stolen. Doing that hurts the people who have to pay more to buy things at the store.

Activity E — Effect of Stealing on Thief

Tammy: That helps. Does stealing have any affect on the thief?

Doctor: I'm glad you asked that, Tammy. Our research shows that stealing has a great affect on the thief. Deep down inside each of us we have two. . .we'll call them invisible charts. If I may use your board, I'll illustrate. (Doctor draws a large happy face.) One chart says, "I like myself." (Draw a sad face.) The other says, "I don't like myself." Even if you get away with stealing — let's say, a candy bar — and no one knows you took it except you, deep down inside of yourself you put a mark on the "I don't like myself" side. (Illustrate on the board.)

If, as you grow up, you put many marks on this side, you will begin to feel badly about yourself. As you know, from all you've talked about in PSE, how you feel about yourself or your self-esteem is the key to doing well in school — making friends, being happy, and being able to care about others. The point isn't whether I think you are a good or bad person, but how you feel about yourself.

Tammy: That's very interesting, Doctor, but I have a question: If you get a mark on your "I don't like myself" side, can you erase it?

Doctor: The answer is YES! You can erase it. We are all making mistakes as we grow. We learn from our mistakes. In the case of stealing: When you give something back, pay for it, or tell the person you are sorry, you are admitting your mistake and doing something to patch it up. This DOES erase the mark from the "I don't like myself" side. (Demonstrate on the board.)

Tammy: Thank you, so much, Dr. Knows-A-Lot.

So, we have clearly seen, that there IS a difference between stealing and borrowing. The difference has to do with asking permission. And, we have seen that even though stealing hurts other people, the person who gets hurt the most is the thief. We are going to switch now to Pamela Problem-Solver who will join the kids in the classrom to talk about TEASING.

Activity F — Define and Give Reasons for Teasing

Pamela: Wonderful, Tammy. I am really impressed with these (name of school) kids. Their sharing is teaching us a great deal. Kids in the classroom, we need to ask you a few questions. First, what is teasing? We usually know when it happens to us, but how would you define teasing? (bother, irritate, annoy, bug) Why do you think people tease? (as a put-down, for revenge, for fun, to get a response, to make someone notice you, sometimes its' just a habit because you don't feel good about yourself) Thanks, kids. Now back to Tammy...

Tammy: Pamela, thank you. We have another studio guest, Tilly Teased-A-Lot. Hello, Tilly. I hear you get teased a lot, do you?

Tilly: Yes

Tammy: What do you do when you get teased?

Tilly: Oh...I chase the kids...or call them names...or scream, "You stop that!" Sometimes I tell the teacher or my mom.

Tammy: Do you ever ignore them?

Tilly: I did once, but they kept on teasing.

Tammy: Do you think if you always ignored them that it would get boring to tease you?

Tilly: Well, I guess so...

Tammy: The truth is, the only people who get teased are those who are fun to tease. People who tease to hurt do not feel good about themselves. Tilly, we can also communicate our feelings to the teaser. Let's go back to Pamela Problem-Solver and the kids in the classroom to make a list of some topics used for teasing.

Pamela: OK, Tammy. Now, kids in the classroom, we don't want to embarrass or hurt anyone's feelings so we ask you not to name names or give any specific examples. What types of things do people get teased about? (being tall, being short, being fat, being skinny, having glasses, or braces, having big ears, nose, etc.) If you are ever teased, we hope you will remember:
1. What do you know about the person who always teases other people?
2. Does that person feel good about self? (no)
3. Does the person who teases have high or low self-esteem? (low)
4. Do you care what the person who doesn't like him/her self thinks about you? (maybe do, maybe don't)
5. What is the best way to handle being teased? (ignore it)
6. Everyone is special, right? (right)
7. Why are you special? (There is no one just like me.)
8. If there is no one just like you, there are differences. What kind of person will tease people about their differences? (low self-esteemers)
9. Are differences OK? (yes)

Therefore, if you have something obvious which is different about you, someone...somewhere...sometime may tease you about that difference. Ignore them. It's OK to have differences. We need to learn to talk to each other. Thanks kids, you've helped a lot.

Tammy: Wonderful, just wonderful. Thanks from me too, kids. Our second case of CLEAN the new laundry magic goes to Marvin Mushmouth for this enlightening poem:

> If you do not talk straight
> Use teasing without end
> You'll damage someone's feelings
> And might even lose a friend.

Thank you reporters and kids in (teacher and grade level) grade class. We have learned a great deal about stealing and teasing. We will leave these two winning poems with you to help remind you of these two important subjects. While we are gone, we want you to make a list of ten ways to be good to yourselves and ten ways to be good to each other.

We'll see you in two weeks. Meanwhile, be good to yourself and to each other.

———————————————— **Lesson 11** ————————————————

Review: Final Lesson

HINT: The content of the final lesson is your choice. Listed below are suggestions devised by PSE teams.

Suggestions For Lesson

1. Go over students' papers "ten ways to be good to yourselves and ten ways to be good to each other." Write their ideas on the chalkboard or butcher paper so the class will have its own list.

2. Ask students to fill out and hand in an evaluation form. (The master for this form is at the end of the chapter.)

3. Use topics from previous PSE lessons and/or the evaluation in this lesson and do the following:

   a) Write the topics on pieces of paper for a drawing.

   b) Place the topic sheets in boxes labeled number one, two and three.

   c) Ask students go to their groups.

   d) Have a member of each group choose a topic slip.

   e) Get the whole group to work on a skit that demonstrates the topic on the slip. Optional: Have props and costumes available for use.

   f) Ask the group to perform the skit for the entire class.

   g) Discuss the point of the lesson demonstrated at the end of each skit.

   h) Repeat if time permits.

4. Hand out "I Am Special" awards. Be certain to give one to the classroom teacher. (The master for this award may be found at the end of the chapter.)

5. Form small groups and check goals.

6. Refer back to Lesson 12 of the 2/3 PSE program for additional activity suggestions.

7. Closing

HINT: Each PSE volunteer may take a line or one person may say the entire closing

---

We've enjoyed our year with you.
Thank you for all your sharing throughout the year.
Have a wonderful summer.
Each and every day, remember to
    Be good to yourself
    and to each other.

Suggested list of topics: Introduce Self Using Positive Adjective; Valuing Differences; Goal Setting; Giving and Receiving Compliments; Smileys; Magic Glasses Story; Pioneer Game; Stress Reduction Exercises; Memorizing Something; Feelings Change; High/Low Self-Esteem Behavior; Qualities You Want in a Friend; Listening and Responding; Stealing; Teasing; King Kong/Doormat/Assertive Behavior; Broken Record; and Harmony.

Name _____

Teacher _____

Goal Setting

Set reachable goals.
Write out steps for reaching that goal.
Keep going until you reach your goal.
Give yourself a reasonable time limit.
Evaluate — check your progress.
Compliment yourself.

My goal is _____

4		
3		
2		
1		

Name _____

Teacher _____

Learning The First 15 Presidents of the U.S.

To learn Presidents 11-15:

1. Washington . . . . Whales
2. Adams . . . . Always
3. Jefferson . . . . Juggle
4. Madison . . . . Mice and
5. Monroe . . . . Monkeys

6. Adams . . . . Ants
7. Jackson . . . . Jump
8. Van Buren . . . . Very
9. Harrison . . . . High
10. Tyler . . . . Trees

11. Polk . . . . P_____
12. Taylor . . . . T_____
13. Fillmore . . . . F_____
14. Pierce . . . . P_____
15. Buchanan . . . . B_____

To learn Presidents 11-15:

1. What animal starts with P? (ponies, pigs, polar bears, pelicans, etc.)

2. What does the animal do? Keep it silly — make a crazy sentence.

3. Take a picture in your mind. Learn the names for the letters and memorize.

To remember all the Presidents from 1 to 15:

You are learning the Presidents in groups of five. Now you need to have some way to remember the first word in each group.

1. Take the first word in each of the three groups (Whales, Ants, and your animal).

2. Make a silly picture. For examples, see a whale shooting ants out of its spout and (a polar bear) catching them. Stack the animals or keep them in some sort of order to remember them in order. Each word in your picture starts a new section.

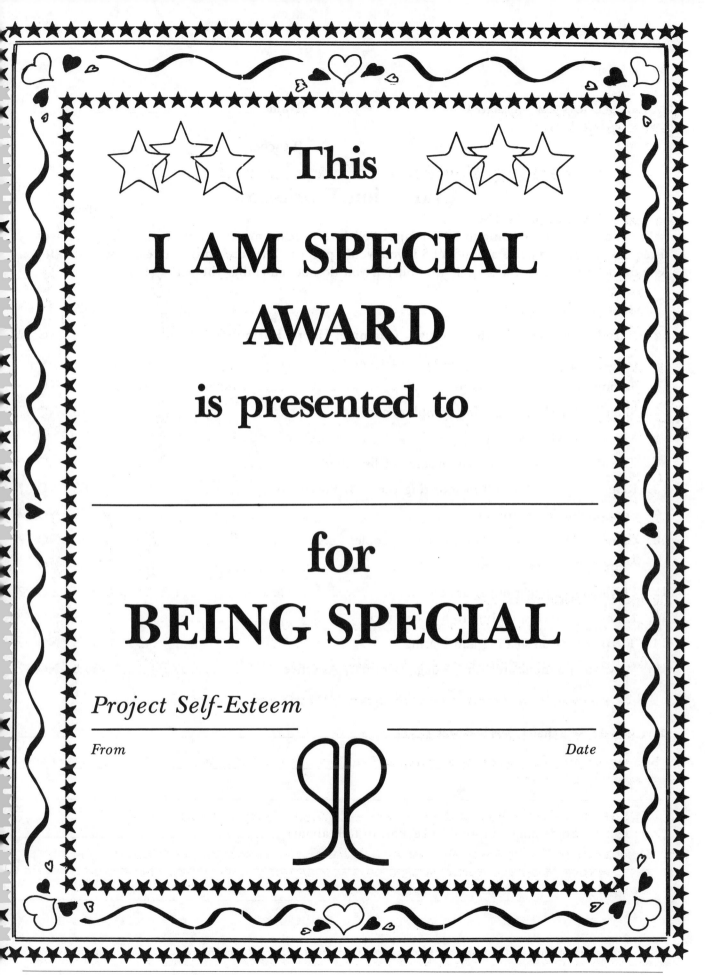

Name _____

Teacher _____

Evaluation Worksheet

Pretend that you are going to be a Project Self-Esteem team member next year. Read each activity listed below. Draw a circle around YES if you would put it in a lesson. Draw a circle around NO if you would not put it in. Draw a circle around ? if you do not remember the activity.

1. Bulletin board sentences . . . . YES   NO   ?

2. Introducing yourself with a positive (example: Happy Harmony) . . . . YES   NO   ?

3. Describing the world if we were all alike . . . . YES   NO   ?

4. Setting goals in small groups . . . . YES   NO   ?

5. Smileys (giving and getting compliments) . . . . YES   NO   ?

6. The Magic Glasses story . . . . YES   NO   ?

7. The Pioneer Game (the importance of listening) . . . . YES   NO   ?

8. Remembering a list and memorizing the U.S. Presidents . . . . YES   NO   ?

9. Stress reduction exercises . . . . YES   NO   ?

10. Charts with high and low self-esteem people . . . . YES   NO   ?

11. Name That Lesson Game . . . . YES   NO   ?

12. Playacting (acting out situations) . . . . YES   NO   ?

13. Listening and responding to a scary story . . . . YES   NO   ?

14. TV program on stealing and teasing . . . . YES   NO   ?

15. Ways to communicate: King Kong, Doormat, Assertive . . . . YES   NO   ?

The PSE Lesson that I like best was _____

_____

_____

Comments: (Something you would like PSE to talk about) _____

_____

_____

Chapter

Grade 5

_____ Lesson 1 _____

Realizing Your Uniqueness

Objectives

- The child will introduce him/herself using a positive adjective.
- The child will interview and introduce one classmate to the group.
- The child will list qualities of low and high self-esteem.
- The child will review Goal Setting steps.
- The child will discuss goal setting in terms of being a better listener.

Suggested Reading

Nelson, Jane. *Positive Discipline,* p. 42. "We should always remember to look for and appreciate the many ways each individual is unique."

Background

It is easy to recall failures because we often tend to focus on what's wrong with us, what we aren't doing well, or how we are not successful. PSE teaches children to focus on successes and to learn from mistakes.

Materials

Harmony, Small piece of writing paper for each child, Chart with success questions, Goal Setting steps   (see Activity E),   New bulletin board strip: Set Reasonable Goals for Improving Your Self-Esteem

Activity A — Volunteers Introduce Themselves, the Program, and Harmony

Welcome to another year of Project Self-Esteem! Raise your hand if you've had PSE before. What is self-esteem?   (how you feel about yourself)   If you feel good about yourself, how will it affect your life?   (more friends, do better in school, be happier, etc.)

We are your PSE team. From now until May   (or the last month of PSE),   we will be coming into your room every other week. I am Mrs. (say your last name).   Each of the PSE volunteers will say their name and tell you one special fact about themselves.

*HINT: Take your time and be sure your introduction is clear. Add
a personal comment or two if you choose.   (My children go to this
school, etc.)*

We are going to be seeing you during this year to talk about self-esteem, so let's
be sure you know what PSE is all about. What do you think Project Self-Esteem is
about? (learning things that assist you in feeling good about yourself) A person
who feels good about him/herself learns more and is happier. We choose to come
here and share this information with you because we care about you and your difficult job of growing up.

(Bring out Harmony.) Welcome Back, Harmony! It's great to see you again!
(Harmony talks.) You missed the students since you were here last year, and you're
excited about learning new ideas this year? We are, too, Harmony. By the way, for
those of you who are new, Harmony is a graduate of PSE. He's a bear who assists us
with our lessons. (Harmony whispers.) Harmony says he knows you played the
game in grade 4, and he wants to learn all of your names, so he wants us to play it
again. Let's do!

Activity B — Positive Adjective Name Game

You may remember the name game. (Pass out paper.) You will pick a positive
adjective that starts with the same letter as your first name — then you may write
down more than one adjective plus your name, and you will circle the one you like
the best. For example, Scott might write: special, super, sensitive and super-
califragilisticexpialidocious. If he likes Special Scott best, he would circle that one.
If you played in fourth grade, why don't you take the PSE challenge and use a different adjective from the one you chose that time. Take a minute to think of an adjective — a positive, complimentary word — to put with your name. Write your ideas
on the paper being given to you. Raise your hand if you are unable to think of one.

*HINT: It saves time if the PSE team creates a list of possible adjec-
tives to go with each letter of the alphabet. Remember to keep the
adjectives in this lesson positive. Give each child a small piece of
paper on which to write the adjectives. Have each child circle the
adjective and name he/she would most like to hear. Students will
take these papers to their group.*

*Begin with the PSE volunteers and go around the room, allowing
each person to say a positive adjective with his/her name. Begin
with the words, "I am . . . (Perky Peggy)."*

If you hear giggling or resistance say something like, "Some of you might feel embarrassed about doing this. Maybe it's hard to give yourself a compliment in front of others. We ask you not to add to that embarrassment with giggles or comments."

Thank you for playing the name game again. Keep your paper for later. PSE wants you to learn to be comfortable in feeling good about yourself. Giving yourself compliments is one way to do that.

Activity C — Students Practice Listening Skills

(Bring Harmony back.)   Harmony says he's Happy Harmony.   (Harmony talks.) Sometimes, he's not happy, and sometimes Harmony says he doesn't even like himself. Everyone has times like that, Harmony. Sometimes we get so busy criticizing ourselves, we forget to compliment ourselves about the many things we do that work well. (Harmony talks.)   Are we going to do the positive adjective and your name again? No. This time, we are going to play a game that requires two important skills: listening and talking.

You will be divided into groups and given partners. All you need to do right now is to listen. You and your partner will be given some time to share a recent success. A success is something you did that you feel good about. It may be something big and exciting or something small that you just feel good about. The important thing is that each of you really listens when your partner is talking because you are going to introduce your partner to your group and tell his or her success story. Stay with me now. Here are the rules. You will share a recent success. Each of you will ask your partner these three questions:

Success Questions
1. What happened?
2. What are three facts about the incident?
3. How did you feel about it?

So, you will each think of a recent success. One person will start, and the other will assist by asking these questions. (Point to chart with three questions.) Then, you will introduce your partner to the group. Watch as we illustrate how you are going to do this.

HINT: Volunteers A and B demonstrate the procedure. A will share a recent success while B listens. B will then turn to the group and introduce A in this manner: "This is . . .   (positive adjective plus name). She cooked a dinner using her new microwave oven. She was very nervous because company was coming to dinner and she wanted everything to turn out just right. Cooking with a micro-wave oven is different from cooking in a regular oven. One more scary thing was that she was using a new recipe. The dinner turned out wonderfully and she felt both proud and happy."

Remind the students of the importance of group support in both comments and body language. There is to be no snickering, side comments, or negative body language.

> 1. *The four PSE volunteers will scatter around the room.*
> 2. *As a team member's name is called, she raises her hand and leaves it up until she has her entire group. Remind students to go quietly to groups, and to take papers on which they wrote their adjectives.*
> 3. *The classroom teacher may preselect the groups so they are balanced. Otherwise, count off to select groups.*
> 4. *The groups may sit on the floor or move desks into a cluster. This choice depends upon classroom space.*
> 5. *The purpose in establishing groups is to provide each child with a significant other with whom to share.*
> 6. *It is important to bond this or any group when it first meets. This is accomplished with an activity that is personal and includes everyone. Establish your group rapport at the beginning of the group work.*
> 7. *Have group members repeat their adjectives and names, say how many brothers/sisters they have, or share their favorite dinner. Please do not eliminate group work!*
> 8. *Show your group the three questions to be used as guidelines.*
> 9. *Allow two or three minutes for partners to interview.*
> 10. *Then ask each student to introduce his/her partner to the group. Have the student introduce his/her partner with the circled positive adjective and name.*
> 11. *When all the students have had a turn, chat with them until each group is finished.*
> 12. *Then have the students return to their regular seats. It is wise to dismiss each group, one at a time, to keep the noise level down.*

Activity D — Looking at Low and High Self-Esteem Qualities

If you had the 2/3 PSE program, you did something similar to what we are about to do. We have a different point to make, so do stay with us.

223

Close your eyes or look down at your desk. Think of someone you think has high self-esteem. You will not share who this person is. Open your eyes. Thinking again about this person with high self-esteem, tell me one quality you admire in that person.

> *HINT: On the chalkboard or butcher paper, put the word "High" at the top and list all the qualities given by the students. Be certain to add the word "listens" to the list as you will need it for a later example. Begin another list with the heading "Low" at the top. Using the "high" self-esteem list, create a list of qualities in a person with low self-esteem. There is a tendency to condense this exercise by saying, "Obviously, a low self-esteem person has the opposite qualities." To the low self-esteem person, it is not obvious. Specific words set specific standards.*

Activity E — Setting Personal Goals for Enhancing Self-Esteem

As you look at the "low" self-esteem list, you might find one or more qualities that you, yourself could improve. Speaking for myself, there is more than one quality on this list I could improve. Too often, we feel embarrassed that we aren't perfect. No one is perfect. If you have one or even a lot of qualities on this list which you could improve, it does not mean you have low self-esteem — it means you can begin here, working to improve these to feel even better about yourself.

Remember in the fourth grade, we talked about setting goals? What is a goal? (Something you want to reach or attain.) In PSE we have six steps for setting goals. Can anyone think of one of these steps?

> *HINT: The goal setting steps are **not** to be given to the students in order. We suggest you write them on separate strips of poster board and put Velcro on the back of each strip. Attach Velcro to a chart-size poster board. Present the steps to the class out of order. Then let the students put them in order as they are discussed. Put them on the chart one at a time.*

Goal Setting
Set a reachable goal.
Write out steps for reaching that goal.
Keep going until you reach your goal.
Give yourself a reasonable time limit.
Evaluate — check your progress.
Compliment yourself.

Let's say you choose how well you listen as a reasonable goal to improve. (Point to the first step.) Next, you would need to write down two or more ways you might improve how well you listen. What's one way I could improve listening to others? (Pay attention, ask questions, use eye contact, etc.) Can someone think of another way I could improve my listening skills? (class response) A reasonable time limit might mean I check myself in a week to see how I am doing as a listener. I know that mistakes are the way I learn, so I keep going, and I compliment myself for improving my listening which helps my self-esteem. You might have noticed I said the steps are slightly out of order — these steps are just guides for you. You can skip one step or change the order and still reach a goal. The important thing to remember is to take goals as little steps to getting what you want for yourself.

When you decide to improve your self-esteem, use the goal setting process to give yourself more self-esteem.

Activity F — Discuss Bulletin Board Strip

We are leaving behind this sentence: Set Reasonable Goals to Improve Your Self-Esteem. It will remind you that you can do something to feel better about yourself.

Activity G — Stress Reduction (read verbatim) and Lesson Ending

If you had PSE in grades two and three, you know we included a stress reduction exercise in each lesson. What is stress? (anything that causes tension or anxiety) What do you think the word reduction means? (to make smaller or lessen) So stress reduction exercises are designed to assist you to lessen the feelings of stress you might have.

Today we are going to breathe deeply for our stress reduction exercise. Watch me and please wait for your turn. Slowly, take air in through your nose. When you think you have enough, take some more — and hold it. Then, making an appropriate noise, let your air out all at once.

Look down at your desk while you are doing this exercise with me. Together, in through your nose . . . and take a little more air in . . . hold it . . . now all at once, let the air out. Be still and quiet. Together, again.

> *HINT: This simple process can assist children in learning to calm down. Encourage the teacher to do this prior to an exam. Repeat the breathing process three or four times.*

We'll be back again in two weeks. Meanwhile, be good to yourself and to each other.

_____ Lesson 2 _____

Goal Setting and Memorizing

Objectives

- The child will contribute to a class discussion about the bulletin board.
- The child will review goal setting steps.
- The child will learn one way to memorize.
- The child will set a goal to memorize eleven states and their capitals.

Suggested Reading

Krueger, Caryl Waller. *Six Weeks to Better Parenting*, p. 296. "As soon as children are able to stand back and look at themselves to see where they need to improve, they set appropriate and often demanding goals for themselves. A child who has realized what needs to be changed is well on the way to making that change."

Background

Teaching children to set goals during their learning process helps them learn to manage their time effectively and reach their goals. Teaching children how to memorize enables them to creatively learn material and retain it for far longer periods of time.

Materials

Harmony, Goal Setting sentence strips and chart from Lesson 1, Flash cards for eleven states (see Activity D), New bulletin board strip: Eleven states and their capitals (see Activity D)

Activity A — Stress Reduction Exercise (read verbatim)

We are going to do a stress reduction exercise. All you need to do is listen. Sit up tall, but comfortably — feet flat on the floor. Make a fist with each hand as tightly as you can. Now tighten all the muscles in your lower arms, upper arms, and shoulders. Keep those muscles tight as you tighten your chest, stomach, and now all the muscles in your legs. Pull every muscle as hard and tight as you can. Make your face and forehead muscles tight. Tighten the muscles in your eyes, mouth and jaw. TIGHT! TIGHT! TIGHT! Now, all at once, relax. Breathe.

In your mind, tell your muscles to relax. Tell your forehead and eyes to relax. Tell your chin and neck to relax. Say relax to your shoulders, your arms and your hands, your chest, your stomach, and the lower part of your body. Tell your legs to relax and say relax to your feet. Just sit still and notice how wonderful it feels to feel relaxed.

Activity B — Review Bulletin Board Materials

We are going to review your bulletin board sentence from last time: Set reasonable goals for improving your self-esteem. Let's see what you did with the sentence we left for you last time.   (Give lots of positive reinforcement).

Activity C — Review of Lesson 1 and Goal Setting

Last time we were here we talked about how important it is to encourage ourselves. When you compliment yourself and share your successes with your friends, you feel better about yourself. What happens when you feel better about yourself?   (do better in school, make friends more easily, take appropriate risks, are happier, etc.)

We learned that people with low self-esteem are just learning to figure out some things that a high self-esteem person already knows. The good news about this is you can help yourself to have higher self-esteem. One way to raise your self-esteem is to set goals and work to improve something you don't do very well. Remember, we worked on being a better listener, last time.

Let's begin by getting the steps for setting a goal onto our chart. Who can think of one step?

> *HINT: Use the same goal setting sentence strips from Lesson 1.*
> *Put the strips on the chart, out of order. Let the students help you*
> *unscramble the steps. When you are finished, the steps should be*
> *in order on the chart.*

Activity D — Goal Setting and Memorizing

Here's Harmony! (Harmony talks.)   Harmony says he is going to night school so he will be a wise and smart bear. That's wonderful, Harmony, but what's your problem?   (Harmony talks to volunteer.)   Oh, he's having trouble remembering all the things he needs to learn for school. Raise your hand if you sometimes have trouble memorizing all the information you need to know.   (Wait for class response.)   At some time in our lives, remembering things can be a problem for all of us. Today's lesson will assist you with learning to memorize quickly and easily. You go over with   (volunteer's name)   and listen with the class, Harmony.   (Hand Harmony to volunteer.)

Let's say you are given the assignment to learn all the states and capitals in the USA, and to do so in two weeks. That could be an awesome task — unless you use the goal setting steps.

HINT: For the following exercise, use the chalkboard, butcher paper, or poster board. Write the steps for accomplishing this specific goal large enough for the whole class to see.

What is the goal?   (to learn the states and capitals in two weeks.)   Let's write down the steps for reaching that goal. How many days do you have?   (fourteen)   We want to be realistic, so out of those fourteen days, how many would you use to study?   (probably ten days if you take out two weekends)   So you will be studying for ten days. How many states are there in the USA?   (fifty)   Ten days, fifty states, how many states will you need to learn each day?   (five)   Now your task is not so awesome. You might decide to learn six or seven states and capitals a day so you don't put a lot of stress on yourself just before the test.

Today, we are going to look at one new way of learning information and most importantly, remembering it forever. Most of the time, we sit in school trying to memorize things by just learning them. Sometimes that works and sometimes it doesn't. Research shows us that "just memorizing" something doesn't last very long. Most of us are not using our creativity in the process of learning. Today you are going to learn to be a creative learner so you can have fun learning things forever!

HINT: It is effective to use flash cards for this part of the lesson. Prepare the flash cards ahead of time using pieces of poster board or large index cards. Handprint a state on one side and the state's capital on the other.

Use two different colors of marking pens — one color for each side. This color differentiation will assist visual learners. The states to be learned and their capitals are listed below. Use them throughout Activities D and E.

**States and Capitals for
Flash Cards and Bulletin Board**

Harrisburg, Pennsylvania	Nashville, Tennessee
Little Rock, Arkansas	Frankfort, Kentucky
Concord, New Hampshire	Springfield, Illinois
Topeka, Kansas	Hartford, Connecticut
Salt Lake City, Utah	Jefferson City, Missouri
Columbus, Ohio	

If you had PSE in the fourth grade, you remember that the capital of Pennsylvania is Harrisburg. (Write Harrisburg and Pennsylvania on the chalkboard or use a flash card.)

Who can remember the video picture we created to assist you in remembering Harrisburg, Pennsylvania? Let's do it one step at a time. What's the first part? (an iceberg covered with hair) That isn't exactly Harrisburg, but hairyburg is close enough to trip your memory into remembering Harrisburg. What comes after an iceberg covered with hair? (a really huge pencil pointing to the iceberg) Remember to make the pencil giant size so it is unusual; your memory will remember the unusual easier. This giant pencil has what running up and down it? (large veins) Stay with me...what is the pencil writing on the iceburg? (the word "ya") Let's go back to the beginning. See a hairyburg, which is Harrisburg. A pencil with veins, writing ya is Pencil-vein-ya. (Wait for groans and class chatter.) You're right, it's silly. Because it is silly, your mind will remember it. Using our hands to illustrate the words, let's do it together. (Put both of your hands together, prayer style, and then push them away from you making a circle and rejoining.) Hairyburg which is Harrisburg, (make a cylinder moving down from right to left) Pencil (wiggle your fingers all through the area where you previously drew the pencil) Vein (script the word "ya") Ya. Now, think of the picture you just created with the hairy iceberg, the giant pencil filled with veins and the word "ya." Using the video camera in your mind, take a picture of that silly picture. What's the capital of Pennsylvania? (Harrisburg) Harrisburg is the capital of which state? (Pennsylvania)

Let's remember another state and capital. Watch me. Think of this picture: A pile of little rocks on top of an ark. An ark is the kind of boat that Noah took lots of animals on in the Bible. Again, lots of little rocks are piled onto an ark. The ark is rocking back and forth on a pile of saws. Reading it from the top you have: Little Rock, Ark-in-saws. Little Rock is the capital of Arkansas. Let's act it out with our hands, (both hands together, fingers wigglng downward) Little Rock... (hands together with palms up, moving away from each other and back again) Ark... (right hand over left hand, wiggling fingers) in Saws.

HINT: Please don't be concerned if you don't understand these directions for hand illustrating the words. The point is to create a picture for the visual learners, to feel it for the kinesthetic learners and to have some fun. Create your own visual picture with your hands.

Remember to use your video camera to take a picture of this silly picture you have created. Close your eyes. Take your picture. All together now... (using your hands to illustrate) Little Rock, Ark-in-saws. (Use the appropriate flash card.) What's the capital of Arkansas? (Little Rock) Little Rock is the capital of which state? (Arkansas)

Let's see if we can do one together. The capital of New Hampshire is Concord. (Write Concord, New Hampshire on the chalkboard or use the appropriate flash card.) What picture do you think of or see when I say the the word Concord? (grapes or someone might say the Concord jet) Sometimes, we can use a picture or symbol for a whole word. In this case, we can use the Concord airplane for the whole word, Concord. New can be something new. Breaking Hampshire into small words, what do you get? (Ham. Sure.) Put what you have together: The Concord jet landing on a new slice of ham...for a sure landing. Sculpture it with your hands as we do it (Let each child do his/her own sculpture.) Take a video of the jet landing on a new slice of ham for a sure landing. See the plane land safely. Look at me, please. (Show flash card.) What's the capital of New Hampshire? (Concord.) Concord is the capital of which state? (New Hampshire.)

(Use flash cards.) What's the capital of...careful now...Arkansas? (Little Rock) How about...Harrisburg is the capital of which state? (Pennsylvania) And last but not least, what is the capital of New Hampshire? (Concord) If you had trouble remembering these states, relax. Go back and take your picture again then practice seeing your video. This is a new way of learning. Some of you will catch on to it faster than others — which has nothing to do with smart or dumb, just the way you learn.

Activity E — Group Work on Creating Mental Videos for States and Capitals

When I finish talking, you are going to move into the same groups we had the last time we were here. When you get into your groups, you will be given two states and capitals. We want you to make a video picture for each of your states. You will discuss your ideas, vote on the one your group wants, and choose one person who will share your idea with the whole class. Your PSE group leader will assist you with this.

> HINT: Move students into groups. Remember to bond the group before you begin. You might ask if they could see the videos in color — and reassure those who didn't have color that some people do, some don't. Show your group only one state at a time. Show both the state and capital. Say the state and capital for them and use the appropriate flash cards. The group leader should be given the flash cards ahead of time. Begin discussing pictures you might get to remember each segment of both words. Go slowly, encourage enthusiasm, discourage "inappropriate" thinking by simply saying, "Remember, this is a classroom. Let's not ruin this fun."

If several suggestions come up for one segment, have the group vote on the one it wants to share. Build a picture, sculpture the picture with your hands, video tape the picture, and choose one person to tell the whole class at a later time. Repeat the process with the second state. Be sure you have some ideas for each of your states, in case your group can't get one.

Divide the list in the following way:

Group A
Topeka, Kansas
Salt Lake City, Utah

Group B
Columbus, Ohio
Nashville, Tennessee

Group C
Frankfort, Kentucky
Springfield, Illinois

Group D
Hartford, Connecticut
Jefferson City, Missouri

Activity F — Sharing Group Work with Entire Class

HINT: The object of this session is to reward each group for its efforts, and to begin the process of the entire class learning these eight states and capitals. Have one person from each group share one state and capital, then have a time for sharing each group's last state. Encourage the child sharing to give the state and capital, sculpture the solution with his/her hands, and create a picture for the class to follow. It is harder to think these than to share them, so be patient and assist wherever possible.

Once the picture is created, have the class take a video. After four states have been shared, ask the whole class either the capital or the state of those given.

Sometimes, someone will say this process of memorizing takes longer than just learning them. That might be true, and research shows us that what you memorize this way will be remembered longer. Besides, doing this will teach you to create video pictures for learning everything you want to know in school and in life.

HINT: Have students share the remaining four states and capitals with the class. Follow the same procedure as before.

If you review these videos in your mind several times before we return, you will know them for life. We will see how many you remember when we visit you in two weeks. Harmony says he will be excited to see what you have learned.

Activity G — Bulletin Board and Lesson Ending

Your bulletin board strip this time is the eleven states we learned today: Harrisburg, Pennsylvania; Little Rock, Arkansas; Concord, New Hampshire; Topeka, Kansas; Hartford, Connecticut; Springfield, Illinois; Frankfort, Kentucky; Columbus, Ohio; Nashville, Tennessee; Salt Lake City, Utah; and Jefferson City, Missouri. When you have some extra time, check to see if you remember your video, then test yourself. We will learn some more states next time.

We'll see you in two weeks. Meanwhile we want you to do two things. . .what are they?   (Be good to yourself and to each other.)

_____ **Lesson 3** _____

Goal Setting and Compliments

Objectives

- The child will review a memorization technique.
- The child will think of a video picture for memorizing two new states and their capitals.
- The child will write out a goal and the steps for achieving that goal.
- The child will write a compliment about two family members.
- The child will make a list of things he/she does well.
- The child will practice giving a compliment to a class member.

Suggested Reading

Padovani, Martin. *Healing Wounded Emotions*, p. 112. "There can never be enough affirmation. If there is a balanced amount of it in anyone's life, self-esteem is nourished and this person in turn can nourish others."

Background

Goal setting provides children with specific means of managing their lives and their own self-improvement. The challenges of life can be overwhelming. Goal setting is one means of bringing life into manageable increments. When one accomplishes a goal, he/she can be more capable. When we feel capable, we feel more lovable.

Learning to feel comfortable about complimenting others and acknowledging one's own worth are invaluable steps towards a higher sense of self-esteem.

Materials

Harmony, Goal Setting sentence strips and chart from Lesson 1, Goal Setting worksheet for each student, Two half sheets of paper per student for compliments, A piece of paper for each student for the list of things he/she does well, a Smiley for each student, New bulletin board strip: Juneau, Alaska and Austin, Texas

Activity A — Stress Reduction Exercise (read verbatim)

Today, we are going to do a stress reduction exercise. All you need to do is follow my words. Sit up tall, but comfortably—feet flat on the floor. Make a fist with each hand as tightly as you can. Now tighten the muscles in your lower arms, upper arms, and shoulders. Keep those muscles tight as you tighten your chest, your stomach, and now all the muscles in your legs. Pull every muscle as hard and tight as you can. Pull your face and forehead muscles tight. TIGHT! TIGHT! TIGHT! Now all at once, relax. Breathe.

In your mind, tell your muscles to relax. Tell your forehead and eyes to relax. Tell your chin and neck to relax. Say relax to your shoulders, your arms and hands, your chest, your stomach, and the lower part of your body. Tell your legs to relax and say relax to your feet. Just sit still and notice how comfortable it feels to be relaxed.

Activity B — Review of Lesson 2

Harmony is with us today.   (Harmony talks.)   He says he has a cousin who lives in the capital city of Missouri, and he can't remember the name of that city. Can anyone tell Harmony both the capital and the video picture you used to remember that city?   (class response: Jefferson City.)   Let's review the other states we learned and go over the video picture for each state.

> *HINT: Using your bulletin board list of states, ask for volunteers to recall the picture of each state and its capital. Keep this section moving at a lively pace to prevent boredom. Include Harmony and have him respond with lots of nods, paw clapping, etc.*

We are going to add two states to this list. As a class, or individually, we want you to think of a video picture for these states. We will ask for your ideas, next time. The new states are: Austin, Texas and Juneau, Alaska. Thank you—and thank you, Harmony.   (Harmony waves.)

Activity C — Learning to Set a Goal

Do you remember the goal setting steps we discussed in the last lesson? Let's put the steps in the correct order.

> *HINT: Show chart with goal setting steps on it, out of order. Go over the process of putting the steps in order on the chart very quickly. The students will be familiar with these steps.*

Now, think of some goal you'd like to work on. A piece of paper is being handed to you.   (Pass out Goal Setting worksheets.)   Write your name on it. After the phrase "My goal is" write the goal you'd like to achieve.   (Pause.)   Beginning at the bottom of the ladder, put your finger on step number one. What is the first step you might take in order to accomplish your goal? We are going to give you a few minutes to write the four steps you could take for achieving you goal. Write one idea on each step of your ladder. If you need assistance, raise your hand.

> *HINT: Allow two or three minutes.*

Goal setting has a lot to do with self-esteem. When you achieve a goal, you feel better about yourself. Look at your goal sheet and see if you can start to work on the first step towards achieving your goal. We will ask you about it next time.

Activity D — Lovable and Capable Are Self-Esteem Feelings

Every single person needs to feel lovable and capable. If we think of it as standing on two legs   (draw the character below), then we understand how important it is to stand on both legs.   (Point to the character you've just drawn.)

HINT: The lovable, capable character looks like this:

A person who does not feel lovable — which means loved by someone, somewhere, just because you exist — will often become the perfectionist, the over-achiever, the person who is never able to do enough. PSE is not against working hard and doing your best. Not feeling lovable is different. It has to do with never relaxing or being satisfied, and with trying to do your best for the wrong reason.

The person who does not feel capable — which is to be able to do something well — will be the people pleaser. This person will try to get along with others at any cost. If you are a people pleaser, you are trying to win friends, rather than just having friends because you are who you are. Being friendly and caring about others does not mean you are a people pleaser. Again, it has to do with trying too hard and not valuing you for you.

The object is to learn enough about yourself and how to feel safe in life so you stand on two legs — so you feel lovable and capable. The things we are sharing with you in Project Self-Esteem are designed to assist you with being balanced in feeling both lovable and capable.

Activity E — Reviewing Compliments

As we said earlier, people who set goals and reach them feel good about themselves. Another part of high self-esteem is giving and receiving compliments. What is a compliment? (When you say something positive about someone that is true.) What response can you give when you receive a compliment? (Say, "Thank you" or return the compliment.)

We are giving you two pieces of paper. You will need a pencil or pen with which to write. I want you to think of one person in your family to whom you wish to give a compliment. It can be your mother, father, brother, sister, aunt, uncle, grandma, grandpa, or cousin. Write the first name of that person in the middle of the top line of one of your two pieces of paper.

On the other piece of paper, write the name of a second person in your family you want to compliment. You will be giving these notes to the people, so be certain your compliments are true.

We want you to begin each compliment with the word "I." Instead of saying something like, "You are a good friend," say "I really like talking to you." Begin your compliment with the word "I" and be sure your compliments are true. You may write as much or as little as you want. When you are finished, please wait quietly.

HINT: The low self-esteem person finds it difficult to accept compliments. Compliments may be superficial, nonspecific and impersonal with "you" messages. When the sender starts with the word "I," he/she tells the receiver: This is a specific message from me and it belongs to you. The receiver might refute a general statement, but cannot so easily challenge a personal opinion. For instance, a child remembering an unkind deed done the day before, might refute the "you" message, "You are kind," but is more likely to accept "I noticed you helped your brother, thank you."

Allow two minutes for each compliment. At the end of two minutes say, "You have two minutes left, begin your second compliment now." At the end of two minutes say, "Take one more minute to finish either of your compliments."

Now comes the really difficult part. Can anyone guess what that part might be? (class response: Remembering to give it to each of the two people.) Who has a suggestion for one way you might remember to take these home and actually give them to the appropriate person? (class response: Put the papers inside of your notebook, etc.) Why don't you take a minute to put these papers in a place that will help you to get them home.

Activity F — Feeling Capable

In order to assist with feeling capable, you are going to recall some of things you do well. A piece of paper is being handed to you. On this paper, you will write: "I (blank) well." Then you will make a list of things you do well. Remember, you will be sharing what you write with the class. Our focus is on what you do — your capable side. (Allow time for participation.) Please look over your list and circle the one for which you would most like to be complimented. When you go to your groups, please take this paper with you.

Activity G — Group Work

We are going to move you into your groups. Watch your leader and please do not move until she calls you.

> HINT: Have a Smiley for all of the children. The group leaders can give each child in their group a Smiley. Discuss the capable item circled on each student's paper. Have students exchange their Smileys along with an "I" compliment. If a student starts to say, "You . . ." stop him or her. The students need to begin the compliment with the word "I." For example, if one person's paper says, "I'm a good kicker," another student might say, "I like the way you made that goal today."

> Remind the students not to throw the Smileys into the air and catch them. Return students to their seats when each group is finished.

Activity H — Lesson Ending with Bulletin Board Strip

Today we talked about using mental videos to remember things we want to know. We talked about giving and receiving compliments. For next time, you have two states and capitals to learn; these are your new states for your bulletin board: Juneau, Alaska and Austin, Texas. Keep going over these states and capitals so you will remember all of them. Also, remember to start working on your own special goal. We want to talk about them during the next lesson.

We'll see you in two weeks. Meanwhile, be good to yourself and to each other.

_____ **Lesson 4** _____

Listening

Objectives

- The child will say the names of two states and their capitals.
- The child will try to name all the states and their capitals presented so far.
- The child will discuss an individual goal and steps taken to achieve that goal.
- The child will name ways to improve the classroom.
- The child will listen carefully during the Space Game.

Suggested Reading

Krueger, Caryl Waller. *Six Weeks to Better*

Parenting, p. 85. "Learning to listen and follow directions bring a child success at school, at home, and later in his career. Listening is a developed art, one that we can teach ourselves and our children."

Background

Most of what needs to be taught to children may be done so in the atmosphere of fun and excitement. Interest is higher when children enjoy what they do, thus retention is greater. Teaching basic skills through a game is an effective way to reach children.

Materials

Harmony, Goal Setting worksheet for each student, Signs for the Space Game (see Activity D), appropriate costumes and props for the Space Game, New bulletin board strip: Think What You'd Hear If You Listened More Often.

Activity A — Review Bulletin Board Strip from Lesson 3

Last time, we left you a bulletin board strip with two more states to learn. Austin is the capital of Texas. Is there a volunteer to share his or her mental video with the class? (Wait for class response.) The second state is Juneau, Alaska. Is there someone who wants to share his or her idea for learning this state? (class response)

> *HINT: Have the student explain the mental video and act it out with his/her hands. Repeat the idea for the class and have the class join you in sculpturing the ideas. Repeat this process for both states.*

Is there anyone who wants to take the PSE challenge which is to name the capitals of *all* the states we have discussed? (class response)

HINT: It is fun to encourage children to learn by providing a measurement of accomplishment. If a child misses a state, say, "Almost! maybe next time. Is there someone else who thinks he/she knows all these states?" When one child is successful, stop the procedure and repeat at another time. After three children try unsuccessfully to name all the states, invite the class to continue working on them for a PSE challenge at another time.

Activity B — Review Individual Student Goals from Lesson 3

During the last lesson, we handed out goal setting sheets and each person wrote down a goal along with the steps toward reaching that goal. Would anyone like to share the results?

HINT: Don't spend more than five minutes on this. If no one volunteers to share, discuss some of the ideas the class had written down.

Activity C — Sharing Goals to Improve Classroom

We are going to talk about one goal you, as a group, could make to improve your classroom. I don't want to hear specific names, or anything that blames anyone for anything. This is not about embarrassing someone. It is about working together to improve the quality of your classroom. What is something all of you could do to improve how this classroom works?   (Wait for class response: Get in line more quickly and quietly, move to groups with less noise, don't talk so much, raise hands before talking, etc.)

HINT:
1)   Make a list of possible group goals to improve the classroom. Include the classroom teacher.
2)   Move the class into groups.
3)   Choose one goal, discuss some steps that the class could do to reach that goal. Discourage specific comments which name or infer a certain person is responsible for the problem. Say, "We're talking about something each one of us can do to improve this classroom."
4)   Pass out Goal Setting papers.
5)   Have students list the steps.
6)   Choose a group representative who will report to the whole class.
7)   When each group is finished, have the students return to their individual seats.

One person from each group is going to come up front and report to the class the goal their group selected and the appropriate steps for reaching that goal.

HINT: Have each of the four people share their group's goal and steps. Discourage negative comments from the class. If another group picked the same goal, have each report and note any differences in their steps.

Have the class vote on the one goal they choose to work on as a group. Review the goal and steps towards reaching that goal. Give the goal papers to the teacher and thank the class for their ideas.

Activity D — Practice Listening Skills with the Space Game

Raise your hand if you remember the Pioneer Game in fourth grade. (class response) We will play a similar game today. You will be divided into five groups. Each group will be given a word and a response for that word. When you hear your group's word, you are to respond as a group. Let's begin with the word for the whole classroom. Whenever I say the word "Earth," all of you will point to the ground and shout together, "That's where we live!" Let's do it together. We live on planet Earth. (class response) There are millions and millions of people on Earth. (class response) OK, let's give you your parts for the game.

HINT: Divide the class into five groups. Tell each group its word and the group's response. Have them practice their part one time. It is sometimes helpful to have a sign for each group, indicating its part. The word and response for each word is listed below.

Words for the Space Game

Group #1 —	Space Voyager —	"That's us!"
Group #2 —	Shuttle —	"Chooo!" (with air in the ooo's)
Group #3 —	Space Station —	"Mmmmmmmmmmm." (deep sound in back of throat)
Group #4 —	Afraid —	"Red alert! Red alert!"
Group #5 —	Attitude —	"You can if you think you can!"
Whole Class —	Earth —	"That's where we live!"

Whenever you hear me say the name of your group, you will say your part. You need to LISTEN so your group stays together. Let's do a practice sentence. LISTEN CAREFULLY! We are going to read a story about a *space station* (pause) that has a *shuttle* (pause), *space voyagers* (pause) and travels a long way from *Earth* (pause). The *space voyagers* (pause) are not *afraid* (pause); their *attitude* (pause) is A-OK.

Now we are going to listen to a story using all of these parts. Pay attention! If you follow your neighbor and he or she gets lost, what will happen? (class response)   The success of this game depends upon how well you listen.

Space Game

It is the year 2050. You are a **space voyager.** You are getting into a **shuttle** to travel from **Earth** to a **space station** where you will live. You are not **afraid.** Your **attitude** is A-OK.

You, the **space voyager,** are in the **shuttle** now, moving away from **Earth. Earth** gets smaller and smaller as you move toward the **space station.** You are still not **afraid.** Your **attitude** remains A-OK.

Suddenly, your **shuttle** starts to spin. The **shuttle's** computer goes berzerk. Your fellow **space voyagers** are **afraid.** You are **afraid.** You don't know where **Earth** or the **space station** are. Your **attitude** begins to slip. Your **attitude** will make the difference. Even though you and the other **space voyagers** are **afraid,** you don't panic. You remember to push the electrical overload button. The **shuttle** stops spinning. You and your **space voyagers** can see **Earth** and the **space station.** You kept your **attitude** A-OK and you could think about what to do. You arrive safely at your **space station.**

HINT: If time permits, change parts and repeat the story. Be sure to promote the idea that mistakes are the way we learn, and support the idea of encouraging each other.

Activity E — Stress Reduction Exercise   (read verbatim)

That game was lots of fun. We are going to do a simple exercise to relax and slow our engines from so much fun. Look down at your desk. Slowly begin to take air in through your nose . . . hold it at the top . . . and let it out all at once, through your mouth. With me . . . in . . . hold it . . . let it out. Again: in . . . hold it . . . let it out. Once more: in . . . hold it . . . let it out. Now tighten every muscle you can, every muscle in your whole body, tight, as tight as you can. Don't forget your head and face muscles. TIGHT! TIGHT! TIGHT! Now all at once, let go and . . . relax.

Breathe in, filling your body with air . . . hold it . . . now, gently let it out. Sit quietly for a minute and just be relaxed. (Wait for one minute.) Look at me, please.

Activity F — Lesson Ending

Today, we talked more about memorizing by using mind videos. We talked about our class goals and steps to take to reach those goals. We LISTENED and played the Space Game. And, finally, we relaxed.

Your bulletin board strip for next time is: Think What You'd Hear if You Listened More Often.

We'll see you in two weeks. Meanwhile, be good to yourself and to each other.

———————————————— **Lesson 5** ————————————————

Communication Skills

Objectives

- The child will learn stress reduction breathing exercises.
- The child will identify anger as a second feeling.
- The child will practice changing "you" messages to "I" messages.

Suggested Reading

Kalab, Jonah and Viscott, David M.D. *What Every Kid Should Know*, p. 56. "A friend is someone who knows what is really important to you because you are close enough to him to share your feelings, dreams, and plans with him. Without friends, people often grow up feeling left out and spend their lives wondering if something is wrong with them. Often, they become adults who feel they don't belong."

Rubin, Theodore Isaac M.D. *Reconciliation — Inner Peace in An Age of Anxiety*, p. 59. "We human beings do not communicate automatically and telepathically, no matter how much we love each other. We MUST tell each other how we feel and we must struggle in order to communicate effectively — that is to give straight messages.

Background

Anger can be an overwhelming feeling that seems to come upon us without any other visible emotion. The truth is some emotion usually precedes anger. Being able to identify the primary feeling as frustration, fear, helplessness, disappointment, etc. enables one to work with an upset situation and not play victim to it. Learning to work with anger instead of denying it will produce a far healthier generation of human beings.

Project Self-Esteem teaches children to communicate with "I" messages instead of blaming and judging with "you" messages. If people learn to communicate clearly and listen to each other, we will have more caring in the world. Also, self-esteem is enhanced with solid communication skills.

Materials

Worksheet for listening game, Worksheet on anger as a second feeling, Harmony, New bulletin board strip: "You" Messages Are War Words.

Activity A — Review of Lesson 4

The last time we were here, you voted on a goal you could work on as a group to improve the class. Does anyone remember what the goal was?   (Wait for class response.)   What steps have been taken towards reaching your goal?   (class response)

> *HINT: Don't spend more than five minutes on this. If the class hasn't started working on the goal, just encourage them for coming up with the idea.*

You also practiced listening skills with a Space Game and that was fun! We learned that listening is an important skill. The PSE team would like to invite you to write a listening game for Lesson 9. When you are finished, you can give the story to your teacher.   (Pass out listening game worksheets.)   This sheet will help you format your story.

When you write your story, first determine six key words — one for each of the five groups and one for the entire class. Make up a statement or a sound for each key word. Be sure to use each key word in the story several times. We really look forward to reading your stories!

> *HINT: Set up an appropriate due date with the teacher. A week should be enough time. Be sure to review the stories before using them! Ask the teacher to collect them, look them over if desired, and then give the stories to the PSE team. Run extra copies of the listening game worksheet to have available in case any students misplace the sheet and ask for another. It might take several reminders, depending on student workload or interest.*
>
> *Some ideas for story topics are: Going on a Treasure Hunt, A Story about Pirates Whose Ship Sank. Topics can also be used from the current Social Studies unit: The Civil War, Famous Explorers, etc. Write these on the board.*

Activity B — Stress Reduction Exercise (read verbatim)

Whenever you are upset and want to calm down, a simple way to do so is a breathing exercise. It is easy and it works. Please look down into your lap. Draw air in through your nose and let it out, very slowly, through your mouth. Do it with me: breathe in through your nose, and breathe out through your mouth. Slowly now — in through your nose, and out through your mouth. Nose . . . in, mouth . . . out. Nose . . . in, mouth . . . out. (Repeat several times.) Now stop. When you are ready, please look at me.

Activity C — Introduce Anger and Upsets as a Second Feeling

Sometimes you or your friends are angry or upset. Being angry or upset can get in the way of thinking clearly, enjoying yourself, and making appropriate choices. One way to understand anger is to realize that some feeling usually comes before the feeling of anger. Let's take a look at that idea and see if we can understand anger as a second feeling.

A small child is playing in the yard. Suddenly, the child darts into the street — just as a car is coming. Brakes squeal and the car stops. The mother rushes out, picks up the child, and begins scolding him. She looks very angry. How do you think the mother felt before she began scolding the child? (frightened, panicky, helpless)

The PSE team is going to pantomime some situations from real life. You are to decide what is the feeling that comes BEFORE anger.

> HINT: Use the same PSE volunteer to get angry in each sentence or skit. Devise one "angry look" (frown, hands on hips) to be used in every skit. One PSE volunteer will read the situation, the other(s) will pantomime.

1. You are all dressed to go somewhere special with your friend and that friend calls to say he/she can't go. You feel angry. (PSE member gives an angry look.) Hold it! If you were this person, what would you feel first? (disappointed)

2. You are trying and trying to find your sneaker. You look everywhere. Your friends, who are waiting to go to school, are getting impatient. You act angry. (Give an angry look.) Hold it! If this were you, what would be your first feeling? (frustration)

3. Your teacher announces he/she had no sleep last night. The class is noisy and restless. Some people are giggling. The teacher acts angry. (Give an angry look.) Hold it! What did the teacher feel first? (tired)

4. Someone on the playground calls you a name. You act angry. (Give an angry look.) Hold it! What feeling came first? (hurt, helplessness, embarrassment)

5. Your friends laugh at you when you make a mistake. You act angry, but what did you feel first? (embarrassed, frustrated, hurt)

> HINT: Write the following on the chalkboard.

First Feeling

disappointment
frustration
fatigue
embarrassment
hurt
helplessness
            then . . . anger

You are going to do a worksheet to practice discovering which feeling might have come before the feeling of anger. When you get your sheet, please put your name and teacher's name at the top. Number one reads: "Clare is having a birthday. She does not invite Maria. Maria seems angry. What did she feel first?" There is a line on which to write what you think Maria's first feeling was.

Put your finger on number four. This one says "My teacher got angry with me (or the class) when..." There is space to write down a time when your teacher got angry with the class or with you. Below, it says "My teacher's first feeling was..." and there is a space in which to write what you think his/her first feeling was. Any questions about how to do this worksheet? Raise your hand if you have a question. Do your own work, please. (Wait four or five minutes depending upon the class.)

We are going to go over number one, two, and three together. Who wants to read number one and say what you wrote? (student response) Who wants to do number two? (student response) Who will do number three? (student response)

Now we are going to pair you off so you can share the rest of the worksheet with a partner. Watch me as I tell you who your partner is. (Pair off class, and allow students four minutes to share.)

HINT: Do NOT share numbers 4-6 on the worksheet as a class.

Activity D — Changing "You" Messages to "I" Messages

When two people are upset with each other they often start using war words. (Bring in Harmony.) Hi, Harmony! (Harmony waves to class then talks to PSE volunteer.) You want to know what a war word is? (Harmony scratches his head.) War words are usually messages that begin with the word "you" and say something negative such as, "You nerd," "You bum," or "You are selfish."

The problem with war words is they do not communicate what's really bothering you. If someone starts firing war words at you, what do you usually do? (send war words back) Now you have two people feeling defensive who are blaming each other and who are not communicating. Nothing will get solved this way.

You see, Harmony, instead of saying "You are selfish," begin with the word "I." For example, "I want a turn, too!" Let's change some "you" messages to "I" statements.

> 1. "You never listen!"
>   I _____ (I want you to listen
>   to what I am saying.)
> 2. "You jerk, you wrinkled my paper!"
>   I _____ (I'm upset that my
>   paper's wrinkled. Please be more careful!)

How are you doing with changing "you" to "I" messages, Harmony? (Harmony talks.) You think you are catching on but you are not sure? Let's practice some more. (Harmony claps his paws.) Turn your worksheets over. I will write a "you" message on the chalkboard. You will change it to an "I" message and will write the "I" message on your paper.

1. You are always late, Dummy! (I don't like being late so I want you to be on time.)

2. You took my bike without asking! (I want to be asked before you use my bike.)

3. You nerd, don't call me a brace face! (I don't like to be teased, please stop.)

4. You're so inconsiderate. You haven't given my record back. (I want my record back today, please.)

> *HINT: It might save time to put the examples on large cards to show to the class. In most classes, it would work to say the sentence a couple of times and have the students change it to an "I" message.*

Let's go over these sentences so you can share how you changed the "you" to an "I" message.

> *HINT: Take as many examples for each of the four sentences as time will allow.*

It is easy to give a disguised "you" message. "I think you don't listen" starts with the word "I." It is still a "you" message. How could you say "I think you don't listen" using an "I" message? (I want you to listen.) Beware of disguised "you" messages!

Do you have something to say, Harmony? (Harmony talks.) Harmony just said, "I think you are a great class." Oops! He also wants to remind you not to disguise a "you" message as an "I" message. What could Harmony say instead of "I think you are a great class?" (I like the way you listen.) I understand Harmony's "you" message now. Thank you, Harmony.

Activity E — Lesson Ending

Today, we talked about anger as a second feeling. We also practiced changing "you" to "I" messages.

Your bulletin board strip says: "You" Messages Are War Words.

We'll be back in two weeks. Meanwhile be good to yourself and be good to each other!

_____ **Lesson 6** _____

Working with Anger

Objectives

- The child will learn that anger is a natural part of being alive.
- The child will learn to calm down by slowing down his/her breathing.
- The child will review that anger is a second feeling.
- The child will write and destroy an angry letter.

Suggested Reading

Zimbardo, Philip G. and Shirley Radl. *A Parent's Guide to the Shy Child*, pp. 116–118. "Children need to express strongly-felt emotions.

If a child is not free to express anger outwardly towards the rightful target, the anger may get misdirected and turned in on the child in the form of lower self-esteem."

Background

Children deal with a multitude of frustrations. If they are given information and practical experience about how to deal with frustrations, upsets, and anger, they will be less likely to become destructive to society or to themselves.

_____

Materials

Harmony, Lined paper for letters, Trash bags, New bulletin board strip: Find an Appropriate Way to Handle Your Anger.

Activity A — Relaxation Exercise (read verbatim)

Frustrations, upsets, and anger are a natural part of life. These feelings often collect and gather inside of us until we explode over something that's really quite small in scope. Do you remember, in second and third grade, the story about Sam's balloon? Who can tell me what happened?   (class response: Sam got upset about lots of little things all day long, and he didn't say anything about the way he felt. Finally, when Chris forgot his mitt, Sam blew up and got really angry.)   The story of Sam's balloon had a point. Who remembers the point of that story?   (class response: If you don't take care of little irritations and upsets, they build up inside until you explode with huge anger.)

Today, we will be talking about some appropriate ways to release your anger. One thing we know is that people breathe differently when they are upset than when they are calm. Often, when you are upset, you breathe from here.   (Put your hand just below the neck to indicate short distance from nose to hand.)   You might sound like this.   (Exaggerate with short wheezing sounds.)

Your body needs oxygen to stay healthy. One thing you can do for yourself when you feel upset is to slow your breathing down and fill your body with oxygen.

Please put your feet flat on the floor, hands in your lap or just hanging to your side.

Now, take in air slowly, through your nose...slowly inhale...take in more air...hold it...and let the air rush out of your mouth. Let it all out. Don't be afraid to let the air make a sound as it rushes out of your mouth. We're going to repeat that whole process several times; be sure to stay with my words. The object is to slow down your breathing and fill your body with air.

Take air in through your nose...slowly...hold it...all at once, let it out.   (Repeat this process four to six more times.)

Whenever you are upset or nervous, stop! Control your breathing. Calm down. Then you can deal with the situation better. Stretch your arms...look up here...and we'll continue with our lesson.

Activity B — Review of Anger as a Second Feeling

In our last lesson we talked about anger as a second feeling. PSE told you that there is some other feeling that usually precedes the feeling of anger. If you suddenly rode your bicycle into the street, a car screeched its brakes, and your mother ran out to angrily scold you...what feeling do you think she would have felt before the anger? (class response: Fear.)   If you were excited about going to some concert, you had saved your money to go, and your friends went to get tickets...only to find the concert was sold out...you might act angry. What might have been your first feeling? (class response: Disappointment/frustration.)

Anger seems like a feeling over which there is no control and about which you can do nothing. Looking for the first feeling is a way for you to look at your anger and decide what to do about it.

Activity C — Writing and Destroying an Angry Letter

Let's bring Harmony out and see what he's doing today. My goodness, you look really angry. (looking at Harmony)   You look like you feel...well, what's happening? (Harmony talks.)   You're too angry to talk. You realize if you keep your anger inside, it will build up and you may go BOOM, just like Sam did...and you don't want to explode. We don't want you to explode either, Harmony. I have an idea which might help. I'm going to include the class so they will learn how to deal with anger in a new way.

While a piece of paper is being handed to you, begin to think of a time you felt really upset or angry. You are not going to share this time with anyone, so let your thoughts roam around until you find something that was really upsetting for you.

HINT: Give each child a piece of lined paper.

Write on one side of this paper, "I felt really upset or angry when..." Take a few minutes to write down some of the details of your upset. You will not hand in or share the information from this paper, so make these notes to help you remember the situation.

HINT: Give the class two minutes to make these notes.

What you are going to do is to write a letter about your anger. You are going to write the letter to the person involved in your anger. When we tell you to do so, you are going to tear up the letter. This is an exercise on releasing angry feelings, not about actually talking to someone about your anger.

There are four steps to keep in mind as you begin to write your angry letter.

HINT: Write the words on the chalkboard:
Anger
Your First Feeling
Concern or Fear
Forgiveness and Friendship

Let's say, just as an example, that I was really angry at a friend for not showing up for a lunch date that we had made. Using the steps, I might write: I'm really angry that you didn't show up for lunch. I thought I could count on you. I hate it when people don't do what they say they are going to do. I really hated sitting there by myself and finally having lunch all alone.

Now, let's look at the first feeling.   (Point to the chalkboard.)   At first, I felt nervous because I didn't know what to do. Then, I felt disappointed and hurt. Then I felt angry.

Let's look at the concern or fear.   (Point to the chalkboard.)   I was afraid that you didn't like me anymore. I was afraid that if we made another appointment, you wouldn't show up again. I was afraid that I couldn't trust you anymore.

Let's look at the last feeling: forgiveness and friendship. (Point to the chalk-board.) I am really glad we are friends. I feel happy when we get to spend time together. I want to be friends with you. I guess anyone can forget a date, and it isn't the end of the world. I think I'll ask you if you are free for lunch next Tuesday.

These steps are to guide you while you write your letter. You do not need to use all of the steps. This is your letter. Do it your way. If writing about these ideas in the steps helps, use them. You are going to take some time to write a letter express-ing your anger about the situation you wrote on your paper. Use the back side of the paper to write your letter. Raise your hand if you need assistance. This exercise can really assist you, if you will give it a chance. Take some time...feel your feel-ings...and write your letters. When you are finished, fold your letter in half and sit quietly until everyone is finished. Please begin.

HINT: Some children may have trouble thinking of a situation, or may hesitate to participate. Encourage and assist to a point, and allow non-participation. A resistant child might be encour-aged to draw a picture about his/her feelings. (Whisper this suggestion or the whole class will want to draw a picture.) Be available for assistance, but do not walk around reading papers. This is private exercise. Please respect the students' rights. Allow eight to ten minutes, or until most of the class is finished. Give a two-minute warning before you end the exercise.

Here comes the fun part. Put down your paper. Now fold your paper in half. Hold the paper in between your two hands, like meat in a sandwich. Close your eyes or look down into your lap. Take a minute to relive what happened to you. This time see a different ending. See a happier ending with you and the person involved being friends. When you have finished giving your story a happier ending, put your papers down on your desk and just wait quietly. Do it now, please.

Hold your paper in your hand. Please stay with me. Altogether, tear your paper in half. Put these two pieces together. Altogether, tear the papers in half. Put the pieces together. Altogether, tear the papers in half. Put the pieces together. Altogether, tear the papers in half. Hold the pieces in your right hand and drop them into the bag when it is brought to you.

HINT: If PSE volunteers use trash bags, the pieces may be col-lected rather quickly. Discourage throwing the pieces around or tearing more than four times.

That might have been difficult or felt awkward to do for the first time. The point is to learn one more way to express your anger so it doesn't build up inside of you. Does anyone want to say anything about how it felt to do that exercise?   (class response)   Thank you. Sometimes, it helps to write and destroy a letter to take care of your anger.

Activity D — Lesson Ending and New Bulletin Board Strip

Today, we talked about releasing upsets and anger. We remembered how Sam blew up when he didn't talk about his feelings. We remembered that anger is the second feeling you feel, and that thinking about the first feeling helps you to feel less helpless. Finally, we learned to write and destroy an angry letter written to release feelings.

> *HINT: If students have turned in stories for the listening game to be used in Lesson 9, thank them. If you have had no response, encourage students to write stories. Remind them that the class will be using them for Lesson 9. You might want to go over some ideas for the stories. Have extra sheets with the sample format from Lesson 5 available to pass out to interested students.*

Your bulletin board strip will remind you of today's lesson. It says: Find an appropriate way to release your anger.

We'll be back again in two weeks to talk more about upsets and anger. Meanwhile, be good to yourself and to each other.

_____ **Lesson 7** _____

Handling Incoming Anger and Upsets

Objectives

- The child will review breathing as a means of calming down.
- The child will recall how to write an angry letter and destroy it.
- The child will learn that it is unnecessary to take on everyone's anger.
- The child will discuss different ways to communicate when upset.
- The child will discuss how to refrain from passing anger along to others.

Suggested Reading

Bedley, Gene. *Climate Creators*, p. 81. "Control needs to lie within, not be based on the external conditions that happen in our world."

Background

Anger. Resentment. Revenge. This unnecessary cycle results from an inability to deal with the anger that comes from around you. Children who learn to handle anger are more likely to respond to circumstances in a responsible manner.

Materials

Harmony, Basket or bucket, Rocks for Martha, New bulletin board strip: Don't Hang onto Anger.

Activity A — Relaxation Exercise (read verbatim)

We are going to begin our lesson with the same relaxation exercise as we did in Lesson 6. People usually breathe differently when they are upset than when they are calm. Often, when you are upset, you breathe from here. (Put your hand just below the neck to indicate short distance from nose to hand.) You might sound like this. (Exaggerate with short wheezing sounds.)

Your body needs oxygen to stay healthy. One thing you can do for yourself when you feel upset is to slow your breathing down and fill your body with oxygen.

Please put your feet flat on the floor, hands in your lap or just hanging to your side.

Now, take in air slowly, through your nose...slowly inhale...take in more air...hold it...and let the air rush out of your mouth. Let it all out. Don't be afraid to let the air make a sound as it rushes out of your mouth. We're going to repeat that whole process several times; be sure to stay with my words. The object is to slow down your breathing and fill your body with air.

Take air in through your nose...slowly...hold it...all at once, let it out. (Repeat this process four to six more times.)

Whenever you are upset or nervous, stop! Control your breathing. Calm down. Then you can deal with the situation better. Stretch your arms...look up here...and we'll continue with our lesson.

Activity B — Review of Lesson 6

Last time we talked about the importance of dealing with anger in an appropriate way. You wrote a letter and then you tore it into pieces.

These were the steps you followed in writing your angry letter: Anger, Your First Feeling, Concern or Fear, Forgiveness and Friendship.

Using the same example as before, I was really angry at a friend for not showing up for a lunch meeting that we had planned. Using the steps, I might write: I'm really angry that you didn't show up for lunch. I thought I could count on you. I hate it when people don't do what they say they are going to do. I really hated sitting there by myself and finally having lunch all alone.

At first, I felt nervous because I didn't know what to do. Then I felt disappointed and hurt. Then I felt angry.

I was afraid that you didn't like me anymore. I was afraid that if we made another appointment, you wouldn't show up again. I was afraid that I couldn't trust you anymore.

Finally, I decided I am really glad we are friends. I feel happy when we get to spend time together. I want to be friends with you. I guess anyone can forget a date, and it isn't the end of the world. I think I'll ask you if you are free for lunch next Tuesday.

When we wrote an angry letter, we remembered that the point in writing an angry letter is to relieve the stress of holding your anger inside. Today we are going to talk about anger and upsets that come into your life.

Activity C — Martha's Rocks

Today, we will talk about a second type of anger — when others are angry or upset with you. In your daily experiences, during your whole life there will always be some anger that comes into your life. Let's get Harmony out so we can talk about this idea. Hi, Harmony! (Harmony waves to the class.) It's nice to see you today. (Harmony talks.) What? You liked writing an angry letter because you feel much better. That's great, Harmony. Today, we have a story for you because we want to talk some more about anger and upsets.

HINT: You may want to choose a child who doesn't normally participate for this part. Use large, flat river rocks for this section. If rocks are not available, use books such as encyclopedias. The student may be given a basket, bucket, or other container for holding the rocks. Have one volunteer hand out the rocks or books, while another volunteer reads the story.

(Student's name)   is going to come up here and assist me. Just stand next to me for now. I want all of you to pay attention because I'm going to ask you for the point of the story when I am finished.

Our story has to do with a girl named Martha. The box next to me has lots of rocks. The rocks stand for the anger that is being directed towards Martha. The rocks stand for other people's anger.

One morning Martha got up and got dressed. Just as she was ready to go to breakfast, her brother stormed into the room, "Have you seen my favorite pen? There it is! You took it! Nothing is safe around here! You stay out of my room!" and he left before Martha could point out he had left the pen in her room himself.   (Give the student a rock.)   Martha walked into the kitchen, looked at her lunch and asked, "What kind of sandwich is it . . . oh, yuck! Egg salad again!" Her Mother snapped, "If you don't like what I fix, make your own lunch, young lady!"   (Hand the student a rock.)   On the way to school, Martha stepped off the curb right in front of a boy zooming along on his bicycle. "Watch where you are going, Moron!" the boy yelled.   (Give the student a rock.)   The person sitting in front of Martha at school said something funny. Martha laughed. The teacher scolded her.   (Give the student a rock.)   Later the teacher scolded Martha for not putting her name on her paper.   (Give the student a rock.)   During P.E., Martha's class was playing kickball. Her team had two outs and two people on base. Whatever Martha did would win or lose the game for her team. Martha kicked the ball as hard as she could — right to the pitcher. It was an easy out. Everyone groaned. "Why don't you play hopscotch or something simple," one boy snapped.   (Give the student a rock.)   Janet, Martha's best friend, had an argument with her brother before school, so Janet was cross with Martha at recess.   (Give the student a rock.)

Martha forgot her sweater on the playground at lunch so she ran back to get it. When she tried to get her place back in line, everyone yelled at her to get to the end of the line.   (Give the student a rock.)   Martha and her friend kept playing after the bell rang, so they had to run to get to class. The principal stopped them in the hall and scolded them.   (Give the student a rock.)   On the way home from school, Martha was thinking about something else so she took one step into someone's garden. That someone was standing right there. You guessed it, Martha got into trouble.   (Give the student a rock.)

Martha hasn't had a very good day so far. She's carrying a huge load of anger with her. (To the student) With that heavy load, do you think you could ride a bicycle? Do your homework? Have any fun? (class response) The truth is, you couldn't do anything well. (Take the basket or bucket full of rocks from the student. Ask the class to give the student a hand.)

What do you think the point of this story is? (class response) You can't do the things you are supposed to do and want to do when you are carrying around everyone else's anger.

Let's look at each thing that happened to Martha and talk about another way she might have handled it:

1. Martha could have called her brother back to tell him the truth.
2. Martha might have used different words about her Mother's lunch. Had she said, "Mom, please don't make egg sandwiches for me after today," there would have been no fight.
3. Martha scared the boy on the bike. When some people are frightened, they yell. Martha needs to watch where she is going, and not worry about the boy's anger.

> *HINT: Continue this process of discussing each of the events. Be sure that Martha takes responsibility for her actions, and discuss any appropriate ways she might release holding on to the anger of others.*

Activity D — Students Playact Stopping Anger

Today, we will take a look at not taking in all the anger that comes into your life. I will read the skit and then we will get some of you to bring it to life.

> *HINT: Read the entire scene. Select appropriate students to act out each part. Volunteer reads. Students pantomime the parts. Be sure the part of the dog is* not *given to a homely child.*

Joey forgot to take out the trash. His father was very angry with him. Joey was so upset that he left for school. When Rod came to get Joey for school, Joey was gone. Rod was very angry and he told Joey a thing or two when he saw him at school. Now Joey was even more angry. He stormed across the classroom only to trip on Margaret's sweater. Joey picked up the sweater and threw it on the floor again. Margaret yelled at Joey. Joey yelled at Margaret. Now the teacher began scolding Margaret and Joey. Sally laughed loudly. Now Margaret, Joey, and the teacher were glaring at Sally. Sally had brought her dog to school to use in a "how to care for your dog" talk. Sally's dog began to bark. All the children started laughing and the teacher was furious.

Activity E — Decide How Each Person Could Choose Not to Pass Along the Anger

Stop the action! Let's give our actors a hand. (class response) Now, I am going to line all these people up in the order they came into the story. We will discuss how each person might have chosen not to pass the anger.

1. Joey could have taken responsibility for forgetting to put out the trash and could realize getting into trouble is a possible consequence of not doing his chores.
2. Rod could have realized it was unlike Joey to leave him and asked what had happened.
3. After seeing Rod and Joey yell at each other, Margaret could have realized Joey had a problem. She might have talked to Joey rather than yelling at him.
4. The teacher, having seen everyone getting angry with each other, might have said, "I think we've had enough upsets in here this morning. Why don't we settle down and get on to more pleasant things."
5. People who laugh at other people do so because they don't remember to be kind. Sally could remember to be kind and not laugh at other people's problems.
6. The dog? Well...dogs are just dogs. The dog would probably still bark.

What we have discovered here is that each person made a choice whether or not to pass on the anger. When anger comes to you, you have the same choice. Will you pass it on or will you let it go? Now you realize the choice is yours.

Activity F — Relaxation Exercise (read verbatim)

Since we've had a lot of excitement today, we will end our lesson with a relaxation exercise.

Please close your eyes. If you don't feel comfortable closing your eyes, look down at your desk. Slowly begin to take in air through your nose...hold it at the top...and let it out all at once, through your mouth. With me...in...hold it...let it out.

Again: in...hold it...let it out. Once more: in...hold it...let it out. Now tighten every muscle you can, every muscle in your whole body, tight, as tight as you can. Don't forget your head and face muscles. TIGHT! TIGHT! TIGHT! Now all at once, let go and...relax. Breathe in, filling your body with air...hold it... now, gently...let it out. Sit quietly for a minute and just be relaxed. (Wait for one minute.) Open your eyes, please.

Activity G — Closing

> *HINT: If students have turned in stories for the listening game to be used in Lesson 9, thank them. If you have had no response, encourage students to write stories. Remind them that the class will be using them for Lesson 9. You might want to go over some ideas for the stories. Have extra sheets with the story format from Lesson 5 available to pass out to interested students.*

Your bulletin board strip today says: Don't Hang onto Anger. We will return in two weeks. Meanwhile, be good to yourself and to each other.

_____ Lesson 8_____

Communicating Assertively

Objectives

- The child will practice a stress reduction exercise.
- The child will learn there are three types of communicators.
- The child will experience the three different types of communicators through playacting.
- The child will learn and practice the Broken Record method of communicating.

Suggested Reading

Palmer, Pat. *Liking Myself*, p. 9. "Being a good friend to yourself means that you can STOP doing something you don't like."
Smith, Manuel J. *When I Say No, I Feel Guilty*, p. 74. "One of the most important aspects of being verbally assertive is to be persistent and to keep saying what you want over and over again without getting angry, irritable or loud."

Background

Extensive research indicates many individuals find themselves in undesirable situations because they do not know how to say no. Learning how to say no when you want to say no is the primary focus of this lesson. The Broken Record method of communication is a valuable tool for each of us to know and use.

Materials

King Kong, Doormat, Assertive chart (see Activity C), One piece of writing paper for each student, New bulletin board strip: Broken Record = Kind Statement Plus Policy Statement.

Activity A — Review Lesson 7

Last time we were here, we listened to a story and one of you held a basket (or bucket) until it was full of rocks. Do you remember what the rocks were for? (They showed the huge load of anger Martha carried.) We also discussed ways to communicate when you are upset. This will help you feel better and will help those people around you, too.

Activity B — Stress Reduction Exercise (read verbatim)

Whenever you are upset and want to calm down, a simple way to do so is a breathing exercise. It is easy and it works. Please look into your lap and keep your head down. Slowly draw air in through your nose and let it out, very slowly, through your mouth. Do it with me. Breathe in through your nose, and breathe out through your mouth. Breathe in through your nose, and slowly breathe out through your mouth. Nose . . . in, mouth . . . out. Nose . . . in, mouth . . . out. (Repeat the words a few more times.) Now stop. When you are ready, please look at me.

Activity C —
Introduce King Kong, Doormat and Assertive Communicators

Types of Communicators

KING KONG — Aggressive: shouts, threatens, calls names, throws a fit, stormy, swears

DOORMAT — Passive: does nothing, withdraws, pouts, feels sorry for self, sulks, whines, begs, cries

ASSERTIVE — Says how he/she feels and states what he/she wants

---

On this chart we have listed three types of communicators. First is the KING KONG type. This communicator uses body language which is powerful and strong. You get an idea of what this person is like by the name, but here are some words which describe a KING KONG COMMUNICATOR: aggressive; shouts; threatens; calls names; throws a fit; storms around; swears loudly. (Point to the chart.)

Then there's the DOORMAT COMMUNICATOR. This person is passive; does nothing; withdraws; pouts; feels sorry for self; whines; begs; cries a lot.

Finally, we have the ASSERTIVE PERSON. This kind of communicator says how he or she feels and states what he or she wants.

Thumbs up for yes, thumbs down for no. Do you think the King Kong Communicator has high self-esteem? (no) How about the Doormat? (no) Assertive? (yes)

These three types of communicators behave in certain ways. Let's do a skit and see how each of them would behave. (One PSE volunteer will be the brother or sister with a loud stereo.) You are trying to study but your brother or sister is playing the stereo so loudly you cannot think. Who wants to show the class how a King Kong Communicator would act? (Remind students: No swearing, even though it is on the list.) How about a volunteer to be the Doormat Communicator? Anyone want to be the Assertive Communicator?

Let's do another example. You are watching a movie in the theater. The person behind you continually kicks your chair and this bothers you.

> *HINT: Have children come up to pantomime: King Kong threatens; Doormat does nothing and just gives a slight glance; the Assertive Communicator says, "That's annoying, please stop."*

260

We need to be careful not to disguise King Kong and Doormat when using Assertive: "I feel upset because you took my pencil and I want you to give it back." You do not shout or threaten as King Kong does. You do not whine or sulk as the Doormat does. The Assertive Communicator is very matter-of-fact, has a strong-but-easy tone of voice, and doesn't use aggressive body language.

> *HINT: Demonstrate an assertive sentence using the King Kong tone first then the Doormat tone.*

Activity D — Introduce Broken Record Technique

Even if you choose to use assertive communication, you may get a King Kong or Doormat back. Watch this example:

A: I feel upset because you took my pencil. I want you to give it back.
KK: So what, nerd!

It is easy, in this situation, to jump right into name-calling. How would you handle this situation? Let's talk about it. Stick to your point and say your sentence again. (Repeat the dialogue for A.)

This technique is called the Broken Record. When a record has a scratch in it, it plays the same section over and over — the technique is the same, over and over. Let's do an example.

> *HINT: Sandy and Peggy meet each other. Sandy wants to borrow Peggy's van. Peggy does not want to loan it and makes one excuse after another: out of gas, dirty, might need it, don't know how to drive a van, etc. For each excuse, Sandy has a solution.*

Stop the action! Peggy is running out of excuses. Raise your hand if you ever said yes when you wanted to say no to a friend. (Wait for class response.) The Broken Record method works well for this and it has two parts. First, you have your policy statement or rule. If a store has a sign saying "No Eating in the Store," the rule is meant for everyone, not just you. A policy statement is a statement for everyone, not just the person you are talking to at the time. Before the policy statement or rule, you make a kind statement which shows you have some understanding, but your policy sticks. Let's replay the van scene. This time Peggy will have a policy statement.

HINT: If the class has a problem with the phrase "policy statement," change the word to "rule." The children love this scene if the borrower really hams it up and literally does anthing she can to get her friend to change her mind. The following are suggestions, only.

Suggested Dialogue

Sandy: Hi, Peggy, I'm glad to see you. You know my daughter is about to have her birthday. She invited a whole bunch of her friends to have a picnic on the beach. Fun, huh? Fun, except she invited more children than will fit into my car. So I thought, being that we're such good friends, you might loan me your van for the afternoon.

Peggy: I understand your problem, Sandy and I never loan my van.

Sandy: Of course you don't...not to others...but we're FRIENDS and have been for a long time.

Peggy: Being your friend is a neat part of my life, and I never loan my van. I'm sorry.

Sandy: What do I do? When the kids arrive do I line them all up and say "You go, you don't, you go, you don't...? Look, I need a favor. Remember the time I loaned you my best, not my junky one, but my best coffeepot for your party?

Peggy: I appreciated using your coffeepot, and my policy is I never loan my van.

Sandy: (Crying, getting angry, pouting, begging — all fair game.)

Stop the action! Peggy held in there with her policy statement. What were some of the kind statements she used? (class response)   Let's do another one.

(Use a PSE volunteer and a student volunteer who is coached by another PSE team member.) Mrs. St.Clair, you are going to talk to Bobby about a book he borrowed and promised to return last week. Mrs. St.Clair's policy statement is, "You promised to return the book by Friday." (PSE volunteer and student act out the skit.)

Stop the action! The important thing to remember is to make a kind statement which may be different each time and a policy statement which is always the same. (Go around the room and ask different children if you may borrow whatever you see on their desk or person. Remind them to use kind and policy statement — making excuses is not allowed.)

Activity E — Broken Record Practice

I am going to divide you into pairs and let you practice this technique. (Divide class.) You decide who will do the Broken Record in the first example...ready? Your friend wants to borrow some money from you but you do not want to loan him or her any money. Remember to make a kind statement then a policy statement. Broken Record people think of your policy statement...and hold the line. Begin! (Allow three minutes.)

What were some of your policy statements? OK, switch parts and let's do this example. Your friend teases you about your clothes. Broken Record people get your policy statement ready. Remember a kind statement first and no war words...begin. (Allow three minutes.)

That one was different. The Broken Record is a great tool to use if someone is teasing you. I know one boy who drove a teaser bonkers by saying over and over, "I'm sorry, I didn't hear you." Whatever your statement or policy statement is, stick to it. It isn't any fun to tease a person who doesn't get upset.

Switch again and let's try this one: One of you wants to steal something from a store, the other does not want to do it. Broken Record communicators, think of your policy statement...begin! (Allow three minutes.) The only statement made is your policy statement. The other person always has his or her right to choose. What were some of your policy statements?

Here's another example: Your friends have some cigarettes and are going to smoke them. You know smoking is harmful and you don't want to join them. One friend tries to argue with you. (Ask students to switch partners and allow three minutes.) What were some of your policy statements?

Activity F — Lesson Ending

Today, we've talked about three different types of communicators. We know that body language, tone of voice, and choice of words are all important things to consider when we want to communicate. We learned the Broken Record technique as a means of saying no when we want to say no and we learned how to be assertive when someone else is doing a King Kong job on us.

Your bulletin board strip for next time is: Broken Record = Kind Statement Plus Policy Statement. See you in two weeks. Be good to yourself and to each other!

——————————————— **Lesson 9** ———————————————

Learning about Handicaps and Listening

Objectives

- The child will review three kinds of communicators.
- The child will review the Broken Record method of communicating.
- The child will practice an activity that will help him/her understand what it's like to be handicapped.
- The child will play a listening game.
- The child will experience a relaxation exercise.

Suggested Reading

LaMore, Gregory S. *Handicapped...How Does It Feel?* "Fear is an emotion that is experienced by children when they don't understand a sit-uation or condition. Through understanding...there can be acceptance."

Background

Sometimes we forget to be king. Sometimes when we want to be kind, we don't have the skills to talk to someone who is handicapped. Compassion is best realized through understanding. *Project Self-Esteem* wants to assist children in treating people who are different with both kindness and compassion.

The art of listening can be practiced best through a game. The value of playing a listening game is to show children that listening is one of the most important skills to develop.

Materials

King Kong, Doormat, Assertive chart from Lesson 8, Aardvark worksheets (which are difficult to read), Lists for group discussion in Activity C, Signs for the student listening game in Activity E, New bulletin board strip: It's Important to Respect the Differences in Others.

Activity A – Review Lesson 8

Last time we were here, we talked about three kinds of communicators. Does anyone remember what they are?

> *HINT: Encourage the students to remember the three types of communicators. If they don't, show the chart. Discuss the various traits. Spend only two or three minutes on this portion of the lesson.*

We also talked about the Broken Record technique. Let's say, for example, someone were to say to you, "May I borrow your coat?" and you knew that you weren't supposed to loan it, what could you say? Remember to use kind words and your policy statement, not war words. (Wait for a few examples, then thank the students for their ideas.)

Activity B — Feeling the Confusion of Being Different

We are putting a paper on your desk, face down. Do not turn it over to look at it. You will need a pencil for this exercise. (Pass out the Aardvark papers.)

(When the papers are all handed out.)   You are to look at me and follow my words exactly with no exceptions. (Say this slowly and deliberately.)   There will be absolutely no talking once this exercise begins. There will be no exceptions to this rule: No talking or sounds are to come out of your mouth.

After I finish talking, not before, you will turn your paper over. You will have exactly two minutes to read the paragraph at the top of the page and answer the questions on the bottom of that page. Do not raise your hand. Under no circumstances are you to make any comment or sound. Look at me please. Two minutes. Turn your paper over and begin.

> HINT: The whole point of this exercise is to give the students an opportunity to feel the frustration of not knowing how to resolve the problem they are having as they try to read the paper. Quickly stop any overt behavior with a single comment, "No talking. Do the best you can." If a student asks if the paper will be graded, respond with, "Just do the best you can."

(At the end of two minutes.)   Please put your pencil down and turn your paper over, face down. Look at me and breathe deeply. (Use a gentle voice.)   Tell me about the experience you just had.   (Allow any and all comments with a minimum of feedback from you.)   So, it was frustrating and nerve-racking and maybe even a little frightening to have the pressure of doing something you were unable to do? Raise your hand if you were worried that everyone else was doing it and you were not.   (Wait for class response.)

Turn your paper over again, please and look at it. Some people who have difficulty reading may look at a page of words and see what you saw and are seeing right now. Imagine how confusing school could be if the words were all fuzzy and mixed up like this. Imagine how much more frightening life would be if you were teased by others about something over which you had very little control.

Activity C — Thinking about Being Handicapped

Having a reading difficulty is only one of the handicaps that many people live with each and every day. Those of us who have no major handicaps very seldom think about how different life would be if we could not see, hear, walk, or speak like other people. Let's take a few minutes to think about how our lives would be different if we were handicapped. Of course, there are many ways that all of us are the same. We will think about those, too. You will break into your groups for this exercise.

HINT: The purpose of group work is to bond. Be sure each group has a PSE volunteer who will take a few minutes to chat with his/her group to bond. Then use the following format for a discussion of handicaps. Make sure you skip any handicap activity that a student might have in a classroom where this lesson is presented. Each volunteer should have a list of the situations below.

Situation #1 — Walter cannot walk.

Here is a list of four things you might do in your day-to-day life: Go to a movie, go to the park, go to school, and go to a party. Let's look at our list of things to do and talk about how each activity would be different for you if you were Walter.

a) How would it be different for you if you couldn't walk to go see a movie?

b) How would it be different for you if you couldn't walk to the park?

c) How would it be different for you if you couldn't walk to school?

d) Of course, Walter could play many games at a party. Some could be changed a little, to be sure that Walter would be included.

Situation #2 — Sim cannot see.

Here is a list of four things you might do in your day-to-day life: Go to a movie, go to the park, go to school, and go to a party. Let's look at our list of things to do and talk about how each activity would be different for you if you were Sim.

a) How would it be different for you if you couldn't go see a movie?

b) How would it be different for you if you couldn't see to play in the park?

c) How would it be different for you if you couldn't see to walk to school?

d) Of course, Sim could go to a party, and could have lots of fun with a little assistance from her friends. How could we assist Sim?

Situation #3 — Tara cannot be easily understood when she speaks.

Here is a list of four things you might do in your day-to-day life: Go to a movie, go to the park, go to school, and go to a party. Let's look at our list of things to do and talk about how each activity would be different for you if you were Tara.

a) How would it be different for you to discuss a movie if others had a difficult time understanding your speech?

266

b) How would it be different for you if it was difficult for you to tell someone you wanted to play in the park? How could you tell someone you wanted to play? (hand gestures, write on paper)

c) If your speech is not easily understood, how could you ask someone to walk to school?

d) How could we assist someone who has difficulty speaking clearly?   (by being a patient listener)

Situation #4 — Alvin cannot learn easily.

Here is a list of four things you might do in your day-to-day life: Go to a movie, go to the park, go to school, and go to a party. Let's look at our list of things to do and talk about how each activity would be different for you if you were Alvin.

a) How would it be different for you if you did not understand all of the movie?

b) How would it be different for you if you didn't understand the rules to a game your friends were playing in the park? How could a friend assist Alvin?

c) How would it be different for you if you didn't always remember the directions to school? What could Alvin do to help himself remember?   (walk with a friend, draw a map)

d) How would it be different for you if you had difficulty understanding a game being played at a party? How could a friend assist Alvin?   (play along with him, suggest an easier game)

So far we have been thinking about how difficult life can be and how different it is for a person with a handicap. Now let's think about how things are the same. For example, I bet almost everyone would like to go to Disneyland. Right?   (Most of us can have our feelings hurt if someone calls us a name—or if we are not included, agree?)   How else are we all alike?

> HINT: It is advisable that each volunteer discuss the above topics ahead of time so that they have thought through the activities and have some means of coaching should the student discussion bog down. Any mockery or negative comment is to be discouraged. The volunteer might say, "This is not the time for that type of comment. We are learning to be kind to others. Sometimes teasing is not kind. Please remember to be kind." Your compassion and sensitivity will set the mood for all of the discussions.

Allow 10 minutes for group discussion time. At the end of the discussion period, do not *return the students to their seats. They will need to stay in groups for the student listening game in Activity E. Conduct the discussion in Activity D with the whole class, where they are seated.*

Activity D — Ways to Be Kind to People

Sometimes, when we think about how different our lives could be, we appreciate what we have more. Another thing that happens is that we develop a desire to assist and include everyone.

Handicapped people say that being different is really hard and sometimes scary. It bothers them to be treated differently or to be ignored. Sometimes, it bothers a handicapped person to have people always staring at them. Remember there are more ways a handicapped person is the same than different.

If you were in the market and you saw a child in a wheelchair, how could you be kind to that person? (Say "Hi" to them. Talk to them. Smile at them. Wave to them, etc.)

If you were on the playground and you heard someone who had trouble talking easily, how could you be kind to him/her? (Listen. Don't make fun of the person. Be patient, be sure to include them in the game.)

If you were in the classroom and you understood something but the person in front of you was totally lost, how could you be kind to that person? (Don't make fun of him/her. Ask your teacher if you could help the person. Tell the person to hang in there. Be patient, etc.)

Sometimes, being kind is simply a matter of thinking how you would feel if you were that person. Everyone is worried about being different. We try to fit in and be just alike. You have learned something in PSE that tells you why it is impossible to be like everyone else. Who remembers why it is so silly to even try to be like someone else? (class response: There are no two people alike, so every one of us is different.) Every one of us is different. Being different is (use slang expressions appropriate for your time)   cool. It is rad. It is boss. Making fun of people who are different is something we need to stop doing. Let's make a pledge to be kind to others.

Activity E — Student's Listening Game

Several lessons ago, we asked you to think of a listening game that we could all play. The game that was chosen was written by (say student's name). Let's give (say student's name) a hand. We are going to play that game now. Each group will have a card to show what they are to say.

HINT: Follow the same procedure for this game that you used in Lesson 4, Activity D of the 5th grade program. Be sure to read the listening game selected, ahead of time, to correct any grammar or language.

Activity F — Relaxation Exercise (read verbatim)

Sit up tall but comfortably. Please look down at your lap and keep looking down for the entire exercise. Take long, slow, deep breaths in through your nose and out through your mouth. You will hear me say "re" on the intake of air and "lax" on the output of air. Look down at your laps and keep looking down please. Take air in through your nose . . . re. Let the air through your mouth . . . lax. In . . . re; out . . . lax. In . . . re; out . . . lax. In . . . re; out . . . lax. In . . . re; out . . . lax. Stop. Sit quietly and enjoy the feeling of being relaxed.

Activity G — Lesson Ending

Today we learned a lot about ourselves, about the abilities of others and how to understand the differences in others. The bulletin board strip for this week is: It's Important to Respect the Differences in Others.

We'll be back in two weeks. Meanwhile be good to yourself and be good to others.

Note: We are indebted to the Helen Irlen Institute for their assistance with this lesson. If you wish to contact this institute for more information, the address and phone number is: 4425 Atlantic Ave., Long Beach, CA 90807   (213) 422-2723.

<hr>

Lesson 10

Stealing and Teasing

Objectives

Stealing:
- The child will demonstrate his knowledge of the difference between borrowing and stealing.
- The child will state the reasons why people steal.
- The child will understand that stealing hurts both himself and the person from whom he steals.
- The child will understand that stealing decreases self-esteem, even if the person stealing is not caught.

Teasing:
- The child will state why people tease.
- The child will conclude that it is often best to ignore the person doing the teasing.
- The child will state that people will tease about things that are different (size, shape, abilities).
- The child will conclude the person who teases most of the time has low self-esteem.

Suggested Reading

Briggs, Dorothy Corkille. *Celebrate Your Self*, p. 94. "Every low and shaky self-esteemer lives with the basic belief: 'I am what I do.' Separate your person from your behavior, thoughts, feelings."

Dreikurs Rudolf M.D. *Children: The Challenge*, p.278. "The act of lying or stealing are symptoms of deeper underlying rebellion."

Background

These lessons were developed at the request of seven classroom teachers who had PSE during our first year. The teachers felt that these subjects are part of the everyday life of a student, and one more approach might help students understand and cope with them. We have used the format of a TV program. You may use any format you wish. However, it has been our experience that it is beneficial to avoid anything that even slightly resembles "preaching" as most students will switch their listening skills to "off."

The information in this lesson gives the individual child another resource in dealing with the temptations and challenges of growing up. Lack of awareness is the same as no choice. Teaching children not to be "victim" to the behavior of others is important. By adding to the individual awareness, we give children a new choice.

<hr>

Materials

Scripts, Props for skits: box of soap powder marked "CLEAN" and a large box marked "washer," Two identical shirts (one dirty), Hats, Glasses, Mikes for TV show, Signs or name tags with character names, New bulletin board: (Use the two Poem Charts from Activity D and F.)

Activity A — Review Lesson 10

The last time we were here, we did an activity to find out how it feels to have a handicap. Can anyone tell me what we did? (Wait for class response.) Can you think of a way you could be a friend to someone with a handicap? (class response)

Activity B — Stress Reduction Exercise (read verbatim)

Whenever you are upset and want to calm down, a simple way to do so is this breathing exercise. It is easy and it works. Please look into your lap and keep your head down. Draw air in through your nose and let it out through your mouth. Do it very slowly. Let's practice together. Breathe in through your nose and breathe out through your mouth. Breathe in through your nose and breathe out through your mouth. Breathe in slowly through your nose, and out through your mouth. Nose . . . in, mouth . . . out. (Repeat several times.) Now stop. When you are ready, please look at me.

Activity C — Introduction of Lesson on Stealing and Teasing (read verbatim)

HINT: PSE volunteers will act out this skit. Visible name tags or signs assist in defining different characters.

Tammy: In other years, we talked about tattling and cheating. Today, PSE-TV will take you to our studios to cover the important subjects of stealing and teasing. First a commercial, then to our PSE studios. Come in, Connie Commercial.

Connie: Boys and girls, we have a new miracle wash powder for you today. It is our new, outstanding, cleaning product. We took CLEAN (show box) to the National Laundry Contest and won first prize. Now for our demonstration. Here we have a very dirty shirt. . .grease spots, chocolate, even bubble gum stains. We place it in the washer (box with word "washer") with some of our spectacular wash powder CLEAN. We will return during our next commercial break and check on the cleaning power of CLEAN!

Activity D — Compare Stealing to Borrowing

Tammy: Good morning (afternoon) boys and girls, this is your very own Tammy-Tell-It-Like-It-Is here to bring you school news. We are broadcasting live from (school) in (teacher's name and grade of class) grade classroom. Today, we will discuss the difference between stealing and borrowing. Let's go to Olive-on-the-Spot and the kids in the classroom to ask, "What is the difference between stealing and borrowing?"

Olive: Olive-on-the-Spot here. Tell us kids, what's the difference between borrowing and stealing? (Stealing is taking something without permission. Borrowing is done with the intention of giving it back.) Thank you kids. But why do people steal? (want something, can't pay for it, to show off or act big, for the challenge, excitement.) Thank you kids. Now back to Tammy.

Tammy: Thank you Olive! Our researchers have put together a list of examples from real life. Would you and your kids in the classroom be willing to decide whether each example is borrowing or stealing?

Olive: How about it kids in the classroom. Would you like to make it into a game?

HINT: Some classes respond better if you simply tell them, "We are going to play a game!"

Olive: OK, if you think the example I read is stealing stand up. If you think the example is borrowing, stay seated. (Write "stealing — stand, borrowing — sit" on the chalkboard. Some classes have used thumbs up and down.) Remember. . .we all know that people make mistakes, so no one needs to laugh if someone makes a mistake. Ready, here's the first one:

    1. Joe took a cookie from Tom's lunch tray. Is he borrowing or stealing? (stealing)

HINT: Under some circumstances, this could be either. Have one student who thinks it is borrowing explain why. (intention)

    2. Carlos asked if he could use Todd's bike; he forgot to bring it back on time. (borrowing)

3. Sam takes his brother's T-shirt out of the drawer. (stealing)

4. You ask your mom if you can take her scissors. (borrowing)

5. John picked up the pencil up from Wong's desk. (stealing)

6. You take a library book without signing it out. (stealing)

7. You put candy in your pocket at the market. You do not pay for it. (stealing)

8. You ask your neighbor to use his skateboard for an hour. (borrowing)

Tammy: Thank you, Olive and kids in the classroom! This week we have two winners in the poem-of-the-week contest, and the first one goes to Nellie Nurd for this little ditty:

If you like to take things
That don't belong to you,
You may end up behind bars
And it won't be at the zoo!

Nellie will be sent a month's supply of CLEAN, the miracle cleaner. Let's check back with Connie Commercial and see how the miracle soap has worked. Connie?

Connie: Here we are, back at the washer demonstration. May I remind you that this laundry soap won first prize as the best stain remover of all laundry soaps. So, the exciting moment is here, where we demonstrate the removal of grease, chocolate, and bubble gum stains. TA-DAH!

HINT: PSE Volunteer playing Connie holds up second shirt which is dirtier than the first. Without looking at the shirt, she continues to talk about the greatness of CLEAN — until kids let her know something is wrong.

Oh, My! Back to the studio...(Looks at shirt in disbelief.)

Tammy: Thank you, Connie, ah, let's go on...Today, boys and girls, we have a special studio guest, Doctor Knows-A-Lot. Dr. Knows-A-Lot is here to give you the latest research data on what stealing does to the person who steals...Welcome, Doctor.

Doctor: Thank you, Tammy. Fact: There is an enormous amount of stealing going on in the world. Research shows many people have not been told what is going on when they choose to steal. My concern is with the fact that people are choosing to hurt other people. You need to realize: If you steal something, you are hurting someone because that's what happens.

Tammy: How does that apply to us, Doctor?

Doctor: For instance, let's say your dad owns (name of a local store) store. I remind you that not just one person, but many people are stealing from this store. In fact, your dad had to hire undercover people to walk around the store trying to catch people stealing. In order to put merchandise into the store, your dad had to buy it. If people steal an item, he spent money he won't get back. If many people steal, it might mean you and your family would not be able to buy something you need. Also, prices on other items will increase. Your father may need to raise the prices to help cover the loss on the things that are stolen. Doing that hurts the people who have to pay more to buy things at the store.

Activity E — Effect of Stealing on Thief

Tammy: That helps. Does stealing have any affect on the thief?

Doctor: I'm glad you asked that, Tammy. Our research shows that stealing has a great affect on the thief. Deep down inside each of us we have two...we'll call them invisible charts. If I may use your board, I'll illustrate. (Doctor draws a large happy face.) One chart says, "I like myself." (Draw a sad face.) The other says, "I don't like myself." Even if you get away with stealing — let's say, a candy bar — and no one knows you took it except you, deep down inside of yourself you put a mark on the "I don't like myself" side. (Illustrate on the board.)

If, as you grow up, you put many marks on this side, you will begin to feel badly about yourself. As you know, from all you've talked about in PSE, how you feel about yourself or your self-esteem is the key to doing well in school — making friends, being happy, and being able to care about others. The point isn't whether I think you are a good or bad person, but how you feel about yourself.

Tammy: That's very interesting, Doctor, but I have a question: If you get a mark on your "I don't like myself" side, can you erase it?

Doctor: The answer is YES! You can erase it. We are all making mistakes as we grow. We learn from our mistakes. In the case of stealing: When you give something back, pay for it, or tell the person you are sorry, you are admitting your mistake and doing something to patch it up. This DOES erase the mark from the "I don't like myself" side.   (Demonstrate on the board.)

Tammy: Thank you, so much, Dr. Knows-A-Lot.

So, we have clearly seen, that there IS a difference between stealing and borrowing. The difference has to do with asking permission. And, we have seen that even though stealing hurts other people, the person who gets hurt the most is the thief. We are going to switch now to Pamela Problem-Solver who will join the kids in the classroom to talk about TEASING.

Activity F — Define and Give Reasons for Teasing

Pamela: Wonderful, Tammy. I am really impressed with these (name of school) kids. Their sharing is teaching us a great deal. Kids in the classroom, we need to ask you a few questions. First, what is teasing? We usually know when it happens to us, but how would you define teasing? (bother, irritate, annoy, bug) Why do you think people tease? (as a put-down, for revenge, for fun, to get a response, to make someone notice you, sometimes its' just a habit because you don't feel good about yourself) Thanks, kids. Now back to Tammy...

Tammy: Pamela, thank you. We have another studio guest, Tilly Teased-A-Lot. Hello, Tilly. I hear you get teased a lot, do you?

Tilly: Yes

Tammy: What do you do when you get teased?

Tilly: Oh. . .I chase the kids. . .or call them names. . .or scream, "You stop that!" Sometimes I tell the teacher or my mom.

Tammy: Do you ever ignore them?

Tilly: I did once, but they kept on teasing.

Tammy: Do you think if you always ignored them that it would get boring to tease you?

Tilly: Well, I guess so. . .

Tammy: The truth is, the only people who get teased are those who are fun to tease. People who tease to hurt do not feel good about themselves. Tilly, we can also communicate our feelings to the teaser. Let's go back to Pamela Problem-Solver and the kids in the classroom to make a list of some topics used for teasing.

Pamela: OK, Tammy. Now, kids in the classroom, we don't want to embarrass or hurt anyone's feelings so we ask you not to name names or give any specific examples. What types of things do people get teased about? (being tall, being short, being fat, being skinny, having glasses, or braces, having big ears, nose, etc.) If you are ever teased, we hope you will remember:
1. What do you know about the person who always teases other people?
2. Does that person feel good about self? (no)
3. Does the person who teases have high or low self-esteem? (low)
4. Do you care what the person who doesn't like him/her self thinks about you? (maybe do, maybe don't)
5. What is the best way to handle being teased? (ignore it)
6. Everyone is special, right? (right)
7. Why are you special? (There is no one just like me.)
8. If there is no one just like you, there are differences. What kind of person will tease people about their differences? (low self-esteemers)
9. Are differences OK? (yes)

Therefore, if you have something obvious which is different about you, someone. . .somewhere. . .sometime may tease you about that difference. Ignore them. It's OK to have differences. We need to learn to talk to each other. Thanks kids, you've helped a lot.

Tammy: Wonderful, just wonderful. Thanks from me too, kids. Our second case of CLEAN the new laundry magic goes to Marvin Mushmouth for this enlightening poem:

> If you do not talk straight
> Use teasing without end
> You'll damage someone's feelings
> And might even lose a friend.

Thank you reporters and kids in (teacher and grade level) grade class. We have learned a great deal about stealing and teasing. We will leave these two winning poems with you to help remind you of these two important subjects. While we are gone, we want you to make a list of ten ways to be good to yourselves and ten ways to be good to each other.

We'll see you in two weeks. Meanwhile, be good to yourself and to each other.

—————————————————————————— Lesson 11 ——————————————————————————

Review: Final Lesson

HINT: The content of the final lesson is your choice. Listed below are suggestions devised by PSE teams.

Suggestions For Lesson

1. Go over students' papers "ten ways to be good to yourselves and ten ways to be good to each other." Write their ideas on the chalkboard or butcher paper so the class will have its own list.

2. Ask students to fill out and hand in an evaluation form. (The master for this form is at the end of the chapter.)

3. Use topics from previous PSE lessons and/or the evaluation in this lesson and do the following:
   a) Write the topics on pieces of paper for a drawing.
   b) Place the topic sheets in boxes labeled number one, two and three.
   c) Ask students go to their groups.
   d) Have a member of each group choose a topic slip.
   e) Get the whole group to work on a skit that demonstrates the topic on the slip. Optional: Have props and costumes available for use.
   f) Ask the group to perform the skit for the entire class.
   g) Discuss the point of the lesson demonstrated at the end of each skit.
   h) Repeat if time permits.

4. Hand out "I Am Special" awards. Be certain to give one to the classroom teacher. (The master for this award may be found at the end of the chapter.)

5. Form small groups and check goals.

6. Refer back to Lesson 12 of the 2/3 PSE program for additional activity suggestions.

7. Closing

HINT: Each PSE volunteer may take a line or one person may say the entire closing

We've enjoyed our year with you.
Thank you for all your sharing throughout the year.
Have a wonderful summer.
Each and every day, remember to
    Be good to yourself
    and to each other.

Suggested list of topics: Introduce Self Using Positive Adjective; Valuing Differences; Goal Setting; Giving and Receiving Compliments; Smileys; Space Game; Stress Reduction Exercises; Memorizing Something; Anger as a Second Feeling; Martha and the Rocks; Changing "You" Messages to "I" Messages; Writing a Letter to Show Anger and then Trashing It; Stealing; Teasing; King Kong/Doormat/Assertive Behavior; Broken Record; and Harmony.

Name _____

Teacher _____

Goal Setting

> Set reachable goals.
> Write out steps for reaching that goal.
> Keep going until you reach your goal.
> Give yourself a reasonable time limit.
> Evaluate — check your progress.
> Compliment yourself.

My goal is _____

4	
3	
2	
1	

Name _____

Teacher _____

_____
title

Words for the Listening Game:

	Name of group	**What group says**
Group #1	_____	_____
Group #2	_____	_____
Group #3	_____	_____
Group #4	_____	_____
Group #5 Entire Class	_____	_____

Story for the Listening Game:

(Circle words that are listed above as keywords. Use each keyword or phrase several times. If you need more space for your story, use the back of this paper.)

_____

_____

_____

_____

_____

_____

Name _____

Teacher _____

Anger as a Second Feeling

1. Clare is having a birthday. She does not invite Maria. Maria seems angry. What did she feel first?

   _____

2. Jack teases Lee about being tall. Lee acts angry. What feeling might Lee have had first? _____

   _____

3. You find out two of your friends are talking about you behind your back. You seem angry. What

   feeling could you have felt first? _____

4. My teacher got angry with me (or the class) when _____

   _____

   _____

   My teacher's first feeling was _____

5. My friend or classmate got angry with me when _____

   _____

   _____

   My friend's or classmate's first feeling was _____

6. I felt angry with a friend when _____

   _____

   _____

   My first feeling was _____

Name_____

Teacher_____

The Aardvark

The aardvark was given it's unusual name, which means "earth pig", by the Dutch who settled in Africa in the 1600's. Although the aardvark's long snout with it's flat end looks like a pig's, that's where the similarity ends. One of the reasons the Dutch may have chosen this name is that the aardvark roots in the ground with its nose to sniff out tasty ants and termites. Pigs also root in the ground for food, and both animals have dirty noses most of the time. After an aardvark finds an ant or termite nest, it rips the nest open with sharp claws. Then the aardvark uses its long, sticky tongue which can be 18 inches long to catch a meal.

An aardvark uses its claws to dig a home because it likes to live underground. It has to dig a deep hole because it is so large. An aardvark can weigh 140 pounds and measure four to six feet long from the tip of its nose to its tail. Few animals can dig a hole large enough to hide in and thus escape from its enemies.

An aardvark is not a fierce animal. To protect himself from humans or lions, this animal just rolls over on its back showing its claws and ardently illustrating its digging techniques. The aardvark sleeps during the day and hunts for food after dark. It usually hunts alone.

Please write your answer to each question in the space provided:

1. What does the aardvark's name mean?

2. What does the aardvark do to defend itself?

3. Who named the aardvark?

Name _____

Teacher _____

The Aardvark

The aardvark was given its unusual name, which means "earth pig," by the Dutch who settled in Africa during the 1600's. Although the aardvark's long snout, with its flat end, looks like a pig's, that's where the similarity ends. One of the reasons the Dutch may have chosen this name is that the aardvark roots in the ground with stiff nose to sniff out tasty ants and termites. Pigs also root in the ground for food and both animals have dirty noses most of the time. After an aardvark finds an ant or termite nest, it rips the nest open with sharp claws. Then the aardvark uses its long, sticky tongue — which can be 18 inches long — to catch a meal.

An aardvark uses its claws to dig a home because it likes to live underground. It has to dig a deep hole because it is so large. An aardvark can weigh 100 pounds and measure four to six feet long from the tip of its nose to its tail. Few animals can dig a hole large enough to hide in and thus escape from its enemies.

An aardvark is not a fierce animal. To protect himself from humans or lions, this animal just rolls over on its back, showing its claws and ardently illustrating its digging techniques. The aardvark sleeps during the day and hunts for food after dark. It usually hunts alone.

Please write your answer to each question in the space provided:

1. What does the aardvark's name mean?

2. What does the aardvark do to defend itself?

3. Who named the aardvark?

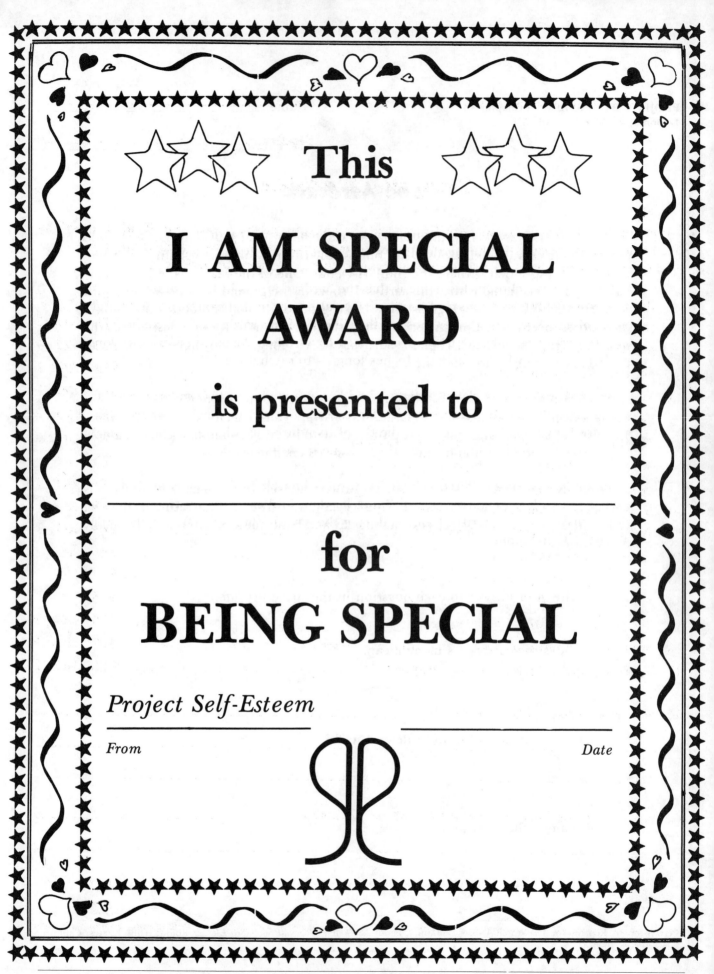

This

⭐⭐⭐ ⭐⭐⭐

I AM SPECIAL AWARD

is presented to

_____

for

BEING SPECIAL

Project Self-Esteem

_____ _____
From   Date

Name _____

Teacher _____

Evaluation Worksheet

Pretend that you are going to be a Project Self-Esteem team member next year. Read each activity listed below. Draw a circle around YES if you would put it in a lesson. Draw a circle around NO if you would not put it in. Draw a circle around ? if you do not remember the activity.

1. Bulletin board sentences . . . . YES NO ?
2. Introducing yourself with a positive (example: Happy Harmony) . . . . YES NO ?
3. Sharing successes . . . . YES NO ?
4. Setting goals in small groups . . . . YES NO ?
5. Smileys (giving and getting compliments) . . . . YES NO ?
6. Setting a goal for yourself . . . . YES NO ?
7. The Space Game (the importance of listening) . . . . YES NO ?
8. Memorizing states and capitals . . . . YES NO ?
9. Stress reduction exercises . . . . YES NO ?
10. Setting a goal from class improvement . . . . YES NO ?
11. Writing letters to express anger . . . . YES NO ?
12. Anger as a second feeling . . . . YES NO ?
13. Playacting (acting out situations) . . . . YES NO ?
14. Writing your own listening game story . . . . YES NO ?
15. TV program on stealing and teasing . . . . YES NO ?
16. Ways to communicate: King Kong, Doormat, Assertive . . . . YES NO ?
17. Learning how it feels to be handicapped . . . . YES NO ?

The PSE Lesson that I like best was _____

_____

_____

Comments: (Something you would like PSE to talk about) _____

_____

_____

Chapter

Grade 6

_____ Lesson 1 _____

Social Skills

Objectives

- The child will recall and relate concepts from prior PSE lessons.
- The child will interview and introduce his/her partner.

Suggested Reading

Buntman, Peter H. and Saris, Eleanor M. *How to Live With Your Teenager,* p. 16. "Self-esteem means a feeling of regard, respect, and affection to one's self."

Norfolk, David. *The Stress Factor,* p. 169. "A fundamental approach to the relief of tension is offered by a wide range of relaxation therapies. . . Most people who faithfully carry out these exercises report an increased feeling of well-being, a greater release of creative energy, and an increased ability to cope with stress and avoid fatigue."

Zimbardo, Philip G. *The Shy Child,* p. 226 (on the subject of starting conversations). "A fringe benefit in being sociable is that when you remain silent in the social encounter, it tends to make YOU just as uncomfortable as it does other people. This feeds your self-consciousness because you dwell on it. Your mind becomes filled with negative thoughts about yourself and truly absurd fears about the various ways you will make a fool of yourself and be rejected by others. On the other hand, when you show interest in another person and LISTEN to what he or she has to say and at least try to respond, the reverse is true."

Background

Students who transfer from sixth grade to junior high school may have some fears about being in a new situation with lots of new people. It is not wise to assume students know basic social skills. It is important to reinforce them even if they do. Lack of awareness is the same as no choice; basic skills training may give students new choices.

NOTE: If you have not taught the 2/3 or 4/5 grade program, it is very important that you read them. You will be called upon to review some concepts taught in these two programs.

These lessons have been designed for a K-6 school, where the students will attend a separate school for seventh grade. If your students will continue in the same school, a few adjustments must be made.

Materials

Harmony, Chalkboard space, Bulletin board strip — Stress: Deal With It.

Activity A — Introduction

I am. . .(Say your name and have the PSE volunteers also introduce themselves.) We are your Project Self-Esteem team for this year. How many of you had PSE last year? (Wait for class response.) What is self-esteem? (how you feel about yourself)

What difference does it make if you have low or high self-esteem? (People with high self-esteem do better in school, don't play victim to other people, are happier and healthier, and enjoy life more.)

Activity B — Review

What do you remember from the Project Self-Esteem lessons you had before? (Wait for class response.)

> *HINT: If the discussion bogs down, remind students of the lesson topics and ask what they remember of those lessons. Keep this section brief but informative enough to assist those new students.*

Wow! I'm amazed at how much you remember. Thanks for sharing. This year, we are going to be talking about lots of different things. What we want is for you to feel good about yourself. If you already do feel good about yourself we want to share ways for you to keep that feeling. We will be here for nine lessons this year.

Activity C — Stress Reduction Exercise (read verbatim)

Let's begin with a stress reduction exercise. What is stress? (class response) What kinds of things can cause stress in your life? (Write responses on the chalkboard.) You may have noticed that many sports personalities use some sort of stress reduction exercises before their event. A skier will follow the slalom course in his mind before he races. A baseball pitcher takes deep breaths and sees himself throwing the perfect pitch. In sports, as in many activities, some stress is helpful. It gets you keyed up to really perform. But too much stress can ruin the quality of what you do. Stress reduction exercises assist in getting you to relax in order to do your best.

If you have not had PSE before, just follow the directions and relax as much as possible. Please sit up straight, but comfortably — feet flat on the floor. We are going to do what is called a tensing exercise. What that means is you will make a muscle really tight, hold it tight, and then relax it. Listen so you will know what to do. Drop your hands to your sides. Look down in your lap so you can concentrate on what you are doing. Squeeze both of your hands into a fist. Hold them as tight as you can while I say TIGHT! TIGHT! TIGHT! TIGHT! TIGHT! Open your hands and let them hang to your sides.

With both hands make a fist again. Bring your fists up by your shoulders like you are showing how strong you are. Make your upper and lower arm muscles TIGHT! TIGHT! TIGHT! TIGHT! TIGHT! Drop your hands and let them hang to your side.

We are going to tighten the muscles in your head. Frown, squeeze your eyes really tight, press your lips together, push your chin down to your chest, and hold all those muscles TIGHT! TIGHT! TIGHT! TIGHT! TIGHT! Let your head hang loose, open your mouth, and just relax for a few seconds. (pause)

Slowly, bring your shoulders up and try to touch your ears. Pull them up hard, hold them there, and drop them. Pull in your chest muscles and stomach muscles. Hold them TIGHT! TIGHT! TIGHT! TIGHT! TIGHT! Let those muscles relax and just sit there quietly for a few seconds.

Pull the muscles tight in your upper and lower legs. TIGHT! TIGHT! TIGHT! TIGHT! TIGHT! And tighten the muscles in your feet. TIGHT! TIGHT! TIGHT! TIGHT! TIGHT! And relax.

Just feel how relaxed your arms feel. And your head. And your chest. And your stomach. And the lower part of your body. And your legs. And your feet. Bringing air in through your nose, take a long slow breath. Hold your breath for a second and while you are letting the air out, please raise your head and look at me.

Activity D — Getting Permission to Use Harmony

If you have had PSE before, you know we use a puppet named Harmony. (Bring Harmony out.) Harmony is a member of the PSE team and he likes to assist us in teaching the lessons. But we know sixth grade is a more sophisticated time in your life, so we don't want to use him unless you feel comfortable about it. (Harmony hides his head.) What's the matter, Harmony? (Bear talks.) As you know, Harmony talks but he only talks to me and I tell you what he says. He's afraid you will vote not to have him and he won't get to come to the sixth grade. (Look at the bear.) I understand your feelings, Harmony, and it's important we give them a choice. Why don't you turn your back. It's better if you don't watch. Please raise your hand if it is OK with you to use Harmony in some of our lessons.

> HINT: The reason we ask permission to use Harmony is to allow
> each class to freely enjoy him. By making him personable and a
> bit "nervous," he appeals to each student's sense of caring. The
> use of Harmony in grade six is optional. Delete Harmony from
> the lessons if the class votes against having him.

Activity E — Learning How to Introduce Friends

Next year you will be going to a new school. We would like to go over a tool which will be helpful, especially at that time. We are going to act out two people being introduced to each other by a third person.

HINT: Three PSE volunteers act out the skit. You can also use two PSE volunteers plus the classroom teacher. They are to fumble around, act like they don't know what to say, and then begin talking about the weather.

Stop the action! What's the matter? (They don't know what to say.) Why? (They don't know each other.) What might we do to assist with this problem? (They could give some information when introduced to each other.) Now we are going to rerun the skit. One team member will introduce the other two and give one piece of information about each person.

HINT: An example for this skit might be: Sandy has a daughter in the same school your daughter attends and Peggy is interested in gourmet cooking. Let the conversation get rolling then stop it.

What kind of things might be used as an example of information about a person? (sports, favorite food, grade, hobby, favorite TV shows, etc.)

There is something important to remember. When I introduce Sandy to Peggy, I need to look at Peggy when I say Sandy's name: "Peggy, I want you to meet   (look at Peggy) Sandy." Sandy already knows her own name, she doesn't need to hear it. Now, when I introduce Peggy to Sandy, where do I look? (at Peggy)

We are going to pair off the class and give each group one minute to discover some facts about each other.   (Write the questions below on chalkboard.)

Questions to Ask

1. What do you like to do in your spare time?
2. What is your favorite food?
3. What is one quality you like in a friend?

HINT: PSE volunteers may give an example before groups are formed. "This is (Susan). She likes to read, loves lamb chops, and wants a friend to be honest." It is fun, where appropriate, to have a PSE teacher do this with the classroom teacher. It sets up the whole exercise and humanizes the teacher.

Now we will have each pair stand and introduce each other, including three facts. (Discourage extracurricular comments from classmates.)

HINT: This exercise may be done at the front of the room or a PSE team member may move about the room to save time. Keep it moving so it is not boring. After two or three pairs have participated, stop and remind about the importance of eye contact. Tell the students one way to get themselves to look at someone's eyes is to check their eye color.

Activity F — Learning How to Introduce Yourself

(Bring out Harmony.) Say "Hi" to Harmony. What's new? (Listen to Harmony.) He wants to meet someone but he doesn't know what to do.   (Talk to Harmony.) You know, Harmony, we all run into situations when it is important to introduce ourselves. These two volunteers have that problem, too. Watch this skit.

HINT: As the two PSE volunteers act out this situation, they are to stumble and fumble around with words and pretend they don't know what to say.

What's the matter? (They don't know what to say.)   How can they improve the situation?   (give information about themselves or ask a question)

HINT: Rerun the skit. This time each PSE volunteer is to give enough information to get the conversation moving.

What kinds of information might you give to someone your own age? (You could give the name of your teacher, a hobby or sport interest you have in common, or you might ask a question such as, "Do you like soccer?")

HINT: Some questions are open-ended (what, when, where, why, how), and require more than a one-word answer. Encourage a child to follow a closed question with one which is open-ended. You may need to give examples.

Let's go back to your orginal pairs. Both of you will pretend to be sixth graders who do not know each other. Take turns introducing yourself, each using different information to get the conversation going. Will one pair volunteer to demonstrate this process in front of the class first? (Have one pair demonstrate the process, and then allow three minutes for the class to practice in pairs.)   One of you will pretend to be the parent of your partner. You will introduce yourself to him or her. Then you will switch and repeat the exercise. (Allow three minutes.)

Activity G — Lesson Ending

So Harmony, knowing how to do something releases some of the fear of doing it, and practice always helps you feel more comfortable. (Harmony talks.) You learned so much you want to go up to (give a famous person's name) and introduce yourself? That's super! You're even going to get his autograph? Wow! that's great!

That was fun, but more important, you now have a tool which will assist you for the rest of your life. We will be back in two weeks. Meanwhile, be good to yourself and to each other!

> *HINT: Bulletin board strips, projects, and folders are optional. This grade level tends to have a pretty full schedule, so you might discuss the pros and cons of their use with the classroom teacher. We will give you suggestions for bulletin board titles and you may choose whether or not to use them.*
>
> *Throughout the sixth grade program it will be very important for you to use terms and examples that apply to your students. For example on page 311 we say someone "butts" in line, in your area they may say "cuts in line"....etc.*

_____ Lesson 2 _____

Social Skills/Choice Making

Objectives

- The child will review the four principles on feelings.
- The child will discover how negative self-talk affects him.
- The child will participate in games of choice making.

Suggested Reading

Buntman, Peter H. and Saris, Eleanor M. *How To Live With Your Teenager*, p. 161-169. Includes a list of positive and negative feeling words.

Cretcher, Dorothy. *Steering Clear*, p. 81. "Children need the ability to make judgments. Making judgments (choices) is partly a matter of understanding and applying relationships. Cause-and-effect relationships are important. Children learn judgmental skills by being involved with mature people who make judgments and who create opportunities for kids to think through what they would do in the same situation."

Kalb, John and Viscott, David. *What Every Kid Should Know*, pp. 10-27. "Everyone has feelings, even if he can't always describe them accurately. Your feelings influence how you think and reason. And they influence your adjustment to everyone and everything around you. Feelings are very, very important."

Background

Probably the most difficult area in relationships of any kind is communication skills. Changing the use of "you" messages to "I" messages is a simple technique which will monumentally enhance the communication level between two people. "You" messages invariably become a name-calling contest and no issues can be resolved by name-calling. Beginning with "I" is a personalized way of saying what you feel. It assists in keeping the other person off the defensive. An "I" message communicates!

Research indicates teenagers who get into trouble with drugs and breaking the law state their number one reason for the problem was that they didn't know what else to do at the time they had to make a choice. "The Choice is Yours" game takes real-life situations and allows the students to explore possible options. If a situation used in the game arises, the students will have a resource of choice.

Materials

Harmony, Chalkboard space, Bulletin board space: Weigh the Risk and Gain in Making a Choice.

Activity A — Stress Reduction Exercise (read verbatim)

Sometimes, when you get rushing around in your lives, it is helpful to just sit, close your eyes, and listen. The object is to take yourself out of motion and simply listen.

Sit up tall but comfortably, with your feet flat on the floor. Bringing air in through your nose, take a long, slow breath. Hold the breath for a moment, and then slowly let the air out through your mouth. Now making no sound whatsoever yourself, simply sit and listen. Relax and just listen to whatever there is to hear. (Pause thirty seconds.) Take a breath in through your nose and let it out through your mouth. One of the ways to relax is to just sit still and listen.

Activity B — Review of Lesson 1

Is there anybody who wasn't here for our first lesson? (Wait for class response.)

HINT: If there is no new student proceed to Activity C.

We are your Project Self-Esteem team. We will be coming into your room every other week from now until May. I am Mrs. Jones, this is Mrs. Landis, and this is Mrs. St. Clair. If you weren't here last time we were in your room, we want to know your name. (Wait for individual student response.)

What is self-esteem? (how you feel about yourself) What difference will having high self-esteem make in your life? (have more friends, do better in school, feel happier, etc.)

Activity C — Review Four Feelings Principles

In earlier PSE lessons, we stated that everybody has feelings. There were three other statements we made about feelings, and we are going to talk about them right now. How many of you like or don't like the weather we're having today? Raise your hands if you have a feeling about today's weather. (Wait for class response.) So, we can say everybody has feelings. Let's say you don't like the weather today. Maybe we will have the same weather tomorrow and for some reason, you might change your feelings. Feelings can change.

Raise your hand if you like today's weather. Raise your hand if you do not like today's weather. One person's feelings can be different from another person's feelings. Let's say you have some memory about another day that was just like today. Maybe the reason you like or don't like the weather today is based upon that memory. Feelings are based upon past experience.

Activity D — Review "You" to "I" Messages

In the PSE program for grades 4 and 5, we talked about changing "you" to "I" messages. A "you" message is usually name-calling. When someone calls you a name, what do you tend to do? (call a name back) When two people stop communicating and start calling each other names, we call those war words. What is the problem with using war words? (Nothing gets solved because there is no real communication.)

Instead of saying "You are so rude!" when someone keeps interrupting you, what could you say? Remember to begin with the word "I." (I want you to listen. I don't like being interrupted, please listen.) Instead of saying, "You are the slowest person on the planet!" use an "I" message and say what? (I want you to hurry. I don't like being late, please move faster.)

Activity E — Review Self-Talk

In grades 4 and 5, we also talked about the ways in which we usually talk to ourself. Does anyone remember what this kind of talk is called? (self-talk) Self-talk is the things you say to yourself. Most of the time, what you say to yourself is not very complimentary. It is unusual if you say to yourself, "That test score is really remarkable!" It is not unusual if you say, "You're such a dummy! That test wasn't that hard! You did terribly!"

> HINT: For this next exercise either use the classroom teacher or one of the PSE volunteers.

Are you right or left-handed? (Wait for a response.) Put your strongest arm to the side so it sticks straight out. I am going to try to push your hand down towards the ground and I want you to resist. Do not let me push your hand down. (Push on hand to test strength of the adult.) You may put your hand down to your side. Think of something you wish you hadn't done. You will not share what it is, just think about it. Nod your head when you have thought of it. (Wait for the adult to respond.) Now, give yourself a "you" message, like "You dummy!" Think the phrase to yourself several times. (Wait for a few seconds.) Keep saying your phrase. When you are ready, raise your hand to the side.

> HINT: Push down on the adult's hand. If the adult is following instructions, his/her arm will be weak and you will be able to push it down easily. If not, continue to coach the adult to use a "you" message and to feel it. Try it with a different adult if unsuccessful.

Now, think of something for which you can compliment yourself. Be your own cheerleader and compliment yourself over and over. (pause) Raise your hand to the side when you are ready.

> HINT: *Push the hand down towards the floor. If the arm is not stronger, continue to coach on giving compliments.*

Are you stronger or weaker now? (stronger) Let's ask the class what they think the message is in this exercise. (You weaken yourself with negative self-talk.)

Watch me. I am going to pair you off, but stay in your seats until I ask you to move. (Pair off the class.) Now listen so you will know what to do. One person will coach, one person will raise his or her arm. Then you will switch roles so each of you will get to do both parts.

1. First test the arm strength of the person who is going to take the arm test.
2. The coach will say, "Think of something you did that you wish you hadn't done. Wait. Now, use a negative "you" message. Say it several times."
3. Test the arm strength of the person saying the negative "you" message.
4. Compliment yourself. Repeat several times.
5. Test the student's arm strength.
6. Switch roles.

> HINT: *It might save time to have these directions written on a chart or on the chalkboard.*

Quietly take your seats. (Wait for a few seconds for the class to be seated.) What did you experience? (class response) What did you learn? (Negative self-talk really does weaken you.) So negative self-talk can harm you physically. How does it make you physically weaker? (You will probably get sick easier. You can't do things well. You will be clumsy, etc.) When you talk to yourself, be kind to you. Be a friend to you. Remember to compliment yourself.

Activity F — Comparing Self-Encouragement to Bragging

(Bring Harmony into the lesson.) Hi Harmony! (Harmony waves, talks, and scratches his head.) You want to know if it is bragging when you give yourself a compliment. Yogi brags all the time and it bothers you? What's the difference? Well, Harmony, let's ask the class what is the difference between bragging and giving yourself a compliment? (Bragging is exaggerated and not always true. People who brag use a "look-at-me" tone of voice.) Most important to remember is the intent behind the statement. A person is trying to impress by bragging. Stating a fact is simply recognizing your worth.

Do you understand the difference between complimenting yourself and bragging now, Harmony?   (Harmony nods.)

Activity G — The Choice is Yours Game: Joining a Group

Every day there are lots and lots of choices each of us makes. Do you realize how many choices you make in a single day? Let's start with getting up this morning. What other choice did you make?   (Make a list on the chalkboard.)   Making choices is a large part of your life. Because of that, we want you to have a tool for choice making. The tool is a game we will play from time to time called "The Choice Is Yours."

For almost everyone, doing something new is scarey. Going to a new school next year might be frightening. For some of you the topic for our Choice is Yours game today might be difficult. Listen to the situation before you raise your hand.

You are a new student in the school. This is your first day. It is recess time and you want to join a group on the playground. If you're the new student, you have some possible choices. Who wants to come up here, and give one possible choice? The PSE team members will be the playground group and I need one volunteer to be the new student.

HINT: PSE volunteers are the group in this activity, to prevent any destructive dialogue towards an individual. As each student gives the choice he or she might make in this situation, the choice is acted out by PSE team. Then the student sits down so another student can come up and take the choice seat. Keep going until the class uses all the possible alternatives. Have a PSE volunteer write the different choices on the chalkboard. This eliminates duplication and gives a visual reminder.

I have a question for you. If the new student wants to do something but chooses to stand there and do nothing, is "doing nothing" also a choice?   (class response)

Whenever you make a choice, you weigh what might happen. You ask yourself: What's the worst that can happen. . .and. . .what could you gain or get out of this?

HINT: Use your right and left hand, like a scale balancing, as you say the two options.

In the situation with the new student, what's the worst that could happen if you tried to join a new group? (rejected) What is the possible gain? (accepted, make new friends) Before you make a choice, decide if it's worth the risk, then make your choice.

Think about which choice you would make from this list. (Point to the chalkboard.) You are not going to share your choice. Just decide for yourself. Raise your hand when you have made your choice. Now let's do another one.

Activity H — Choice Is Yours Game: Going Against the Group

Here is the situation. There is a group of 3 sixth graders. To the side, there is a new student in the school. One of the group members wants to include the new student in the group's activity, but the other group members say "No way!" (Choose two students to act out this. They need to be a reasonable pair who won't steal the scene.) The new student will be imaginary because we don't want anyone to get hurt. I am the one who wants to include the new student. Is someone willing to take my place and act out one possible choice? (Choose another student.)

> *HINT: Possible choices include: leaving the group to be with the new student; asking the new student over anyway; giving into the group's wishes; introducing the new student to someone else; and doing nothing. Each person in the choice seat will say, "Let's invite that new kid over." Monitor the amount of protest from the dissenters so it does not get out of control. Once a choice is made, stop the action and ask for a volunteer to illustrate another choice by taking the choice seat. Keep track of the choices by writing each one on the chalkboard. When all the choices have been made, select one or two from the list on the chalkboard and ask what is the worst that could happen and what is the possible gain. Also, have the students look at the list and decide which choice they would make. A raised hand will tell the PSE volunteers that a decision has been made.*

Activity I — Lesson Ending

Today, we have talked about how negative self-talk can weaken you. We practiced changing "you" to "I" messages. We also talked about making choices and played a game called The Choice is Yours.

We will be back in two weeks. Meanwhile, we hope you will CHOOSE to be good to yourself and to each other. Between now and next time, take a look at your choices and begin to practice weighing the worst that could happen in a choice and the possible gain.

_____ Lesson 3 _____

Assertive Training: Broken Record

Objectives

- The child will experience three ways to communicate.
- The child will practice the assertive training technique of the Broken Record.

Suggested Reading

Booraem, Curtis; Flowers, John; and Schwartz, Bernard. *Help Your Children Be Self-Confident*, p. 12. "In school the child with assertive skills will do better than other children with equal intelligence. They ask more questions of more people to get the information they need. In addition, because they know when and how to refuse, they are not as likely to be influenced to act contrary to their better judgment. Thus, they are able, for example, to withstand group pressure..."

Smith, Manuel J. *When I Say No, I Feel Guilty*, p. 323. "Broken Record: A skill that by calm repetition, saying what you want over and over again, teaches persistence without you having to rehearse arguments or angry feelings beforehand, in order to be "up" for dealing with others. After practice, allows you to feel comfortable in ignoring manipulative verbal side traps, argumentative baiting, irrelevant logic, while sticking to your desired point."

Background

The teenage years are a time where peer pressure steadily increases. Therefore, it is valuable for young people to learn a skill which allows them to say no when they need to say no. The Broken Record's positive statement and policy statement allow students an acceptable way of enhancing their self-esteem.

Materials

Harmony, Chalkboard space, Three Ways to Communicate chart   (see Activity C), Bulletin board strip: Saying No is OK.

Activity A — Stress Reduction Exercise (read verbatim)

Sit up tall but comfortably and, please look down into your lap and keep looking down for the entire exercise. Take long, slow, deep breaths in through your nose and out through your mouth. You will hear me say "re" on the intake of air and "lax" on the output of air. Look down into your lap and keep looking down please. Take air in through your nose . . . re. Let the air through your mouth . . . lax. In . . . re; out . . . lax. In . . . re; out . . . lax. In . . . re; out . . . lax. In . . . re; out . . . lax. Stop. Sit quietly and enjoy the feeling of being relaxed.

Activity B — Harmony Has a Problem

(Harmony is hiding his head and looking sad.)   What's the matter, Harmony? (Harmony talks to PSE teacher.)   Oh dear...your friend Yogi asked to borrow your black tie and now he can't find it?   (Harmony talks to teacher.)   You didn't want to loan it to him in the first place...(Harmony scratches head)...but you don't know what you could have done? Let's take a look at that problem.

(To the class)   Raise your hand if you've ever loaned something to someone when you really didn't want to do it.   (Harmony looks at class then talks to PSE teacher.) Why did they do it, then? I don't know, let's ask them. Why did you loan it if you didn't want to do it?   (afraid of hurt feelings, people being mad at you, didn't know what to say, etc.)   The most common reason, Harmony, is that people don't know what to say. But we have an answer for that, today.

Activity C — Three Ways to Communicate

In most situations, you have three possible ways to communicate.

> *HINT: Show the Three Ways to Communicate chart as listed below. Be sure the lettering is large enough for the whole class to see.*

KING KONG —	Aggressive: raise voice, shout, threaten, calls names, hit
DOORMAT —	Passive: sit, do nothing, hide from, yell "ouch" a lot, pout
ASSERTIVE —	Positive: confident in most everything, will claim or defend his/her rights

Do you think the person who almost always behaves like King Kong has high or low self-esteem?   (Wait for class response.)   Self-esteem is how you feel about self. King Kong has what kind of self-esteem?   (low)   How about Doormat?   (low)   And what about Assertive?   (high)   Remember, a high self-esteemer feels good about him/herself most of the time. Let's look at how you might behave in this situation.

Activity D — Being Bothered in the Library

You are trying to read in the library. Someone is talking loudly. If you were the King Kong type of person, what might you say?   (Stop talking or I will...)   What would the Doormat do? (probably feel angrier and angrier but would do nothing) Assertive? (Use the formula from last year: State feelings and my wants, one or both. Ask the person to talk quietly.)

Activity E — Introduction of the Broken Record

One tool to use in being assertive is the Broken Record method. If a record has a deep scratch or is warped, it plays the same thing over and over. If someone is teasing you, you might choose to ignore him or her or you might say "I don't like being teased and I want you to stop!" Even if the other person continues to tease, you repeat over and over, "I don't like being teased and I want you to stop." It is not fun to tease someone who doesn't respond, so the teaser will soon get bored. What do we know about the person who often teases others? (low self-esteem)

> *HINT: It is fun to use a topic which actually relates to the PSE volunteers. A hilarious lesson came out of trying to borrow a PSE volunteer's new motorcycle. The class knew about the motorcycle and they really loved this section.*

Let's look at another situation. (This time use the PSE team members' names.) Mrs. Mertz wants to borrow Mrs. Irvine's coffeepot. Mrs. Irvine does not want to loan her the coffeepot.

> *HINT: The more lively this skit is presented, the more fun it will be; and correspondingly, the longer it will be remembered. Mrs. Irvine gives excuse after excuse: might dent it, might lose cord, might need it, someone else might need it, didn't get it back last time, etc. But Mrs. Mertz has a solution for each excuse. (Do five or six excuses.)*

What's happening here? (Mrs. Irvine will run out of excuses.) Let's rerun this situation. Notice what Mrs. Irvine does this time.

> *HINT: Use the Broken Record this time. Make a kind statement first and then your policy statement. You might say for example, "I understand your problem, and I never loan my coffeepot." If that is not true, and you just don't want to loan this person your coffeepot, say, "I don't feel comfortable loaning you my coffeepot." Choose one policy statement and use several different examples of kind statements. The PSE team will act out the example.*

Mrs. Irvine: I can see you have a problem, and I never loan my coffeepot.

Mrs. Mertz: Of course you don't — not to other people — but you know what a careful person I am.

Mrs. Irvine: You're a very careful person. I never loan my coffeepot.

Mrs. Mertz: Remember the time you had that big, big party and I loaned you my serving trays?

Mrs. Irvine: You saved my day and I appreciate it. I never loan my coffeepot.

Mrs. Mertz: Well, what do you expect me to do. . .serve water?

Mrs. Irvine: I can hear your frustration. I never loan my coffeepot.

Mrs. Mertz: I thought we were friends! A friend would help another friend!

Mrs. Irvine: I'm really glad we're friends. I never loan my coffeepot.

(Write on the board "kind statement plus policy statement.")   The policy statement states a rule which is to be used or followed all of the time, no matter who is involved. For example, a store might have a "No Food Permitted Inside" rule. That means no matter who comes inside, food is not to be brought into the store. A policy statement needs to be said in a matter-of-fact voice so you convey the choice is not a personal one. That is, it does not apply only to the person to whom you are talking, but to everyone, without exception! If a situation comes up where you usually do loan something and you do not want to loan it to this person, change your policy statement just a little and say "I like being your friend. I don't feel comfortable loaning my coffeepot." (Write these sentences on the chalkboard.)   Before giving your policy statement you say "I don't feel comfortable. . ." Let's practice.

> *HINT: A PSE volunteer walks around the room selecting, at random, students with whom to practice the Broken Record. Try to borrow a sweater, a watch, a pen, a bicycle, money, etc.) Keep the pace moving and animated so it isn't boring.*

Activity F — The PSE Challenge: Practicing the Broken Record

> *HINT: If appropriate, ask the classroom teacher to play the adult part with the following exercise. She will try to borrow the bike.*

Now we're ready for the big challenge. Mrs. Irvine will challenge any sixth grade student to see if she can get that student to loan his/her bicycle. Who will accept the PSE challenge? (Select one volunteer.)   Remember to use both a kind statement and a policy statement.

> *HINT: The PSE member can use any and all of the following techniques: being a buddy-buddy, begging, buttering-up, intimidating, being upset, putting down, being selfish, crying. The more you get into this, in terms of persuasion, the more the class will learn from it. It is helpful if another PSE volunteer stands near the student to remind him/her to stay with the policy statement.*

Is there a second person in this room who wants to take the PSE challenge? (This is optional according to time allotment.)

Let's use the Broken Record in a situation where two students wish to borrow cassette tapes from another student. The third student, for whatever reason, does not want to loan his/her cassettes. PSE is not saying: Do not loan your cassettes. The point we are making is: It's important to have a tool to use for saying no when you want to say no.

> *HINT: Ask for two student volunteers who want a third student to loan his/her cassette. Tell the students to use lots of pressure. (You can come to the party. We can't have the party without music, etc.) Assist the third student in developing a policy statement and sticking to it.*

Sometimes, when you don't do what someone wants you to do, that person will threaten to take away his/her friendship. How would you feel if the people in this group (pointing to two students) said, "Keep your ol' cassettes, but you can forget about being our friend?" (A friendship based upon doing what the other person wants you to do isn't worth much.) Remember, a person has the right to loan his/her cassettes, or not. Threatening to take away a friendship is not honoring those feelings.

There are other times when knowing about the Broken Record is valuable. One time is when someone wants you to do something you don't want to do. For example: A friend wants you to go to a movie and you don't want to go.

> *HINT: Discuss with the class a possible kind and policy statement. (I heard it is a good movie. I don't want to go to a movie tonight.) Have two students playact this situation.*

Activity G — Practicing the Broken Record

Being assertive means you stick to the issue or point and stay with what you want. We will divide you into groups of two to practice some examples. (divide into pairs) Listen to my instructions. I will tell you when to begin.

1. A wants to borrow money from B. B does not want to loan the money. The issue is not whether B has the money or doesn't have it. B has the money but doesn't want to loan it. Remember to make your kind statement first, then keep saying your policy statement. Remember, don't make any excuses. You may begin.
2. Someone is teasing you because you do not wear name brand clothes.
3. A friend wants you to ride down a very steep hill on your bicycle.
4. You are accused of something you didn't do. (Use a specific example in your accusation.)
5. A friend wants to copy your homework. It is against school rules.
6. A friend wants you to smoke a cigarette after school.

HINT: At the end of each example ask for some of the policy statements. Allow enough time, but do not let this section drag. Each time, partners switch.

(Bring Harmony back.) Now Harmony, do you understand what you might say to Yogi if he asks to borrow something again? (Harmony nods.) We'll be back in two weeks. Remember if you have an opportunity to use the Broken Record so we can talk about it next time. Remember to be good to yourself and to each other.

_____ Lesson 4 _____

Assertive Training: Fogging

Objectives

- The child will playact the assertive training technique of the Broken Record.
- The child will participate in the use of the assertive technique called Fogging.

Suggested Reading

Smith, Manuel J. *When I Say No, I Feel Guilty,* p. 323. "Fogging: A skill that teaches acceptance of manipulative criticism by calmly acknowledging to your critic the probability that there may be some truth in what he says, yet allows you to remain your own judge of what you do. After practice, fogging allows you to receive criticism comfortably without becoming anxious or defensive, while giving no reward to using manipulative criticism."

Background

Teenagers tend to be brutally judgmental toward each other. One of the most difficult aspects of life for teens is not knowing how to deal with criticism. Fogging is a technique designed for this purpose. Its purpose is to maintain one's own power in what might otherwise be a powerless situation.

We are grateful to Manuel J. Smith for giving us permission to use his material in our program.

Materials

Harmony, Chalkboard space, Note cards for Activity E, Bulletin board strip: If Someone Puts You Down, Fog Them.

Activity A — Stress Reduction Exercise (read verbatim)

We are going to do a new stress reduction exercise. You need to stand up, so please get out on the right side of your desk. Listen to my words before you move. You are going to try to take up as little space in this room as you can. Get yourself squeezed into as tight of a package as you can. Do it now, please. Be very still and hold your muscles tightly in your little space. (Wait for silence.)

Listen to my words before you move. You are now going to do exactly the opposite. You will stand up and take as much room as you can without touching anyone or anything. Keep your feet on the floor. Quietly do it now, please. Stretch all your muscles as far as you can. Quietly sit down. Look into your lap and slowly begin breathing in through your nose and out through your mouth. (Wait one minute.) Now look at me, please.

Activity B — Introduce Fogging

What do you do when someone picks on you? (Write all options on the chalkboard.) When one person attacks, the natural response is to defend yourself and the inevitable result is WAR ZONE! Fogging is an effective means of refusing to play victim. What does victim mean? (being cheated, fooled, damaged by someone or something or being pushed into fighting when you do not want to fight)

We're going to do a Choice-Is-Yours situation. Listen before you volunteer. Two people are going to a birthday party. One says to the other, "That's a dumb outfit to wear to a birthday party!" (Have a PSE volunteer be the criticizer.) Who wants to have the choice seat?

> *HINT: Have each student in the choice seat demonstrate his/her choice. Keep reminding the class each time a new student comes up that you are looking for different ways of handling criticism. Possible responses are: "What you have on is dumb, too!" or "What do you know?" Other choices could be: ignore, punch out, walk away, joke about it, or agree. Students might use excuses like "Mom made me wear it." If one of the choices given by the students is to agree or say "You could be right," skip the next paragraph.*

There is one more way to handle this situation. It is called Fogging and is an assertive training technique. Watch this PSE skit (Two PSE volunteers do this.)

A: That's a dumb outfit to wear to a party.
B: You could be right.

Stop the action! Does saying "You could be right" mean you agree? (Write "you could be right" on the chalkboard. Wait for class response.) You are not agreeing, just saying it is possible. The point is not to engage in war over someone else's opinion. You do not need to play victim to other people's put-downs. Fogging is like a fog bank. (Write the word "Fogging" on the chalkboard.) If you throw a rock into a fog bank, it isn't thrown back. The rock doesn't hurt the fog, either. You can be a fog bank with people who use put-downs. Fogging is used in the following way:

1. If what the person picking on you says is true "You're late to class," you respond "You're right!" or "That's true!"

2. If what the person picking on you says is not true you respond, "You could be right," "You might be right," "That's possible," "Maybe so," or "Probably so." For example, if someone said "You're stupid," you certainly would not answer "You are right," but you could say "That's possible."

Back to our Choice-Is-Yours example. The comment was, "That's a dumb outfit to wear to a party!" Using Fogging, what could you say? (You could be right.)

> *HINT: Be careful to watch for anything that resembles sarcasm.*
> *Fogging is a bland response to criticism.*

Usually, the person teasing will not stop with one assault; more put-downs will follow. You may continue to use Fogging, or there is another assertive training technique you might use. What is it? (Broken Record) The main point is to stay with Fogging and not become defensive. Watch this skit.

> *HINT: Two PSE team members act out skit.*

A: That's a dumb outfit to wear to a party!
B: You could be right.
A: People will laugh at you.
B: Maybe they will.
A: No one will invite you to a party again!
B: That's possible.
A: You'll be so embarrassed when everyone stares at you.
B: Maybe so.

No one likes to be put down. Here's Harmony! (Harmony waves and talks.) When someone puts you down you may get a knot in your stomach because you don't like put-downs? Nobody likes a put-down, Harmony. But you can change your response to put-downs and you can choose to not let them hurt your self-esteem. One way to do that is to use Fogging. (Harmony begins opening and closing his arms, moving slightly backwards.) What are you doing, Harmony? (Harmony talks and volunteer laughs.) He's trying to look like a fog bank. Harmony, you don't need to look like a fog bank. You act like a fog bank by not using war words and fighting back. (Harmony scratches his head.) We'll practice this again in this lesson so you'll understand.

Activity C — Practice Fogging

Mrs. Newberry and I are going to take turns going around the room challenging some of you. You are to use the Fogging technique on us and keep doing it until we give up.

HINT: It is important to keep the pace moving and be really lively in this exercise. Objects for criticism are jewelry, haircut, clothes, pen or pencil (especially a chewed one), way someone is sitting, etc. Be sure you think the opposite of what you are saying. In other words, if you pick on a haircut do so to one you really do like. The object is to teach Fogging, not to intimidate children. Here is an example:

A: I noticed you weren't listening. If you don't listen you won't learn.

B: You could be right.

A: Of coarse I'm right. If you don't learn you won't go to college.

B: That's probably true.

Activity D — Review the Broken Record

Last time we were with you, we discussed the Broken Record as a way of communicating. What is the Broken Record? (a way to say no when you want to say no.) What are the two rules for using this technique? (Make a kind statement first. Then give your policy statement.)

Let's do some playacting to assist in remembering this important technique. The situation is that A wants to borrow a book from B. B does not want to loan it. Which two students want to playact this idea? (Choose two. Help them make a policy statement and remind them about the kind statement.)

HINT: The point in this section is to reinforce the processes the students have been taught. Do more than one example if desired. Ask if anyone had an opportunity to use the Broken Record since last time and allow time to share. If a child says he/she used it with a parent, let them know that communication between adults and children is different than communication between students. The Broken Record may be perceived as rude by adults unless used carefully. Suggest the classroom teacher set up practice sessions for Broken Record use during the regular day.

One apsect of teaching the Broken Record, which is often overlooked, is to be aware of your body language and tone of voice. It's good to keep your body language and tone of voice neutral.

Activity E — Using the Broken Record and Fogging Techniques

HINT: To keep this section interesting, walk around the room like you did in the Fogging practice. Switch giving criticism and asking to borrow or do something. Have the class identify what is happening and which technique is to be used in the example below.

A: That watch doesn't go with your outfit. Stop! What am I doing? (criticizing) Which technique do you use for criticizing? (Fogging) That watch doesn't go with your outfit.

B: You could be right.

A: I like your watch. It would go really well with this outfit. May I borrow it? Stop! What am I doing? (borrowing) Which technique do I need to use? (Broken Record) May I borrow your watch?

B: I'm glad you like it and I never loan my watch.

A: Just for an hour. I'll give it back in an hour.

B: I'm sure you'd keep your word and I never loan my watch.

We are going to challenge you. You will need to decide whether to use Fogging or the Broken Record.

First decide what's happening. If it is criticizing, use Fogging. If it is borrowing or trying to get you to do something you don't want to do, use the Broken Record.

HINT: In the following exercise, use 9 3" x 5" cards. Place one example on each card. Give the cards out to students who feel comfortable reading them aloud.

Have the students read the examples. Then ask what technique they would use and have them give an example of the technique.

1. I can't believe you got a D on that test. It was easy. (Fogging)
2. You must be the one who broke my pencil. You're the only one sitting here. (Broken Record)
3. Don't you know how to print? Everybody knows how to print! (Fogging)
4. That's a funny haircut! (Fogging)
5. You're waiting in line. Someone cuts in front of you. (Broken Record)
6. I can't read your handwriting. You should be able to write by now! (Fogging)
7. Boy, that was a dumb comment. You made a fool of yourself! (Fogging)
8. Your family rules are that you are at home at a certain time. It is now a little past that time. Your friend says, "Come on, let's go to the store." You want to go home. (Broken Record)
9. Hey, look what I found in your parent's refrigerator . . . beer! "Let's have one!" You say no to the beer. (Broken Record)

Now you have two tools that will assist you with many of life's situations. Who can name one of these tools? (class response: Broken Record.) Who can name the other? (class response: Fogging.) It is also important for you to remember that it is unlawful in most states for anyone under twenty-one to drink alcohol.

Activity F — Lesson Ending

You see, Harmony, how important it is to use our words? (Harmony nods.) Now you can handle it when your bear-pals pick on you and you know how to say no when you want to say no. It's time to go now; Will you say good-bye? (Harmony talks.) You understand it is time to go but you like this class and you want to stay? Which technique is Harmony using with me? (Broken Record) We feel that way about this class, too, Harmony. But. . .you understand it's time to go and you want to stay here longer? I think we have a problem here. (Cover Harmony's mouth.) We'll. . . ah. . .see you in two weeks. Meanwhile be good to yourself and to each other.

_____ Lesson 5 _____

Peers and Conformity

Objectives

- The child will define conformity.
- The child will participate in a game of choice making.
- The child will participate in a demonstration of the effects of peer pressure.

Suggested Reading

Briggs, Dorothy Corkille. *Your Child's Self-Esteem*, pp. 154-157. "The need to belong is so central that when a teenager appears completely indifferent to group opinion, he may be covering feelings of isolation and estrangement. On the other hand, overwhelming conformity suggest undue insecurity. Withstanding some group pressures comes easier for the youngster who knows he is adequate and belongs unquestionably. He usually becomes a pacesetter. Ordinarily, only the secure dare to be noticeably different."

Buntman, Peter H. and Saris, Eleanor M. *How to Live With Your Teenager*. p. 14. "Another psychological need that is crucial to the adolescent is his need for peer group acceptance."

Dobson, Dr. James. *Preparing for Adolescence*. p. 41. "The word 'conformity' refers to the desire to be just like everyone else — to do what they do and say what they say . . . In our society, there is tremendous pressure on all of us to conform to the standards of the group."

Background

There is a lot of talk about peer pressure. The desire for a teenager to conform is a natural part of development. This lesson clearly shows how influential peer pressure can be and the importance of choosing friends with similar values to your own.

Materials

Pill bottle that rattles, Chalkboard, Harmony, Cards with lines on them (see Activity F), Bulletin board strip: Choose Your Friends Wisely.

Activity A — Stress Reduction Exercise (read verbatim)

Sit up straight, feet flat on the floor; but this time let your hands hang loosely at your sides. Beginning with your feet we are going to tighten every muscle. Pull your feet in tight and hold them. Tighten the muscles in the lower part of your legs, the top part of your legs, and pull your stomach muscles in really tight. Tighten the muscles in your chest, and your shoulders. Make a fist with your hands. Tighten your arms. Pull in your chin and make a face as you tighten those muscles. Pull every muscle in your body really tight. TIGHT! TIGHT! TIGHT! And let go. And relax. Slowly begin taking deep breaths, in through your nose and out through your mouth. Again. Sit quietly and enjoy feeling relaxed. (Allow thirty seconds.)

Activity B — Review Broken Record and Fogging

In our last lesson we talked about two assertive training techniques. Do you remember what we called them? (Broken Record and Fogging) When do we use the Broken Record? (when someone wants to borrow something and you don't want to lend it, or when someone wants you to do something you don't want to do) Let's see if I can get someone to loan me something that he/she doesn't want to loan. (Do a few examples, reminding students to keep a matter-of-fact voice.)

The second assertive technique is Fogging. When do you use Fogging? (when someone is criticizing you) Do I have a volunteer who is willing to practice Fogging? (Do a few examples, reminding students to keep answers emotionless.) Knowing how to use these techniques may or may not make a difference in your lives, but they cannot assist you unless you use them.

We have talked about choices — how many different choices you make in each day, how you weigh the gain, and the worst that can happen whenever you make a choice. Today, we are going to talk about the effect of peer pressure on you and your choices.

Activity C — Peers and Conformity

When you were a baby, you COUNTED ON the people in your home for survival. As you grew up and got older, you slowly learned to be more independent. You learned to COUNT ON YOURSELF more.

During the next few years some of your peers will influence your choices. (Write "peers" on the chalkboard.) Who are your peers? (people your age) Most people will be influenced by some of their peers and that's OK.

You will probably conform with some of your peers. What does conform mean? (Write "conform" on the chalkboard.) Yes, it means a desire or need to be like everyone else — dress, think, say, do the same. You will probably conform with some of your peers, and that's OK.

What are some of the ways people in this school conform? (Write each answer on the board. Put a check by a response which is repeated so it is acknowledged.)

Conforming to what other people do is not always wrong. In fact, it can be the right thing to do. When is it right to conform? (when you have homework to do) The problem comes when you go against your own standards and values to conform. Then you feel badly about yourself.

Activity D — Choice is Yours: Accepting Changes in Friends

> *HINT: This game is designed to provide all possible choice options in a situation which may come up in an individual student's life. Statistics show peer pressure is the number one influence in choice making. Not being able to think of alternatives when placed in a given situation is the second dilemma facing youth. "The Choice is Yours" becomes a reference for youth.*
>
> *The game is played by having the student in the choice seat make one choice and act it out. The PSE volunteer thanks him/her, asks that student to sit down, and says, "Is there somone else who wants to take the choice seat and act out one other way to handle this situation?" Call on students until all options have been exhausted. Keep emphasizing, "Does someone have a NEW or DIFFERENT way of handling this?" Each choice needs to be recorded on the chalkboard by another PSE team member.*

Students in the sixth and seventh grades are beginning what are called the teen years. Lots of changes occur during these years, and those changes affect friendships.

Your bodies will be changing a lot. Some of the changes will be external and visible, and many will be internal or inside. We are not going to talk about physical changes, but we are going to focus on some possible changes which affect friendships. We'll do that by playing a game called "The Choice is Yours."

> *HINT: There are three main concepts to be learned from this game.*
> 1. *To realize people change.*
> 2. *To allow each other to do so.*
> 3. *To not take other people's changes personally — which is not easy for anyone to do!*

This is the situation: For whatever reason, or even for no reason you can see, a friend acts like he/she doesn't like you. Your friend always eats with you at school. But today he/she goes over to eat with someone else.

Who wants to be the friend who goes elsewhere to eat? (Choose one student volunteer.) Now, we need someone who will come up and show us one choice that could be made. (Choose one student.) The question is: What do you do if this happens to you? (join your friend anyway, ask why, go sit with someone else, pout, etc.)

> *HINT: Write each choice on the chalkboard. Accept all answers.*

In every situation where a choice is to be made, it is appropriate to weigh what is the worst that can happen and what is the possible gain. In the situation of (choose one example from the chalkboard), what is the worst that could happen? What is the possible gain? (Wait for class response.) What about this choice? (Point to a second choice from chalkboard.) What is the worst that could happen? What is the possible gain? (Wait for class response.)

Think about which choice you would make from this list. You are not going to share your choice. Just decide for yourself. Raise your hand when you have made your choice. (Wait one minute.)

Part of growing up is to see that friends change. Maybe two people will not be best friends anymore. This can hurt — and hurt a lot. It can damage your self-esteem. But the fact is we need to allow people to change.

The point is that people change as they grow. Sometimes friendships change. It is easy to take changes in friendships personally — to think something is wrong with you. Change is very difficult, but change is OK. When other people change, it may have nothing to do with you. You could still like your friend even when you don't like his/her action.

Activity E — More Choices

(Bring Harmony into the lesson.) Hi Harmony! You look worried. What's the matter? (Harmony talks to PSE volunteer.) Some of your pals have been taking drugs. You know that drugs can hurt them and you're worried. (Harmony talks.) That's true, Harmony, sometimes it is difficult to say no if the group is going to take drugs. Maybe, if we do a Choice Is Yours about saying no to drugs we can talk more about this important issue.

> HINT: Arrange some classroom chairs as if they were seats in a car. Put two chairs in the front, for a driver and a passenger, and three in back. Designate the middle seat in the back as the "choice seat."

This is the situation. The driver says, "A friend gave me these." He shows the other students a bottle and continues, "My friend said they make you feel really up (or any positive slang word appropriate for the time)." "Let's try one." Who would like to be the driver? (Choose one volunteer student.) Now, we need three passengers who will try to convince the person riding in the "choice seat," the back middle seat, to join the others in taking the pills. (Choose three more volunteer students.)

> HINT: If class gets very excited, it helps to say, "I will only call on people who have their hands raised and are quiet."

315

Who would like to be in the choice seat? (Call on one student.)   Remember, whatever happens, you do NOT want to take the pills because you know they are bad for your body. Make one choice as to how to handle this situation and act it out. Do you understand? (Wait for student's response.) OK, Action! (PSE team member writes the choices on chalkboard.) Who has a different choice (Continue until all choices have been demonstrated: pretend to take the pills, throw the bottle out the window, use the Broken Record, get out of the car, etc.)

Whenever you make a choice, you weigh what might happen: What's the worst that can happen, and what could you gain or get out of it.

> HINT: Use your right and left hand, like a scale balancing, as
> you say those two options.

In this situation, what's the worst that could happen?   (Use an example from the board.)   What is the possible gain? Before you make a choice, decide, is it worth the risk? Think: What are the possible consequences of this choice? Then, make your choice. Raise your hand when you have decided which choice is yours.

Whenever you go against your own wants and values to conform, you feel badly about yourself. What difference does it make if you feel badly about yourself? (Wait for class response.)

> HINT: Here's some information you can use in this discussion —
> but ONLY IF IT IS TOTALLY APPROPRIATE. (From Your
> Child's Self-Esteem by Dorothy C. Briggs, p. 3.) "A person's judg-
> ment of self influences the kinds of friends he/she chooses, how
> he/she gets along with others, the kind of person he/she marries,
> and how productive he/she will be. It affects his creativity,
> integrity, stability and even whether he/she will be a leader or
> follower. His/her feelings of self-worth form the core of his/her
> personality and determine the use he/she makes of his/her
> aptitudes and abilities. Self-esteem is the mainspring that slates
> each individual for success or failure as a human being."

Activity F — Skit Showing the Affect of Peer Pressure

> HINT: Rather than telling this information, you are going to act
> it out, using the whole class. Visual learning provides the greatest
> retention. Two PSE volunteers will be needed. One will be Person
> A and one will be Person B.

316

We are going to tell you about an experiment which was actually done. Because it will be difficult for you to believe what happened in the experiment, we are going to act it out. Person A, will you please leave the room for a few minutes? (PSE team member leaves.)

I'm going to hold up some cards. On each card are three lines. Line 1, Line 2, and Line 3. Each line is a different length. In some cases Line 2 will be the longest and in some cases, Line 3 will be the longest. When Person A comes back, I will ask all of you to raise your hand when I point to the LONGEST line of the three. What I want you to do is listen to what I say, but actually raise your hand when I point to the SECOND longest line. Remember, I will ask you to raise your hand when I point to the longest line. But as I am pointing to the second longest line, you are to raise your hand indicating you think IT IS THE LONGEST. Don't think about it, just do it. You need to be very serious about this. Do you understand?

Ask Person A to come in and take a seat, please. (The PSE volunteer playing A is to sit toward the back of the room.) Now, I am going to hold up a card and I want you to raise your hand when I point to the LONGEST line of the three. I repeat: I am going to hold up a card and I want you to raise your hand when I point to the longest line.

> HINT: Hold up a card with lines 1, 2, 3 on it. Point to the second longest line and say, "If this is the longest line of the three, raise your hand." Person A will act surprised, show disbelief, and ultimately raise his/her hand to join the crowd. Repeat the procedure using a new card.

Remember, we are acting out something that actually happened. In fact, SEVEN-TY-FIVE PERCENT of those who were asked to leave the room agreed that a short line was longer than a long line. Tell me why? (They were not able to risk going against the crowd.)

Now, we are going to rerun this scene with one important difference. Person A and Person B (PSE volunteer) will go out of the room together.

> HINT: Remind the class they are to follow the same directions you gave them when A was out. Repeat the process, this time pointing to the LONGEST line first. Seat Person B near Person A when they come back into the room. This time, both A and B will show disbelief, but B will raise her hand and A will follow. Person A and Person B will go against the crowd.

Remember, we are acting out an actual experiment. When there was only one person in each experiment who disagreed with the rest, the percentage of individuals who went against the crowd's vote was not very high. But more people went against the crowd's decision when one person joined them.

What does this experience tell you? (If you have even one friend stand up with you against the crowd, it gives you more courage. It is important to choose friends who support you.)

Let's apply this to your life. Since you know smoking is harmful to you, it would be helpful for you to find friends who do not smoke. What other example can you think of? (Drugs, alcohol, stealing, gossiping)

Activity G — Lesson Ending

Because friendship is such an important part of life, especially in what is called the teen years, we will talk about it again next time. Meanwhile, be good to yourself and to each other.

_____Lesson 6_____

Friendship and Assertive Apology

Objectives

- The child will practice using the assertive technique called the Assertive Apology.
- The child will participate in a game where he/she makes a choice concerning listening.
- The child will compile a list of rules for listening.

Suggested Reading

Buntman, Peter H. and Saris, Eleanor. *How to Live With Your Teenager,* pp. 22-25. "Knowing how to listen is probably the most important communication tool there is. To listen, we must be attentive. We must be still, and yet encourage thought in others. Our full attention must be directed to the person who is speaking."

Wassmer, Arthur C. *Making Contact,* pp. 71-97. "People are not born skillful listeners. Skillful listening is a fairly complex activity."

Background

Most of us are never taught to listen well. Rules for listening can be guidelines for improving this important skill. As is true in learning any skill, it is essential to practice.

Making mistakes is natural part of living. Teaching children to be responsible for their choices and to apologize assertively gives them a useful tool for daily life.

Materials

Chalkboard, Harmony, Bulletin board strip — Recipe for Having a Friend: Be One.

Activity A — Stress Reduction Exercise (read verbatim)

Sit up tall but comfortably and please look down at your lap and keep looking down for the entire exercise. Take long, slow, deep breaths in through your nose and out through your mouth. You will hear me say "re" on the intake of air and "lax" on the output of air. Look into your laps and keep looking down please. Take air in through your nose . . . re. Let the air through your mouth . . . lax. In . . . re; out . . . lax. In . . . re; out . . . lax. In . . . re; out . . . lax. In . . . re; out . . . lax. Stop. Sit quietly and enjoy the feeling of being relaxed.

Activity B — Review of Lesson 5

Last time, we talked about peer pressure. What's a peer? (someone you're own age) What does it mean to conform? (to do what everyone else is doing) We showed an actual experiment in which there were three lines — one long line, a medium-sized line, and a short line. Who can tell me what happened in the experiment? (The class voted the second shortest line to be the longest and the person who had been outside voted with the class.) This happened in 75% of those tested. What did the second experiment tell you? (Peer pressure is very strong. If you have one friend who agrees with you, it is easier to stand up against a crowd.) Today, we are going to talk about listening and apologizing.

Activity C — Choice is Yours Game: Friend Doesn't Listen

We are going to play The Choice is Yours. The situation is this: one person begins talking about what he/she did last night, the second person doesn't listen.

> *HINT: The PSE team acts out the situation. The PSE volunteer who isn't listening looks away, looks at watch or nails, straightens clothing, slumps, yawns, etc. The other PSE person sits in the "choice seat."*

OK, I have the choice seat. I may choose to respond to this situation in several ways. Who wants to take my place and demonstrate one possible way of handling this situation? (stop talking, ask a question, make a ridiculous statement, walk away, etc.)

> *HINT: Repeat until all options are given. Write each choice on the chalkboard. Point to one choice, ask what is the worst that could happen and the possible gain. Have students decide which choice they would make and ask them to raise their hands when they have made a decision.*

There are studies being done on how to listen. Most of us have not been taught to listen well. Let's see if we can put together a list of rules for effective listening. What could each of us do to be a better listener?

> *HINT: It is most helpful to elicit possible rules from the class. The amount of material gathered will depend upon the nature of each class. PSE volunteers may interject any ideas which seem important. The following are some suggestions.*

320

1. **USE EYE CONTACT.**
   What does that mean? Looking into a person's eyes can be scarey. If it is difficult for you to look into someone's eyes, especially at first, play a game and check to see what color eyes the person to whom you are talking has. What else could you do to help you use eye contact? (Wait for class response.)

2. **RESPOND TO WHAT THE PERSON IS SAYING.**
   If it gets boring to just stand and look at someone, you could do the following: nod your head; smile; ask appropriate questions; say "Oh, " "Ah," "Uh-huh," etc. Who wants to tell me what you did last night and I'll respond. (Use eye contact and respond appropriately.) What was the difference between this time, when I listened to (student's name), and the time I listened to (PSE volunteer's name)? Are there two people who want to come up here — one to talk about what you did last night and the other to respond? (Choose two volunteers and coach or point out proper use of responses. Repetition is appropriate.)

3. **USE BODY LANGUAGE.**
   What body language tells you someone is listening? (head leaning forward, nodding head, etc.)

4. **STAY WITH WHAT THE SPEAKER IS SAYING. DON'T DAYDREAM.**
   Use rules one and two to accomplish this point. People who don't listen well have not been taught to listen. It is frustrating when someone doesn't listen. You need to tell that person it bothers you, but do so in a way which does not create a WAR ZONE! How could you tell a friend to listen better? (I feel frustrated because it doesn't seem like you're listening. I want you to listen to me, do you understand?) Being honest with each other is very difficult. Most of us aren't honest because we are afraid to talk to each other and we worry about the consequences. We think people might get upset when we tell them things they don't want to hear. It could damage our self-esteem when we don't say what we want to say. Choose friends with whom you can be honest.

Activity D — Choice is Yours: Assertive Apology

Have you ever made a mistake in which someone else was involved? (Wait for class response.) Often, it is very difficult to apologize. We are going to learn a way to apologize which won't hurt your self-esteem and yet will allow you to take the responsibility for your mistakes.

Let's do another Choice is Yours. The situation is this: There are two friends. One borrowed the other's watch and broke it. One person says, "Did you bring back my watch?" The other responds, "Yes, but I broke it." That's where the action begins. Who would like to volunteer? (Name), you be the person who owns the watch. (Name), you are returning the broken watch. This is the choice seat. You choose how to handle returning the broken watch to your friend. (Students act this out.)

HINT: Write each choice on the board and follow Choice is Yours procedure. (Possible choices: make excuses, say it might have been already broken, promise to replace it, apologize, etc.)

Take some of the choices and ask what might be the worst that could happen. Then ask what possible gain there might be. Have students decide which choice they would make. Then, when they have decided, ask them to raise their hands.

Here's Harmony! (Bring Harmony in, have him wave to the class, and then talk to the PSE volunteer.) You were hearing the lesson and realized something? Yesterday you broke a friend's toy and you didn't know what to do. The Choice is Yours gave you some options, and you still feel uncomfortable about talking to your friend?

Well, Harmony, whichever choice you made you would probably apologize. Let's ask the class how the Doormat would apologize. (grovel, make excuses, blame) What about King Kong? (blame the other, probably wouldn't apologize) The assertive person would use the following steps:

1. Apologize by saying how he/she feels. "I feel badly."
2. Pat self on back. "I usually don't . . ."
3. Show intention . . . "I will replace it.

HINT: Students may ask, "Why can't I say I'm sorry?" Tell them they can but they need to be careful. "I'm sorry" can become so overused it becomes meaningless.

Sometimes it isn't appropriate to use all three steps, but you need to use at least two of them. It is important to be completely honest so you are believable in your response. Don't say "I usually don't . . ." if you usually do. Are there two of you who want to come up here and demonstrate the proper use of the assertive apology? (Choose two student volunteers.) Here's the situation. (Name), you borrowed his/her paper with an important English assignment written on it. You not only forgot to copy the assignment, but you also lost the paper. (Name), you are not pleased. OK? (Name of second student), you begin by asking for the paper.

HINT: The second student will ask for the paper, and the first student will give an Assertive Apology. It is not realistic to have the second student give up at this point. Encourage the second student to keep voicing his/her upset, and then invite the first student to use either the Broken Record, Fogging and/or the Assertive Apology technique.

Let's have two more students demonstrate a third example. I need one person to be a neighbor and a second person to play yourself. Your neighbor is upset because you broke a flower pot. (You actually did break it.) Go! (Repeat as mentioned in the hint above.)

Do you feel more comfortable about talking to your friend now, Harmony? (Harmony nods and talks.) That's true. No one likes to apologize. It IS easier when you have practiced.

Activity E — Practice Assertive Apology

Let's pair off and practice. Decide who will give the Assertive Apology. Here's the situation. You agreed to return a book to your teacher today. You forgot and did not bring back the book. OK, go ahead. (Allow two minutes.)

Who wants to share your apology statement? (I feel badly, I forgot. I promise I'll bring it tomorrow.) What happens if you promise and then don't do it the next day? (won't believe/trust you)

Switch roles and try another example. Your friend told you a secret. You told someone else, and it got back to your friend. OK. Let's start. (Allow two minutes.) What were some of your apology statements? (I feel embarrassed, I usually keep secrets and didn't this time. You have every right to be annoyed. I will keep my mouth shut next time.)

Apologizing can become an excuse. What happens when someone is always making an apology but never changes? (People learn not to trust him/her. People do not like to be around someone who always makes excuses.)

Apologizing may not be easy to do. One reason it's difficult is we forget that making mistakes is one of the ways we learn. Some people have a tendency to be hard on themselves when they make a mistake, rather than realizing that this is an important part of learning. Apologize by stating your feeling, then pat yourself on the back, and finally state your intention.

Activity F — Lesson Ending

Today, you learned to apologize assertively. You also learned some steps to assist you in listening effectively. These tools will assist you in feeling good about yourself, which is what PSE is all about. We'll be back in two weeks. Between now and then, practice your assertive techniques and be good to yourself and to each other.

_____ Lesson 7 _____

Alcohol and Drug Abuse

Objectives

- The child will increase his/her awareness of the negative mental and physical effects of alcohol, tobacco, and marijuana.
- The child will understand the importance of saying no to drugs.
- The child will learn to assist friends in saying no to drugs.
- The child will participate in games of making choices concerning drugs.

Suggested Reading

Film or Video: *"How Do You Tell?"* MTI Teleprograms, Inc. 108 Wilmot Road, Deerfield, Illinois 60015. This is a 13-minute film which informs students of the dangers of drug abuse, particularly alcohol, tobacco and marijuana, and encourages them to say no to drugs. It also encourages students to use positive peer pressure to encourage others to say no.

Film: *"A Step in Time."* Southerby Productions, Inc., 500 East Anaheim Street, Long Beach, California 90804, (213) 498-6088. This is a 29-minute film stressing decision-making for grades 5-8.

Cretcher, Dorothy. *Steering Clear*, p. 26. "The most important factor in beginning to use drugs is the influence of a close friend or friends."

Background

Research indicates teenagers who make inappropriate choices often do so because they can't think of something else to do. Information based upon true-life experiences gives students resources for alternatives.

Materials

Film *"How Do You Tell?"* (see review at end of lesson) or another film or video on drug abuse, Projector, Screen or TV/VCR, Bulletin board strip: Say NO to drugs.

Activity A — Stress Reduction Exercise (read verbatim)

Sometimes, when you get rushing around in your lives, it is helpful to just sit and listen. The object is to take yourself out of motion and simply listen. Sit up tall but comfortably, with your feet flat on the floor. Bringing air in through your nose, take a long, slow breath. Hold the breath for a moment, and then slowly let the air out through your mouth. Now, making no sound whatsoever yourself, simply sit and listen. Relax and just listen to whatever there is to hear. (Pause thirty seconds.) Take a breath in through your nose then let it out through your mouth. One of the ways to relax is to just sit and listen.

Activity B — Review the Assertive Apology From Lesson 6

During our last lesson we talked about using an Assertive Apology. Did anyone use an Assertive Apology since we were last here?   (Wait for class response.)

> HINT: Write on chalkboard: 1. Apologize by stating your feelings. 2. Pat self on back. 3. State intention.

You need to use at least two of three steps.   (Point to chalkboard.)   Let's do some playacting. I need two volunteers.   (Select two students.)   You two are going to have an argument on the phone.   (Name), hangs up the phone. Soon, you decide to call back, using the Assertive Apology. What can you say? Go!   (I feel badly I hung up on you. When I get really upset I can't think. Let's talk about it later, OK?).

The Assertive Apology was the third assertive technique we've talked about. Does anyone remember the other two?   (Broken Record and Fogging)   Today, we are going to discuss a subject where you may find it helpful to know these techniques. Our subject for today is alcohol and drug abuse.

Activity C — Show Film or Video "How Do You Tell?"

> HINT: There are several sources for this or other drug abuse films and videos. Contact your principal or a parent group formed to fight teenage substance abuse. The high school in your area will probably be able to give you this information. You may wish to use the MTI film/video, "Just Say No" (if it is not being used in a JSN Club). Also, (for a young sixth grade) MTI Teleprayers, "The Wizard of No" is an appropriate substitute. (Ask the class if they would change the ending on the Wizard film and if yes, how?) Be sure to preview the film or video and obtain district permission to use before showing it.

We have a film for you today called "How Do You Tell?" While you are viewing the film, we would like you to consider the following question: What do you think the real messages are in this film?

Activity D — Follow-up Questions

1. What do you think the real messages are in the film?

2. How do you tell someone you like that you think he/she is doing something that could hurt him/her? Is it any of your business? Is it an easy thing to do?

3. Why do people want to smoke pot? What effects does marijuana have on those who use it?

4. What happens when marijuana and alcohol are mixed?

> *HINT: Questions and answers may vary depending upon the availability of this film. The purpose of this activity is to allow the students time to discuss questions. Use only as many as time permits.*

Activity E — The Choice is Yours Game

Now we are going to play the game "The Choice is Yours." Here is the situation. You are at a baseball game when a group of friends ask you if you would like to go with them and buy a six-pack of beer. You really don't want to do it. It is unlawful for you to use alcohol or drugs.

> *HINT: Have several students act as the persuasive group and ask some other students to come up and act out ALL possible alternatives with each situation. Use "The Choice is Yours" procedure.*

Sometimes peer pressure is very subtle and you aren't aware that it is being applied. What are the choices is this situation? You walk into a party and everyone has a can of beer in his or her hand. The host or hostess greets you and, without asking if you want one, hands you a beer. You don't want to drink alcohol. Several people watch to see what you will do. Who would like to be the host or hostess? (Choose one student.) We need two volunteers to be party-goers. Now we need someone to be the new arrival, who is handed a beer. What would you choose to do? (Choose students with different alternatives.)

Here's another situation: You are walking home from school and see a friend smoking but he/she does not know that you see him/her. What would you do? (Be sure to act this out, even though there is only one speaking part.)

> *HINT: Follow each situation by discusssing risk and gains. Remember to have individual students make a commitment to which choice he/she would be most likely to make. Then ask students to raise their hands when they have made a choice.*

We'll be back in two weeks with another PSE lesson. Meanwhile, be good to yourself and to each other.

Review of Film "How Do You Tell?"

Since this film may not be available to you, we are providing a synopsis so that similar information may be used.

"How Do You Tell?" is a delightful, entertaining film which combines cartoon with interviews of sixth and seventh grade students. The first question asked of the students is "How do you tell friends you really like that they are doing something dumb or something that will hurt them?" The students are refreshingly honest and caring when they answer "I like you too much to see you hurt yourself." Several important questions are discussed in the film

1. Why do kids smoke? (to act "cool", to feel grown up) The film tells kids scientists have proven that smoking is bad for your lungs, and causes cancer, lung, and heart disease. It is difficult to stop smoking.

2. Why do kids smoke marijuana? (friends do it, want to be part of the group, don't feel good about selves, think it will bring good feelings, avoiding problems)

3. What is the "dark side" of marijuana? (You can become a pot head. You lose energy and strength. Your physical and mental growth processes slow down and there is damage to lungs and brain.) Scientists have also found out that heavy, long-term marijuana use causes brain burnout.

4. How can you tell if a person is involved in substance abuse? (You can tell if a friend is using drugs or alcohol because his eyes will be glassy, he won't make sense, he may stagger, or may act mean.)

5. What do you do if you are offered drugs? (If you are offered drugs you can say: "No, I don't want to mess up my life," or "No, it is not good for you, either," or "No, I want to stay the way I am, I like myself.")

The film very clearly shows that combined use of dope and alcohol can be very harmful. Because of what these chemicals do to the body, they are more than just twice as harmful. The real advantage of this film is that it shows kids talking to kids. No adult is lecturing, and the dialogue seems very authentic.

Distributed by MTI Teleprograms Inc.
108 Wilmot Road
Deerfield, Ill. 60015
(800) 621-2131. In Illinois, Alaska and Hawaii, call collect:
(312) 940-1260.

_____ **Lesson 8**_____

Review of PSE Principles

Objectives

- The child will determine which assertive training technique to use in a given situation.

- The child will participate in a review game.

Materials

Envelopes with possible situations on strips for practice — one envelope for each group of students (see Activity C), Harmony, Optional: Envelopes with PSE topics strips (see Activity D)

Activity A — Stress Reduction Exercise (read verbatim)

Sit up tall but comfortably and, please look down into your lap and keep looking down for the entire exercise. We are going to do a breathing exercise. As you take long, slow, deep breaths in through your nose and out through your mouth, you will hear me say "re" on the intake of air and "lax" on the output. Take air in through your nose . . . "re." Let the air through your mouth . . . "lax." In . . . re; out . . . lax. In . . . re; out . . . lax. In . . . re; out . . . lax. Stop. Sit quietly and enjoy the feeling of being relaxed. (Allow thirty seconds.)

Activity B — Review of the Movie from Lesson 7

In our last lesson we saw a movie about drug abuse. What were some of the main ideas of the movie? (say no to drugs and alcohol) How could the assertive techniques of the Broken Record and Fogging help you say no to drugs and alcohol?   (use them when others offer drugs and alcohol)

Activity C — Using the Broken Record, Fogging, and Assertive Apology

> *HINT: Write the steps for Assertive Apology on the board. They are: 1. Apologize by stating your feelings. 2. Pat self on back. 3. State your intention.*

The steps for the Assertive Apology are on the board. Let's add the rules for the Broken Record (kind statement + policy statement — repeat over and over.) We'll also add the rules for Fogging (to agree or agree with the possibility) First, you will listen to the example and decide what to say. Let's do one. Your friend wants you to go to a play. You don't want to go. Now, decide which assertive training technique would you use? (Broken Record) What would you say? (I understand you want to go to the play, I don't want to go tonight.) Let's try one more. You borrowed your friend's book. You forgot to return it. Which assertive technique would you use? (Assertive Apology) What would you say? (I feel badly, I forgot your book, I don't usually do that. I'll bring it tomorrow.)

> *HINT: For this next exercise divide the class into three groups. There must be one PSE volunteer for each group. Pass out the envelopes. (Remember to collect them when finished.) As one student draws a slip and reads it, the PSE volunteer will playact the situation with the student and then ask the group to identify which technique is being used.*
>
> *Monitor the class activity. Students may need to be reminded to keep the noise down since all three groups will be talking at the same time. Topics for group slips are at the end of this lesson so you can duplicate, cut, and use.*

This time, we are going to break you into three groups. Each group will be given an envelope. Each envelope has strips with possible situations in which you might use the Broken Record, Fogging, or the Assertive Apology. Sometimes you will use more than one technique. One person will draw a strip, read it to the group, and then decide which technique to use. The PSE volunteer will playact the situation with you. The group will decide which assertive technique was used. The envelope will be passed around so each person gets an opportunity to practice. This is for practice, and is to be fun. It may seem stilted, and not at all like real life, but the purpose is to practice so that you can handle any and all situations in real life.

Activity D — Review of Material in PSE Program

> *HINT: A review lesson may be handled in any way the PSE team desires. This is one place we try to tap your creativity. Therefore, the following is a suggestion only.*

Review Lesson Suggestions

1. Divide class into groups of three.
2. Have possible topics in an envelope. Have one person in each group draw a strip with an idea or topic to be acted out.
3. Topics will be acted out so the class can guess from which lesson the idea came and discuss whatever they remember about that idea.

Hi Harmony! (Bring Harmony in and have him wave to the class.) How are you? (Harmony scratches head, moves in a circle, and jumps backward. PSE volunteer laughs.) You have been learning so much so fast in the PSE lesson, you are not sure if you can remember it all? Maybe it's time for a review. (Harmony claps paws.)

Class, this is our next-to-the-last lesson. We thought it would be fun to review some of the lessons. We will give each group an envelope which contains a slip with one of the PSE topics. Your group is to think of a way to act out this topic. The rest of the class will guess the topic and then we will have a short discussion. If you have any questions, raise your hand and we will come to your group. (Pass out envelope. Allow three or four minutes.)

Here we go, folks, with the (school name) school's version of EVERYTHING YOU WANT TO KNOW ABOUT PSE BUT DIDN'T ASK."

Possible Ideas and Topics for Playacting As a Review

1. Introducing two people to each other.
2. Introducing yourself to someone you don't know.
3. King Kong
4. Doormat
5. Broken Record
6. Fogging
7. Assertive Apology
8. Peer Pressure
9. Listening to each other
10. Stress reduction exercise
11. Be good to yourself and to each other

HINT: Call one group at a time to act out their strip. Encourage comments and discussion regarding the topic material. Keep it moving to cut down on class restlessness. Be lively! Have fun! Enjoy!

Activity E — Lesson Ending

We had fun reviewing, today. You have some new tools to use in your life. When you use them, life will be easier. The next lesson is our last one for this year. We will be bringing in some seventh and eighth graders to talk to you about the differences between elementary school and junior high. We'll see you then. Meantime, be good to yourself and be good to each other.

Strips for Review of Broken Record, Fogging and Assertive Apology: (Activity C)

1. You trip and fall. Someone calls you clumsy.

-- -- -- -- -- -- -- -- -- -- -- -- -- -- -- -- -- -- -- --

2. A friend wants you to go to a show. You don't want to go.

-- -- -- -- -- -- -- -- -- -- -- -- -- -- -- -- -- -- -- --

3. You agree to meet a friend every day to ride bikes to school and you forget.

-- -- -- -- -- -- -- -- -- -- -- -- -- -- -- -- -- -- -- --

4. Another person tries to sell you something that you do not want.

-- -- -- -- -- -- -- -- -- -- -- -- -- -- -- -- -- -- -- --

5. A friend says to you, "How could you eat an egg salad sandwich? I'd rather starve!"

-- -- -- -- -- -- -- -- -- -- -- -- -- -- -- -- -- -- -- --

6. One person says to another "You're such a jerk!"

-- -- -- -- -- -- -- -- -- -- -- -- -- -- -- -- -- -- -- --

7. Someone says you lied when you really didn't.

-- -- -- -- -- -- -- -- -- -- -- -- -- -- -- -- -- -- -- --

8. You throw a ball and it hits someone.

-- -- -- -- -- -- -- -- -- -- -- -- -- -- -- -- -- -- -- --

9. A friend wants you to loan him/her money. You really don't want to loan your money.

-- -- -- -- -- -- -- -- -- -- -- -- -- -- -- -- -- -- -- --

10. You knock over a glass of milk. Your friend says, "That was a dumb thing to do!"

-- -- -- -- -- -- -- -- -- -- -- -- -- -- -- -- -- -- -- --

Answers: Broken Record = BR, Fogging = F, Assertive Apology = AA

1. F and BR, 2. BR, 2. AA, 4. BR, 5. F, 6. F, 7. BR, 8. AA, 9. BR, 10. F.

_____ Lesson 9 _____

Introduction to Junior High

Objectives

- The child will listen to junior high students talk about going to seventh grade.
- The child will write a question about going to junior high school.
- The child will participate in a group discussion about going to junior high school

Background

Often, the best antidote for fear is information. New situations are fearful for many students. The purpose of this lesson is to let kids talk to kids about the way it really is in junior high school.

Materials

Slips of paper for questions

Activity A — Meet with Junior High Students

> HINT: This whole activity has to be carefully orchestrated. At the end of this lesson we've included a list of suggestions to be sure it runs smoothly.

Doing something for the first time is often frightening. This lesson was planned to help alleviate some of the fear you might have of going to junior high. We've invited several junior high students to speak to you. Each of them would like to talk briefly and then you may ask questions.

> HINT: First introduce the moderator and the guest speakers, then tell a little about each of them. Allow time for the seventh graders to speak.

Thank you (names of guest students), we really learned a lot. We are going to distribute slips of paper (One PSE team member distributes paper as the other explains directions to class.) Please write a question concerning anything that the panel did not cover. You don't need to put your names on the slips. If you don't have a question, you can write a compliment to the group.

HINT: Allow one or two minutes and then collect the papers. Select slips one at a time, in random order. You might want to have the moderator screen them first. Allow time for all questions to be answered.

This has been very interesting. Let's thank the guest speakers and the moderator with our applause.

Activity B — Lesson Closing

Many of you have been in Project Self-Esteem since the second grade. We hope you have learned useful ideas for your whole life through PSE. Remember, we were here because we care about you and your sometimes difficult job of growing up. In the weeks and years ahead, remember to be good to yourself and to each other.

Steps to Take When Inviting Guest Speakers

1. **Meet with the principal of the local junior high school.**
   a. Ask him to invite all sixth graders to the junior high school's Open House, if possible. Do this early in the year and let the kids know about this invitation well in advance. A reminder or two wouldn't hurt.
   b. Ask the principal if you can invite several junior high school students to speak to the sixth graders. (You will need 4 seventh graders to speak and 1 eighth grader to be a moderator. Give the specific date and time.)
   c. You will want high self-esteem students as guests. Ask the junior high school principal and the teachers at your school to suggest people to use for this activity. Suggest that the students be ones that graduated from your elementary school, if possible.

2. **Set up a meeting with the junior high students at their school.**
   a. You will want to ask them to think about several questions the sixth graders might be considering. (Was the change of school scarey for them? What would they have liked to have known? What did they need to know?) The object is to inform and alleviate fears, not to create more fear.

3. **Make a list of categories to help the junior high students.**
   a. Academic (homework, what subjects students have the first year, grades.)
   b. PE/Sports (type of dress for gym, what sports available, showers, etc.)

c. Routine (Go through one day in the life of a seventh grader — especially the first day.)

d. Miscellaneous (How does one behave in the beginning as teachers are forming their opinion about you? What are some junior high rules and consequences? How do you get to lunch? Information on bells, extra curricular activities, clothing.)

HINT: Allow seventh graders to choose categories to be covered in a brief talk for the sixth graders. Give the students your phone number in case of questions, illness, or problems.

4. **Arrange transportation to the elementary school. Be sure to clear it through the principal.**
   a. Be certain each student has a permission slip.
   b. Ask students to be sure to be on time.

5. **Arrange transportation back to the school or to individual student homes.**
   a. It's fun to treat the junior high school students to ice cream and talk about the day when they are finished.
   b. Write a thank you note to each seventh and eighth grader who participated.

Chapter

Teacher's
Guide

Chapter VIII

Teacher's Guide

Introduction

The following pages are suggestions for individual teacher use of the Project Self-Esteem program. The outline follows the lessons for grades 2/3, 4, 5, and 6. The Kindergarten and First Grade lessons are short enough to be taught in their entirety during 5 twenty-five minute sessions for each grade level. You can teach the PSE lessons for grades 2-6 in two ways:

- in increments of 12 forty-minute lessons
- in shorter increments — by dividing most of the lessons into two parts

Because we know that you often teach subjects in short time slots, we have divided the 2/3, 4, 5, and 6th grade lessons into two sections (where possible), for your convenience. The stress reduction exercises are repeated since they have such a calming effect in the classroom. You'll find that the length of each lesson will be dependent upon the amount of student participation. Our suggestion plan includes:

- 2/3 grades — 3 forty-minute lessons and 18 twenty-minute lessons
- 4th grade — 3 forty-minute lessons and 16 twenty-minute lessons
- 5th grade — 5 forty-minute lessons and 12 twenty-minute lessons
- 6th grade — 1 forty-minute lesson and 16 twenty-minute lessons

You are encouraged to use the scripted material as a guideline for presentation. However, you are in no way asked to memorize or present the material verbatim. The stress reduction exercises, Lesson 11 in the 2/3 program, and Lesson 10 in both the 4th and 5th grade programs are the exception to this statement and are to be read verbatim.

Bulletin board strips are recommended for follow-up work. You may want to develop your own individualized program for continued use of the Project-Self-Esteem principles. Difficulties or problems which arise in the classroom may be addressed with the use of Harmony, the bear hand puppet. There are unlimited possibilities, within the curriculum, for creating your own follow-up activities. For example, a classroom in California put notes saying "You Are Special!" into helium balloons and let them go. Return addresses were included in the notes, and the response from the longest distance away, to date, is Missouri.

In specific instances (which are clearly stated in your outline), it will be difficult for that section of a lesson to be taught by one person. PSE is designed to be taught by three or four persons. Please follow the stated suggestions and/or use your own resources.

The most common statement made by classroom teachers who have had Project Self-Esteem in their classroom is "After PSE, the children are nicer to each other." So, we welcome you to a delightful experience with your class which will reward you all in immeasurable ways.

2/3 Grade Program

Lesson 1 — Realizing Your Uniqueness

Do the whole lesson.

Lesson 2 — Gratitudes and Changes/Attitude

First half — Do: A, B, C, and D.

> *ACTIVITY D: This skit requires two people. Use yourself and one capable student.*

Second half — Do: E, F, G, and H.

Lesson 3 — Compliments

First half — Do: A, B, C, D, and E.

Second half — Do: E   (Review), F, G, and H.

> *ACTIVITY F: Instead of doing group work, the children can practice giving compliments with the teacher.*
>
> *1. Skip opening the box of Smileys.*
>
> *2. Begin with appropriate material   (for grade 2 or 3.)*
>
> *3. Teacher takes the role of the person receiving the compliment. For example: "Peggy, your mother fixed your favorite dinner. What might you say to your mom?"*

Lesson 4 — Rumors and Stress Reduction

First half — Do: A and B.

Second half — Do: C, D, E, and F.

Lesson 5 — Feelings

First half — Do: A, B, C, D, and E

> *ACTIVITY E: Look at one item in a box and write the first feeling.*

Second half — Do: B   (Review), E, F, and G.

> *ACTIVITY E: Look at one item in a box and write the first feeling.*

Lesson 6 — Person and Actions Are Separate

First half — Do: A, B, C, and D.

ACTIVITY D: Requires two people. Prepare ahead of time with capable student. Do only one playacting example this time.

Second half — Do: B (Review), E, F (worksheet), and G.

ACTIVITY E: Do the two remaining playacting examples.

Lesson 7 — Communication Skills, Part I

First half — Do: A, B, C, D, and E.

Second half — Do: B (Review), F, G, H (worksheet), and I.

Lesson 8 — Communication Skills, Part II

First half — Do: A, B, and C.

Second half — Do: A (Review), D, E, and F.

ACTIVITY D: Requires two people. Prepare ahead of time with capable student.

Lesson 9 — Friendship, Part I

First half — Do: A, B, and C.

Second half — Do: B (Review), D, and E.

Lesson 10 — Friendship, Part II

First half — Do: A, B, C, and D.

Second half — Do: B (Review), E, F, and G.

Lesson 11 — Tattling and Cheating

Do the whole lesson. This lesson needs several people to play all the parts. You might ask three parents or three other teachers to do this lesson with you.

Lesson 12 — Review: Final Lesson

Do the whole lesson. Follow the suggestions given in the lesson.

4th Grade Program

Lesson 1 — Realizing Your Uniqueness

First half — Do: A, B, and C.

ACTIVITY C: Divide class into pairs instead of groups. Introduce to the whole class.

Second half — Do: D, E, F, and G.

> *ACTIVITY F: If this is the students' first experience with the stress reduction exercises, it would be wise to include part of the 2/3 program, Lesson 4 (D and E). Your lesson time will be increased by ten minutes or more.*

Lesson 2 — Goal Setting

First half — Do: A, B, C, and D.

Second half — Do: A (Review), E, F, and G.

> *ACTIVITY F: The class may be divided into four groups which could be seen at four different times (segmented as during a normal reading group lesson). It is easier to give personal attention in a small group situation.*

Lesson 3 — Goal Setting and Compliments

First half — Do: A, B, C, and D.

Second half — Do: A (Review), D (Review), E, F, and G.

> *ACTIVITY D: Give the Smileys out to each student in the SECOND half of the lesson.*

> *ACTIVITY E: This segment is designed for group work. It may be done with the entire class or in the group situation you created for Lesson 2, Activity F.*

Lesson 4 — Listening and Stress Reduction

Do the whole lesson.

> *ACTIVITY A: This part of the lesson is optional and need not be included unless there is a long vacation between lesson three and four.*

Lesson 5 — Learning to Memorize

First half — Do: A, B, and C.

Second half — Do: A (Review), D, and E.

Lesson 6 — Feelings

First half — Do: A, B, C, and D.

Second half — Do: B (Review), E, F, and G.

> *ACTIVITY E: This segment is designed for group work. Use the same format as you did in Lesson 2, Activity F.*

Lesson 7 — High and Low Self-Esteem: Review

First half — Do: A, B, and C.

Second half — Do: B (Review), D, E, and F.

Lesson 8 — Communicating Assertively

First half — Do: A, B, and C.

Second half: Do: B (Review), D, E, and F.

Lesson 9 — Friendship

First half — Do: A, B, C, and D.

Second half — Do: B (Review), E, F, and G.

Lesson 10 — Stealing and Teasing

Do the whole lesson. This lesson needs three or four people to play all the parts. We suggest using four parents or four teachers, recruited to assist you.

Lesson 11 — Review: Final Lesson

Do the whole lesson. Follow the lesson suggestions.

5th Grade Program

Lesson 1 — Realizing Your Uniqueness

First half — Do: A, B, and C.
>   *ACTIVITY C: Divide class into pairs instead of groups. Introduce to the whole class.*

Second half — Do: D, E, F, and G.
>   *ACTIVITY G: If this is the students' first experience with the stress reduction exercises, it would be wise to include part of the 2/3 program, Lesson 4 (D and E). Your lesson time will be increased by ten minutes or more.*

Lesson 2 — Goal Setting and Memorizing

First half — Do: A, B, C, and D.

Second half — Do: A (Review), E, F, and G.
>   *ACTIVITY E: The class may be divided into four groups which could be seen at four different times   (segmented as during a normal reading group lesson). It is easier to give personal attention in a small group situation.*

Lesson 3 — Goal Setting and Compliments

First half — Do: A, B, C, and D.

Second half — Do: A (Review), E, F, G, and H.

ACTIVITY G· This segment is designed for group work. It may be done with the entire class or in the group situation you created for Lesson 2, Activity E. Give the Smileys out to each student in the SECOND half of the lesson.

Lesson 4 — Listening

Do: B, C, D, and F.
ACTIVITY A: This part of the lesson is optional and need not be included unless there is a long vacation between lesson three and four.

Lesson 5 — Communication Skills

First half — Do: A, B, and C.

Second half — Do: B   (Review), D, and E.

Lesson 6 — Working with Anger

Do the whole lesson.

Lesson 7 — Handling Incoming Anger and Upsets

First half — Do: A, B, and C.

Second half — Do: B   (Review), D, E, F, and G.

Lesson 8 — Communicating Assertively

First half — Do: A, B, and C.

Second half — Do: B   (Review), D, E, and F.

Lesson 9 — Learning about Handicaps and Listening

Do the whole lesson. Activity C: This activity can be done as a whole class exercise rather than separating into groups.

Lesson 10 — Stealing and Teasing

Do the whole lesson. This lesson needs three or four people to play all the parts. We suggest using four parents or four teachers, recruited to assist you.

Lesson 11 — Review: Final Lesson

Do the whole lesson. Follow the lesson suggestions.

6th Grade Program

Lesson 1 — Social Skills

First half — Do: A, B, C, D, and E.

Second half — Do: C (Review), E (Review), F, and G.

Lesson 2 — Social Skills/Choice Making

First half — Do: A, B, C, D, and E.

Second half — Do: A (Review), F, G, H, and I.

Lesson 3 — Assertive Training: Broken Record

First half — Do: A, B, C, D, and E.

Second half — Do: A (Review), F, and G.
>   *ACTIVITY F: Use sixth grader or another adult (parent or teacher), for this part.*

Lesson 4 — Assertive Training: Fogging

First half — Do: A, B, and C.

Second half — Do: A (Review), C (Review), D, E, and F.

Lesson 5 — Peers and Conformity

First half — Do: A, B, C, and D.

Second half — Do: A (Review), E, F, and G.
>   *ACTIVITY F: Requires two students. Prepare ahead of time.*

Lesson 6 — Friendship and Assertive Apology

First half — Do: A, B, and C.

Second half — Do: A (Review), D, E, and F.

Lesson 7 — Alcohol and Drug Abuse

First half — Do: A, B, C, and D.

Second half — Do: A (Review), D (Review), E, and F.

Lesson 8 — Review of PSE Principles

First half — Do: A, B, and C.

Second half — Do: A (Review), D, and E.

Lesson 9 — Introduction to Junior High

Do the entire lesson as written.

Chapter

Parent
Program

Chapter IX

Parent Program

From the beginning, we realized that the most viable means of reaching and assisting children is through the home and school working together. This parent section is a vital part of the Project Self-Esteem program and serves as an outline for teaching the PSE principles in the home.

• It informs the parents of the philosophy and teaching of the program. Parents may reinforce and add to these concepts with values and morals of their own.

• Since the school program is limited to no more than twelve lessons during the year, the Parent Program provides important follow-up and enrichment.

• Parents whose children are not in the PSE program may use the parent section to strengthen their own family teachings.

The Parent Program is designed to reach as many different types of families as possible. Additional ideas for family use may come out of our suggestions. Some families may not choose to use all of the ideas presented in this program.

We have seen children who have had very little to say suddenly become verbal fountains when asked about Harmony or some PSE lesson. Family ties are strengthened by communicating, sharing, and being together. One objective of the Parent Program is to provide a catalyst for closer association between a parent and child.

The parent page for the Kindergarten and First Grade programs consists of a one-page explanatory letter. This same letter can also be sent home to parents of students in grades 2-6 who are new to the PSE program. Don't forget to date and sign the master before sending the letter home. The parent pages for the 2/3, 4, 5, and 6th grade programs cover each individual lesson and coordinate with the PSE lesson taught at school.

Individual schools will determine how the Parent Program is to be sent home. Some schools may send the sheets home after each lesson. Some may send all the Parent Program pages home at once — or give them out at Back-to-School Night. Each team leader can work with the school principal to choose the best means of seeing that the Parent Program reaches the people for whom it is intended...the parents!

This program is designed to encourage parents and schools to work together to give children every possible means of becoming capable, contributing, loving human beings.

Dear Parents:

Your child is about to participate in a program called Project Self-Esteem or PSE. The purpose of Project Self-Esteem is to provide children with information which will assist them in their daily lives. Project Self-Esteem's goal is to allow new choices for children.

The greatest value of the Parent Program is that it allows parents the opportunity to reinforce their own family morals and values along with the PSE concepts. Sample lesson topics include:

- **Kindergarten and First Grade —**
  Being a Friend, Taking Care of Yourself, Being Kind to Others

- **Second and Third Grade —**
  Realizing Your Uniqueness, Gratitude, Giving Compliments, Communication Skills, Friendship

- **Fourth Grade —**
  Goal Setting, Listening, Learning to Memorize, High and Low Self-Esteem, Communicating Assertively

- **Fifth Grade —**
  Practicing Listening Skills, Learning to Memorize, Stress Reduction, Handling Anger, Understanding Handicaps, Handling Stealing and Teasing

- **Sixth Grade —**
  Social Skills, Choice Making, Assertive Training, Peers and Conformity, Understanding Alcohol and Drug Abuse

The PSE team members appreciate your support.

Sincerely,

PSE Team Leader

_____ **Lesson 1** _____

Realizing Your Uniqueness

Background

Every human being needs to feel LOVABLE and CAPABLE. Feeling lovable comes primarily from the knowledge that we are loved unconditionally by significant others. Feeling capable means we know we are able to do something well. High self-esteem, then, is a balance of feeling lovable and capable.

In a society which is "do" oriented (do this, do that), it's easy to get swept up in the belief that there is a need to DO something to be special. The truth is, each human being is an unrepeatable happening in the universe. EACH OF US is special. What we do is what we are learning. Being special is a gift no one can take away. Feeling special is not an ego trip. Each and every person is special so there is no need to compete. We are all special so let's celebrate together!

If Your Child Is in the Project Self-Esteem Program

1. Who is Harmony? (a puppet)

2. What do you have to do in order to be special? (Nothing. One of a kind is as special as you can get.)

3. Can you be more special than someone else? (No! Everyone is one of a kind. Each of us is special no matter what we do.)

Family Activities

1. Have a family plate which is only used as a celebration of the acknowledgement for being lovable (celebrate being you), or capable (something done well).

2. Give each child some one-to-one time every day (even a five-minute backrub before sleep).

3. Each child needs to have one-to-one time with the father and the mother as often as possible. It can be small like going to the market or big like "Just us, out to dinner."

4. Keep a photo album or scrapbook (a personalized reminder of his/her past) for each child. Let the child assist with the creation of this book.

5. Make periodic cassette recordings of your child talking.

6. Use humor in a note to remind your child of an unfinished chore. Examples of such messages are: "The Health Department will inspect this room at 4:00 p.m. today" or "These ice cubes will not clone themselves, please fill the trays."

_____ **Lesson 2** _____

Gratitudes and Changes/Attitude

Background

In any given situation, each person has a choice. Attitude IS THE DIFFERENCE. A person's outlook substantially influences how he/she approaches anything. A child with a learning difficulty needs to be approached FIRST in terms of attitude. One means of dissecting a problem, be it with a person or a situation, is to examine attitude.

Often we want to change the world around us to make it easy. Sometimes we cannot change situations or how others treat us. Working with a child's attitude allows him/her something to do as an alternative to feeling sorry for self and being immobilized.

If Your Child Is in the Project Self-Esteem Program

1. What could be changed in the skit about the girl Nancy whose clock was slow and in the skit where the ball got popped? (attitude)

2. Discuss: What is something you can't change? (cleaning your room) How could you change your attitude about that? (make a game of it)

3. Will you sing "You Are Special and You Know It" for me? (You are special and you know it, clap your hands...)

Family Activities

1. Talk about some things for which you are grateful. Then discuss the things you would change. (world, school, etc.) Think about how you could change your attitude about each thing on your "change" list. (Do what you can do. Don't spend time worrying about what you can't do.)

2. Discuss home chores. Discover ways of making distasteful tasks more fun. For example, everybody could work together to clean the kitchen before the timer goes off.

3. List chores to be done on separate pieces of paper, put strips in a bag, and then have each family member draw one. Be sure everyone has at least one job, toddlers included. The "too busy" child may be given a time period (by five o'clock on Sunday) in which to have a job completed.

4. Discuss: If a child in the neighborhood is teasing you and you can't change the child, how can you change your attitude to feel better about the situation? (You could ignore the teasing and not let yourself be bothered. You could remember that a person who teases is upset about something and is trying to get you upset.)

_____ Lesson 3 _____

Smileys and Compliments

Background

Everyone likes compliments. However, the tendency is to focus on what people do incorrectly. Consequently not enough attention is given to what is done correctly. This lesson teaches there is good in everyone. People thrive on encouragement. Sincere compliments assist people in feeling good about themselves.

We encourage the use of "I" messages in giving compliments. This means a compliment is begun with the word "I." Normally, people say "You look nice." Use of the word "you" is judgmental. Judging sets up people-pleasing. People-pleasing decreases self-esteem. So, from "You look nice," we change the "you" to "I" and say "I really like that color on you!" To say "You're a good friend!" is an empty phrase. It is much more personal to hear, "I feel better having talked to you. I'm glad we are friends." Beware of disguised "you" messages such as, "I think you are rude."

If Your Child Is in the Project Self-Esteem Program

1. Can you tell me about Molly? (Molly was someone to whom we gave compliments. She could do some things well but there were other things she couldn't do. We talked about finding good in everybody.)

2. What is a Smiley? (a yarn ball) What does a Smiley stand for? (a compliment) What can you do when you receive a compliment? (say thank you or sincerely return the compliment)

3. In the story "The Rarest Gift," what was inside of the box? (Allison)

Family Activities

1. Write the name of some family member not living in your home (grandmother, grandfather, aunt, uncle) or a close friend of the whole family on the top of page. Have each person write an "I" message compliment for that person on the paper. Mail or give the paper to that person.

2. At the dinner table, ask each member to give a compliment to the person on his/her right. Begin each compliment with the word "I."

3. Write each family member's name on a piece of paper and draw one from a box or a hat. Have each family member give that person a compliment beginning with the word "I."

4. On the week of someone's birthday, tape a paper bag to that person's bedroom door. Slips of paper with "I" message compliments may be put into the bag all week. The bag of compliments may be saved for a "down" day.

_____ **Lesson 4** _____

Rumors and Stress Reduction

Background

The tendency is to say "rumors happen," but each of us has a responsibility in dealing with rumors: (1) Not to believe everything we hear (2) Not to pass a rumor (3) Not to "mirror" passing rumors to our children especially in the form of gossip.

People think they relax by watching TV or reading a book. Though these activities can be relaxing, they are not enough. Research tells us that we are a stress-oriented nation. Techniques have been developed by stress clinics, the medical profession, and a number of other groups for the purpose of teaching people to relax. Scientific research is proving that being relaxed affects health, attitudes, and performance in all walks of life. The stress reduction techniques used in Project Self-Esteem are based on careful research and were chosen to assist children in relaxing.

If Your Child Is in the Project Self-Esteem Program

1. What's a rumor? (something said about someone which may or may not be true)

2. What do you do if you hear a rumor? (don't believe it, don't pass it on.)

3. Show me how to breathe properly. (hands above stomach, breathe deeply, fingers spread apart, and stomach pushed out)

4. When could you do a stress reduction technique? (whenever you want to calm down and relax)

Family Activities

1. Talk about a time someone gossiped about you and discuss how you felt about it. Talk about why people pass rumors and how harmful they can be.

2. Have the whole family practice relaxing together. Begin by taking a long slow breath in through your nose, holding it for a moment, and then slowly letting it out through your mouth. Do this four times in a row. Talk about other things you can do to feel calm and relaxed.

3. Look through magazines and newspapers and discover articles about stress management. Discuss ways you, as a family, can work together to use stress reduction exercises.

Lesson 5

Feelings

Background

Feelings are friends. They give information about what is important to us. If someone is mean, our feelings of hurt are telling us that we like to be treated kindly. When someone loves us just for being ourselves, we feel happy inside. Sadness tells us we want something to go differently than it did.

Many people try to keep their feelings all bottled-up inside. But feelings are all hooked up together. They are like a string of Christmas lights: when one goes out, the whole string goes out. In the same way, when a person closes off one feeling such as sadness or love, all other emotions close down as well.

If Your Child Is in the Project Self-Esteem Program

1. Why was Jack afraid of dogs? (One jumped on him when he was little.) Was Jack always afraid of dogs? (No. He was given a puppy and learned to trust dogs.)

2. What was in the box? (varies from school to school)

3. Did everyone have the same feeling about what was in the box? (No. There were lots of different feelings.)

4. How could people have so many different feelings about the items in the box? (Not everyone feels the same about any one thing, and that's OK.)

Family Activities

1. Go around the family and have each person discuss one time they felt happy. Repeat this activity with proud, important, sad, and other feelings. Please accept what is said without judgment. Any teaching may be done at a later date. This is to be a safe place for sharing.

2. Ask everyone to think of something about which they are afraid (snakes, heights, public speaking, etc.). You might take time to share these fears. No one is to try to change, judge, or comment negatively about anything said. The object is to realize that everyone has fears and that people have different fears.

3. Have everyone think of something about which they were once afraid but are no longer. Share and discuss. Note: feelings can change.

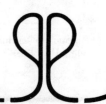

_____ **Lesson 6** _____

Person and Actions Are Separate

Background

To call someone a "jerk" is to put that person into a box. It is one thing to have "jerky" behavior and quite another thing to be a "jerk." I can, if I choose, change "jerky" behavior, but to change "BEING A JERK" is nearly impossible. It is important to separate the person from his/her actions. "I" messages are an effective means of separating a person from actions. Instead of "You're a slob!" say, "this is a recording: I want you to put your toys on the shelf so I can walk into the room without getting insurance." It is important to remember to give constructive criticism, focusing on behavior and not the person. This is a difficult area for many parents as most of us were raised with "you" messages. The most constructive way of learning to use "I" messages is to practice. . .don't give up!

If Your Child Is in the Project Self-Esteem Program

1. Why was Harmony upset? (He missed the children while he was in hibernation.)

2. Why was the PSE volunteer upset with Harmony? (He misbehaved during the lesson.)

3. Did the PSE volunteer still like Harmony when he misbehaved? (yes) What didn't she like? (his actions)

Family Activities

1. As a family, list often-heard "you" messages (with no reference as to who gives them). Discuss how to change those "you" messages to "I" messages.

2. Whenever a child is upset with another person, discuss how he/she can state feelings in a way that clearly illustrates the problem. (I'm upset that you borrowed my toy.)

3. Make a family agreement to use "I" messages when disagreeing or fighting. Discuss a workable method of switching from "you" to "I" messages.

4. Focus your comment on what the person does rather than the person. (When your chores are consistently not done, I really get upset.) It is wise to set up a plan of action to remedy the situation. (I want you to vacuum your room within the next hour. Do you agree?)

5. Discuss, as a family, specific times you felt upset outside of the home. Change language about the incident from "She's a scumball!" to "I really didn't like it when she sneered at me."

_____ Lesson 7 _____

Communication Skills, Part I

Background

Many psychologists tell us that lack of communication is one of the primary problems facing human beings today. Assisting children in getting in touch with their feelings and wants and in learning to express both is important.

When a person tells another person about his/her feelings and wants, this may not alter the situation. The value is in having a means of standing up for your own rights. People who know how to express their feelings and wants tend to be victimized less by those people who want to tease and manipulate them.

If Your Child Is in the Project Self-Esteem Program

1. You talked about body language. Do you remember how to say yes, happy, no, without any words?

2. If someone took your pencil what two things would you say? (One answer might be, "I feel upset and I want you to return my pencil.")

3. When you ask for what you want, do you always get it? (No. The other purpose is to express feelings so you don't keep them inside.)

Family Activities

1. Research indicates up to 95% of what we say is communicated through body language. Have family members give examples of some uses of body language (thumbs up for yes, shaking finger for no, etc.)

2. Stating feelings is important. Stating wants does not mean you get what you want. The purpose in expressing feelings and wants is to clearly communicate your thoughts. Example: A friend borrows your bike without asking. You might say, "I feel frustrated. I want you to ask me first." Discuss what to say:

• The kids' room is a mess. (I feel annoyed when I walk into your room and I want you to clean it right now.)

• Someone was late picking you up and you will be late to the meeting. (I hate being late and I want you to know how upset I feel.)

• Your mother baked cookies. (Wow! Am I hungry! I want to eat a dozen of your great cookies!)

_____ **Lesson 8** _____

Communication Skills, Part II

Background

Careless use of words causes many problems in interpersonal relationships. Communication skills give children an alternative in the way they speak to others. Being aware that we com- municate more through body language and tone of voice than words assists us in being alert to what others are communicating as well as to what message we are sending

If Your Child Is in the Project Self-Esteem Program

1. When we use our hands, face, legs, and whole self to communicate, it is called _____ language. What goes into the blank? (body)

2. The tone of voice is also an important part of how you communicate. Can you say "Hi, Mom" and sound happy? Say the same words and sound unhappy. How about excited?

3. Was Harmony in the lesson? (yes) When the PSE volunteer was talking to Harmony, she wouldn't do something. Do you remember what it was? (look at him)

Family Activities

1. The tone of voice is important in communication. Ask a question such as, "How was school today?" Have the child respond with "fine" while the family guesses what is being felt. Have the child transmit unhappy, happy, worried. Ask "Did you like the show?" and have a family member say "Yeah," transmitting that he/she loved it or was bored.

2. Often we say "fine" when we don't mean "fine." It is important to communicate openly and honestly. Discuss what could be said to "How was school today?" and "Did you like the show?" in a way to communicate true feelings.

3. Practice communicating using "I feel" and "I want."

4. List ten ways to be good to yourself and ten ways to be good to others in the family.

Permission to Reprint for Classroom Use: © McDaniel, Sandy & Bielen, Peggy, *Project Self-Esteem:* Rolling Hills Estates, California, Jalmar Press, 1990.

_____ Lesson 9 _____

Friendship, Part I

Background

Learning to get along with people is best developed through friendships. It is important that students learn to choose their friends wisely, to communicate effectively, and to be respon- sible friends themselves. Peer pressure has a huge influence on the individual child, so it is impor- tant to have supportive friends with the same values and morals

If Your Child Is in the Project Self-Esteem Program

1. What was one quality you put to complete the sentence "I like it when a friend _____?"

2. What is one quality you put to complete the sentence "It bothers me when a friend _____."

3. Which bulletin board strip (or bumper sticker) did you choose to make?

Family Activities

1. Discuss the qualities you like in a friend. Make a family list, in order of preference, of those qualities you value in friends.

2. Go to your local library. Look under "friendship" in the card catalogue. Appropriate stories are a positive way of supporting your child.

3. At dinner name one friend and three qualities you like in him or her. Discourage negative comments from other members of the family. One person's feelings may be different from another person's feelings.

4. Discuss ways in which to be a friend to yourself.

5. Listen. Hear where your child is, what he/she is doing, what's important, and what's being said.

Permission to Reprint for Classroom Use: © McDaniel, Sandy & Bielen, Peggy, *Project Self-Esteem:* Rolling Hills Estates, California, Jalmar Press, 1990.

_____ **Lesson 10** _____

Friendship, Part II

Background

Communication skills are taught with the intent of giving a child appropriate tools to use in support of his/her own values and ideals. Learning to express frustrations rather than holding them inside is a vital skill for all ages.

Knowing that there is an appropriate time, place and way to communicate will assist the individual child. Like learning any skills, practicing communication techniques makes them more available for daily use.

If Your Child Is in the Project Self-Esteem Program

1. Why did Sam blow up? (He stored his upsets with Chris until they blew up inside of him.)

2. What did Sam need to do so he wouldn't explode? (communicate his feelings.)

3. If someone takes your pencil what could you say to him or her? (I feel upset you took my pencil and I want you to give it back.)

4. Which appropriate sentence is being broken if you are arguing with a friend in the classroom? (Choose an appropriate time, place, and way.)

Family Activities

1. Using "Choose an appropriate time, place, and way" as your guideline, discuss which part of the rule would be broken if two kids begin hitting each other at a baseball game. (all of it) Also discuss how an upset might be solved in a positive way.

2. Discuss how difficult it is to say what you feel and want to a friend. Talk about the risks and gains of speaking the truth.

3. Write a note to a friend. Tell that person how much you value him/her. If the family has one friend in common, everybody could write a personalized compliment on a piece of paper and mail it to that person. Be sure to use "I" messages.

4. Everyone choose one way to be good to themselves tomorrow. Set as a goal that you will be good to yourself in that certain way.

_____ Lesson 11 _____

Tattling and Cheating

Background

Project Self-Esteem teaches when you are concerned with someone's safety or harm you are reporting, anything else is tattling. Once the difference between tattling and reporting is defined, the procedure is as follows. A child comes up to you and says "Johnny and Susie are talking." You reply "Is that tattling or reporting?" Continue to ask that same question until the child acknowledges tattling is occuring. In this way the responsibility for the action of tattling is placed with the person who is tattling. Cheating is also handled as an act which hurts the individual who cheats.

If Your Child Is in the Project Self-Esteem Program

1. Reporting is when you are concerned about someone else's what?   (safety or harm)

2. Tattling is minding someone else's what? (business)

3. Sally Sneaks-A-Look was crying. Why? (She cheated a lot in school. She got behind in her work, so she felt lost.)

Family Activities

1. Discuss the PSE statement from the background section concerning the definition of tattling and reporting. Take turns thinking of possible situations. One example would be: John tells his mother that Nancy took a cookie. Family members show thumbs up if tattling, thumbs down if reporting.

2. Sometimes cheating occurs because of strong family pressure to excell. If a child gets a low grade, rather than saying "You got a D! How did you get a D?" ask "How do you feel about that grade? What would you do differently if you could do it over again? What did you learn? Is there something I can do to assist you with this class?" We all make mistakes. The value of a mistake is to learn from it.

3. Discuss the effects on a person who chooses to cheat. Talk about how each family member feels about cheating. Talk about different forms of cheating (school, at games, not doing something the way you know it is to be done, etc.). Discuss how each person feels about being around someone who cheats. Include in your discussion any family morals or values concerning cheating.

Realizing Your Uniqueness

Background

Self-esteem means feeling good about our-selves. It is easy for parents to underestimate how vital respect and love are to their child. By treating each child as a valued individual, you enhance that child's self-esteem. One way to respect individuality is to refrain from verbally comparing your child.

If Your Child Is in the Project Self-Esteem Program

1. When you introduced yourself with a positive word that started with the same letter as your first name and then gave your first name, what did you say?

2. What did you decide to take with you on the space station?

3. What qualities did you decide you liked in someone else?

Family Activities

1. Using a positive word that starts with the same letter as your first name say, "I am...," that word, and your first name. Each person in the family will say his/her special name.   (I am Special Sandy.)

2. Pretend you and your family are going to move far away. You can only take one thing that belongs to you. Basic necessities will be provided. Nothing can be shipped or mailed. What will you take? The purpose of this exercise is to teach values without lecturing. By discussing each person's choice you can discover what he/she really values.

3. Have each family member take turns complimenting other people in the family. Focus on one person at a time. For example "What I appreciate about you is..." The person receiving the compliment can only say "Thank you."

4. Read with your child. The book selection may be a combination of "for pleasure" books and required reading as well. Take turns reading a page aloud for each other. It is important to be patient and supportive and allow the child to read at his/her own pace.

Lesson 2

Goal Setting

Background

The question arises "Can someone have too much self-esteem?" This is usually said in reference to someone who seems overconfident. Self-esteem is a quiet sense of well-being. The braggart is usually hiding a lot of insecurity. To become aware of our strengths is not to give up being humble; it is to value our own identity even more. It is important to stop rating ourselves as good or bad and to start seeing ourself as someone who is learning and growing.

Everyone needs to feel lovable and capable. Goal setting focuses on the individual feeling of being capable. The six guidelines for goal setting are: (1) Set reachable goals. (2) Write out the steps for reaching that goal. (3) Keep going until you reach your goal. (4) Give yourself a reasonable time limit. (5) Evaluate — check your progress. (6) Compliment yourself.

If Your Child Is in the Project Self-Esteem Program

1. What is a goal? (when you want to do or be something)

2. How do you set a goal for yourself? (Decide what you want to do and write down steps on how to do it.)

Family Activities

1. A common deterrent to progress of any kind is the feeling of being overwhelmed. Teaching goal setting enables the individual to live life in one-step-at-a-time increments. Work with each child in picking a goal for contributing to the upkeep of the home (hanging up clothes, putting things where they belong, keeping room neater, etc.). List each goal plus four to six steps for achieving it. Have a weekly progress talk.

2. Each family member could write a personal goal on a piece of paper and put it into an envelope. Open the envelope at the end of the month and discuss how you worked on or achieved those goals.

3. Use your imagination and decide what the number one goal would be if you were:
(a) A baker (chocolate chip cookies with very little dough)
(b) A reindeer (fly with Santa)
(c) A doctor (cure an illness)
(d) A dog in a pet store (to get taken home)
(e) The President of the United States (to assist in bringing peace to the world).

_____ Lesson 3 _____

Goal Setting and Compliments

Background

Just as you talk to other people, you also talk to yourself. Mostly, you comment on how you are doing in life and sometimes might say, "That was a dumb thing to do!" Talking to yourself is called self-talk. Sometimes self-talk is negative. We need to learn to give ourselves positive self-talk as well.

What is the difference between bragging and complimenting yourself? Feeling good about yourself is a quiet sense of well-being. Bragging is when people try to impress others. They pretend to be something that they are not. Self-assured people do not brag excessively and are able to recognize their strengths.

An important life resource is to teach children to see something through to completion. Goal setting is a process of resourcefully accomplishing certain tasks or changes.

If Your Child Is in the Project Self-Esteem Program

1. It is important to see and value the positive aspects of you. Therefore, you need to be kind to yourself, true or false? (true)

2. What's a Smiley? (a fluffy ball) What does it stand for? (It stands for a compliment and compliments give you a reason to smile — inside and out.)

3. What could you say when you receive a compliment? (Thank you. Return the compliment.)

4. What did Kathleen and Scott see when they looked through Uncle Fred's glasses? (good in everybody)

Family Activities

1. Everyone in the family is to give themselves a compliment. Start with "I am. . ." Discourage any negative comments. Discuss the difference between giving yourself a pat on the back and bragging.

2. A car has a license plate for identification. If you could use eight letters or less, what would your license plate say so people would know something positive about you? (kind, IMLUVABLE, happy, etc.)

3. Write ten things you really like in yourself. Put each on a separate piece of paper. On a "blue" day, take out your slips and read them to yourself

_____ Lesson 4 _____

Listening and Stress Reduction

Background

A large percentage of a child's success in school is dependent upon his/her ability to listen. Listening skills are best taught by modeling them. If teaching a skill such as listening becomes too academic, it turns out to be boring and ineffectual. Using a game to practice a skill is a successful method of instruction.

When your child has a problem or a concern that is important to him/her, **take it seriously.** Do — STOP what you are doing, LOOK at your child's eyes, and LISTEN with your mind and heart. Don't — give advice unless asked, try to "fix it," or share how very difficult it was for you, way back then.

If Your Child Is in the Project Self-Esteem Program

1. Which group were you in when you played the Pioneer Game? (These are the various groups: pioneers, west, oxen, wild animals, afraid, soldiers, attitude.)

2. What skill did you use for the Pioneer Game? (listening)

3. Which stress reduction exercise did you use today? (tensing the muscles in your body and then letting them relax)

Family Activities

1. Do this stress reduction exercise as a family: Take a long, slow breath — in through your nose and then slowly let it out through your mouth. Repeat six times. Discuss other ways you can give yourself the gift of time to relax each day.

2. Make up a story. One family member begins then stops, and another family member continues. The person talking will choose the next one to continue the story, so everyone needs to listen.

3. Everyone close their eyes. One person makes a sound (close a book, open a soft drink can, rub sandpaper, etc.) The family members guess what made the sound.

Permission to Reprint for Classroom Use: © McDaniel, Sandy & Bielen, Peggy, *Project Self-Esteem:* Rolling Hills Estates, California, Jalmar Press, 1990.

_____ **Lesson 5** _____

Learning to Memorize

Background

School children are told, over and over, to memorize. But many children are not given enough assistance on ways to learn. We've taught the children three techniques for memorization. We chose to memorize the first 15 Presidents of the United States because it is a common task many children will tackle in school. The simple techniques we shared have opened a whole new world of learning. Children have discovered that memorization need not be a drudgery.

If Your Child Is in the Project Self-Esteem Program

1. Do you remember what you were to get at the market? (The key word is SCREAM. S-soap, C-cereal, R-raisins, E-eggs, A-apples, and M-milk.)

2. Do you remember the sentence to write the first presidents of the United States? I think the first word is Whales. (Whales Always Juggle Mice and Monkeys.)

3. Using W for whales, A for always, J for juggle, M for mice and M for monkeys, can you name the first five presidents of the United States? (Washington, Adams, Jefferson, Madison, and Monroe. We suggest you use paper to do this exercise.)

Family Activities

1. Tell a story where you use a noun (person, place or thing) several times. For instance, if the word is "house," you will use the word "house" as many times as you can without being too obvious. Family members will guess what the noun is. The object is to weave the word into the story so you can talk a long time before the word is guessed.

2. Pretend you need to go to the store and get the following: toothpaste, sugar, light bulb, almonds and Band-Aids. (1) Scramble the first letter of each word to see if you get a word. (2) Make a silly picture out of the objects. Work together to learn the list. Practice these techniques with a list of your own.

3. Talk about something specific one family member needs to memorize. Assist with a fun way to remember that task.

_____ **Lesson 6** _____

Feelings

Background

Feelings tell you valuable information about yourself. One way of dealing with feelings is to realize that feelings can change. For example, almost every child is afraid of the dark at one time or another. To honor a fear as a valid feeling, even if you think it is silly, is an important way to begin walking a child through those fears.

_____

If Your Child Is in the Project Self-Esteem Program

1. Can you fill in the blanks?
Everyone has _____. _____ are based upon a past experience. One person's _____ can be different from another person's _____. _____ can change. (feelings)

2. One person might feel fine about snakes while another person feels scared. Can you sometimes have feelings different from other people? Is that OK? (yes)

3. How are you doing with your goal in PSE? Do you want to share what your goal is and how you are doing?

Family Activities

1. Make cards with these words on them: happy, sad, angry, proud, frustrated, scared and any other feeling words. Draw one card and have everybody share, "One time I felt. . . ." It is important to honor feelings. Any issues may be resolved on a one-to-one basis at a later time.

2. Set a family goal (clean the garage) and add a reward (go to a special place for dinner).   Write three to five steps for accomplishing that goal. Discuss each person's part. Follow through. Be sure to keep your agreement as to the reward. The family goal may be personalized   (everyone will give more compliments to each other).

3. Talk about feelings you use to have which have changed (scared of the dark, going to a party, etc.). It is important that parents share equally.

Permission to Reprint for Classroom Use: © McDaniel, Sandy & Bielen, Peggy, *Project Self-Esteem:* Rolling Hills Estates, California, Jalmar Press, 1990.

——————— Lesson 7 ———————

High and Low Self-Esteem/Review

Background

The high self-esteemed person is able to: share self; make positive comments about self; give genuine compliments easily; know he/she doesn't have to be good in everything; understand we learn from our mistakes; laugh at self; and listen. The low self-esteemed person: excludes others; frequently tattles; brags about accomplishments; continually puts self down; bullies others; starts rumors; frequently teases others; continually puts others down; and tries to people-please all the time. No one is perfect. The high self-esteemed person expresses positive qualities most of the time.

If Your Child Is in the Project Self-Esteem Program

1. Do you remember three actions a person with high self-esteem has? (able to share self, can compliment self, gives and receives compliments involving others easily, etc.)

2. Do you remember three actions a person with low self-esteem has? (tattles, brags about accomplishments, constantly puts self down, bullies others, starts rumors, etc.)

Family Activities

1. Each person decides on one thing they want to change about themselves (be on time more often, don't put self down so much etc.). Share. Discuss steps that may be taken towards making this change. The point is to encourage each other. Discuss progress.

2. The Pioneer Game was designed to practice listening. The class was divided into groups and given a word with a body movement or sound to go with that word. For instance, the group with the word **west** stood up and pointed towards the left with their right hand shouting, "Thata way!" As a family, pick a theme for your own story and choose an appropriate word for each family member. One member could have more than one word. Together, write a short story in which the selected words are used over and over. One person might read the story and everyone else will do his/her part. Enjoy this exercise!

3. Discuss the story "The Magic Glasses." The point of this story is a person's attitude affects how he/she sees other people. With the magic glasses on, a person can see the good in others. Make an agreement for the whole family to see the good in each other for one day. Remind each other to stay on track with, "Oops! Put on the magic glasses!" At the end of the day, discuss how it felt.

—————————————————— Lesson 8 ——————————————————

Communicating Assertively

Background

The Broken Record is an assertive training technique which is used when you want to express yourself. It has two steps (1) A kind statement (2) A policy statement. It is an especially effective means of teaching children how to say no when they want to say no. It may also be used when someone is aggressive or when a person wants to hold his/her point.

The Broken Record is a wonderful technique for parent use. It eliminates arguing and lecturing. Some parents may be concerned they will hear the Broken Record when the child is asked to do a household chore. Rules for the appropriate use of this technique need to be discussed.

If Your Child Is in the Project Self-Esteem Program

1. The ways people communicate are Assertive, Doormat, and what is the rough-tough one? (King Kong)

2. Why do they call the part where you say a kind statement and a policy statement the Broken Record? (You say the same thing over and over.)

3. If I want to borrow your bicycle and you do not want me to, what is your kind statement? (I understand you like my bicycle.) And what is your policy statement? (I never loan my bicycle.) What do you do if the person who wants to borrow your bike argues? (Repeat your kind and policy statement over and over.)

Family Activities

1. Attempt to borrow something from each other. Use the Broken Record technique.

2. Discuss situations in your life when you could use the Broken Record. Talk about how you would use the technique in order to say no (salesman on the phone, someone invites you to do something you think is dangerous, someone wants you to donate money to a cause you do not want to support, someone asks you to eat or drink something that you know is not good for you, someone asks you to go somewhere and you don't want to go, etc.) Act out each situation and enjoy it! It is important to keep your tone of voice even at all times when using the Broken Record technique.

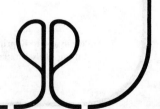

_____ Lesson 9 _____

Friendship

Background

Peer pressure is an increasing influence on the individual child. Therefore, it is important to continually reevaluate one's choice of friends. A simple way of accomplishing this is to list the qualities valued and not valued in a friend.

When friends listen to each other there is a feeling of being valued. One aspect of listening which is not frequently taught is responding. The person who is talking receives feedback as an expression of interest in what is being said. By practicing this skill in a fun-filled manner it is more likely to be remembered and used in daily life.

If Your Child Is in the Project Self-Esteem Program

1. Which stress reduction exercise did you do today? (We took some breaths in through our nose, and let them out through our mouth.)

2. What qualities do you remember that your class put on the "My Kind of Friend" chart?

3. In the listening story, who was following the lady in her car? (her neighbor)

4. What was the point of telling the scary story? (It was a story to teach us to respond while listening.) What did the person listening to the story do? She/he responded to what was being said.)

Family Activities

1. Everyone will interview two or more people for qualities they want in a friend. The question to ask is "What three qualities are most important to you in a friend?" Compile a group list of qualities your family rates as most desired in a friend.

2. Make a list of five or more ways you can be a friend.

3. One person begins to tell a spooky story. Each member will add to the story. The people listening are to respond with "oohs" and "aahs" where it is appropriate to do so.

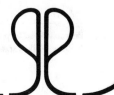

_____ Lesson 10 _____

Stealing and Teasing

Background

Taking something without permission is stealing. Borrowing is done with the intention of giving it back. The intent of this lesson is to give information about stealing (it hurts someone), and the effects it has on people even if they are not caught (damages your self-esteem).

A second issue which is talked about in this lesson is teasing. Relentless teasers have enormous power because they can hurt people's feelings and get others to fear them. The purpose in this lesson is to reveal the frequent teaser as a person with low self-esteem who, because he or she feels badly about self, tries to harm others.

If Your Child Is in the Project Self-Esteem Program

1. PSE teaches that the best thing to do with someone who teases is _____. (ignore them)

2. What do people who tease choose to tease about? (differences)

3. How do you keep from being hurt by a person's teasing? (Don't be concerned about what the person who is teasing thinks about you.)

Family Activities

1. Discuss the following situation and the consequences of each choice. What would you do if you were with a friend who put something into his/her pocket in a store? (You could be equally liable if caught.)

2. Discuss the following situation. A lady drops an expensive earring. Your friend picks it up and indicates he/she is going to keep it. What do you do? (Note: Please acknowledge peer pressure as a large factor in this choice.)

3. Discuss the following situation. You get a new pair of shoes that are different in some way. How might you handle any teasing at school?

4. If your child does not like to be teased, teach him/her to think these words while being teased, "No matter what you say or do, I'm still a worthwhile person." This thought should be repeated several times. As the child being teased focuses on this valuable statement, the teaser discovers he/she is not getting any feedback and generally stops the behavior.

— Lesson 1 —

Realizing Your Uniqueness

Background

Self-esteem means feeling good about ourselves. It is easy for parents to underestimate how vital respect and love are to their child. By treating each child as a valued individual, you enhance that child's self-esteem. One way to respect individuality is to refrain from verbally comparing your child.

If Your Child Is in the Project Self-Esteem Program

1. When you introduced yourself with a positive adjective that started with the same letter as your first name and then gave your first name, what was your name and adjective?

2. When someone introduced you to your group and told of a success you had, what success did that person tell about?

3. What are some of the goal setting steps you discussed? (The steps are: set a reasonable goal, write out steps for reaching that goal, keep going until you reach your goal, give yourself a reasonable time limit, check your progress, compliment yourself.)

Family Activities

1. Choose a phrase or word that everyone can use when a mistake is made, like "Oops!" or "Wish I hadn't done that!" (The tendency, when one makes a mistake, is to talk negatively and harshly to oneself. Negative self-talk is destructive. While one needs to be mindful of the consequences of one's actions and take responsibility for behavior change, this may be done effectively without self-abuse.)

2. Go around the dinner table and have each person think of a positive adjective to go with their last name. The adjective needs to begin with the same letter as the last name: the Super Smiths! or the Caring Carsons!

3. Ask each person to share a recent success. This success can be a "big deal" or something small and meaningful to the individual. This is an opportune time to teach compassion. Negative comments or body language, snorts or other non-supportive messages destroy the point of the whole exercise — which is to encourage.

—————————————— Lesson 2 ——————————————

Goal Setting and Memorizing

Background

The question arises "Can someone have too much self-esteem?" This is usually said in reference to someone who seems overconfident. Self-esteem is a quiet sense of well-being. The braggart is usually hiding a lot of insecurity. To become aware of our strengths is not to give up being humble; it is to value our own identity even more. It is important to stop rating ourselves as good or bad and to start seeing ourself as someone who is learning and growing.

Everyone needs to feel lovable and capable. Goal setting focuses on the individual feeling of being capable. The six guidelines for goal setting are: (1) Set reachable goals. (2) Write out the steps for reaching that goal. (3) Keep going until you reach your goal. (4) Give yourself a reasonable time limit. (5) Evaluate — check your progress. (6) Compliment yourself.

If Your Child is in the Project Self-Esteem Program

1. Can you tell me the way you learned in school to remember that Harrisburg is the capital of Pennsylvania?

2. What kind of picture did you make in your mind to memorize the capital of Arkansas?   (The capital of Arkansas is Little Rock.)

3. What are the word pictures for some of the other capitals and states you discussed in class?   (These are the other capitals and states introduced to the class: Concord, New Hampshire; Topeka, Kansas; Salt Lake City, Utah; Columbus, Ohio; Nashville, Tennessee; Frankfort, Kentucky; Springfield, Illinois; Hartford, Connecticut; and Jefferson City, Missouri.)

Family Activities

1. Set a family goal   (clean the garage, pick up the family room, etc.). Discuss each person's role, set a time limit, and think of ways to turn the job into a game. After the job is completed, discuss how it went with gentle comments about how to improve the activity next time. Have a family reward   (go for a treat)   at the end.

2. Ask each person to set one personal goal and share it with the family. Set a time limit to accomplish the goal and listen to suggestions from the family members for ways to accomplish that goal.

3. Discuss the state and capitals of the places where parents, grandparents, and other relatives were born. Have the student who participated in the Project Self-Esteem lesson, teach the family how to build a crazy picture for remembering the states and their capitals.

—————————————— **Lesson 3** ——————————————

Goal Setting and Compliments

Background

Just as you talk to other people, you also talk to yourself. Mostly, you comment on how you are doing in life and sometimes might say, "That was a dumb thing to do!" Talking to yourself is called self-talk. Sometimes self-talk is negative. We need to learn to give ourselves positive self-talk as well.

What is the difference between bragging and complimenting yourself? Feeling good about yourself is a quiet sense of well-being. Bragging is when people try to impress others. They pretend to be something that they are not. Self-assured people do not brag excessively and are able to recognize their strengths.

An important life resource is to teach children to see something through to completion. Goal setting is a process of resourcefully accomplishing certain tasks or changes.

If Your Child Is in the Project Self-Esteem Program

1. Can you tell me the goal you set for yourself in class and the steps you've decided upon to reach that goal?   (The students had a goal sheet to write down the goal and the steps.)

2. What is the first word you use in a compliment.   (A compliment begins with the word "I."

3. What compliment did someone tell you in your group? Remember it began with the word "I."

Family Activities

1. Compliments need to begin with the word "I." A compliment is specific and true. Go around the family table and have each person think of someone in his or her life who is special. Pick someone in the family and ask him/her to be one of the special people selected by a family member. Have another family member give the "pretend" person a compliment. Repeat this with other family members, using their "special person" to compliment.   (When giving compliments is practiced in the safe atmosphere of home, it is easier and more natural to do it in public. Having good manners is often a combination of *both* confidence and thoughtfulness.)

2. Talk about the family goal from the last lesson. Set a new family goal. Write down all the steps it will take to achieve the goal. Have family members volunteer for specific jobs. Set a time to do it and discuss a family reward as an incentive.

3. Play a family game in which everyone looks for things to compliment each other about — for one whole day. The focus will be only on the positives for that day. Later, discuss how it felt to be both supportive of others and supported by others.

_____ **Lesson 4** _____

Listening

Background

A large percentage of a child's success in school is dependent upon his/her ability to listen. Listening skills are best taught by modeling them. If teaching a skill such as listening becomes too academic, it turns out to be boring and ineffectual. Using a game to practice a skill is a successful method of instruction.

The stress reduction techniques are designed to teach children how to cope with stress and relax. These simple tensing exercises may be used in the child's daily life.

If Your Child is in the Project Self-Esteem Program

1. Tell me about the goal you and your classmates decided upon to improve the classroom.

2. Which group were you in when you played the Space Game?   (These are the various groups: space voyager, shuttle, space station, afraid, attitude, Earth.)

3. Which stress reduction exercise did you do today?   (tensing the muscles in the body and then letting them relax)

Family Activities

1. Tell a child to do something. Have the child repeat back to you what was heard.   (This process is a way of training people to listen and it will quickly let you know which child you need to communicate with in more detail.)

2. Play a listening game. One person says a sentence, the other person repeats what was just said. Be sure to keep the sentence length consistent with each child's maturation level.

3. Play another listening game. Begin with the sentence, "I'm going (to Hawaii, on a camping trip, to the jungle, to the beach, to the park, etc.) and I'm going to take   (blank)." Fill in the blank with a word that starts with each letter of the alphabet, beginning with the letter A. Give everyone a chance to add to the list, until all the letters of the alphabet have been used.

_____ **Lesson 5** _____

Communication Skills

Background

Upsets seem to come without any other visible emotion. The truth is, some other emotion usually precedes the feeling of being upset. For example, a small child runs out in the street causing a car to screech to a halt. The mother might act upset but what was her first emotion? (fear) One way to work through an upset feeling is to recognize it as a second emotion.

A "you" message is a judgment. Even a positive "you" message such as "You're a good girl for cleaning your room," is judgmental. The opposite of good is bad. If the child had not cleaned her room would he/she be a bad person? Personalized messages beginning with "I" enhance self-esteem. "I notice you picked all the toys off the floor. It looks wonderful!" is a personalized message of validation.

If Your Child is in the Project Self-Esteem Program

1. If you were all dressed and ready to go somewhere special with your friend and that friend called to say he or she couldn't go, what feeling would you have? (anger)

2. What was the first feeling you would have had, though? (disappointment)

3. Instead of "You took my bike without asking!" what could you say? Remember to use an "I" message. ("I want to be asked before you use my bike.")

Family Activities

1. Make a list of all possible emotions which could come before an upset feeling (frustration, disappointment, helplessness, hurt, rejection, embarrassment, etc.) Without listing specific instances, discuss things you feel upset about (when someone teases) and what the first feeling might be. (helplessness)

2. Without using specific instances, make a list of the types of "you" messages some people give. (you're lazy, you're inconsiderate, you're a good boy, etc.) Discuss ways to change each one to an "I" message.

3. Discuss things to do with friends that do not cost anything. Make a list and post that list on the refrigerator. (This is especially helpful to do prior to summer. To the phrase, "I'm bored!" respond, "Why don't you check your list of things to do and choose one.")

_____

_____ **Lesson 6** _____

Working with Anger

Background

Children deal with a multitude of frustrations. If they are given information and practical experience about how to deal with these frustrations, upsets, and anger, they will be less likely to become destructive to society or to themselves.

Children who learn to handle anger are more likely to respond to circumstances in a responsible manner. Practicing "I" messages at home is wonderful training for learning both how to communicate clearly and how to defuse anger.

If Your Child is in the Project Self-Esteem Program

1. What relaxation exercise did you do today?   (breathing in and out slowly)

2. What is one thing you could do to release anger?   (Write a letter telling how angry you are.)

3. What do you do with that letter?   (Put it in the trash.)

Family Activities

1. Make an agreement that there will be no name calling in your family. If an argument occurs, ask family members to use an "I" message and focus on the behavior. An example would be, "I feel really angry when something is missing from my room." Using "I" messages is a difficult process. Using the formula of stating feelings first and then wants is helpful. I (feeling) and I want you to (whatever). It is important to note that the purpose of this activity is to clearly express a problem. Be patient with each other in this learning process.

2. Practice changing these "You" messages to "I" messages:
   a) You are such a lazy slob, I can't believe it! (The "I" message could be: I am tired of seeing the house in such a mess, and I want it to be cleaned up.)
   b) Watch where you're going, you klutz! (The "I" message could be: I don't like it when you trip over my feet. Please watch where you are going.)

Lesson 7

Handling Incoming Anger and Upsets

Background

Most people are not responsible for *all* of the anger that comes into their lives. Teaching children how to release the stress of pent-up frustration and upsets is important. This process begins by realizing we are not responsible for everyone's upsets.

If Your Child is in the Project Self-Esteem Program

1. Can you tell me the story about Martha? (Martha had many upsets during the day. In class we used a container to put a small rock in every time someone got upset with her.)

2. What could Martha have done when her brother accused her of taking his pen? (She could have called her brother back to tell him the truth.)

3. What could Martha have done when she discovered she had an egg salad sandwich? (She could have asked her mom politely not to make egg sandwiches for her anymore.)

Family Activities

1. Talk about appropriate ways to release anger in your family (exercise, punching bag, etc.). Children who are given permission to defuse their anger in an appropriate manner tend to be less prone to depression and resentment. Point out that some people have a longer "fuse" than others.

2. Discuss the fact that we often express anger toward other people who actually had no part in the original problem. When "uninvited anger" comes into your life, you can detach yourself from it by thinking of yourself as swiss cheese (let the anger pass *through* you, not *into* you) or as superman (let the anger bounce *off* of you, not *into* you).

3. Discuss ways to handle incoming anger with solutions that are consistent with your family morals and values.

_____ **Lesson 8** _____

Communicating Assertively

Background

The Broken Record is an assertive training technique which is used when you want to express yourself. It has two steps (1) A kind statement (2) A policy statement. It is an especially effective means of teaching children how to say no when they want to say no. It may also be used when someone is aggressive or when a person wants to hold his/her point.

The Broken Record is a wonderful technique for parent use. It eliminates arguing and lecturing. Some parents may be concerned they will hear the Broken Record when the child is asked to do a household chore. Rules for the appropriate use of this technique need to be discussed.

If Your Child is in the Project Self-Esteem Program

1. What are the three ways people often communicate? (Assertive, Doormat, or King Kong)

2. What are the two parts to the Broken Record way of communicating? (You say a kind statement and then a policy statement.)

3. If someone wanted to copy your homework and you used the Broken Record idea, what would be your kind statement? (I know you don't like to do this work.) And what would be your policy statement? (I will not let you copy my homework.) If the person argues, what do you do? (Repeat the kind statement and policy statement over and over.)

Family Activities

1. Attempt to borrow something from each other. Use the Broken Record technique.

2. Discuss situations in your life when you could use the Broken Record. Talk about how you would use the technique in order to say no (salesman on the phone, someone invites you to do something you think is dangerous, someone wants you to donate money to a cause you do not want to support, someone asks you to eat or drink something that you know is not good for you, someone asks you to go somewhere and you don't want to go, etc.) Act out each situation and enjoy it! It is important to keep your tone of voice even at all times when using the Broken Record technique.

Permission to Reprint for Classroom Use: © McDaniel, Sandy & Bielen, Peggy, *Project Self-Esteem:* Rolling Hills Estates, California, Jalmar Press, 1990.

_____ **Lesson 9** _____

Learning about Handicaps and Listening

Background

Sometimes we forget to be kind. Sometimes when we want to be kind, we don't have the skills to talk to someone who is handicapped. Compassion is best realized through understanding. Project Self-Esteem wants to assist children in treating people, who are different, with both kindness and compassion.

If Your Child is in the Project Self-Esteem Program

1. What activity did your class do to get a feeling of what it's like to be handicapped? (The class tried reading a paper that was fuzzy and unclear.)

2. How did you feel when you did this activity?

3. What are some of the things you could do to help a person who might have a problem like this?

Family Activities

1. Blindfold one person and ask them to do an ordinary activity (get something from the kitchen, go to a specific place, etc.). Protect that person from danger with a "beep" sound that means "stop and head in another direction."

2. Talk about how your life would be different if you were blind.

3. Watch a movie or video about the life of a handicapped person. Ask family members to discuss their feelings after the movie.

Lesson 10

Stealing and Teasing

Background

Taking something without permission is stealing. Borrowing is done with the intention of giving it back. The intent of this lesson is to give information about stealing (it hurts someone), and the effects it has on people even if they are not caught (damages your self-esteem).

A second issue which is talked about in this lesson is teasing. Relentless teasers have enormous power because they can hurt people's feelings and get others to fear them. The purpose in this lesson is to reveal the frequent teaser as a person with low self-esteem who, because he or she feels badly about self, tries to harm others.

If Your Child is in the Project Self-Esteem Program

1. What is the difference between borrowing and stealing? (When you ask someone for an item and get permission to take it, that is borrowing. When you take something without asking, that is stealing.)

2. What does teasing have to do with self-esteem? (If you have a high self-esteem, you don't feel the need to tease.)

3. If you tease a friend what could possibly happen? (You might lose the friend.)

Family Activities

1. Discuss the following situation. What would you do if you were with a friend who put something into his/her pocket in a store? (You could be equally liable if caught.)

2. Discuss the following situation. A lady drops an expensive earring. Your friend picks it up and indicates he/she is going to keep it. What do you do? (Note: please acknowledge peer pressure as a large factor in this choice.)

3. Discuss the following situation. You get a new pair of shoes that are different in some way. How might you handle any teasing at school?

_____ **Lesson 1** _____

Social Skills

Background

If your child is going to junior high school next year, he/she will be meeting lots of new people.

New situations cause stress. Practicing social skills can ease that stress.

If Your Child Is in the Project Self-Esteem Program

1. When you introduce yourself to someone, it can be awkward. What can you do to feel less awkward? (Give your name, some information about yourself, and ask a question which cannot be answered in one word: What, when, why, where, how. An example would be, "Hi! I'm Sara Velasquez. I'm having trouble with my locker. Do you know where I can go for help?")

2. When you introduce one person to another how can you get a conversation started? (offer information about each person along with their names)

3. Do you remember which person you look at when you are introducing two people? (look at the person who doesn't know the name, not the person who owns the name)

Family Activities

1. Pretend your family members do not know each other. Introduce one member to the other, remember to give some information about each one.

2. Pretend one family member is someone famous. Playact introducing self to that person.

3. Discuss a situation in which you felt stress. What do you think caused the stress? Let your child know how you handled the situation.

4. Make a list of situations which cause stress (doing something for the first time, taking a test, etc.). Discuss appropriate ways for handling stress in each situation.

_____ Lesson 2 _____

Social Skills/Choice Making

Background

In every situation we are making choices. These decisions are made with the influence of morals, values, and peer pressure. PSE teaches children to weigh the risks and gains as they view their possible choices. This process teaches them to think before they act.

"The Choice is Yours" is a game wherein students practice making responsible choices.

When asked, "why?" the majority of teenagers who get into trouble with drugs, alcohol, etc. say, "I didn't know what else to do." Based upon real-life situations, "The Choice is Yours" gives possible alternatives to situations, so if the same or a similar circumstances later occur in a student's life, he/she will have a resource for action.

If Your Child Is in the Project Self-Esteem Program

1. What is the difference between bragging and giving yourself a compliment? (Bragging is exaggerated, not always true, and the person bragging uses a "look-at-me" tone of voice. Trying to impress someone is bragging. Quietly stating a fact is recognizing your worth.)

2. When you have a choice of doing one thing or another, how is "doing nothing" a choice? (You choose to do nothing.)

Family Activities

1. Think of a time when you chose to "do nothing" as your choice. What was the outcome?

2. Play "The Choice is Yours" with the following situation. A new kid on the block phones and asks your child to play. Your child does not want to play. What could a young person do? (Say you are busy, say you have other plans, say "I can't play, but thanks for asking me!", etc.) After all possible responses are given, discuss the risk and possible gain with each choice. Discuss which choice would be made if this situation arose.

3. Repeat the "Choice is Yours" procedure with the following situation. You need to do a chore within the next hour. Your friend who talks a lot phones. What do you do?

— Lesson 3 —

Assertive Training: Broken Record

Background

We have put communicators into three possible categories: King Kong (the really aggressive person), Doormat (the person who does not stand up for him/herself), and the Assertive Person (one who stands up for self and his rights in an appropriate way.)

In PSE, being assertive means to stand up for oneself in a way which respects the rights and feelings of others. The three Assertive techniques PSE teaches are (1) The Broken Record, (2) Fogging (3) The Assertive Apology.

The Broken Record is a technique designed to enable a person to say no when he/she wants to say no. Simply stated, it is a kind statement plus a policy statement repeated several times. (I understand you want to borrow my bicycle and I never loan my bicycle.)

If Your Child Is in the Project Self-Esteem Program

1. The three types of communicators are Assertive, King Kong, and what is the passive or non-assertive one called? (Doormat)

2. Why is the part where you say a kind statement and a policy statement called the Broken Record? (You say the same thing over and over.)

3. If I ask you to go to a movie and you do not want to go, what is your kind statement? (I like being with you.) And what is your policy statement? (I don't want to see a movie tonight.) What do you do if the person argues with you? (Repeat your kind and policy statements over and over.)

Family Activities

1. Attempt to get each other to do something you don't want to do. Use the Broken Record technique.

2. Discuss situations in your life when you could use the Broken Record. Talk about how you would use this technique in order to say no (salesman on the phone, someone invites you to do something you think is dangerous, someone wants you to eat or drink something, someone asks you to go somewhere and you don't want to go, etc.) Act out each situation and enjoy it! It is important to keep your tone of voice even at all times when using the Broken Record technique.

3. Someone asks to borrow something. You usually say yes, but for reasons of your own you want to say no. Use the Broken Record in this way, "I understand you want to borrow my watch, and I don't feel comfortable loaning it." Act out a situation in which you might say yes to some people but you want to say no to this person (borrowing something, going somewhere you don't want to go etc.). Discuss different ways of using the Broken Record.

--- **Lesson 4** ---

Assertive Training: Fogging

Background

As sixth grade students approach adolescence they are entering a period of excessive put-downs. Though put-downs are a normal part of this age period, a student's self-esteem may be damaged by constant negative input. Assertive training techniques give students resources for handling criticism.

The Fogging technique assists students by giving them a specific way to handle a given situation. The student is taught to think of himself/herself as a fog bank, and to think of criticism as a rock. When a rock is thrown at the fog bank the fog is in no way damaged. The fog bank does not throw the rock back, either. Thus, use of the Fogging technique enables the student to remain untouched by the criticism. Knowledge relieves their frustration level which can play havoc with self-esteem.

If Your Child Is in the Project Self-Esteem Program

1. When do you use Fogging? (when someone is putting you down)   If their statement is definitely true, how do you answer? (You simply agree. If someone says "You have big feet," I would answer "You're right, I do"). If what is said could or could not be true, how do you answer? (If someone says, "You have the biggest feet I've ever seen!" I would answer, "That could be true.")

2. How do you think Fogging assists you and your self-esteem? (You remain calm and do not get defensive.)

3. When might you combine Fogging and the Broken Record? (When someone persists in putting you down.)

Family Activities

1. Practice using Fogging with these statements: (a) You giggle too much, (b) That's really an ugly shirt, (c) You tell the dumbest jokes, (d) You're a real nerd.

2. Talk about specific situations in the past which were hurtful and discuss how your child could have used Fogging.

3. Any practice has its appropriate place and use. Discuss situations in which the use of Fogging would not be appropriate (teacher tells you you need to do your homework, or Mom says your room is a mess, etc.)

_____ **Lesson 5** _____

Peers and Conformity

Background

There is a great deal of talk about peer pressure. The teenager's desire to conform is a natural part of development. Since friends become such an important influence in a teens life, Project Self-Esteem stresses to students the importance of choosing friends who support them in the value systems they've learned from home.

If Your Child Is in the Project Self-Esteem Program

1. Can conformity be useful or helpful? (Yes)

2. When is conformity a problem? (When you go against your own values, you feel badly about yourself.)

3. In the classroom experiment where you chose the longest line, a surprising 75% of the students went along with an obviously wrong answer. When one person agreed with that person, only 35% went along with the crowd. What does this tell you about choosing friends? (need to choose friends who have similar values)

Family Activities

1. Have each member of the family discuss what they like in a friend. (honesty, sense of humor, trustworthiness, etc.)

2. Have each family member tell a time when having a friend "saved the day."

3. Discuss places in your life where peer pressure is obvious (clothes, not getting all A's, keeping up with the Jones).

4. Discuss times when conformity might be useful or helpful. (traffic laws, dress, etc.)

_____ **Lesson 6** _____

Friendship and Assertive Apology

Background

Friendships are important to everyone but they are especially critical to teenagers. If preteens and teens understand how many rapid physical changes their bodies are making, they will begin to understand how "normal" the ups and downs of this period are. It will assist them to know that changes in relationships need not always be taken personally, that it is perfectly natural to change friendships, and that usually there is no fault or blame to be assumed when these relationship changes occur. This knowledge relieves their frustration level which often can play havoc with self-esteem.

If Your Child Is in the Project Self-Esteem Program

1. People change as they grow. Sometimes friendships can change. What do you want to remember if a friendship changes? (not to take it personally and that sometimes friends change)

2. What are some of the ways to listen? (Look in the eyes of the person. Show interest with verbal responses. Ask questions.)

3. What are the three parts of the Assertive Apology? (apologize, pat self on back, and state your intention) What happens if you state your intention and then fail to follow through? (others won't believe you next time)

Family Activities

1. Make a list of effective ways to listen. Place the list in a prominent place as a reminder to all family members.

2. PSE teaches mistakes are a natural part of living. We learn from making mistakes. Discuss one time you made a mistake and what you learned from it. Be careful to curtail any negative comments.

3. At dinner time ask "Who has something to share?" Be sure everyone listens and that each person gets a turn.

4. Practice the Assertive Apology in these situations: (a) One family member borrows something and forgets to return it. (I feel badly that I didn't return it. I will remember next time. Here it is.) (b) One family member keeps everyone waiting. (I feel embarrassed that everyone had to wait. I'm sorry I am late. I will be on time next time.)

Lesson 7

Alcohol and Drug Abuse

Background

Parents and educators are becoming more and more aware of the importance of assisting students to recognize the physical and emotional complications involved in the use of alcohol and drugs.

Research indicates teenagers who make inappropriate choices often do so because they can't think of anything else to do. Information based upon true-life experiences gives students resources for alternatives. A student of high self-esteem is more apt to withstand peer pressure and make choices consistent with his/her values and morals.

If Your Child Is in the Project Self-Esteem Program

1. What is one reason alcohol, marijuana, and non-perscription drugs are harmful to kids and teens? (body is growing rapidly, so teens can get addicted faster than an adult)

2. What can you do if your friends make fun of you for not drinking? (Use the Broken Record, leave, find new friends.)

3. Did you see a film about drug abuse? What do you remember about the film? (individual response dependent upon which film is used)

Family Activities

1. Discuss your family policy for alcohol and drugs. It is important children know the consequences of inappropriate alcohol or drug use BEFORE a problem arises. Be firm and specific in your feelings and wants.

2. Discuss alternatives to riding home with someone who has been drinking. (Call parents, call a cab, phone a friend, etc.)

3. There is a national move to curtail drug and alcohol abuse. Discuss why you think this is happening. (Remember to practice listening skills and allow each person his/her right of opinion.)

Bibliography

Books

Anglund, Joan Walsh, *A Friend Is Someone Who Likes You.* New York: Harcourt and Brace, 1985.

Axline, Virginia M., *Dibs: In Search of Self.* New York: Ballantine Books, 1967.

Barksdale, Lilburn S., *Essays on Self-Esteem.* Idyllwild, California: The Barksdale Foundation, 1977.

Baron, Jason D., M.D., *Kids and Drugs.* New York: The Putnam Publishing Group, 1983.

Barun, Ken and Bashe, Philip, *How to Keep the Children You Love Off Drugs.* New York: The Atlantic Monthly Press, 1988.

Bedley, Gene, *The ABCD's of Discipline.* Irvine, California: People-Wise Publications, 1979.

Bedley, Gene, *Climate Creators.* Irvine, California: People-Wise Publications, 1982.

Berne, Eric, M.D., *What Do You Say After You Say Hello?* New York: Grove Press, 1971.

Booraem, Curtis; Flowers, John; & Schwartz, Bernard, *Help Your Children Be Self-Confident.* Englewood Cliffs, New Jersey: Prentice-Hall, Inc., 1978.

Branden, Nathaniel, *The Psychology of Self-Esteem.* New York: Bantam Books, 1969.

Briggs, Dorothy Corkille, *Your Child's Self-Esteem.* Garden City, New York: Doubleday, 1967.

Briggs, Dorothy Corkille, *Celebrate Your Self.* Garden City, New York: Doubleday, 1977.

Buhler, Rich, *Love No Strings Attached.* Nashville, Tennessee: Thomas Nelson Publishers, 1987.

Buntman, Peter H., *How to Live With Your Teenager.* New York: Ballantine Books, 1979.

Buscaglia, Leo, *Living, Loving & Learning.* Thorofare, New Jersey: Charles B. Slack, 1982.

Buscaglia, Leo, *Love.* Thorofare, New Jersey: Charles B. Slack, 1972.

Clems, Harris and Bean, Reynold, *Self-Esteem The Key to Your Child's Well-Being.* New York: Putnam, 1981.

Coopersmith, Stanley, *The Antecedents of Self-Esteem.* San Francisco: Freeman, 1967.

Cretcher, Dorothy, *Steering Clear.* Minneapolis: Winston, 1982.

Crow, Lester and Alice, *How To Study.* New York: Collier Books, 1980.

Curran, Delores, *Traits of a Healthy Family.* Minneapolis: Winston, 1983.

Davis, Lois and Joel, *How to Live Almost Happily with Your Teenagers.* Minneapolis: Winston, 1982.

Dobson, James. *Preparing for Adolescence.* Santa Ana, California: Vision House, 1978.

Dodson, Dr. Fitzhugh, *How to Discipline With Love.* New York: Rawson Associates, 1977.

Dreikurs, Rudolf, M.D., *Children: The Challenge.* New York: Hawthorne, 1964.

Dyer, Dr. Wayne W., *Pulling Your Own Strings.* New York: Avon Books, 1978.

Fensterheim, Herbert, *Don't Say Yes When You Want to Say No.* New York: Dell Publishing Co., 1975.

Fox, C. Lynn, Ph.D. and Weaver, Francine Lavin, *Unlocking Doors to Friendship.* Rolling Hills Estates, California: B.L. Winch & Associates, 1983.

Freeman, Jodi, M.Ed., *How to Drug-Proof Kids.* Albuquerque, New Mexico: The Think Shop, Inc., 1989.

Gardner, James E., *The Turbulent Teens.* Los Angeles: Sorrento Press, Inc., 1983

Ginott, Haim, *Teacher and Child.* New York: Avon, 1972.

Glasser, William, *Schools Without Failure.* New York: Harper & Row, 1969.

Gordon, Thomas, *Parent Effectiveness Training.* New York: Peter H. Wyden, 1974.

Harris, Thomas A., M.D., *I'm OK — You're OK.* New York: Avon, 1967.

Holt, John, *How Children Learn.* New York: Delta Books, 1967.

James, Muriel and Jongeward, Dorothy, *Born to Win.* Menlo Park, California: Addison-Wesley, 1971.

Jampolsky, Gerald G., M.D., *Teach Only Love.* New York: Bantam, 1983.

Kalb, Jonah and Viscott, David, M.D., *What Every Kid Should Know.* Boston: Houghton Mifflin, 1974.

Keirsey, David and Bates, Marilyn, *Please Understand Me.* Del Mar, California: Prometheus Nemesis, 1978.

Knight, Michael E.; Graham, Terry Lynne; Juliano, Rose A.; Miksza, Susan Robichaud; Tonnies, Pamela G. *Teaching Children to Love Themselves.* Englewood Cliffs, New Jersey: Prentice-Hall, 1982.

Krueger, Caryl Waller, *Six Weeks to Better Parenting.* Rancho Santa Fe, California: Belleridge Press, 1980.

Kuczen, Barbara, *Childhood Stress.* New York: Delacorte, 1982.

LaMore, Gregory S., *Handicapped . . . How Does It Feel?* Rolling Hills Estates, California: B.L. Winch & Associates, 1984.

Lorayne, Harry and Lucas, Jerry, *The Memory Book.* New York: Stein and Day, 1974.

Maslow, Abraham, *Toward a Psychology of Being.* New York: D. Van Nostrand, 1962.

Miller, Gordon Porter, *Teaching Your Child To Make Decisions.* New York: Harper & Row, 1984.

Miller, Mary Susan, *Childstress!* Garden City, New York: Doubleday & Company, Inc., 1982.

Montessori, Maria, *The Discovery of the Child.* Notre Dame, Indiana: Fides, 1967.

Nelson, Jane, Ed.D., *Positive Discipline.* Fair Oaks, California: Sunrise Press, 1985.

Newman, Mildred and Berkowitz, Bernard, *How to Be Your Own Best Friend.* New York: Random House, 1973.

Nierenberg, Gerard I. and Calero, Henry H., *How to Read a Person Like a Book.* New York: Hawthorne, 1971.

Norfolk, Donald, *The Stress Factor.* New York: Simon & Schuster, 1977.

Padovani, Martin H., *Healing Wounded Emotions.* Mystic, Connecticut: Twenty-Third Publications, 1987.

Palmer, Pat, *Liking Myself.* San Luis Obispo, California; Impact, 1977.

Palmer, Pat, *The Mouse, The Monster, and Me.* San Luis Obispo, California: Impact, 1977.

Parrino, John J., *From Panic to Power — The Positive Use of Stress.* New York: John Wiley & Sons, 1979.

Paul, Jordan and Margaret, *Do I Have to Give Up Me to Be Loved by You?* Minneapolis, Minnesota: CompCare Publications, 1983.

Peale, Norman Vincent, *You Can If You Think You Can.* Pawling, New York: Foundation For Christian Living, 1974.

Powell, John, *Why Am I Afraid to Love?* Chicago, Illinois: Argus Communications Co., 1972.

Reasoner, Robert W., *Building Self-Esteem.* Palo Alto, California: Consulting Psychologists Press, Inc., 1982.

Richards, Arlene Kramer and Willism, Irene, *Boy Friends, Girl Friends, Just Friends.* Atheneum, New York: McClelland & Stewart, Ltd., 1979.

Rubin, Theodore Isaac, M.D., *Reconciliation — Inner Peace in An Age of Anxiety.* New York: The Viking Press, 1980.

Satir, Virginia, *Peoplemaking.* Palo Alto, California: Science & Behavior Books Inc., 1972.

Saunders, Antoinette, Ph.D. and Remsberg, Bonnie. *The Stress-Proof Child.* New York: New American Library, 1984.

Schuller, Robert Charles, *Self-Esteem: The New Reformation.* Waco, Texas: Word Books, Inc., 1982.

Selye, Hans, M.D., *The Stress of Life.* New York: McGraw-Hill, 1976.

Shaffer, Martin, Ph.D., *Life After Stress.* New York: Plenum Press, 1982.

Simpson, Bert K., Ph.D., *Becoming Aware of Values.* La Mesa, California: Pennant Press, 1973.

Skoguland, Elizabeth R., *To Anger With Love.* New York: Harper & Row, 1977.

Smith, Manuel J., *When I Say No, I Feel Guilty.* New York: Bantam, 1975.

Ungerleider, Dorothy Fink, *Reading, Writing and Rage.* Rolling Hills Estates, California: Jalmar Press, 1986.

Vennard, Jane, *Synergy.* Novato, California: Academic Therapy Publications, 1978.

Vitale, Barbara Meister, *Unicorns Are Real.* Rolling Hills Estates, California: Jalmar Press, 1982.

Viscott, David, M.D., *The Language of Feelings.* New York: Pocket Books, 1976.

Wahlross, Sven, *Family Communication.* New York: Macmillan Publishing Co., Inc., 1974.

Waitley, Denis, *The Winner's Edge.* New York: Berkley Publishers, 1983.

Warren, Neil Clark, *Make Anger Your Ally.* Garden City, New York: Doubleday, 1983.

Wassmer, Arthur C., *Making Contact.* New York: Dial Press, 1978.

Winn, Marie, *Children Without Childhood.* New York: Pantheon Books, 1981.

Zimbardo, Philip G. and Radl, Shirley, *A Parent's Guide to the Shy Child.* New York: McGraw-Hill, 1981.

Pamphlets

U.S. Department of Health and Human Services, Public Health Service, National Institute on Drug Abuse. *Adolescent Peer Pressure.* Rockville, Maryland, 1983.

U.S. Department of Health and Human Services, Public Health Service, National Institute on

Special Training Aids From Harmony and His Friends...

Peggy Bielen, Harmony, and Sandy McDaniel

PSE Workshop Video Tape — A Perfect Training Tool

A comprehensive VHS video tape designed to provide special training for your Project Self-Esteem team. Filmed at a recent workshop conducted by the authors, this 3½-hour, full-color tape helps to visually train team members and give them that extra boost of confidence for a successful program. The workshop tape includes:

- Background Information
- Importance of Self-Esteem
- Program Philosophy & Implementation
- Full Lesson Demonstration
- Excerpts from Actual Class Presentations
- Tips on Working with Children

| BW6689 | Project Self-Esteem Video Tape | $75.00 |
| JP9059-1 | Project Self-Esteem Book | $39.95 |

Harmony Bear Puppet

Add extra enrichment to your program with the child-safe, freindly Harmony hand puppet. His gentle demeanor, fuzzy warmth, and lovable face will add that special sparkle to your lesson teaching. Brown fur, approximately 12" high.

BW6688   Harmony Bear Puppet $22.95

Special Price

Buy 1 PSE book plus a Harmony Bear Puppet

JP9600   PSE Book & Puppet $55.90

Experiential Workshops on Self Esteem

Keynote Addresses and Talks for Adults

Founders of Project Self-Esteem
Peggy Bielen and Sandy McDaniel

Helping Our Children Feel Lovable and Capable

5 hour workshop for Parents and Teachers

An experiential workshop, to focus on eight ways to enhance your self-esteem and the self-esteem of children with whom you work or live. This informative, fun-filled day will assist in bridging the gap between parents and teachers, giving each a common basis for communication/working with children.

A Double Feature
Enhancing Learning Through Self-Esteem

Afternoon session (3 hours suggested) for Teachers

A warm experiential workshop for educators. Including such topics as: The Fundamentals of self-esteem, Teaching children how to memorize, Communicating more effectively, The art of encouragement. This practical workshop will give educators new resources for their lives and classrooms.

Beyond Coping

2 Hour Night session for Parents

In a delightful setting of information and sharing, this workshop, filled with parenting skills, is a must. It is recommended this event be opened to the community-at-large.

Beyond Coping

2 Hour Workshop for Parents

Parents and people who work with children will take home many new ideas for their own lives and for assisting children. A workshop based on the experience of raising five children, the examples are real-life and highly entertaining.

3-5 Hour Workshops

For people planning to teach PSE

Based on the PSE concepts and principles, participants will be trained to understand and present the comprehensive Project Self-Esteem program ranging from Kindergarten through grade 6.

Keynote Addresses

1-2 Hour Workshops — Talks for:

- Church Groups
- Educators
- Business Organizations
- Medical Associations
- Civic Groups
- Staff Development
- General Public
- Banks

Organizations which have used these services:

- California State Women's Clubs
- Conference for Professionals in Guidance and Human Services
- California State PTA
- Santa Clara and Los Angeles Conference on Self-Esteem
- National Council for Self-Esteem
- YPO • CADFY
- National Council on Alcoholism
- IU7 in Greensburg, Pennsylvania
- Crittenton Center and Jr. League of Kansas City, Kansas/Missouri·
- San Jose, Calif. School District

What people have said about their work:

"Sandy and Peggy are two of the finest presenters on self-esteem around. Their work is warm, loving, humorous, dynamic, entertaining, engaging and most importantly practical and usable. I highly recommend them to you."

Dr. Jack Canfield
Author 100 Ways to Enhance Self-Concept in the Classroom

"Sandy and Peggy are two of the most dynamic, warm, inspiring presenters that I know. Those who have the opportunity to attend one of their classes/ workshops/talks count themselves fortunate and truly enriched."

Dr. Connie Dembrowski
Chairperson
National Council for Self-Esteem

About the Presenters

Sandy McDaniel and Peggy Bielen are former teachers and founders of the successful program PROJECT SELF-ESTEEM. Well-received for their dynamic practical approach to presenting information, Sandy and Peggy have talked to thousands of people in the USA and Canada.

PROJECT SELF-ESTEEM was piloted in over 200 schools in California. It has been purchased in over 45 states and in Canada. The original program ranged from grade 2-6. The Kindergarten-First Grade component is currently being piloted and will be printed by Spring of 1988.

For more information about Project Self-Esteem — and — for information about workshops, talks and presentations write or call.

Lack of Awareness is the Same as No Choice

Order NOW 10% Discount On 3 Or More Titles!

At Last . . . You Can Be That
"MOST MEMORABLE" PARENT/TEACHER/CARE-GIVER
To Every Person Whose Life You Touch (Including Your Own!)

20+ YEARS
AWARD WINNING
PUBLISHER

HELP KIDS TO: ❖ IMPROVE GRADES ❖ INCREASE CLASS PARTICIPATION ❖ BECOME MORE ATTENTIVE
ENCOURAGE & INSPIRE THEM AND YOU TO: ❖ TACKLE PROBLEMS ❖ ACHIEVE GOALS
AND
IMPROVE SELF-ESTEEM — BOTH THEIRS AND YOURS

Our authors are not just writers, but researchers and practitioners. Our books are not just written, but proven effective. All 100% tested, 100% practical, 100% effective. Look over our titles, choose the ones you want, and send your order today. You'll be glad you did. Just remember, our books are "SIMPLY THE BEST." *Bradley L. Winch, Ph.D., JD — President and Publisher*

Sandy Mc Daniel &
Peggy Bielen

Newly revised

Naomi Drew, M.A.

Gerry Dunne, Ph.D.

V. Alex Kehayan, Ed.D.

Project Self-Esteem, Expanded *(Gr. K-8)*

Innovative *parent involvement program.* Used by over 2000 schools/400,000 parti-cipants. Teaches children to respect them-selves and others, make sound decisions, honor personal and family value systems, develop vocabulary, attitude, goals and behavior needed for *living successfully* , *practicing responsible behavior* and *avoiding drug and alcohol use.* VHS, 1½ hrs. **$75.00**

0-915190-59-1, 408 pages, **JP-9059-1 $39.95**
8½ x 11, paperback, illus., reprod. act. sheets

Esteem Builders *(Gr. K-8)*

Teach self-esteem via curriculum content. Best K-8 program available. Uses 5 building blocks of self-esteem (*security/ selfhood/affiliation/mission/ competence*) as base. Over 250 grade level/curric. content cross-correlated activities. Also assess. tool, checklist of educator behaviors for model-ing, 40 week lesson planner, ext. biblio-graphy and more.

Paperback, 464 pages, **JP-9053-2 $39.95**
Spiral bound, **JP-9088-5 $49.95**, 8½ x 11, illus.

Michele Borba, Ed.D.

NOT JUST AUTHORS BUT RESEARCHERS AND PRACTITIONERS.

Learning The Skills of Peacemaking:
Communicating/Cooperation/Resolving Conflict (Gr. K-8)
A completely revised and expanded how-to guide for teachers and parents for bringing the skills of peacemaking to real-life situations. New section on how to create a peer mediation program, training guide, mediation scripts, role plays, and 59 activities to teach kids the skills they need to get along. Activities now coordinated with major content areas.

1-880396-42-4, 272 pages, **JP-9642-4 $29.95**
8½ x 11, paperback, illus., reprod. act. sheets

Peaceful Classroom in Action: *Integrating Literature and Writing into the Peacemaking Process(Gr. K-6)*

Great companion to Learning the Skills of Peacemaking. Features 22 easy to use lessons and multiple other activities. Uses literature and writing to access the peace inside of each student. Helps create a climate of respect that aids students in resolving their own conflicts. Covers collaboration and diversity.

1-880396-61-0, 176 pages, **JP-9661 $24.95**
8½ x 11, paperback, illus., biblio, appendices

Naomi Drew, M.A.

NOT JUST WRITTEN BUT PROVEN EFFECTIVE.

Preventing Violence in our Schools: *Essential Skills for Students (Gr. 4-12)*

Help students stop violence inside themselves--where it starts. Themes include: healthy vs unhealthy affiliations and influences; anger and impulse awareness and control; defusing potential violence; empathy; relating to diverse individuals and groups. Contains developmentally appropriate activities and discussions.

1-880396-65-3, 208 pages, **JP-9665 $21.95**
8½ x 11, paperback, illus., reprod. act. sheets

6 Vital Ingredients of Self-Esteem: *How To Develop Them In Your Students (Gr. K-12)*

Put self-esteem to work for your students. Learn practical ways to help kids manage school, make decisions, accept consequences, manage time, and discipline themselves to set worthwhile goals...and much more. *Covers developmental stages from ages 2 to 18, with implications for self-esteem at each stage.*

0-915190-72-9, 192 pages, **JP-9072-9 $21.95**
8½ x 11, paperback, biblio., appendices

Bettie B. Youngs, Ph.D.

100% TESTED — 100% PRACTICAL — 100% GUARANTEED.

Self-Awareness Growth Experiences
(Gr. 7-12)

Over 593 *strategies/activities* covering affective learning goals and objectives. To increase: self-awareness/self-esteem/social interaction skills/problem-solving, decision-making skills/coping ability /ethical standards/independent functioning/ creativity. Great *secondary resource.* Useful in counseling situations.

0-915190-61-3, 224 pages, **JP-9061-3 $19.95**
6 x 9, paperback, illus., 593 activities

Partners for Change: *Peer Helping Guide For Training and Prevention (Gr. K-12)*

This comprehensive *program guide* provides an excellent *peer support program* for program coordinators, peer leaders, professionals, group homes, churches, social agencies and schools. *Covers 12 areas,* including suicide, HIV / Aids, child abuse, teen pregnancy, substance abuse, low self esteem, dropouts, child abduction. etc.

Paperback, 464 pages, **JP-9069-9 $44.95**
Spiral bound, **JP-9087-7 $49.95**, 8½ x 11, illus.

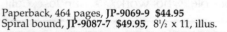

ORDER FROM: B.L. Winch & Associates/Jalmar Press, PO Box 1185, Torrance, CA 90505
Visit our website at: http://www.jalmarpress.com or CALL TOLL FREE — (800) 662-9662 • Add 10% shipping; $4 minimum

7/99

DISCOVER materials for positive self-esteem.

CREATE a positive environment in your classroom or home by opening a world of understanding.

Esther Wright, M.A.

Good Morning Class - *I Love You (Staff)*

Contains thought provoking quotes and questions about *teaching from the heart*. Helps love become an integral part of the learning that goes on in every classroom. Great for new teachers and for experienced teachers who sometimes become frustrated by the system. Use this book to begin and end your day. Greet your students every day with: *"Good morning class - I love you."*

0-915190-58-3, 80 pages, **JP-9058-3 $7.95**
5½ x 8½, paperback, illus./**Button $1.50**

Enhancing Educator's Self-Esteem:
It's Criteria #1 (Staff)

For the educator, a *healthy self-esteem* is job criterion No. 1! When high, it empowers us and adds to the vitality of our lives; when low it saps energy, erodes our confidence, lowers productivity and blocks our initiative to care about self and others. Follow the *plan of action* in this great resource to develop your self-esteem.

0-915190-79-6, 144 pages, **JP-9079-6 $16.95**
8½ x 11, paperback

NEW
Enhancing The Educator's Self-Esteem
It's Your Criteria #1

Bettie B. Youngs, Ph.D.

NOT JUST AUTHORS BUT RESEARCHERS AND PRACTITIONERS.

Bettie B. Young, Ph.D.

Stress Management for Administrators: *A Guide to Manage Your Response to Stress (Administrators)*

When you are in a leadership position, hardly a day goes by without feeling pressured and stretched to capacity. This book helps you examine the stress engendered in leadership roles and shows you practical ways to reduce that stress. Dozens of effective strategies are provided to make your leadership role more fulfilling.

0-915190-90-7, 112 pages, **JP-9090 $16.95**
8½ x 11, paperback, illustrations, charts

Stress Management for Educators: *A Guide to Manage Our Response to Stress (Staff)*

Answers these significant questions for educators: *What is stress?* What causes it? How do I cope with it? What can be done to manage stress to moderate its negative effects? Can stress be used to advantage? How *can educators be stress-proofed* to help them remain at *peak performance?* How do I keep going in spite of it?

0-915190-77-X, 112 pages, **JP-9077-X $16.95**
8½ x 11, paperback, illus., charts

STRESS MANAGEMENT
A Guide to Manage Your Response to Stress
By Bettie B.Youngs

Bettie B. Youngs, Ph.D.

NOT JUST WRITTEN BUT PROVEN EFFECTIVE.

Eva D. Fugitt, M.A.

He Hit Me Back First: *Developing Personal Responsibility. (Gr.K-8) Revised*

By whose authority does a child choose right from wrong? Here are *activities* directed toward *developing* within the child an *awareness* of his own *inner authority* and ability to choose (will power) and the resulting sense of *responsibility*, freedom and *self-esteem*. 29 separate activities.

0-915190-64-8, 120 pages, **JP-9064-8 $16.95**
8½ x 11, paperback, appendix, biblio.

Let's Get Together! *(Gr. K-6)*

Making friends is *easy* with the activities in this thoroughly researched book. Students are paired, get to know about each other, produce a book about their new *friend*, and present it in class. Exciting activities help discover commonalities. Great *self-esteem booster*. Revised after 10 years of field testing. Over 150 activities in 18 lessons.

0-915190-75-3, 192 pages, **JP-9075-3 $21.95**
8½ x 11, paperback, illustrations, activities

NEW
LET'S GET TOGETHER!
Activities for Developing Friendship and Self-Esteem in the Elementary Grades

C. Lynn Fox, Ph.D.

100% TESTED — 100% PRACTICAL — 100% GUARANTEED.

FEEL BETTER NOW

Chris Schriner, Rel.D.

Feel Better Now: *30 Ways to Handle Frustration in Three Minutes or Less (Staff/Personal)*

Teaches people to *handle stress as it happens* rapidly and directly. This basic requirement for *emotional survival* and *physical health* can be learned with the methods in this book. Find your own recipe for relief. Foreword: Ken Keyes, Jr. *"A mine of practical help"* — says Rev. Robert Schuller.

0-915190-66-4, 180 pages, **JP-9066-4 $9.95**
6 x 9, paperback, appendix, bibliography

Peace in 100 Languages: *A One-Word Multilingual Dictionary (Staff/Personal)*

A candidate for the Guinness Book of World Records, it is the *largest/smallest dictionary ever published*. Envisioned, researched and developed by *Russian peace activists*. Ancient, national, local and special languages covered. A portion of purchase price will be donated to joint U.S./Russian peace project. **Peace Button $1.50**

0-915190-74-5, 48 pages, **JP-9074-5 $9.95**
5 x 10, glossy paperback, full color

PEACE
IN 100 LANGUAGES
By:
M. Kabattchenko,
V. Kochurov,
L. Koshanova,
E. Kononenko,
D. Kuznetsov,
A. Lapitsky,
V. Monakov.
L. Stoupin, and
A. Zagorsky
Shalom · Paz
PEACE
Paix · Vrede

ORDER NOW FOR 10% DISCOUNT ON 3 OR MORE TITLES.

THE TURBULENT TEENS

James E. Gardner, Ph.D.

The Turbulent Teens: *Understanding Helping, Surviving (Parents/Counselors)*

Come to grips with the difficult issues of rules and the limits of parental tolerance, recognizing the necessity for *flexibility* that takes into consideration changes in the adolescent as well as the imperative *need for control*, agreed upon *expectations* and *accountability*. A must read! Useful in counseling situations.

0-913091-01-4, 224 pages, **JP-9101-4 $8.95**
6 x 9, paperback, case histories

Hilde Knows: *Someone Cries for the Children (Staff/Personal)*

We're all aware of the growing problem of child abuse. In this book, a dashound, is kidnapped from her happy family. The dog sees child abuse firsthand, when the parents abuse their daughter. Psychiatrist Dr. Machlin, outlines how caring adults can use the book with a child.

1-880396-38-6, 48 pages, **JP-9638-6 $6.95**
7 x 8½, fully illustrated

Someone Cries For the Children

Lisa Kent
Illus. by Mikki Machlin

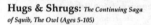

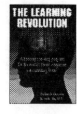

The Parent Book

Counselors/Teachers: Help parents meet the needs of their children in all the areas of Emotional Intelligence (EQ). Assist them in *identifying* each area of EQ in which their children are challenged and *provide* exactly the response needed to help the children grow by leaps and bounds in maturity.

The Parent Book

Ages 3-15, Counselors /Teachers/ Parents
Harold Bessel, Ph.D., & Thomas P. Kelly
Raising Emotionally Intelligent Children
Give parents the five easy steps to improve positive bonding with their children: listen to the feelings, learn the basic concern, develop an action plan, confront with support, and spend one-to-one time in each identified area of EQ development.
208pp, **JP9015, $9.95**, 8.5x11, paperback

identify

AWARENESS TRAITS (18)

A-1 Knowing one's own feelings
My child is aware of and able to report his/her own feelings with accuracy. (p.53)
☐ Rarely ☐ Sometimes ☐ Usually ☐ Often ☐ Very Often

A-4 Ability to discuss personal feelings
My child is able to discuss personal feelings with accuracy and is willing to do so.(p.57)
☐ Rarely ☐ Sometimes ☐ Usually ☐ Often ☐ Very Often

A-5 Coping with mixed feelings
My child accepts the inevitability of having mixed feelings and copes effectively with them. (p.60)
☐ Rarely ☐ Sometimes ☐ Usually ☐ Often ☐ Very Often

A-9 Coping with anger
My child is aware of his/her feelings of anger, and copes with the situation in effective ways. (p.67)
☐ Rarely ☐ Sometimes ☐ Usually ☐ Often ☐ Very Often

A-13 Coping with uncertainty
My child accepts some degree of uncertainty as inevitable and retains a positive and willing attitude about dealing with it. (p.78)
☐ Rarely ☐ Sometimes ☐ Usually ☐ Often ☐ Very Often

RELATING TRAITS (18)

R-2 Getting attention constructively
My child gets his/her needs for attention met in constructive ways> (p.92)
☐ Rarely ☐ Sometimes ☐ Usually ☐ Often ☐ Very Often

R-9 Coping with peer pressure
My child is able to sacrifice the seeming acceptance of the group by refusing to go along with something he/she knows is wrong. (p.106)
☐ Rarely ☐ Sometimes ☐ Usually ☐ Often ☐ Very Often

R-10 Expressing dissatisfaction constructively
My child is able to express complaints or criticism in ways that are supportive of the other person. (p.109)
☐ Rarely ☐ Sometimes ☐ Usually ☐ Often ☐ Very Often

R-14 Resolving conflicts constructively
My child, without sacrificing his/her own rights, uses peaceful and constructive means for resolving conflicts. (p.117)
☐ Rarely ☐ Sometimes ☐ Usually ☐ Often ☐ Very Often

R-17 Coping with mixed feelings toward people
My child recognizes, accepts and deals constructively in dis appointments and disagreements with other people. (p.125)
☐ Rarely ☐ Sometimes ☐ Usually ☐ Often ☐ Very Often

provide

COMPETENCE TRAITS (18)

C-4 Showing Initiative
My child initiates and implements ideas and projects. (p.139)
☐ Rarely ☐ Sometimes ☐ Usually ☐ Often ☐ Very Often

C-7 Showing self-reliance
My child relies upon his/her own resources to meet objectives. (p.146)
☐ Rarely ☐ Sometimes ☐ Usually ☐ Often ☐ Very Often

C-11 Being responsible
My child, without reminding, fulfills obligations (p.154)
☐ Rarely ☐ Sometimes ☐ Usually ☐ Often ☐ Very Often

C-15 Being cooperative
My child combines his/her talents well with those of others to achieve a common benefit. (p.163)
☐ Rarely ☐ Sometimes ☐ Usually ☐ Often ☐ Very Often

INTEGRITY TRAITS (15)

I-1 Showing self-control
My child's controls prevail over impulse. (p.171)
☐ Rarely ☐ Sometimes ☐ Usually ☐ Often ☐ Very Often

I-3 Being truthful
My child is natural, spontaneous and sincere when describing events. (p.173)
☐ Rarely ☐ Sometimes ☐ Usually ☐ Often ☐ Very Often

I-4 Coping with unpleasantness
My child shows a positive attitude about coping with unpleasantness, pain or discomfort. (p. 177)
☐ Rarely ☐ Sometimes ☐ Usually ☐ Often ☐ Very Often

I-8 Being reliable
My child consistently fulfills his/her commitments. (p.182)
☐ Rarely ☐ Sometimes ☐ Usually ☐ Often ☐ Very Often

I-12 Willing shares in the work
My child willing carries his/her share of the work load.(p.189)
☐ Rarely ☐ Sometimes ☐ Usually ☐ Often ☐ Very Often

HELPING YOU WITH THE TOUGH STUFF

JALMAR PRESS   **JALMAR PRESS**

P.O. Box 1185 Torrance CA 90505   tel:(800) 662-9662   (310)816-3085   fax:(310)816-3092   e:blwjalmar@worldnet.att.net   website:www.jalmarpress.com